Race, Reform, and Rebellion

The Second Reconstruction in Black America, 1945–1990

SECOND EDITION

Manning Marable

M

First edition 199–84

Published by
MACMILLAN EDUCATION LTD
Houndmills, Basingstoke, Hampshire RG21 2XS
and London
Companies and representatives
throughout the world

Printed in the United States of America

ISBN 0–333–564332

British Library Cataloguing in Publication Data is available from
the British Library.

Race, Reform, and Rebellion

Contents

Dedication

To all women of color, everywhere, who embody the spirit of
  freedom . . .
For Sojourner Truth,
For Harriet Tubman,
For Lucy Parsons,
For Ida B. Wells,
For Mary Church Terrell,
For Mary McLeod Bethune,
For Claudia Jones,
For Fannie Lou Hamer,
For the women fighters of the ANC, SWAPO, FRELIMO, PLO, PAIGC, and the
  Sandinistas,
For Assata Shakur,
For Sonia Sanchez,
For Alice Walker,
For Joan Little,
For Angela Davis,
For Sandra Neely Smith,
For Toni Cade Bambara,
For Shirley Graham DuBois,
and for my friend, co-worker, lover and wife,
  For Hazel Ann.

Acknowledgments

The author and publishers wish to thank the following who have kindly given permission for the use of copyright material:

Harper & Row, Publishers, Inc. for an extract from *Why We Can't Wait* by Martin Luther King, Jr. Copyright © 1963 by Martin Luther King, Jr.

Hughes Massie Ltd on behalf of the author, and Random House, Inc. for the poem 'Un-American Investigators' from *The Panther and the Lash* by Langston Hughes. Copyright © 1967 by Langston Hughes.

Hutchinson Publishing Group Ltd and Random House, Inc. for an extract from *The Autobiography of Malcolm X* by Malcolm X, with the assistance of Alex Haley.

Johnson Publishing Company Inc. for the poem 'Junglegrave' by S. E. Anderson from *Negro Digest*, 1968.

William Morrow & Company Inc., for an abridgement of the poem 'Nigger. Can You Kill' and extract from 'Ugly Honkies' from *Black Feeling, Black Talk, Black Judgement* by Nikki Giovanni. Copyright © 1968, 1970 by Nikki Giovanni.

Every effort has been made to trace all the copyright holders. If any have been inadvertently overlooked, the publishers will be pleased to make the necessary arrangement at the first opportunity.

Preface

The original edition of *Race, Reform, and Rebellion* was written largely in 1982, during the second year of the Reagan Administration. It reflected two perspectives: the thoughts of the social historian, seeking to explain the successes and failures of the modern civil rights and Black Power movements; and the commentary of the political theorist and social activist, searching among the ruins of black protest formations to unearth the reasons for the demise of militancy and activism among African-Americans in the post–1975 period. The devastating economic and social impact of Reagan's domestic policy agenda was being felt in dozens of black communities, and traditional civil rights leaders seemed to lack creative proposals for effective resistance. Even as the initial preface was being written, and as the book was being published in the United Kingdom in early 1984, the prospects for reviving the black protest movement were unclear. The growth of a small but vigorous conservative current within the black middle class, which was absorbed into the margins of mass conservatism, was equally disconcerting.

All of this appeared to change in the mid-1980s, with the eruption of Jesse Jackson's insurgent presidential campaigns in 1984 and 1988; the widespread resistance to Reagan's policy of support for apartheid South Africa, which led to nonviolent, direct-action demonstrations; and the successful election of powerful black leaders into high office—the mayoral victories of Harold Washington in Chicago in 1983 and 1987, the New York mayoral election of David Dinkins, and the gubernatorial victory of Doug Wilder in Virginia, the so-called cradle of the Confederacy. Yet despite this rebirth of activism in the electoral system, the trends contributing to social and economic deterioration of the black working class and lower-income communities continued to worsen. Crack cocaine produced a social devastation and violence between black Americans that had never before been witnessed. Single-parent households continued to proliferate; the number of African-Americans imprisoned in federal and state institutions exceeded the total number of black male college students; the black homeless population doubled in less than a decade. These statistics of human poverty, social disruption and hunger were not accidental, nor did they derive from the absence of a black "work ethic"; they were the consequences of deliberate federal and corporate policy. The irony of these new realities was that the latest structures of domination no longer assumed the classical form of "Jim Crow" racial segregation. No Reagan Administration official would dare utter the term "niggers." No corporate official, moving his firm's productive resources and jobs out of the inner city, would justify economic divestment in crudely racist terms. Blacks, Hispanics and other people of color were being more thoroughly oppressed in economic, political, social and educational institutions, without being stigmatized specifically in "racial" terms. This paradox of desegregation in the 1980s and early 1990s meant that black oppression was more systematic and sophisticated than before, and that only a fragile élite had been granted opportunities and privileges the white middle class had long taken for granted.

The original edition anticipated some, but not all, of these developments. Certainly I did not recognize that the demise of racial segregation in the legal sphere would be followed by an intense urban crisis which would foster social disruption as well as collective resistance and electoral protest. The revised edition takes advantage of the new information and perspectives drawn from the bitter years of the Reagan Administration, and its ambiguous but largely negative aftermath under George Bush. This information presumes the profound influence of national political culture and government on the contours of African-American society, perhaps at the expense of other cultural and social variables that directly affect the organic evolution of black life and institutional development. Yet my primary purpose has been to explain problems largely of a political nature: the factors behind collective protest; the agendas, strategies and tactics employed by political formations, labor unions, parties and civil rights groups; the impact of governmental policy, corporate decision-making, and national parties upon the current and projected status of African-Americans. This revision incorporates the new evidence of the continuing burden of race, class and gender inequality within contemporary American society, illustrating that the distance which separates blacks and other people of color from full human equality and social justice still exists, regardless of the passage of civil rights laws abolishing racial segregation.

Another purpose has motivated me to revise my earlier work. Part of the paradox of desegregation is what could be termed "historical amnesia" or "cultural illiteracy" on the part of younger African-Americans about their own legacy of resistance to oppression. King and Malcolm X are widely recognized, but political reform organizations such as the Student Nonviolent Coordinating Committee and Black Power formations such as the Black Panther Party, the League of Revolutionary Black Workers or the

Republic of New Afrika are all but unknown. The accomplishments and the errors of these and hundreds of other political and social protest groups are generally forgotten among those blacks who did not personally experience segregation. History's greatest dangers are waiting for those who fail to learn its lessons. Any oppressed people who abandon the knowledge of their own protest history, or who fail to analyze its lessons, will only perpetuate their domination by others. In this context, therefore, the writing of political history assists in prefiguring the conditions essential for future protests. This is not to suggest that social science functions solely as propaganda; the integrity of evidence and collection of data from a variety of subject areas and interpretations is an essential part of reconstructing the political and social experiences of any people. As DuBois suggested in *Black Reconstruction in America*, however, we must be "able to use human experience for the guidance of mankind." Our understanding of the realities of the past must inform corrective public policies in the present, to create more democratic and pluralistic possibilities for the future. Scholarship does not have the luxury of standing apart from the gritty human problems of poverty, racism, sexism, unemployment and hunger, whether in theory or practice. I hope that this slender reader, which presents some of the essential details of the African-American movement for human equality and political empowerment, will inspire members of the next generation to join a very long and rich tradition of resistance. In this faith, I dedicate this revised edition to my children: Malaika, Sojourner and Joshua.

MANNING MARABLE
1 August 1990

Race, Reform, and Rebellion

1. Prologue: The Legacy of the First Reconstruction

In two historic instances, Negro Americans have been beneficiaries—as well as victims—of the national compulsion to level or to blur distinctions. The first leveling ended the legal status of slavery, the second the legal system of segregation. Both abolitions left the beneficiaries still suffering under handicaps inflicted by the system abolished.

C. Vann Woodward, *The Strange Career of Jim Crow*

What is the object of writing the history of Reconstruction? Is it to wipe out the disgrace of a people which fought to make slaves of Negroes? Is it to show that the North had higher motives than freeing black men? Is it to prove that Negroes were black angels? No, it is simply to establish the Truth, on which Right in the future may be built.

W. E. B. DuBois, *Black Reconstruction in America, 1860–1880*

I

During two brief moments in history, the United States experienced major social movements which, at their core, expressed a powerful vision of multicultural democracy and human equality. The first was developed before the seminal conflict in American history, the Civil War (1861–65), and came to fruition in the twelve-year period of reunion, reconstruction and racial readjustment which followed (1865–77). Almost a century later, a "Second Reconstruction" occurred. Like the former period, the Second Reconstruction was a series of massive confrontations concerning the status of the African-American and other national minorities (e.g., Indians, Chicanos, Puerto Ricans, Asians) in the nation's economic, social and political institutions. Both movements brought about the end of rigid racial/caste structures which had been used to oppress blacks for many decades. Both elevated articulate and charismatic black leaders from the African-American working class and fragile middle class. Both were fought primarily in the southern U.S. although in certain respects both inspired major socio-economic reforms in the northern states as well. In both instances, the federal government was viewed as a "reluctant ally" of the blacks and their progressive white supporters, whereas the opponents to black equality were primarily white Southern Democrats and substantial numbers of white small-business and working-class people. Both movements pressured the federal courts and Congress to ratify and to validate legislative measures which promoted greater racial equality and an improvement in the material status of blacks and poor whites. Finally, both movements eventually succumbed to internal contradictions, the loss of northern white support, and the re-emergence of the South's tradition of inequality and racial prejudice as the dominant theme of U.S. public policies *vis à vis* blacks. History never repeats itself exactly, so it would be foolish to view the period of racial rebellion from 1945 to the present strictly through the prism of the past. Nevertheless, no real understanding of modern America is possible without an analysis of this nation's ongoing burden of race and class, a social and economic dilemma which was created by almost 250 years of chattel slavery. The racial patterns of the present and the possibilities for the future are buried in that past, in the myriad of successes and failures of the Civil War, and the First Reconstruction. It is here that our assessment of modern American race relations must begin.

More than any other modern nation in the world, with the possible exception of South Africa, the United States developed from the beginning a unique socio-economic structure and a political apparatus which was simultaneously racist, stubbornly capitalist, and committed to a limited form of bourgeois democracy: a racist/capitalist state. In electoral politics, free blacks from the eighteenth century onward found it difficult if not impossible to exercise the franchise. North Carolina permitted some blacks to vote in 1667, for example, but repealed the measure in 1715. At the election of George Washington in 1789, no southern state permitted blacks to vote. In the nineteenth century, northern states passed anti-black voting restrictions as well. In 1823, New York established a stiff property qualification which effectively eliminated blacks from voting. Pennsylvania and Indiana denied black males the right to vote in 1838 and 1851, respectively. In most states, blacks were forbidden by law to pursue certain vocations. Free blacks in South Carolina, for example, could not work as clerks; Maryland blacks were forbidden to sell wheat, corn or tobacco without a state license after 1805; Georgia's free blacks briefly lost the right to own or sell property in 1818. The primary source for all discriminatory legislation, North and South, prior to the Civil War, was the omnipresence of slavery. The "peculiar institution" was the South's chief mode of agricultural production, and its existence, and the unquenching demand for servile black labor, directly and indirectly influenced the shape of every state's laws and relations with blacks. The growth of the slavery mode of production generated increasing political and social conflicts within American society over a period of eight decades, which culminated in the Civil War.

The white North did not wage the Civil War "to free the slaves." Most Republicans, including Lincoln, expressed absolutely no support for the idea of social and political equality between the races. This was, at first, clearly a "white man's war," fought to preserve federal authority. Throughout the conflict, blacks in the North continued to experience racist assaults. When blacks were hired to work on riverboats in 1862, for example, white residents of Cincinnati, Ohio, were so outraged that they looted and burned the city's black districts. In July 1863, white New Yorkers destroyed black-owned stores, burned a black orphanage, and lynched black women and men in a four-day racist rampage. It was only after white military casualty figures mounted that an alarmed white public began to accept the suggestion that northern blacks should be permitted to join the Union army in combat units. The Enlistment Act of July 1862 ordered that black troops should receive half the amount of salary that whites received. Despite this insult, about 186,000 blacks enlisted in the Union army during the conflict. Half of these troops were from the South. In a series of bitter engagements with the Confederate army, they fought with courage and distinction which amazed racists on both sides of the struggle. Partially due to the brutal policy of "no quarter" which many southern troops exercised when fighting blacks, 38,000 black soldiers were killed in the war.

By the battle of Shiloh in April 1862, it became evident to the Lincoln administration that a disruption of the South's labor force was a necessity in order to win the war. In July 1862, Congress legally freed any slaves who had run away from the plantations to join the Union army. Three months earlier, Congress abolished slavery in Washington, D.C. and provided up to $300 per slave to the former owners. On 1 January 1863, Lincoln freed all slaves who lived in rebel territory not yet controlled by the Union army. Technically, slavery as a legal institution did not end in the United States until the ratification of the Thirteenth Amendment in December 1865. Practically, black emancipation occurred not by fiat, but by the direct actions of the slaves themselves. Thousands waited, watching for the first opportunity to escape. Northern and southern whites began to understand what virtually every black American, slave or free, had first comprehended. "After the first few months," noted black scholar W. E. B. DuBois observed, "everybody knew that slavery was done with; that no matter who won, the condition of the slave could never be the same after this disaster of war."[1] As nameless chattels, they had been raped, whipped, sold on the auction block, worked in the hot fields of endless cotton rows from dawn to dreary dusk. As men and women, they departed defiantly, with every expectation that their ordeal would soon end, and the freedom was close at hand. "To win the war," DuBois wrote, "America freed the slave and armed him; and the threat to arm the mass of black workers of the Confederacy stopped the war."[2]

Reconstruction actually began barely one year after the conflict started, when in July 1862, one Union general, Rufus Saxon, confiscated plantations along the Carolina coast and promoted the development of black-owned family farms. General William T. Sherman issued Order No. 15 in January 1865, which seemed to promise land to the former slaves. Other Union officers and politicians held property rights as superior to whatever claims blacks made for a just return for 250 years of unpaid labor power. General Nathaniel P. Banks ordered Louisiana blacks to return to their masters and to accept absurdly low wages. After Lincoln's assassination, President Andrew Johnson, a southerner, promptly voided most of the land transfers to blacks, and returned the property to wealthy whites. In 1866, the governor of Mississippi complained that the presence of 9,000 black troops in his state promoted the rumor that former slaves would be given property. President Johnson ordered all black troops out of the state within five months. Despite these and other problems, blacks attempted to purchase land wherever and whenever possible. By the early 1870s, Virginia black farmers had purchased 80,000 to 100,000 acres. A decade after the war, Georgia blacks owned approximately 400,000 acres, worth $1.3 million. The failure of the federal government to recognize the necessity for massive land redistribution, along the lines of what blacks themselves called "forty acres and a mule," would be the principal reason for the failure of the First Reconstruction. In most southern counties by the mid-1870s, 5 percent of the white farmers controlled at least 40 percent of the productive agricultural land. The upper one-tenth of the white farmers in most states owned anything from one-half to two-thirds of the farmland. Racial equality could not occur in political and social relations when economic power was held in relatively few hands.

In non-economic matters, however, Reconstruction produced major changes in the social status of blacks. The federal government launched the Freedmen's Bureau, which provided food and clothing to millions. The Bureau opened 46 hospitals for blacks across the South. By 1870, its educational institutions claimed one-quarter of a million students and almost 10,000 instructors. A number of Bureau-sponsored colleges became the basis for African-American higher education: Howard University of Washington, D.C., Atlanta University, Fisk University, and Hampton Institute are among the most prominent examples. Prior to the Civil War, most southern states had no real public school systems. With blacks as voters and legislators, the public school was made accessible to the poor of both races. Mississippi's constitution of 1868 created a biracial public school system for the entire state, and legislators set about the task of constructing hundreds of school buildings. The delegates at South Carolina's constitutional convention that same year ratified a proposal for universal education, and proposed $900,000 in expenditures for the public schools. Black religious organizations, notably the African Methodist Episcopal Church, were actively involved in educational and health care efforts. From 1865 to 1869, black churches established 257 black schools in North Carolina alone, which served 15,600 black students. State legislatures passed legislation creating orphanages and other public charities for blacks and whites.

The electoral defeat of congressional Democrats in November 1866, and the subsequent impeachment of Johnson, shifted effective power from the president to the "Radical Republicans." The effect of this political transition was felt almost at once: the passage of the Fourteenth Amendment, which guaranteed blacks civil rights; the Fifteenth Amendment, which allowed black male adults the electoral franchise; and the federal government's acceptance of black legislative representation, both in the state and nation. Reconstruction state governments, as a rule, tended to have a smaller percentage of blacks as merited by their respective numbers in each state. Only one southern state, Mississippi, appointed or elected blacks to the U.S. Senate. Only fourteen blacks were elected to the U.S. House of Representatives during Reconstruction. Most of the states' top offices were filled by white southerners. White historians, dismayed by the phantom of "Negro rule," have tried to claim that these men were unfit for public office. Even their white contemporaries, influenced by the deep racism of the day, knew otherwise. Four of the sixteen elected to Congress had received college diplomas; five were prominent lawyers. Francis L. Cardozo, who served as South Carolina's secretary of state from 1868 to 1872, was a former student of the University of Glasgow. Mississippi's two black U.S. senators, Hiram R. Revels and Blanche K. Bruce, were superior in intellect and political acumen to most of their counterparts. Revels was trained in an Ohio seminary and attended Knox College in Illinois. During the war he served as a chaplain in the Union army, and in the late 1860s he emerged as the leader of Natchez, Mississippi's black community. Bruce had served as tax collector, sheriff and state superintendent of schools before his election to the U.S. Senate in 1874. He purchased hundreds of acres of farmland in the state's "blackbelt" region and became one of the most affluent public figures in the South. Between 1869 and 1901, a total of 816 black men were elected as federal and state legislators. Of these, 63 percent came from just four southern states: South Carolina (218); Virginia (93); North Carolina (82); and Louisiana (122). Some southern and border states with substantial black populations had few or no black elected officials: Kentucky (0); Maryland (0); Tennessee (12); West Virginia (1).

The drive for biracial democracy could not be contained in the South. Northern blacks fought for the repeal of every law which discriminated by race. Gradually, northern states were forced to amend or abolish many racist regulations. In 1865, Illinois finally permitted blacks to testify in courtrooms. Blacks in Washington, D.C., in 1865, led by the fiery abolitionist Sojourner Truth, led a boycott of public transportation facilities which practiced Jim Crow. Philadelphia blacks fought successfully to bar segregation in the city's streetcars. Rhode Island blacks forced state officials to desegregate public schools in 1866. Northern blacks pressured their white congressmen to ratify the Enforcement Act of May 1870, and the Civil Rights Act of March 1875, which further protected blacks' civil liberties. The period even brought black women leaders to the center of national attention. Frances Ellen Watkins Harper, for instance, travelled and spoke throughout the South from 1865 to 1871, raising capital for black schools and hospitals. In the 1870s, she became assistant superintendent of the YMCA school in Philadelphia, and subsequently helped to establish the National Association of Colored Women. Across the nation, blacks in commerce, politics and education were building new institutions with incredible energy. Between 1865 and 1900, to take a single example, over 1,200 black-owned newspapers were established. This fact alone, from a population which was 90–95 percent illiterate in 1860, is awesome.

The decline and demise of the First Reconstruction grew apparent before the Panic of 1873 and the economic recession which lasted for four years afterward. Northern capitalists recognized that they did not have to condone biracial rule in the South in order to develop the predominantly rural region. Conservatives in the Republican Party found that their own interests converged with those of the former planter class to a greater extent than they did with poor blacks. As historian Lawrence Goodwyn observes, "the bankers, manufacturers, shippers, and merchants" who ran the Republican Party "soon wearied of their attempt to build a postwar party in the South based on black suffrage. As elected victories in the 1860s and 1870s proved that the [Republicans] could rule with a basically northern constituency, Negroes, their morale declining, and white radical abolitionists, their numbers thinning, lost the intra-party debate over Southern policy."[3] White southern hostility towards blacks expressed itself dramatically with race riots in Meridian, Mississippi, in 1871, and in Savannah, Georgia, and Hamburg, South Carolina, in 1872. White terrorists organized a series of vigilante groups, including the Ku Klux Klan and the Knights of the White Camelia, to intimidate black voters and elected officials. In the disputed presidential election of 1876, the Republicans secured their narrow victory by promising to curtail civil rights measures and to allow the re-establishment of white supremacy in the South. After the so-called Compromise of 1877, federal troops were eventually ordered to leave the South.

The end of Reconstruction produced a political and social climate of fear and intimidation for every black person in the South. Despite a brief period from the late 1880s, to the mid-1890s when black and white southern farmers attempted to develop a biracial opposition to the planters through the Populist Party, the conditions of black life and labor deteriorated rapidly. Politically, the federal government abandoned any commitment to biracial democracy. In 1883, the Supreme Court declared the Civil Rights Act of 1875 unconstitutional. The principle of "separate but equal," America's legal justification for domestic *apartheid*, was ordained by the Supreme Court in the *Plessy v. Ferguson* decision of 1896. By the 1890s, southern states had begun to rewrite their Reconstruction-era constitutions, denying blacks and many poor whites the right to vote. The effect of these new state constitutions was as striking as it was undemocratic. In Alabama, for example, there were 181,000 blacks who were eligible to vote in 1900; two years later, merely 3,000 were noted as registered voters. Republican presidents supported the creation of a "Lily White" wing of their party in the South, which would deny blacks the right to participate even in their own political organizations. Political disfranchisement was also facilitated by extra-legal means. Between 1882 and 1903, 2,060 blacks were lynched in the United States. Some of the black victims were children and pregnant women; many were burned alive at the stake; others were castrated with axes or knives, blinded with hot pokers, or decapitated.

II

The experiment in biracial democracy was effectively at an end. For many millions of black farmers, the only hope for political survival and economic self-sufficiency was in an exodus from the South. The earliest migrants left in the 1870s. Benjamin "Pap" Singleton, a black mortician, led over 7,000 blacks from Kentucky and Tennessee into Kansas. In 1879, a second wave of 60,000 black farm families walked and rode from the lower Mississippi River Valley into Kansas. Many blacks later migrated to Oklahoma Territory; between 1891 and 1910 more than two dozen all-black settlements were established in the state. The vast majority who fled, however, moved to the North. The flood of black humanity increased steadily: 170,000 migrants in 1900–1910; 454,000 in 1910–20; 749,000 in 1920–30. Black migration dropped during the Great Depression decade, 1930–40, with only 349,000. From 1940–50, the movement accelerated again, totalling 1,599,000 for the decade. In the thirty years between 1910 and 1940, the black population in Illinois increased from 109,000 to 387,000; in New York from 134,000 to 571,000; in Pennsylvania from 194,000 to 470,000. In 1940, 22 percent of all blacks lived in the North, compared to 10 percent in 1910. This major demographic shift produced dramatic changes in the labor patterns of blacks. In 1890, 63 percent of all black males were agricultural workers, 22 percent were domestic servants, and only 14 percent worked in transportation, communications, and/or manufacturing. In 1930, the percentage of black male agricultural workers declined to 42. Only 11 percent were domestics, but 36 percent were employed in manufacturing, transportation and communications. The small, black middle class which emerged after slavery had begun to multiply. The number of black public and private schoolteachers more than doubled from 1910 to 1940. The number of black-owned businesses between 1904 and 1929 grew from 20,000 to over 70,000. Between 1900 and 1914, 47 black-owned banks were established. The percentage of black youth between the ages of 5 and 20 enrolled in school increased from 33 in 1890 to 65 fifty years later. In the same period, black illiteracy dropped from 61 percent to 15 percent. The migration from the rural South to the urban Northeast and Midwest, and the growth of a black urban working class throughout the nation, brought an improvement in health care, education, economic and political life for millions of black people. Nevertheless, the substantial gap between the socio-economic and political status of whites and blacks still existed and was reinforced across the nation by the rule of Jim Crow.

Even these marginal improvements in the material existence of many blacks did nothing to halt the proliferation of brutal white violence. The Jim Crow system of racial exploitation was, like slavery, both a caste/social order for regimenting cultural and political relations, and an economic structure which facilitated the superexploitation of blacks' labor power. Unlike slavery, Jim Crow was much more clearly capitalistic, since white owners of factories did not have to purchase entire black families in order to obtain the services of a single wage-earner. However, in caste/racial relations, both systems were dependent upon the omnipresence of violence or coercion. Throughout the early twentieth century, white politicians, business leaders and most workers defended the necessity to discipline the black working class via lynchings, public executions, and the like. One particularly brutal moment occurred immediately after World War I, when whites across the country committed an array of bestial acts against blacks, unheard of even in slavery. In the "Red Summer of 1919" 70 blacks were lynched, including ten soldiers who had fought "to preserve democracy against the Kaiser." Eleven of these blacks were burned alive. In the Chicago race riot of 1919, 38 persons were killed, and 537 were injured. Up to 1,000 black families were burned out of their homes in the city. Whites in Knoxville, Tennessee, destroyed black property worth $50,000. Dozens of black cottonfarmers and laborers were shot in Elaine, Arkansas. An Omaha, Nebraska, white mob attacked a black man suspect accused of raping a white woman. The man was shot over 1,000 times, and the corpse was lynched in the city's central district. Throughout the carnage, the federal government remained blind and mute. State governments increased stringent segregation laws to the point of high absurdity. South Carolina insisted that black and white textile workers could not use the same doorways, pay windows, bathrooms or even the same water buckets. Many cities passed ordinances which kept blacks out of public parks and white residential districts. Atlanta outlawed black barbers from clipping the hair of white children and women in 1926. There were soon segregated zoos, baseball clubs, buses, taxicabs, restaurants, and race tracks. Historian C. Vann Woodward noted one extreme case: A Birmingham ordinance got down to particulars in 1930 by making it "'unlawful for a Negro and a white person to play together or in company with each other' at dominoes or checkers."[4] For all practical purposes, the black American was proscribed by the state from any meaningful political and social activity for two generations. Behind this powerful proscription, as always, was the use of force.

The first four decades of the twentieth century witnessed major social, cultural and economic changes for most black Americans. Yet after two world wars and a devastating economic depression, the barrier of the color line still existed in the United States. Most white Americans, looking backward at Reconstruction, cautioned Negroes not to demand abrupt changes in their caste status too quickly. Jim Crow would gradually be allowed to decline after another century or two of racial improvement and social adjustment. But in growing numbers, blacks and other national minorities looked at America's experiment in multicultural democracy as the harbinger for a better life in the immediate future. In the prophetic words of W. E. B. DuBois, the campaign for freedom had hardly begun:

> This the American black man knows: his fight here is a fight to the finish. Either he dies or wins. If he wins it will be by no subterfuge or evasion of amalgamation. He will enter modern civilization here in America as a black man on terms of perfect and unlimited equality with any white man, or he will enter not at all. Either extermination root and branch, or absolute equality. There can be no compromise. This is the last great battle of the West.[5]

2 The Cold War in Black America, 1945–1954

It is the problem of the Russian People to make changes there. We cannot advance a progressive development by threatening Russia from the outside. . . . America is incomparably less endangered by its own Communists than by the hysterical hunt for the few Communists there are here. In my eyes, the "Communist conspiracy" is principally a slogan used in order to put those who have no judgment and who are cowards into a condition which makes them entirely defenseless. Again, I must think back to the Germany of 1932, whose democratic social body had already been weakened by similar means.

Albert Einstein, open letter to Norman Thomas, 1954

There are class divisions among Negroes, and it is misleading to maintain that the interests of the Negro working and middle classes are identical. To be sure, a middle-class NAACP leader and an illiterate farmhand in Mississippi or a porter who lives in Harlem all want civil rights. However, it would be enlightening to examine why the NAACP is not composed of Negro porters and farmhands, but only of Negroes of a certain type.

Harold Cruse, *Rebellion or Revolution*

I

The aftermath of any war affects those on the side of its victors even more than it does those who have lost. For many African-Americans who celebrated V-J Day in the late summer of 1945, there was an intense sense of joy and dread: fears that there might be another anti-black "Red Summer" such as had swept the nation in 1919; hopes that the progressive economic changes that had occurred for blacks during the wartime era could be expanded; unanswered questions about the new administration of Harry S. Truman, its commitment to the modest social democratic policies of Franklin D. Roosevelt and to the limited pursuit of civil rights. Two decades later, black social critic Harold Cruse described his feelings at that ambiguous moment in history:

> World War II shattered a world irrevocably. But people who thought as I did were called upon in 1945 to treat the postwar era with intellectual and critical tools more applicable to the vanished world of the thirties—a world we had never had time to understand as we lived it. I spent the years from 1945 to about 1952 wrestling with this perplexity.[1]

The crimes of the Third Reich against European Jews had shocked the nation, and the popular ideology which inspired public opposition to Hitler was rooted in an anti-racist and democratic context. The blatant contradiction between the country's opposition to fascism and the *herrenvolk* state and the continued existence of Jim Crow in the States after 1945 was made perfectly clear to all. Blacks and an increasing sector of liberal white America came out of the war with a fresh determinaton to uproot racist ideologies and institutions at home. But few at the time were precisely clear as to what measures were required to turn this egalitarian commitment into public policy.

Part of the dilemma which confronted black leaders resided in the ambiguous legacy of the late president, Franklin D. Roosevelt (1933–1945). By most standards, the Democrat had been the most liberal chief executive in regard to the civil rights of national minorities in American history. The number of black federal employees was increased from 50,000 in 1933 to 200,000 by 1946. Roosevelt had appointed a small group of prominent middle-class blacks, including lawyers Robert C. Weaver and William H. Hastie, journalist Robert L. Vann, and educator Mary McLeod Bethune, to administrative posts. Government agencies in the "New Deal" administration of Roosevelt were organized on strictly segregated lines. Youths who worked in the Civilian Conservation Corps camps were segregated by race; provisions in the Public Works Administration which mandated certain percentages of black workers in the construction of buildings were blatantly ignored; benefits from the Agricultural Adjustment Administration were often denied to black rural farmers through fraud and outright corruption. Roosevelt resisted blacks' demands that the federal government should pressure defense contractors to hire greater numbers of minorities. It was only under the direct threat of a black workers' march on Washington, D.C., co-ordinated by black labor leader A. Philip Randolph in 1941, that Roosevelt signed Executive Order 8802 which met the blacks' concerns in a limited respect.

In a real sense, the watershed of African-American history occurred during the 1940s. Thousands of black men working as sharecroppers and farm laborers were drafted into the army with the outbreak of World War II. Over three million black men registered for the service, and about 500,000 were stationed in Africa, the Pacific, and in Europe. Fighting as customary in segregated units, black troops again distinguished themselves on every front. At home, the war effort brought another million black women and men into factory lines of production. Some white workers viewed this racial turn of events with greater alarm than the specter of fascism. Between March and June 1943, a series of "hate strikes" against the upgrading of blacks in industries contributed to a total 100,000 man-days lost. Philadelphia streetcar workers refused to work with blacks in 1944, and Roosevelt was forced to order 5,000 federal troops into the city to restore order. Partially through the militant labor-organizing efforts of the American Communist Party, the number of black union members rose from 150,000 in 1935 to 1.25 million by the end of the war. Even in many southern cities black and white workers formed biracial unions and fought for higher wages and improved working conditions. In 1943–1944, 11,000 black and white tobacco workers at the R. J. Reynolds plant in North Carolina struck successfully to upgrade the salaries of black employees. In politics, blacks evinced for the first time since the demise of Reconstruction a growing leverage on state and national affairs. Northern black voters had largely shifted their political allegiances from the Republican to the Democratic Party during the Great Depression. In 1934, Arthur W. Mitchell of Chicago became the first black Democrat elected to Congress in American history. Ten years later, a Harlem minister and militant political activist, Adam Clayton Powell, was elected to the House. Black northern votes for Roosevelt in the presidential election of 1944 accounted for his margin of victory over Republican New York governor Thomas Dewey in eight states, including Michigan and Maryland. The major civil rights organization in the country, the National Association for the Advancement of Colored People (NAACP), founded by DuBois in 1910, more than tripled its membership in 1934–44. The NAACP Legal Defense Fund had gained considerable success in the repeal of Jim Crow state legislation through its appeals to the Supreme Court. By 1945, a growing number of white Americans in the North had concluded that the system of racial segregation would have to be modified, if not entirely overthrown.

In the months immediately following World War II, blacks made decisive cracks in the citadel of white supremacy. By 1946, there were over two dozen blacks who were serving in state legislatures in northeastern states (New York, Massachusetts, Pennsylvania, New Jersey, and Vermont), in the Midwest (Illinois, Kansas, Nebraska), the West (California and Colorado) and even in border states (West Virginia and Kentucky). In 1945, Truman appointed a black attorney, Irvin C. Mollison, as associate judge of the U.S. Customs Court. In 1946, William H. Hastie was named governor of the Virgin Islands, and black sociologist Charles S. Johnson was appointed to the national commission advising the U.S. State Department on participation in the United Nations Education, Scientific, and Cultural Organizations (UNESCO). Ralph J. Bunche, a former socialist and co-organizer of the militant National Negro Congress in the 1930s, was named to the Anglo-American Caribbean Commission of the State Department. Across the country, blacks were participating openly in electoral politics in heretofore unprecedented numbers. In Harlem, black Communist Party leader Benjamin J. Davis was elected to the New York City Council. By 1947, 12 percent of all voting-age blacks in the South were registered, up from only 2 percent in 1940. Blacks in the upper South— Virginia, North Carolina, and Tennessee—began to be elected in small numbers to city councils and school board posts. Congress reflected this trend towards a more liberal to moderate segregationist policy. Against 1937–38, when only 10 bills which were considered favorable to desegregation and civil rights were introduced in Congress, by 1949–50, 72 bills were being proposed. After 1946, several northern states passed local restrictions against racial discrimination in employment.

During the 1940s, there was also a marked improvement in the quality and accessibility of black education. In the 1930s, the incomes of private black colleges had decreased by 16 percent, and private gifts declined by 50 percent. In October 1943, a group of black college presidents, led by Tuskegee Institute president Frederick D. Patterson, established the United Negro College Fund to save these institutions. During 1944, 1945 and 1946, about a million dollars a year was raised. Black public schoolteachers campaigned to equalize the pay schedules between blacks and whites in a number of states and cities. In 1943, black teachers in Tampa, Florida, sued successfully in federal court to overturn unequal salary schedules. This was followed by similar legal actions by black teachers in Charleston, South Carolina, in 1944, and in Columbia, South Carolina, Newport News, Virginia, Little Rock, Arkansas, and Birmingham, Alabama, in 1945. Black parents attempted, with less success, to increase state allocations in support of black segregated public schools. On balance, greater progress in improving black educational prospects was achieved in these few years than during the previous three decades. By 1950, 83,000 black women and men between the ages of 18 to 24 were enrolled in universities, 4.5 percent of their age group.

In the labor force, a similar picture of change emerged. Philip S. Foner notes that "the median income of nonwhite wage- and salary-earners had risen from 41 percent of the white median in 1939 to 60 percent in 1950; the percentage of male black workers in white-collar and professional jobs had risen from 5.6 in 1940 to 7.2 in 1950, and that of craftsmen and operatives from 16.6 percent of the total in 1940 to 28.8 percent in 1950."[2] By 1946, there were 450,000 black members of the American Federation of Labor (AFL) in the South, and another 200,000 in the rest of the country. Substantial numbers of blacks were in many sectors of the workforce that were unionized before the war and afterwards: 17 percent of all semi-skilled meatpacking workers were black, 9.2 percent of the coalminers, and 68 percent of the tobacco workers. By 1946, blacks were also well represented in the more progressive Congress of Industrial Organizations (CIO). The largest numbers of black workers who were organized were in the Steelworkers of America–CIO (95,000 blacks); the Automobile, Aircraft, Agricultural Implement Workers of America–CIO (90,000); Hodcarriers and Common Labor–AFL (55,000); Marine and Shipbuilding Workers–CIO (40,000); and the United Electrical, Radio and Machine Workers–CIO (40,000). The nation's most influential black trade unionist, A. Philip Randolph, was a leading force for desegregation both inside the House of Labor and within the largest society. By 1955, he was named vice-president of the merged AFL-CIO.

The growing social and economic power of the black working and middle classes seemed to many to provide the basis for an entirely new political relationship between blacks and whites. In early 1948, NAACP political theorist Henry Lee Moon predicted with stunning accuracy that the potential weight of this emerging black force could no longer be ignored by either the Democratic or the Republican parties. The ballot is "the indispensable weapon in the persistent fight for full citizenship . . . a tool to be used [against] Jim Crow," Moon declared in *Balance of Power: The Negro Vote*. "By 1936, after four years of the New Deal, colored voters in the urban centers of the North and East had caught up with the procession. The mass migration out of the Republican camp was in response to the Roosevelt program which . . . made an effort to meet some of their urgent needs."[3] Moon observed that the black vote would be delivered in the future only to those candidates of either party who addressed civil rights issues and strengthened the social and economic reform programs initiated by the Roosevelt Administration. He also cautioned Democrats not to take the black voter for granted and sensed that, even in any election year, blacks could easily move their allegiances. In retrospect, Moon seriously overemphasized the volatility of the black electorate; but at the time, no white candidate could be absolutely certain that blacks would remain basically Democrats. During the early post-war years, blacks had occupied positions of minor-level influence in the trade unions, in municipal and state politics, and were in many formerly all-white universities. It was apparent to every observer, particularly the national leaders of the Democratic Party, that the black electorate's interests would have to be accommodated at the expense of the South and Jim Crow.

II

The democratic upsurge of black people which characterized the late 1950s could have happened ten years earlier. With the notable exception of the *Brown* decision of 17 May 1954, which ordered the desegregation of public schools, most of the important Supreme Court decisions that aided civil rights proponents had been passed some years before. In May 1946, for example, the high court ruled that state laws requiring segregation on interstate buses were unconstitutional. In *Smith v. Allwright*, delivered 3 April 1944, by an eight to one margin, the Supreme Court ended the use of the all-white primary election. By the spring of 1946, there were 75,000 black registered voters in Texas and 100,000 black voters in Georgia. Yet the sit-ins, the non-violent street demonstrations, did not yet occur; the façade of white supremacy was crumbling, yet for almost ten years there was no overt and mass movement which challenged racism in the streets. This interim decade, between World War II and the Montgomery County, Alabama, bus boycott of December 1955, has also generally been ignored by black social historians. I think that the answer to the question, Why were mass popular protests for desegregation relatively weak or nonexistent in the period 1945–54?, is precisely the answer to the second question: Why have historians of the black movement done so little research on the post-war period? The impact of the Cold War, the anti-communist purges and near-totalitarian social environment, had a devastating effect upon the cause of blacks' civil rights and civil liberties. As this chapter will illustrate, the paranoid mood of anti-communist America made it difficult for any other reasonable reform movement to exist. The sterile legacy of anti-communism, felt even today, has so influenced many American historians that they are not even able to comment on the facts before them.

By the end of 1946, the Soviet Union and the United States had reached a clear breaking point in their relations. From the Soviets' perspective, the Americans were ungrateful for their preeminent role in the anti-fascist war effort, and lacked any critical understanding of their domestic and foreign requirements needed to restore peace and economic order. The Soviets had lost 20 million men and women in World War II. During the summer of 1946, the worst drought of the twentieth century dried up all the crops in the Ukraine and Volga lands, and millions were on the verge of starvation. Urban consumption declined to only 40 percent of 1940 totals. "In the coal-mines of the Donetz Basin men were still pumping water out of the shafts. . . . The steel mills, rattling with wear and tear, turned out only

12 million tons of ingot, a fraction of the American output. Engineering plants were worked by adolescent semi-skilled labour. People were dressed in rags; many were barefoot."[4] The Soviet Union was simply in no condition to fight another war, but it did feel that its national interests had to be preserved. The Americans were driven by other motives. For many political conservatives and emigrants from Eastern Europe, World War II had been "the wrong war against the wrong enemy," writes social historian David Caute. "These groups were joined after 1944 by others initially favorable to the war but subsequently appalled by the spread of Soviet communism in Eastern Europe and by the reduction of [these] nations to satellite status. Here Catholic indignation ran high." Anti-communist liberals in both major political parties "soon developed a determination to halt Soviet encroachment by every available means and to deal roughly with elements at home—communists, fellow travelers, progressives—who foolishly or wickedly adopted the Soviet point of view."[5] American corporate interests were concerned about expanding investments abroad and reducing or eliminating all pro-labor legislation sponsored by the New Deal at home. The anti-communist campaign permitted them to do both, as well as to flush suspected leftists out of positions of trade union authority. A great many post-war politicians, such as Wisconsin Senator Joe McCarthy and California Senator Richard M. Nixon, simply "recognized a good thing when they saw it, [and] cynically manipulated public hysteria for their own political purposes."[6]

Noted playwright Lillian Hellman accurately describes the post-war "Red Scare" period as a "Scoundrel Time":

> It was not the first time in history that the confusions of honest people were picked up in space by cheap baddies who, hearing a few bars of popular notes, made them into an opera of public disorder, staged and sung, as much of the congressional testimony shows, in the wards of an insane asylum. A theme is always necessary, a plain, simple, unadorned theme to confuse the ignorant. The anti-Red theme was easily chosen . . . not alone because we were frightened of socialism, but chiefly, I think, to destroy the remains of Roosevelt and his sometimes advanced work. The McCarthy group . . . chose the anti-Red scare with perhaps more cynicism than Hitler picked anti-Semitism.[7]

In March 1947, Truman asked Congress to spend $400 million in economic aid and military hardware to halt leftist movements in Turkey and Greece. In the following years, five million investigations of public employees suspected of communist sympathies were held. Trade unions were pressured to purge all communists and anti-racist activists with leftist credentials. By July 1947, union leader Philip Murray ordered the CIO executive committee, "If communism is an issue in your unions, throw it to hell out, and throw its advocates out along with it."[8] The CIO convention of 1949 expelled the 50,000-member United Electrical, Radio, and Machine Workers union for being dominated by leftists; within months, eleven progressive unions with nearly one million members were purged from the CIO. In 1949, 15 states passed "anti-subversion laws." "Writing or speaking subversive words" in Michigan was a crime punishable by a life sentence in prison. In 1951, Tennessee mandated the death penalty for the espousal of revolutionary Marxist ideas. That same year, Massachusetts required a three-year term in the state prison for anyone who allowed a Communist Party meeting to be held in their homes. Georgia, Indiana, Pennsylvania and Washington outlawed the Communist Party. The U.S. Attorney General, Tom Clark of Texas, warned all Americans in January 1948: "Those who do not believe in the ideology of the United States, shall not be allowed to stay in the United States."[9]

"The wealthiest, most secure nation in the world was sweat-drenched in fear," Caute writes. "Federal, state and municipal employees worried about their pasts, their student indiscretions, their slenderest associations. . . . Some hastened to save their own skin by denouncing a colleague. In schools, universities, town halls and local professional associations, a continuous, pious mumbling of oaths was heard—the liturgy of fear."[10] For black Americans, the "Scoundrel Time" was refracted through the prism of race, and was viewed in the light of their own particular class interests. For many black industrial and rural agricultural workers, the communists were the most dedicated proponents of racial equality and desegregation. In the 1930s, they had organized a vigorous defense of the Scottsboro Nine, a group of young black men unjustly convicted of rape in Alabama. The Party had sponsored Unemployed Councils, and provided the major force to desegregate American labor unions. For the aspiring black middle class, the image of the Communist Party was entirely different. Many black preachers had often denounced Marxism because of its philosophical atheism. Black entrepreneurs were dedicated to the free enterprise system, and sought to enrich themselves through the existing economic order. Many black leaders had condemned the Party during World War II for urging blacks to maintain labor's "no strike" pledges. Foner notes, "It was to be exceedingly difficult for the communists to overcome the resentment among blacks created by the Party's wartime policies. The communists never completely erased the feeling in sections of the black community that they had placed the Soviet Union's survival above the battle for black equality."[11] In general, black middle-class leaders attempted to divorce themselves from the communists as the reactionary trend was building across the country.

The most prominent black leaders were affected in different ways by the outbreak of the domestic Cold War. Randolph was the doyen of the black labor movement. During World War I, he and his radical associate Chandler Owen had edited the militantly socialist journal the *Messenger*, and were known throughout Harlem as the "Lenin and Trotsky" of the black movement. During the Red Summer of 1919, President Woodrow Wilson had denounced Randolph as "the most dangerous Negro in America." During the mid-1920s Randolph had organized the Brotherhood of Sleeping Car Porters, and began to moderate his leftist views considerably. His fierce struggle with the Communist Party over the leadership of the National Negro Congress from 1935 and 1939 left a bitter anti-communist bias in his entire political outlook. During the war, he had continued to urge black workers to adopt a "strategy and maneuver (of) mass civil disobedience and non-cooperation" to fight racism.[12] But Randolph opposed, certainly from this point onward, any co-operation or "united front" activity with the communists. In 1947, he organized the Committee Against Jim Crow in Military Service and Training, and threatened the Senate Armed Services Committee that he would direct a massive civil disobedience effort if the U.S. armed forces were not promptly desegregated. But in the post-war years, Randolph deliberately eschewed any political or organizational links with revolutionary Marxists. In his speeches and writings, he denounced the domestic communist "conspiracy" at every opportunity. By clearly separating the interests of black labor from the radical left, he believed that he could gain the political support of many anti-communist liberals and the Truman Administration. As Randolph declared before a congressional committee in 1948, racial segregation "is the greatest single propaganda and political weapon in the hands of Russia and international communism today."[13]

Although elected to Congress only in 1944, Adam Clayton Powell, Jr., quickly emerged as the most influential black public official for the next two decades. Almost twenty years younger than Randolph, Powell had acquired his reputation as a dedicated militant during the Great Depression. As the son of the leader of one of the largest black churches in the nation, Harlem's Abyssinian Baptist Church, Powell led a series of popular boycotts which called for black jobs and greater welfare and social services. A charismatic speaker whose entire "way of life" was "an act of rebellion," Powell had at first no reservations about joining with the communists who defended the interests of black poor and working people.[14] The practical contributions of the Party were praised by Powell in a 1945 statement: "There is no group in America, including the Christian church, that practices racial brotherhood one-tenth as much as the Communist Party."[15] Once in Congress, Powell led the fight against anti-communism. In early 1947, when two congressional contempt citations were passed against com-

munists who refused to divulge information to the House Un-American
Activities Committee (HUAC) by votes of 370 to 1 and 357 to 2, only Powell
and progressive New York Congressman Vito Marcantonio voted against
the majority. Powell recognized that every defender of racial segregation in
Congress was also a devout proponent of anti-communist legislation, and
that the Negro had no other alternative except to champion the civil liberties of the left in order to protect the black community's own interests.
This advanced perspective, which would prove to be correct in later years,
found little support among the black middle class, despite Powell's continued personal popularity. Within Congress itself, Powell was contemp-
tuously dismissed as a political pariah for fifteen years.

Since 1930, the leader of the NAACP had been Walter White. Under his
direction the organization had grown in numbers and political influence.
During the 1920s, he had written a provocative investigative report on
lynchings in the South. As an assistant secretary to James Weldon Johnson
he had served tirelessly, and with Johnson's retirement White slowly moved
the NAACP to the right. Internally, co-workers who resisted any of White's
initiatives were soon fired. In DuBois's words, White was absolutely self-
centered and egotistical to the point that he was almost unconscious of it.
He seemed really to believe that his personal interests and the interest of
the race and organization were identical. This led to curious complications
because to attain his objects he was often absolutely unscrupulous."[16] In
1933–34, White feuded with DuBois over the NAACP's lack of coherent
economic policy for blacks to deal with the Great Depression. In despair
and outrage, DuBois resigned as editor of the NAACP journal, the Crisis, in
June 1934, after 24 years of service. DuBois returned to the NAACP after an
absence of ten years as research director, but with the outbreak of the Cold
War, White pressured the board to fire him within three years because of
DuBois's "radical thought" and progressive activities in international
peace and Pan-Africanist movements. White's bitter relationship with Du-
Bois was manifested in his opposition to the entire American left generally.
From the beginning of his tenure at the NAACP, he had fought any influence of communists or independent radicals in the organization. He supported the early "witch-hunts" to exclude communists from all levels of
the federal government. When in late 1947, a poll of the NAACP national
office revealed that 70 percent of the staff intended to support former vice
president Henry Wallace on the Progressive Party ticket in opposition to
Truman, White warned DuBois and other Wallace advocates not to take
part in any electoral campaign. Simultaneously, White was already "making a nationwide drive for Truman, by letter, newspaper articles, telegrams and public speech." Like Randolph, White attempted to identify
the struggle for black equality with the anit-communist impulse.[17]

The most prominent black supporters of progressive and leftist politics were DuBois and the famous cultural artist-activist Paul Robeson. DuBois had been an independent socialist since 1904, but had experienced a series of volatile confrontations with revolutionary Marxists. In the wake of the Bolshevik Revolution, he denounced the entire concept of the "dictatorship of the proletariat," and told the readers of the *Crisis* that he was "not prepared to dogmatize with Marx and Lenin."[18] As late as 1944, DuBois had written that "the program of the American Communist Party was suicidal."[19] Yet after extensive travels in the Soviet Union in 1926, 1936 and 1949, DuBois's view on matters shifted considerably. He concluded that the Soviets' anti-imperialist positions promoting the necessity for African political independence from European colonial rule were genuinely progressive; he was impressed with the Soviet Union's extensive domestic educational, social and technological gains. By the late 1940s, he believed that the black liberation movement in America had to incorporate a socialist perspective, and that blacks had to be in the forefront in promoting peaceful co-existence with the Soviet bloc. Robeson was politically closer to the communist movement for a greater period of time. In the late 1930s, he supported the progressive government of Spain against the Nazi-backed Spanish fascists in that country's bloody civil war. He recognized earlier than Dubois that the rise in domestic anti-communism would become a force to stifle progressive change and the civil rights of blacks. In early 1949, in a controversial address in Paris, he declared that U.S. policies toward Africa were "similar to that of Hitler and Goebbels." The Soviet Union "has raised our people to full human dignity." These and other statements led to Robeson's wide public censure. His noted career as a Shakespearean actor and singer, which was described by American critics as the most gifted of his generation before 1945, crashed in short order. To muffle Robeson's impact, HUAC quickly called black baseball player Jackie Robinson before the committee to denounce him. Robeson had been a "famous ex-athlete and a great singer and actor," Robinson admitted, but his subversive statements gave support to the communist cause. "We can win the fight [against segregation] without the Communists and we don't want their help."[20]

As the presidential election of 1948 approached, the Truman Administration recognized that the Negro electorate would play an unusually decisive role in the campaign. More than Roosevelt, Truman privately viewed the blacks' goals of social and political equality with great contempt. But the administration's aggressively anti-communist polemics could not create a sufficient electoral bloc among white voters which would guarantee victory that November. Democratic party disaffections grew on the left and right, with Wallace's Progressive Party and the southern-based States'

Rights Party, which nominated hard-line segregationist Strom Thurmond of South Carolina. The Republicans renominated popular New York governor Thomas Dewey as their standard-bearer, a politician who had run a very creditable race against Roosevelt in 1944. Presidential advisers informed Truman that he might even win the popular vote, but without critical black support in the industrial Northeast, the Midwest, and California, he would lose the electoral college count to Dewey—or, as in 1800 and 1824, a disastrous statement could occur and the House of Representatives might have to select a president in 1949. Thus, for the first time since 1876, it seemed apparent that blacks would decide the national election. Truman immediately responded to blacks' interests by publicly calling for new civil rights legislation. He promised to promote fair employment procedures and to press federal contractors aggressively to comply with desegregation guidelines. On 26 July 1948, the president issued an executive order to the effect "that there shall be equality of treatment and opportunity for all persons in the armed forces without regard to race, color, religion or national origin."[21] Randolph promptly suspended the Committee Against Jim Crow in Military Service and Training's plans for a proposed boycott. White and his NAACP supporters exhorted blacks to reject the Wallace campaign, and urged them to vote for Truman in the interests of civil rights. White's efforts were a triumph for Cold War liberalism. In Harlem, Truman received 90,000 votes to Wallace's 21,000 votes, even though the Progressive Party's anti-racist platform was far superior to that of Truman's. In Pittsburgh, only 2,000 blacks cast ballots for Wallace. In California, Ohio and Illinois, black voters provided the decisive electoral edge for Truman over Dewey. Overall, Truman carried about two-thirds of the black vote, and with that margin he won the election. True to his campaign promises, in 1949 Truman continued to promote modest biracial reform efforts at the federal level, while at the same time escalating the Cold War at home. Truman's victory silenced and isolated black progressives for many years, and committed the NAACP and most middle-class black leaders to an alliance with Democratic presidents who did not usually share black workers' interests, except in ways which would promote their own needs at a given moment. Accommodation, anti-communism, and tacit allegiance to white liberals and labor bureaucrats became the principal tenets of black middle-class politics for the next decade.

III

Without much public fanfare or notice, a series of new political formations created by blacks and liberal whites began to emerge at this time. Blacks in South Carolina formed the Progressive Democratic Party to challenge the

whites-only state Democratic Party. By May 1944, the Progressive Democrats had organized chapters in 39 of the state's 46 counties, and had begun
an independent electoral strategy to expand the number of registered black
voters in South Carolina. That same year, the biracial Southern Regional
Council was formed in Atlanta, a coalition of clergy and professionals who
supported the gradual but steady abolition of Jim Crow. The most important new biracial group, however, was the Congress of Racial Equality
(CORE), established in 1942 by the pacifist Fellowship of Reconciliation,
directed by A. J. Muste. Of CORE's 50 charter members, at least a dozen
were black, including a Howard University divinity school graduate,
James Farmer. The black youth secretary for the Fellowship of Reconciliation, social democrat and pacifist Bayard Rustin, gave political purpose
and direction to the young formation. One of CORE's first actions was a
confrontation with barbers at the University of Chicago who in November
1942 refused to cut Rustin's hair. From these modest beginnings, CORE developed into a civil rights group which emphasized non-violent direct action, rather than the litigation and moral suasion techniques of Walter
White and the NAACP. Unlike the older organization, it was democratic,
and most funds raised by chapters remained at the local level. By 1947,
there were 13 CORE chapters, mostly in Ohio, New York, Illinois, Kansas,
and Minnesota. CORE chapters staged a series of non-violent boycotts to
desegregate lunchcounters and schools in a series of northern and midwest
cities. White Methodist student leader George Houser and Rustin developed a plan for CORE to test desegregation laws on interstate buses in the
upper South during the late autumn of 1946. Perhaps hearing about the
proposed "Journeys of Reconciliation," NAACP leaders, including attorney
Thurgood Marshall, warned that: "A disobedience movement on the part
of Negroes and their white allies, if employed in the South, would result in
wholesale slaughter with no good achieved."[22] Walter White, true to form,
refused to provide any financial support for the effort. On 9 April 1947, a
small party of 8 blacks and 8 whites left Washington, D.C. determined to
sit in whites-only sections of the buses. In the journeys, CORE members
were repeatedly arrested and intimidated by southern police, bus drivers,
and the local courts. Rustin and other activists were sentenced to serve 30
days on North Carolina's jail gang. The Journeys of Reconciliation failed to
overturn the South's racial codes, but in the process they established a pattern of civil rights protest which would be revived with greater effectiveness as the Freedom Ride movement in the 1960s.

By the early 1950s, the progress towards civil rights began to slow down
perceptibly. The number of registered black southern voters reached 1.2
million by 1952. Yet "in the lower South, apart from a very few cities,"
C. Vann Woodward writes, "little change in Negro voting or office-holding

could be detected. By one means or another, including intimidation and terror, Negroes were effectively prevented from registering even when they had the courage to try."[23] On 2 June 1946, a black army veteran, Etoy Fletcher, was flogged publicly in Brandon, Mississippi, for attempting to register. Senator Theodore Bilbo of Mississippi boasted that only 1,500 out of 500,000 black potential voters were registered in his state. "The best way to keep a nigger away from a white primary is to see him the night before," Bilbo declared. The *Jackson Daily News* (Mississippi) warned the state's few registered black voters: "Don't attempt to participate in the Democratic primary anywhere in Mississippi. . . . Staying away from the polls will be the best way to prevent unhealthy and unhappy results."[24] Southern registrars employed Kafkaesque tests to determine whether blacks were "literate" enough to vote. One white registrar in Forest County, Mississippi, asked black potential voters this question: "How many bubbles are in a bar of soap?"[25] As one Alabama political leader explained, the vote of even one black person in the deep South was an intolerable threat to the entire structure of Jim Crow. "If it was necessray to eliminate the Negro in 1901, because of certain inherent characteristics, it is even more necessary now because some intellectual progress makes the Negro more dangerous to our political structure now than in 1901. The Negro has the same disposition to live without working that his ancestors had in the jungle 10,000 years ago."[26] Most of these racist politicians were still leading figures in the national Democratic Party, and were represented in powerful posts in the Truman Administration.

Truman himself was virtually silent from 1946–53 as white racist vigilante groups proliferated. As the black population in Los Angeles County, California, reached 200,000 by 1946, the Ku Klux Klan began to appear on the West Coast. Klan organizations were formed throughout the South, and were reported active in Pennsylvania and New Jersey. In New York, the state attorney general estimated that there were 1,000 Klansmen in his state alone in the late 1940s. In the face of growing racist opposition, the NAACP counselled continued reliance upon the Truman Administration, legal challenges to segregation laws, and a general policy which spurned direct action. The failure and tragedy of this conservative approach to social change was in its parochial vision and tacit acceptance of the Cold War politics. By refusing to work with Marxists, the NAACP lost the most principled anti-racist organizers and activists. Instead of confronting the racists politically, with the commitment of a Robeson or a DuBois, they accepted the prevailing xenophobia of the times, and in the end undercut their own efforts to segregate society. The anit-communist impulse even affected CORE, to its detriment. A few CORE chapters, in Columbus, Ohio, and Chicago, encouraged Marxist participation in the early 1940s. In 1949, however, when Trotskyists joined the San Francisco chapter, the national office voided its affiliation. In 1948, Houser and CORE's executive committee drafted a "Statement on Communism," which was passed unanimously by its convention that year. CORE denounced any ties with "Communist-controlled" groups, and CORE members were ordered not to co-operate or work with so-called communist-front organizations. As CORE's historians noted, this action did not prevent "conservatives and racists from continuing to attack CORE as Communist-controlled. Despite its vigorous anticommunist position, CORE suffered considerably from the McCarthyite hysteria of the period. The Red Scare, by labeling radical reform groups subversive, seriously impeded CORE's growth."[27] By 1954, CORE had all but ceased to exist as an organization.

IV

As the Cold War intensified, the repression of black progressives increased. Aided by local and state police, a gang of whites disrupted a concert given by Paul Robeson in Peekskill, New York in 1948. HUAC witnesses declared that Robeson was "the black Stalin among Negroes."[28] In August 1950, the U.S. government revoked his passport for eight years. Officials prevented Robeson entering Canada in 1952, although no passport was necessary to visit that country. DuBois ran for the U.S. Senate in New York in the autumn of 1950 on the progressive American Labor Party ticket, and denounced the anti-communist policies of both major parties. Despite wide public censure, he received 206,000 votes, and polled 15 percent of Harlem's ballots. The Truman Administration finally moved to eliminate DuBois's still considerable prestige within the black community. On 8 February 1951, DuBois was indicted for allegedly serving as an "agent of a foreign principal" in his anti-war work with the Peace Information Center in New York. The 82-year-old black man was handcuffed, fingerprinted, and portrayed in the national media as a common criminal. Before his trial, the New York *Herald-Tribune* convicted him in a prominent editorial: "The DuBois outfit was set up to promote a tricky appeal of Soviet origin, poisonous in its surface innocence, which made it appear that a signature against the use of atomic weapons would forthwith insure world peace. It was, in short, an attempt to disarm America and yet ignore every form of Communist aggression."[29] An international committee was formed to defend DuBois and his colleagues at the Peace Information Center. Threatened with a fine of $100,000 and a five-year jail term, DuBois continued to denounce the Truman Administration while out on bail. In November 1951, a federal judge dismissed all charges against DuBois, when the government failed to introduce a single piece of evidence that implied that he was a communist agent.

Despite DuBois's acquittal, the government had accomplished its primary objectives. DuBois's voluminous writings on Negro sociology, history and politics were removed from thousands of libraries and universities. The State Department illegally withheld his passport for seven years. Black public opinion moved even further to the right. One leading black newspaper which had carried DuBois's essays for decades, the *Chicago Defender*, declared that "it is a supreme tragedy that he should have become embroiled in activities that have been exposed as subversive in the twilight of his years." The oldest Negro fraternity, which DuBois had helped to found in 1906, Alpha Phi Alpha, did not rally to his defence. Only one of thirty Alpha Phi Alpha chapters expressed public support for DuBois. Virtually every black college president except Charles S. Johnson of Fisk University, DuBois's *alma mater*, said nothing about the case. The NAACP was especially conspicuous in its moral cowardice. White told NAACP board members that the government had definite proof which would convict DuBois. The NAACP Legal Defense lawyers made no overtures to provide assistance. The central office contacted NAACP local chapters with strongly worded advice about "not touching" DuBois's case. Black schoolteachers' groups and the black National Baptist Convention took no action. The entire ordeal left DuBois in bitter doubt about the political future of the Negro middle class:

> The reaction of Negroes [to the case] revealed a distinct cleavage not hitherto clear in American Negro opinion. The intelligentsia, the successful business and professional men, were . . . either silent or actually antagonistic. The reasons were clear; many believed that the government had actual proof of subversive activities on our part; until the very end they awaited their disclosure. [These blacks] had become american in their acception of exploitation as defensible, and in their imitation of American "conspicuous expenditure." They proposed to make money and spend it as pleased them. They had beautiful homes, large and expensive cars and fur coats. They hated "communism" and "socialism" as much as any white American.[30]

On many black college campuses, the Red Scare was reflected in a growing exclusion of radical views from classroom discourse. Any faculty member who had a history of militant activism, either in the Communist Party or in other suspicious groups, could be fired. Two examples from Fisk University can be cited. Giovanni Rossi Lomanitz had been an active Party member in the early 1940s, working in the Federation of Architects, Engineers, Chemists and Technicians. A former associate of J. Robert Oppenheimer, Lomanitz taught at Cornell and in the late 1940s began an appointment at Fisk. In 1949 HUAC subpoenaed Lomanitz, and before the committee he refused to testify against himself, citing the Fifth Amendment. In twenty-four hours, despite the support of faculty and students, president Charles S. Johnson dismissed Lomanitz without due process. Five years later, Fisk mathematics professor Lee Lorch was summoned before HUAC. Lorch pointedly denied being a member of the Communist Party during his tenure at Fisk, and refused to answer questions about his alleged Party membership before 1941 by evoking the First Amendment. Johnson issued a public statement stating that Lorch's position before HUAC "is for all practical purposes tantamount to admission of membership in the Communist Party." Out of a faculty of 70, 48 urged Fisk's Board of Trustees to retain him, as did 22 student leaders and 150 alumni. Fisk instead ended Lorch's contract, as of June 1955.[31]

A number of black former actisists agreed to become informers against the communists. In the federal trial of twelve leading Party officials, which included two blacks, New York City councilman Benjamin J. Davis and Henry Winston, staged in New York City during July and August 1948, one of the government's black witnesses was an autoworker, William Cummings. Cummings joined the Party in 1943 for the FBI in Toledo, Ohio, and told the jury that communists "taught militants that one day the streets would run with blood." The defendants received sentences ranging from three to five years in federal prisons, and were ordered to pay fines of $5,000 each. Some of the Party's oldest black recruits turned into agents for the government. William O. Nowell, born in a southern sharecropper's family, joined the Party in the late 1920s. Trained in the Soviet Union, he rose as a Party leader in Detroit's trade union struggles. When he was expelled from the Party in 1936, he promptly worked as an agent in Henry Ford's "goon squad," threatening and beating other autoworkers. From 1948 until 1954, Nowell became a "professional anti-communist," testifying in approximately 40 trials and hearings. Manning Johnson entered the Party in 1930, and quickly climbed to its national committee in the ten years before his departure. Johnson repeatedly perjured himself at numerous trials, later claiming with pride that he would lie "a thousand times" to protect "the security of the government." The U.S. Justice Department paid Johnson $4,500 a year for his services. Ex-communist Leonard Patterson received $3,800 a year for two yeras, testifying against his former comrades before HUAC and in the courts. North Carolina black attorney Clayton Clontz joined the Party after the war, and covertly informed the FBI on its activities from August 1948 until February 1953. In the trial of one communist, Clontz made the astonishing claim that he was told that Soviet troops would land in the U.S. if America "declared war on [U.S.] communists in the revolution."[32]

The purge of communists and radicals from organized labor in 1947–50 was the principal reason for the decline in the AFL-CIO's commitment to the struggle against racial segregation. In the wake of the NAACP's stampede to the right, a left of center space on the political spectrum was open, and militant black workers took advantage of the opportunity. In June 1950, nearly 1,000 delegates met in Chicago at the National Labor Conference for Negro Rights. Robeson gave a moving plenary address which condemned the Cold War and supported deténte with the Soviet bloc countries. Black delegates from AFL unions noted that the federation still maintained all-white unions, and black veterans of the CIO argued that their organization had all but abandoned the struggle for Negro rights. The Chicago conference established a steering committee for the coordination of future work, which included Coleman Young, a Detroit leader of the Amalgamated Clothing Workers, UAW activist William R. Hood, and Cleveland Robinson, vice president of the Distributive, Processing, and Office Workers Union. In 1950 and 1951, the committee helped to develop 23 Negro Labor Councils, each fighting to end segregated facilities at the workplace, expanding black job opportunities, and attacking racism in the unions. The militant Detroit Council, led by Hood, inspired the call for the creation of a new black progressive labor organization. In October 1951, the National Negro Labor Council was formed in Cincinnati, Ohio. The delegates at the convention represented unions expelled from the CIO for retaining communists, as well as members of both the AFL and CIO. Hood emerged as the president, and Young was elected executive secretary. Almost immediately, the National Negro Labor Council came under direct attack. CIO leaders denounced Hood, Young and other black labor activists as the "tool(s) of the Soviet Union." Lester Granger of the National Urban League criticized the council as "subversive." In its brief history, the organization pressured to desegregate jobs in major U.S. firms; organized campaigns to increase black workers' salaries and to upgrade their job ranks; led pickets against hotels and companies practicing Jim Crow; and challenged the unions to advance more black workers into leadership positions. The pressure against the Congress's pickets and protest activities was enormous. By December 1954, HUAC denounced the "pro-communist ideology" of the organization. It is true that communists participated in the National Negro Labor Council, but in no way were the desegregationist programs it carried out dictated or even directly influenced by the Party. By 1956, however, due to political pressures from the

U.S. government, corporations and white labor leaders, the National Negro Labor Council had disappeared.[33]

Besides Robeson, DuBois, and the militant workers of the National Negro Labor Council, few examples or models of black resistance existed, except in the Communist Party. Black communist leader Henry Winston was confined during his 1948 trial in a poorly ventilated, closet-like cell. Despite two heart attacks, and following this, the judge's denial that he be seen by his family doctor, Winston's will to fight remained strong. At the April 1952 trial of black communists Pettis Perry and Claudia Jones, Perry described himself "as a victim of a frameup so enormous as to resemble the Reichstag Fire trail" of 1933. Secretary of the Party's Negro Commission, Perry defiantly asked the court, "How could a Negro get justice from a white jury?" A native West Indian Marxist, Jones "delivered a long indictment of America's treatment of black people." Convicted, Perry received three years and a $5,000 fine; Jones, one year and one day in jail, and a $2,000 fine. Claude Lightfoot, secretary of the Illinois party, was arrested in June 1954, and had to stay in jail four months until $30,000 bail money could be collected. Convicted in January 1955, the black World War II veteran was given five years and a $5,000 fine. Prison life for these black revolutionaries was difficult physically, but their resistance remained uncompromised. Claudia Jones's acute asthmatic and cardiac conditions were made worse by having to work at a prison loom. In ten months she was sent to a hospital, and she died not long after her release. Prison doctors refused to treat Winston's eyesight, and as a result he became blind. Confronted with segregated accommodation in the federal prison at Terre Haute, Indiana, Benajmin Davis filed a suit against prison officials. Despite being placed on "round-the-clock administrative segregation," Davis refused to be defeated.[34]

The black middle class's almost complete capitulation to anti-communism not only liquidated the moderately progressive impulse of the New Deal years and 1945–46; it made the Negroes unwitting accomplices of a Cold War domestic policy which was, directly, both racist and politically reactionary. When paranoid librarians took DuBois's works off their shelves, they did not stop there—banned literature often included black publications such as the *Negro Digest* and the NAACP's *Crisis*, as well as the *New Republic*, *The Nation*, and other white-oriented liberal journals friendly to desegregation causes. When Robeson was blacklisted along with Lillian Hellman, director Dalton Trumbo and the "Hollywood Ten," did blacks think their feeble voices praising American patriotism would save black actors and artists? The wife of Adam Clayton Powell, Hazel Scott, a talented singer and pianist, could not obtain employment for years. Black television actor William Marshall, stage performer Canada Lee, and others were victimized by blacklists. When Randolph defended anti-communism at home, did he not recognize that in doing so he became a tool for American interests and power abroad? In 1952, Randolph travelled with socialist leader Norman Thomas to Asia under the auspices of the Congress for Cultural Freedom. Speaking in Japan and Burma, he denounced Russia's "slavery" and emphasized the progress made in U.S. race relations. In 1967, it was revealed that the Congress for Cultural Freedom was a subsidized front for the U.S. Central Intelligence Agency (CIA). Historian Christopher Lasch's criticisms of Thomas could be made with equal vigor of Randolph: "He does not see that he was being used [for different purposes] from the ones he thought he was advancing. He thought he was working for democratic reform . . . whereas the CIA valued him as a showpiece, an anti-Communist who happened to be a Socialist."[35] By serving as the "left wing of McCarthyism," Randolph, White and other Negro leaders retarded the black movement for a decade or more.

V

Another dimension to America's traditional racial dilemma became more prominent after the war. Blacks were by far the largest single racial minority group in the nation, but they were not alone. In the Far West, Chinese peasants were brought into California to labor in the mines and for railroad companies after the Civil War. Before the Depression of 1893 roughly 30,000 worked as low-paid laborers on California ranches and farms. In the 1890s, a trickle of Japanese immigrants expanded into a flood. By 1898, 60,000 Japanese lived in Hawaii; between 1886 and 1908 the number of Japanese on the mainland increased from 4,000 to over 100,000. The 1924 immigration legislation passed under President Calvin Coolidge effectively prevented Japanese entering the U.S. mainland, but new waves of cheap workers were found by American businesses in the Philippines. By the end of the 1920s, about 25,000 impoverished Filipino farm workers were employed in California's Salinas and San Joaquin valleys. At the beginning of World War II, some 78,000 Chinese-Americans and 127,000 Japanese-Americans were living on the West Coast. In the eastern U.S., colored workers were drawn from the Caribbean. The Puerto Rican population in New York City alone increased from barely 60,000 in 1940 to 240,000 in 1950. The majority of these newer national minority groups experienced a system of rigid racial segregation, residential discrimination, political oppression and low wages which blacks had known intimately for generations. As early as 1906–7, anti-Japanese riots erupted in San Francisco, as racist whites pillaged the Japanese community. In 1942 over

100,000 Japanese-Americans, mostly native-born U.S. citizens, or Nisei, were forcibly removed to internment camps for the duration of World War II. Most lost their homes and all of their personal belongings. The American general who supervised their mass arrests justified U.S. policy in bluntly racist language: "A Jap's a Jap. It makes no difference whether he is an American citizen or not."[36] Puerto Rican workers were often victimized by policies of crude racial discrimination by unions and managers like. Compounding this problem of ethnic competition for jobs was a fresh influx of European and Asian immigrants after 1945. Between 1948 and 1953, the Displaced Persons Act brought 410,000 Slavic and Germanic people into the country. Another 50,000 Hungarians and 31,000 Dutch-Indonesians arrived several years later. Thus by the Cold War period, the problem of the color line was not simply a social equation of black and white.

Despite the wide diversity of the national minorities which lived and labored in the U.S. there were two specific oppressed groups with which blacks had a special relationship, by both historical experience and economic status—Mexican-Americans (or Chicanos) and American Indians. The Spanish had colonized the American Southwest almost 200 years before slavery effectively took root in the Carolinas and Virginia. Slavery was officially abolished by Mexico in 1829, a move designed primarily to halt the immigration of white slaveholders into Texas. After the Mexican War of 1846–48, the United States seized roughly half of the nation of Mexico as its territory, and within a generation, thousands of Mexican peasants worked as peons and wage-laborers for white American settlers. The "Anglos" systematically weakened or destroyed the Spanish-built missions and other institutions of Mexican culture. Mexican ranches were seized, usually by illegal means, and became the property of white Americans. Mexican sheep herders were often denied access to pasture lands and water for their flocks, and in the early 1880s scores were murdered by rampaging white ranchers in the Graham–Tewksbury War in Arizona. As heavy industry moved into the region by 1900—railroads, mining, smelting—white corporations relied upon the Mexican population as their principal reservoir of cheap labor. In times of economic expansion, Mexicans were used as strike-breakers or scabs during periodic conflicts between white laborers and managers. In periods of recession and depression, they became the "reserve army of labor," the first to be fired from their jobs, as blacks were in the South. During the 1930s, almost half a million Mexicans were forcibly deported "as unemployed Anglos claimed Mexican jobs."[37] Racist and nativist groups, including the American Federation of Labor, the American Legion, the Daughters of the American Revolution and the Veterans of Foreign Wars, fought vigorously for the exclusion of additional Mexican workers from the country. The Ku Klux Klan in Texas, New Mexico and Arizona attacked and sometimes killed Chicano men and women with legal impunity. Despite these assaults and legal restrictions, the number of Mexican-Americans continued to increase. Between 1900 and 1930, approximately 1.5 million Mexicans settled in the United States—more than the total number of Europeans who colonized the U.S. east coast between 1607 and 1790.

Throughout the early twentieth century, the political, economic and social status of Mexican-Americans was scarcely distinguishable from that of blacks. Like African-Americans, Chicanos attempted to improve their economic status by joining trade unions. Mexican-Americans participated in the Knights of Labor and several, including Manuel Lopez, a master workman of the Fort Worth, Texas local, emerged as key leaders. During the Great Depression, Chicano working-class activists were part of the Congress of Industrial Organizations, and were particularly influential in fighting racial prejudice as leaders of the United Cannery, Agricultural, Packing, and Allied Workers Union. Generally, however, the social controls imposed by both capital and the Anglo political and caste system remained effectively to check Mexican-American resistance. A dual pay structure in Arizona mines and in southwestern ranches perpetuated the income gap between Chicanos and Anglos. Chicanos were generally denied basic constitutional rights and civil liberties even when they had been born inside the U.S. In electoral politics, their votes were often manipulated or discounted. One typical example of this occurred routinely during the 1930s and 1940s in southern Texas. Political bosses, or "jefes," determined whether Chicanos were "qualified" to vote on a case-by-case basis. As political scientist V. O. Key observed in 1949, the jefe often paid the Chicano voter's "poll taxes" and held "the tax receipts until election day to insure discipline and orderly procedure. Economic dependency often makes the control easier, and in south Texas there are large landholdings with whole communities employed on a single ranch." In Duval County, Texas, such regimentation of the Chicano vote ensured electoral margins for favored Democratic Party candidates of at least 90 percent. The Duval vote in the Democratic Party senatorial primary of 1948, for example, was 4,662 votes for the then Congressman Lyndon Johnson to 40 votes for his opponent. The common judgment among most white Texas politicians, therefore, was that the Mexican-American electorate had "only the most remote conception of Anglo-Saxon governmental institutions." Among Chicanos, Key wrote, one finds "a high incidence of political indifference, ignorance, timidity, and sometimes venality."[38] People subjected to such racist contempt are inevitably the victims of violence. During August 1942, Los Angeles police illegally raided the growing Latino barrio (ghetto) of that city and arrested 600 Chicanos. In June 1943, fourteen off-duty policemen established a "Vengeance Squad" and began attacking Los Angeles Chicanos at random. Joined by hundreds of white sailors and tourists, they "toured the barrios in convoys of taxi cabs, in bars and restaurants and movie houses" as white police officers "looked the other way." History records the incident as the "Zoot Suit Riots," named for the style of clothing then worn by young Chicano males: in fact, it was a racist pogrom not unlike that waged by whites against the black community of Atlanta in 1906, or against Chicago blacks in 1919.[39]

The special plight of the Native Americans at the hands of European settlers predated American slavery itself. A succession of colonial, state and federal government treaties with various Indian nations, from the seventeenth century to the mid-nineteenth century, were invariably violated by whites in an effort to eradicate the Indian from the frontier. By the end of President Andrew Jackson's administration, the majority of Native American nations had been defeated militarily and forcibly removed west of the Mississippi. After the Civil War, the U.S. government pursued a policy against the Indians of the West which can only be termed genocidal. General William T. Sherman's 1866 orders to his troops were specific: "At least 10 Indians are to be killed for each white life lost. You should not allow the troops to settle down on the defensive but carry the war to the Indian camps, where the women and children are . . . [You] should not delay the punishment of the Indians as a people."[40] The contemporary Indian nationalist movement of the 1970s and 1980s was born here, over a century ago, in the fierce determination of Native American people to resist their own extermination. The Athabascan people of the Southwest (Apaches and Navajos) waged an unrelenting campaign to maintain their way of life and culture, as did the Sioux and other Indian nations of the Great Plains. By the end of the century, however, the sheer numbers of settlers and the superiority of white military power overwhelmed and crushed the Indian resistance movement. Indian leaders and guerrilla generals—Sitting Bull, Crazy Horse, Geronimo—were imprisoned, murdered or assassinated. Women and children were butchered by government troops at the Wounded Knee massacre of 1890. Unique cultural forms of resistance, such as the Native American Church, were criticized by American officials for fostering Indian unity. The role of African-Americans in the political and territorial suppression of the Indian people is, at best, mixed. There were numerous instances of Black-Indian military and political co-operation along the American frontier, most notably among the Seminoles of Florida. For several decades, runaway slaves and Indians fought successfully against federal troops, defeating white soldiers decisively in several battles, before they succumbed in the 1840s. Con-

versely, black soldiers in the Ninth and Tenth Regiments of the U.S. army
were used against Indians on the Great Plains in the 1870s and 1880s. At
one point, about one out of five American troops ordered to "suppress
civil disorders," to chase "Indians who left the reservation out of frustration or in search of food," "arrest rustlers and guard stagecoaches" were
black. Called the "Buffalo Soldiers," these black troops "paradoxically
helped bring the white man's law and order to the frontier," and in doing
so, aided the process of destroying Indian civilization.[41] Over the entire
century, the Indian population was cut from two million to barely 200,000.

A crude type of "American apartheid" was imposed upon Indians, with
the expressed purpose of destroying Indian political unity and regimenting
indigenous culture. Indians were scattered across the country, designated
to live in so-called tribal areas or reservations. The Dawes Act of 1887 di-
vested Indians of huge tracts of land, "impoverish[ing] large numbers of
people who then became beggars or wards of the various states." The Reor-
ganization Act of 1934 "enabled tribes to achieve corporate status through
charters, thereby enabling them to continue their existence in a collective
form." Still, all major power was controlled in Washington, D.C. by the
paternalistic Bureau of Indian Affairs.[42] By World War II, the 350,000 Indians had become the most marginalized of all national minority groups.
Alcoholism, high rates of infant mortality and severe malnutrition were
prevalent in the reservations. Desperate young Indian men by the thousands left the reservation in search of work in major cities. Conditions for
Native Americans became even worse with Cold War domestic policies
aimed at minorities. In 1953, upon congressional orders, the Bureau of Indian Affairs proposed the "termination" of thirteen Indian "groupings."
The Termination Act was a modern version of Sherman's policies towards
the Indian. In brutal violation of existing treaties, thousands of Indians
were swiftly relocated to specific urban enclaves or centers in Los Angeles,
San Francisco, Denver, Phoenix, and Cleveland. As Indian scholar Roxanne Dunbar Ortiz notes, "in the cities, the mostly young Indian re-
locatees experienced grueling urban poverty and unemployment in place
of the grinding rural poverty and unemployment, with the added inevi-
tability of losing their homelands and their existence as people."[43] Tens of
thousands of Indians were "thrown into white society without the skills or
means to survive; a sizeable proportion of Indian land was again appropri-
ated and most of it sold to whites; and those tribes that were terminated
were subject to state and local taxation without an economic base from
which to pay the taxes."[44]

With the growth of the post-war black freedom movement, however,
came a concomitant awakening of political and social consciousness among
all other national minorities. Among Chicanos, the American GI Forum

and the Community Service Organization were created to register voters and to urge members of their community to take a more active role in the electoral system. The Mexican-American Political Association was founded in California in 1958, and four years later, the Political Association of Spanish-Speaking Organizations was established in Texas. The major political forum of the Mexican-American middle class remained the League of United Latin American Citizens (LULAC), which had been established three decades before. Assimilationist in cultural outlook and inclined towards the liberal wing of the Democratic Party, LULAC shared many characteristics of the NAACP. LULAC members eschewed political militancy of any type. Their construction prohibited "any radical and violent demonstrations which may tend to create conflicts and disturb the peace and tranquility of our country." LULAC leaders "always emphasized American citizenship, education, equality, and the use of the English language rather than the Spanish language."[45] Puerto Rican immigrants had begun to establish a series of small businesses in New York City's boroughs, and Puerto Rican workers soon emerged in increasing numbers as trade union officials, civic and neighborhood political leaders. On the West Coast, Japanese-American leaders, supported by progressive whites, led a successful fight in 1946 to defeat an anti-Nisei constitutional provision. Despite the loss of millions of dollars worth of property, Nisei pooled their meager resources collectively to compete with whites in both business and professional fields. Between 1945 and 1960, the percentage of Japanese-American professionals among their male workforce had increased four times, reaching roughly the level among whites. Due to their strenuous opposition, Indian leaders forced the federal government to halt the Termination Act by 1961, giving Indian activists a renewed sense of their potential power. The forces of racial repression had not been halted, and like the African-American, other national minorities continued to labor beneath the burden of caste oppression and economic exploitation. But between the lines, a new level of political courage and commitment among all people of color had been achieved, even during the period of McCarthyism.

VI

In the early spring of 1946, an event of symbolic significance occurred which, in time, would touch the lives of several million rural African-Americans and Chicanos. In Montgomery County, Alabama, on the 7,700-acre plantation of the McLemore Brothers, black fieldhands were busy preparing for the new year's crop. The McLemores proposed to have an experiment. Setting aside a 150-acre tract, the white planters decided to see whether cotton could be processed from seed to market "without touching human hands." In a one-man operation, newly purchased farm machinery prepared the land, and subsequently "planted, fertilized, chopped, weeded, defoliated and picked" every boll of cotton on the 150-acre plot. Tuskegee Institute social scientists noted, "this is probably the first time that the human hand rarely touched the cotton from the time plans were made until the burlap-wrapped bale of cotton was delivered from the gin process."[46] The South had traditionally lagged well behind the rest of the nation in agricultural technology. By 1945, 30.5 percent of all U.S. farmers had tractors; tractor-ownership percentages in the South were considerably lower—South Carolina, 5.4 percent; Georgia, 5.9 percent; Alabama, 4.5 percent; Mississippi, 4.1 percent. A typical Southern white owner-operated farm averaged only 122 acres; but farms owned by corporations and managed by whites averaged 2,126 acres. In the past, large and small white farmers kept black farmworkers' wages at subsistence levels; but low salaries allowed them to hire the maximum numbers of black workers. As late as 1945, the average hourly salaries of non-white men on southern farms was only 0.23 cents, compared to 0.66 cents for white males. The larger farms increasingly relied upon machines to replace black labor in the cotton fields during the 1940s. Within ten to fifteen years, the smaller white farms would follow their lead. Expendable, despite his/her low wages and long hours (an average workday of 9.7 hours), the black farmworker was rapidly becoming extinct. "Labor-intensive" farming was giving way to "capital-intensive" farming.

The mechanization of southern agriculture was a decisive reason why the black migration north continued. From 1940–50, the number of non-southern blacks increased from 2.4 million to 6.4 million. In most industrial cities in the Midwest, the black population growth rate was between 500 to 1,000 percent above that for whites. The drive, to the North was inspired also by the promise of higher wages and better working conditions; but these factors were dependent upon the availability of employment. During the last five years of Truman's administration, non-white unemployment averaged 6.9 percent, compared to 4 percent for white workers. By 1954 and 1955, non-white unemployment had jumped to 9.3 percent v. 4.5 percent for whites. In 1954, 16.5 percent of all non-white youths in the job market were unemployed. The black ghettoes of the North, first taking shape with the industrial demand for Negro labor a half century before, were beginning to become stagnant centers for joblessness and despair.

By the spring of 1954, nine years after Roosevelt's death, there was a feeling of unfulfilled ambitions and expectations among many blacks. The legalistic strategy of the NAACP had proved successful, yet there was still much dissatisfaction with the now elderly Walter White's authoritarian style and dependence on the anti-communist liberal wing of the Democratic Party. CORE and the National Negro Labor Council had almost disappeared from public view, for very different reasons. Republican Dwight David Eisenhower had been elected president in 1952. No friend of the armed forces desegregation decision of 1948, the former five-star general wanted to slow down the pace and retard the movement for civil rights. Dewey's vice presidential running mate of 1948, California governor Earl Warren, had been named chief justice of the Supreme Court. For blacks, he was best known for placing 100,000 Japanese-Americans into concentration centers during World War II. Neither Eisenhower, the NAACP, nor black America would yet discover that this same Republican politician would become the strongest defender of blacks' rights in Supreme Court history. No one could realize completely the new phase of American history that would dawn on 17 May 1954, in a legal decision which would mark the real beginning of the Second Reconstruction.

3. The Demand for Reform, 1954–1960

. . . a little rebellion, now and then, is a good thing. . . . It is a medicine necessary for the sound health of government.

Thomas Jefferson to James Madison, 1787

Racial integration, [is] a great myth which the ideologues of the system and the Liberal Establishment expound, but which they cannot deliver into reality. . . . The melting-pot has never included the Negro.

Harold Cruse

I

Black parents and civil rights lawyers in Virginia, Kansas, Washington, D.C., South Carolina, and Delaware had challenged the legality of segregated public school systems during the early 1950s. By late 1952, all these cases had reached the Supreme Court. After a year and a half of hearings, the high court finally handed down a unanimous decision in what was popularly known as *Brown v. Board of Education of Topeka, Kansas*. The Court ruled that "we cannot turn the clock back . . . to 1896 when *Plessy vs. Ferguson* [the decision which validated the separate-but-equal principle] was written. We must consider public education in the light of its full development and its present place in American life." Chief Justice Earl Warren and other justices were persuaded by the writings of black sociologists that racial segregation did irreparable damage to black schoolchildren both socially and psychologically. "In the field of public education the doctrine of 'separate but equal' has no place. Separate educational facilities are inherently unequal." Warren and his colleagues thus overturned the legal justification for one of the principal pillars of white supremacy.[1]

The *Brown* decision marked the end of a long phase in the legal war of attrition between the NAACP and the defenders of racial inequality. As early as 1938, the Supreme Court had ordered Missouri to guarantee its black residents who applied to state schools that equal educational provisions would exist. In 1948, the Court voided any real estate agreements which racially discriminated against purchasers. One year later, *Sweatt v. Painter* ruled that Texas's segregated law school for blacks was inherently unequal and inferior in every respect to its law school for whites. *McLaurin v. Oklahoma* declared in 1950 that Oklahoma had to desegregate its law school. The Supreme Court stated that racial restrictions of this type "impair and inhibit" the Negro student's "ability to study, engage in discussions and exchange views with other students and, in general, to learn his profession."[2] Thus, even before *Brown*, a pattern of desegregation had been set into motion by the Court. By 1953, blacks attended 10 formerly all-white public colleges and 23 graduate schools in the South. By Truman's second term, many Southern Democrats understood that they could forestall court-ordered desegregation only if they spent millions of dollars in upgrading all-black public schools. Expenditures soared 800 percent between 1939 and 1952 in the South's futile efforts to build new black schools. After *Brown*, it became apparent that the all-black public school system was legally intolerable. Upper South states led the way in desegregation efforts. Baltimore, Washington, D.C., cities in Delaware and West Virginia desegregated their public schools by September 1954. On 31 May 1955, the Supreme Court ordered boards of education to draw up desegregation plans "with all deliberate speed." Within the next twelve months 350 school boards representing nine southern states had desegregated without much white opposition. By January 1956, the Supreme Court had overturned segregation laws in Tennessee, Arkansas, Florida, and Texas. Lower courts generally tried to cater to southern whites by interpreting the time frame for desegregation as indefinite; but they had no legal recourse except to carry out desegregation mandates of the high court. By the 1956–57 school year, 723 southern school districts had been desegregated, and 300,000 black children were either attending formerly white schools or were part of a "desegregated" school district. Despite these gains, there were at this point 2.4 million black southern children still enrolled in Jim Crow schools, and 3,000 white school boards expressed every intention of maintaining the color line in spite of the Supreme Court's mandates.

Within several years Congress reinforced the Supreme Court's desegregation initiatives with the passage of the first civil rights legislation since the demise of Reconstruction. The Civil Rights Act of 1957, as first designed, was a fairly strong federal commitment to blacks' rights. One section of the act required federal guarantees for the voting rights of blacks, and authorized the Justice Department to sue states and local interests which supported segregated schools or perpetuated racial restrictions in elections. The Democratic majority leader in the Senate, Texas senator Lyndon B. Johnson, a former segregationist, was chiefly responsible for maneuvering the bill through fierce southern and conservative opposition in the upper house. In the weakened version which was eventually passed, federal judges were permitted to arrest state and local officials who kept blacks from voting. The act also mandated a Commission on Civil Rights which developed an agenda for federal action. In May 1960, a second Civil Rights Act was passed over bitter opposition and a filibuster led by Southern Democrats, or Dixiecrats. Federal judges were now permitted to select "referees" who could bypass local white registrars who kept blacks from voting. These referees were empowered to register black voters. The law also included federal sanctions and penalties for racists who used violent measures to disrupt the orderly process of voting and desegregation.

II

For many blacks, the drive for desegregation still seemed agonizingly slow. In Deep South cities steeped in *apartheid*-style social relations, the black population was humiliated and exploited to the breaking point. In Montgomery, Alabama, the median annual income for the average black worker was under $1,000 in 1956; only 2,000 black adults were registered to vote. In early December 1955, when Mrs. Rosa Parks was arrested for sitting in a "whites-only" section of a municipal bus, black civic leaders led by E. D. Nixon decided to act. A boycott of local buses was held to protest against the city's segregation code, and this challenge to racism blossomed into an international event. Emerging as the principal leader of the boycott was a young black doctor of divinity, the Reverend Martin Luther King, Jr. Ably assisted by the Reverend Ralph David Abernathy and activist Bayard Rustin, King urged local blacks to employ nonviolent protest tactics. Throughout 1956, approximately 95 percent of Montgomery's blacks refused to use the buses. White police and local officials arrested 92 black organizers on a variety of charges in the effort to frustrate the boycott. Black and white liberal activists were vindicated by a Supreme Court ruling of 13 November 1956, which outlawed segregation on Montgomery buses. Overnight, King became the charismatic symbol of the political aspirations of millions of colored people across the world. Domestically, the success of the Montgomery bus boycott reinforced a similar effort begun in Tallahassee, Florida, and sparked a fresh boycott in nearby Birmingham, Alabama.

In Little Rock, Arkansas, blacks seemed to be making greater progress towards desegregation. Integration had occurred in some of the state's schools, and the capital city of Little Rock had begun to implement plans for a gradual, grade by grade desegregation of its public schools. The state governor was a racial moderate, Orval E. Faubus, who had defeated a rigid racist named James D. Johnson in the 1956 Democratic primary elections. Indeed, Faubus's greatest electoral support came from blacks and middle-to-upper-class whites. Less than a week before the schools opened, the Arkansas state court ordered Little Rock not to initiate the desegregation plan. A federal court overruled the state jurists, but Governor Faubus ordered the state's national guard to forbid nine black children to enter the high school. Armed with automatic rifles, the soldiers and a mob of unruly whites pelted and pushed blacks away from the schoolhouse before national television cameras. Arkansas's militant defiance of federal authority forced Eisenhower reluctantly to support the civil rights of blacks. In late September 1957, the president ordered the state's 10,000 guardsmen to submit to federal authority, and U.S. army troops were called to disperse the angry whites blocking the high school. Little Rock schools were closed in 1958–59, and blacks did not actually attend the high school until August 1959.

By 1956, southern white opposition to desegregation had begun to mushroom at every level of society. In Congress, North Carolina Senator Sam Ervin, Jr., drafted a racist polemic, the "Southern Manifesto," on 12 March 1956, which vowed to fight to maintain Jim Crow by all legal means. Ervin succeeded in obtaining the support of 101 out of 128 members of Congress from the eleven original Confederate states. In electoral politics, rabid segregationists attacked moderate to liberal New Deal Democrats as the white public shifted increasingly to the far right. Two moderate Democrats in Congress from North Carolina who did not support the Southern Manifesto were thrown out of office in the 1956 election. That same year, the white supremacy States' Rights Party collected 7.2 percent of the popular vote in Louisiana, 17.3 percent in Mississippi, and 29.5 percent in South Carolina. National and state politicians in both the Democratic and Republican parties catered to the militantly white racist trend. In a crass attempt to win some segregationist votes, Eisenhower campaigned throughout Dixie. In one South Carolina appearance, he evoked "rebel yells" by standing smartly to attention when the band played the Confederate anthem "Dixie." A few southern populists tried to resist the racist tide. In 1958, circuit judge George C. Wallace ran for governor of Alabama as a moderate on racial issues and a progressive on economic policies. His opponent, Attorney General John Patterson, campaigned as an advocate of an American-version of *apartheid*, and won easily. Wallace had received the support of the meager black electorate, and had even won the quiet backing of the state's NAACP. In the wake of his defeat, Wallace

swore, "they out-niggered me that time, but they'll never do it again."
Four years later, Wallace won the state's gubernatorial election by taking
the most extreme racist position since the capitulation of populist Tom
Watson to racism a half century before. Ironically, by the 1960s, it was
Wallace who personified the white South's commitment to racial bigotry,
more than any other major public figure.[3]

A reign of white terror was hurled at the proponents of black freedom in
the guise of new organizations and regulations. In 1955–59, White Citizens' Councils were initiated in almost every southern city, comprised
chiefly of middle-to-upper income whites in business, white-collar professions and the clergy, who vigorously opposed desegregation. In early 1956,
five southern legislatures passed at least 42 Jim Crow laws reinforcing separate black public schools. In Mississippi, state laws declared that it was
illegal for a black child to enter a white primary, elementary, or secondary
school. Georgia laws required that "any school official of the state or any
municipal or county schools" which "spend tax money for public schools
in which the races are mixed" was committing a felony. South Carolina's
legislature publicly condemned "the illegal encroachment of the central
government" by its demands for black equality. Alabama politicians overwhelmingly voted to "nullify" the Supreme Court's *Brown* decision for
any schools within its borders. Mississippi and Louisiana even "amended
their state constitution to provide that to promote public health and morals
their schools be operated separately for white and Negro children."[4]

As the movement towards desegregation gained momentum, the measures employed the white supremacists and terrorists became more violent. In December 1951, civil rights proponents received a foretaste of
events to come with the bombing in Miami, Florida, of the home of state
NAACP leader Harry T. Moore. Moore was murdered in the attack, and
many Christian, veterans' and civil rights agencies asked the Truman Administration to investigate the killing. But Truman, who could not be a
candidate in the next election, had little political motivation to co-operate,
so the federal government did nothing. Thousands of local black leaders
were threatened, arrested, intimidated and harassed. Mississippi assumed
its traditional role in this respect as the South's crucible for racist violence.
NAACP leaders were bludgeoned, pistol-whipped and shot at. The president of the Belzoni, Mississippi, NAACP chapter was assassinated on the
city's courthouse lawn in 1955. In other southern states, a similar pattern
of overt violence occurred. Louisiana courts ordered the NAACP to halt all
public meetings in the state. South Carolina legislators declared the NAACP
a "subversive organization." The Ku Klux Klan reasserted itself as a
powerful secret organization, committing a series of castrations, killings,
and the bombing of black homes and churches.

Woodward accurately describes this period as a time when "all over the South the lights of reason and tolerance and moderation began to go out":

> A fever of rebellion and malaise of fear spread over the region. Books were banned, libraries were purged, newspapers were slanted, magazines disappeared from stands, television programs were withheld, films were excluded. Teachers, preachers, and college professors were questioned, and many were driven out of the South. . . . Words began to shift their significance and lose their common meaning. A "moderate" became a man who dared open his mouth, an "extremist" one who favored eventual compliance with the law, and "compliance" took on the connotations of treason. Politicians who had once spoken for moderation began to vie with each other in defiance of the government.[5]

Desegregation across the South ground to a standstill. In 1958, 13 school systems were desegregated; in 1960, only 17. Despite their concessions, white racists in the government and other institutions began to perceive dimly that the forces for biracial democracy could be defeated, and that legal segregation in most civic relations might continue for many decades to come.

III

Beyond the civil rights battlefield, new trends in black culture and intellectual thought began to reveal themselves during the 1950s. For some white sociologists and cultural historians, the decade under Eisenhower and the Cold War has seemed a sterile and vacuous period of social conformity. The "Silent Generation" of the white middle class began moving from the urban centers to the suburbs; the populace and politicians alike were preoccupied with televisions, automobiles, and other mass consumer goods. For black America, however, this conservative cultural description does not apply. In the creative arts, in literature, in intellectual work, there was a significant outpouring of energy, talent and hope for the future.

Some of the most provocative contributions to black culture occurred in literature. As early as 1937, black novelist Richard Wright, who was at the time a member of the Communist Party, predicted the new cultural directions which black writers would later pursue, in the essay, "Blueprint for Negro Writing." Wright declared that the real goal of black writing was political and social advocacy, "molding the lives and consciousness of [the black] masses towards new goals." It should not simply be "the voice of the educated Negro pleading with white America for justice."[6] Wright would become in many respects the seminal new Negro intellectual: breaking with the Communist Party in 1944; authoring the searing *Native Son* (1941), *Black Boy* (1945), and *The Outsider* (1953). Turning bitterly against the left during the Cold War, Wright was increasingly influenced by the European existentialist movement. From his exile in Paris during the 1950s, Wright spoke through his character Cross Damon on his fears for the oppressed:

> There is no escaping what the future holds. We are going back to something earlier, maybe better, maybe worse, maybe something more terrifyingly human? These few hundred years of freedom, empire building, voting, liberty, democracy—these will be regarded as the *romantic* centuries in human history. There will be in that future no trial by jury, no writs of habeas corpus, no freedom of speech of religion—of all of this being buried and not by Communists or Fascists alone, but by their opponents as well. All hands are shoveling clay onto the body of freedom before it even dies, while it lies breathing its last. . . .[7]

Most black intellectuals did not share Wright's pessimistic and even nihilistic vision of a world thrown into political chaos. Yet the generation of black writers born during the 1920s and coming into maturity during the post-war era were all influenced by his sweeping style and idealism.

The two black intellectuals most affected by Wright were undoubtedly Ralph Ellison and James Baldwin. Ellison's *Invisible Man* (1952), which evoked the existential tones of Doestoevsky and Camus, was viewed by many white critics as the most powerful fiction work written by an American in the post-war period. In *Go Tell It on the Mountain* (1953), Baldwin described the black exodus from the rural South into the North's ghettoes. After the *Brown* decision, Baldwin's considerable talent as a political critic was revealed in *Notes of a Native Son* (1955), *Nobody Knows My Name* (1960), and *The Fire Next Time* (1963). Other black novelists began to find a new audience for their work. Chester Himes's *If He Hollers, Let Him Go* (1945) discussed the intense racism of white workers levelled against blacks during World War II. Arna Bontemps, a veteran novelist of the Harlem Renaissance, a productive period of black cultural creativity in the 1920s, wrote a moving study of black adjustment in the North in *They Seek a City* (1945). Harlem novelist and cultural critic John Oliver Killens's novel of black southern society and struggle, *Youngblood* (1954), won critical praise. As in the Harlem Renaissance, black women writers also played a critical cultural role in the 1950s. Ann Petry, a journalist in Harlem during the war, described the outrage and frustrations of inner city black youth in her first novel, *The Street* (1946). Petry subsequently produced two more novels, *Country Place* (1947) and *The Narrows* (1953), as well as a series of works for children and black teenagers.

In the field of black poetry, the two most popular intellectuals were Langston Hughes and Gwendolyn Brooks. Hughes, like Bontemps, was a product of the Harlem Renaissance, and his position as the "poet laureate"

of the African-American people was secure well before the 1950s. As a political progressive, Hughes could scarcely tolerate the growing climate of
fear and repression which existed during the Cold War. In one poem entitled "Un-American Investigator," Hughes revealed his long commitment
to human freedom and democracy:

> The Committee's fat,
> Smug, almost secure
> Co-religionists
> Shiver with delight
> In warm manure
> As those investigated—
> Too brave to name a name—
> Have pseudonyms revealed
> In Gentile game
>   Of who,
>   Born Jew,
>   Is who?
> Is not your name Lipshitz?
>   Yes.
> Did you not change it
> For subversive purposes?
>   No.
> For nefarious gain?
>   Not so.
> Are you sure?
> The committee shivers
> With delight in
> Its manure.[8]

Brooks's first collection of poetry appeared in 1943, *A Street in Bronzeville*.
Her second collection, *Annie Allen* (1949), won a Pulitzer prize in literature. Brooks's other works of the period include a short novel, *Maud Mar-
tha* (1953), two poetry volumes, *The Bean Eaters* (1960) and *Selected Poems*
(1963), and a children's book, *Bronzeville Boys and Girls* (1956). Other significant black novelists and poets of the 1940s–50s included Margaret
Walker; Melvin B. Tolson, author of *Heart-Shape in the Dust* (1940) and
Rendezvous with America (1944); the witty and prolific Zora Neale Hurston,
author of the autobiographical *Dust Tracks on a Road* (1942), and the novels *Man of the Mountain* (1942) and *Seraph on the Suwannee* (1948); novelist Paule Marshall, *Browngirl, Brownstones* (1959); and poets Robert Hayden and Sterling A. Brown.

   An even younger group of black writers emerged during the mid-to-late

1950s, born in the Depression, and developed politically during the outbreak of the Second Reconstruction. Chief among them was Lorraine
Hansberry. The daughter of a prosperous, upper-middle-class black Chicago household, Hansberry attended school at the University of Wisconsin, Mexico's University of Guadalajara, and Chicago's Roosevelt University. In the mid-1950s she became a young writer for Harlem's radical
Freedom newspaper. Her meteoric rise to prominence came with the production of her acclaimed play on the struggle of a poor black Chicago family seeking to move into a white neighborhood, *A Raisin in the Sun* (1959).
Hansberry described herself as part "of the generation that grew up in the
swirl and dash of the Sartre-Camus debate of the post-war years. The sil-
houette of the Western intellectual poised in hesitation before the flames of
involvement was an accurate symbolism of some of my closest friends,
some of whom crossed each other leaping in and out, for instance, of the
Communist party." Hansberry had come to reject Wright's existentialism
as an exaltation of "brutality and nothingness" because he had abandoned
"the reality of our struggle for freedom." For her, and for many other
young black intellectuals, the decisive human conflict was not against
communism, but with Jim Crow and America's racial stereotypes of black
life. Ironically, her call for a politically relevant black art echoed Wright's
own 1937 essay.[9]

In black music, the post-war era also brought powerful changes to many
aspects of popular culture. During the war, several "poor, unknown and
unprepossessing" black musicians developed a group that played in Harlem nightclubs—a set whose members included trumpeter Dizzy Gillespie, saxophonist Charlie Parker, and pianist Thelonius Monk. These men
would revolutionize America's most creative indigenous music tradition,
jazz. Before his death at the age of 35, Parker would become a living legend among musicians. As critic LeRoi Jones wrote in 1963, "Parker was
the soul and fire of the bebop era. After Parker, trumpet players, piano
players, guitar players, bass players, etc., all tried to sound like him, in
much the same fashion as all kinds of instrumentalists had once tried to
sound like Louis Armstrong. Both Gillespie and Monk developed popular
bands which featured, at different times, Parker's worthy successor on the
saxophone, the innovative stylist John Coltrane. Other brilliant black musicians making their stamp on jazz in the 1950s included trumpet soloist
Miles Davis, tenor saxophonist Sonny Rollins, also saxophonist Ornette
Coleman, and pianist Cecil Taylor. It cannot be emphasized too strongly
that jazz played a powerful role in the cultural education of millions of
young blacks and whites during this time. Listening to the beauty of Coltrane and Parker, established critics were often at a loss for words. The
"bebop" of the 1940s had given way, by the late 1950s, to an *avant-garde*

described by some as "the new music." Coltrane was viewed in the last ten years of his brief life as a musical "James Joyce," a man whose preeminence as an artist was "being acclaimed great by fellow artists, critics and the public . . . not only while he [was] alive, but when he [was] also just *beginning* to prove that greatness concretely."[10] For white American youth, especially from the suburban homes of the upper classes, jazz symbolized a cultural creativity they could not find within their own placid lives. It inspired the literature and lifestyle of a white "beat" subculture which consciously rejected the "Silent Generation's" crass materialism and political apathy. For blacks, jazz represented on the "cultural front" what the Montgomery boycott, demonstrations and the new militant mood were in politics. It shattered established conventions; it mocked traditions; in form and grace, it transcended old boundaries of life and thought. It became the appropriate cultural background for their activities to destroy Jim Crow.

In the 1950s, the image of Africa as a cultural and political entity began to reassert its impact upon African-American intellectuals and artists. Prior to 1950, the general relationship between black Americans and Africans had taken three very different forms. Black Christian missionaries from the Congregationalist American Board of Commissioners for Foreign Missions had been sent to Liberia by 1821. During the nineteenth and early twentieth centuries, hundreds of black Baptists, Episcopalians, Methodists and Presbyterians were sent to proselytize across the continent. There religious missions served as a bridge for young Africans who came to the United States to attend universities and professional schools. During the 1920s, the militant black nationalist movement of Marcus Garvey embraced Africa as the symbolic home of all New World blacks. Garvey's organization of several millions, the Universal Negro Improvement Association, attempted unsuccessfully to establish a beachhead in Liberia for the emigration of U.S. and West Indian blacks. Two decades earlier, DuBois had initiated a series of political meetings between African-Americans, West Indians and Africans, the Pan-African Conferences of 1900, 1919, 1921, 1923, 1927 and 1945. The final conference, held in Manchester, England, brought DuBois together with some of the African intellectuals who would soon become the leaders of their nations' anti-colonialist movements. By the late 1950s, economic and political pressures had finally forced France, Belgium and England to end their direct rule over the continent. Many of the new African leaders were familiar to black American intellectuals, politicans, and civil rights leaders: Nnamdi Azikiwe of Nigeria had attended Howard University, and in 1932 received an M.A. degree in philosophy and religion at Lincoln University of Pennsylvania; Ghana's Kwame Nkrumah, another Lincoln University graduate, was the protegé of New World Pan-Africanist scholar/activists C. L. R. James, George Padmore and, to a lesser extent, DuBois.

Black American newspapers during the Cold War gave prominent coverage to the battle to end European colonialism. Richard Wright travelled across Africa to observe the groundswell of activisim, and produced his strongest political statement from his experiences in *Black Power*. Black politicians, including Adam Clayton Powell, writers and journalists went to the conference of Third World and non-aligned nations at Bandung, Indonesia, in 1955. Hundreds of black professionals trained in the natural and social sciences emigrated to African nations to support the cause. The most significant African political events during the decade, the development of Nkrumah's Convention People's Party of Ghana and that nation's independence in 1957, and the rise of Egypt's Gamal Nasser as the leader of the Third World, influenced almost every African-American intellectual and activist. For King, Egypt's 1956 defiance of England seemed to have direct parallels to the U.S. struggle for desegregation. "They have broken loose from the Egypt of colonialism and imperialism, and they are now moving through the wilderness of adjustment toward the promised land of cultural integration," King wrote in 1957. "As they look back they see the old order of colonialism and imperialism passing away and the new order of freedom and justice coming into being."[11] DuBois saw Africa quite differently. In his private correspondence with Nkrumah in 1957, he urged that Ghana's leader should "avoid subjection to and ownership by foreign capitalists who seek to get rich on African labor and raw material, and should try to build a socialism on old African communal life." An independent, non-aligned Africa could "teach mankind that Non-violence and Courtesy, Literature and Art, Music and Dancing can do for this greedy, selfish, and war-stricken world."[12] Even black middle-class groups such as the NAACP, who had traditionally eschewed any programmatic links with black Africa, began to perceive the necessity for close co-operation. The contradiction of a "free" Africa and their "unfree" descendants in the U.S. was an immediate and important parallel which was reiterated by many civil rights advocates.

IV

In the aftermath of the destruction of the National Negro Labor Council, black workers had few organizational tools to protest against the AFL-CIO's institutional racism. At the founding convention of the merged AFL-CIO in 1955, delegates ratified Article 11 to their constitution, which declared that the organization would "encourage all workers, without regard to race, creed, color, national origin or ancestry, to share equally in the full benefits of union organization." Another section of the constitution man-dated the creation of a Committee on Civil Rights which would have "the duty and responsibility to bring about at the earliest possible date the effective implementation of the principle . . . of non-discrimination." Black delegates led by Randolph fought to obtain a greater commitment to racial equality from the labor bureaucrats. Many pointed out that the con-stitution authorized the AFL-CIO's Executive Council to expel any labor af-filiate which was "dominated, controlled or influenced in the conduct of its affairs" by Marxists, yet made no comparable statement on unions which deliberately excluded blacks from membership. AFL-CIO president George Meany opposed the ban of overtly racist unions, and the proposal was easily defeated. At the convention, Michael J. Quill, president of the Transport Workers Union–CIO, condemned the constitution as "a license for discrimination against minority groups."[13] The delegates did attempt to make token concessions to blacks, however, by appointing Randolph and Willard S. Townsend, president of the United Transport Service Em-ployees–CIO as the only two blacks on the Executive Council. James B. Carney, secretary-treasurer of the CIO, was appointed to chair the AFL-CIO Committee on Civil Rights. Carney was not permitted, however, to deliver a blistering address on desegregation before the convention.[14]

In public, the white leaders of the AFL-CIO gave liberal "lip-service" to desegregation. In April 1960, for example, Meany criticized the moderate Civil Rights Bill before Congress as an insult to "the will of the vast major-ity of Americans who believe in, and wish to implement, the basic consti-tutional rights which properly belong to all Americans regardless of race or color or national origin." Meany demanded that the federal authorities "press forward vigorously in the full enforcement of civil rights laws, both old and new."[15] Privately, it was clear to black trade unionists that Meany and many other white labor leaders would do virtually nothing to support the desegregation struggle both within organized labor and within the gen-eral society. Apologists for Meany argued that the AFL-CIO could not expel racist unions, because in the words of socialist Gus Tyler, "the power of the Federation is moral, resting on consensus and persuasion."[16] Even if this was the case—and the rigidly anti-communist directives on expulsion proved that it was not—it did not explain the AFL-CIO's tepid stance towards the desegregation campaigns in the South during the 1950s. The only unions which actively assisted the Montgomery bus boycott of 1955–56 were Randolph's Brotherhood of Sleeping Car Porters; several small United Auto Workers locals; the United Packinghouse Workers, District 65; and Local 1199 of New York, Southern union members played visible and active roles in the Massive Resistance. In Montgomery, the all-white Bus Drivers Union and the Montgomery Building Trades Council took part in the vigilante attacks against civil rights leaders. Southern locals refused to process grievances of black members. When AFL-CIO unions were invited to participate in Martin Luther King's "Prayer Pilgrimage for Freedom" in Washington, D.C., in May 1957, most refused or simply ignored the event.

Inside the AFL-CIO, the lack of union support for desegregation led Carney and another black member of the Civil Rights Committee to resign from their positions. The AFL-CIO did nothing, they complained, effectively to combat union racism even in the North. In Detroit, for example, a city with a major black working class population, less than 2 percent of all apprentices in craft unions were black. Kansas City, Missouri, blacks were effectively barred from employment as steam fitters, plumbers, electricians, operating engineers, and sheet metal workers. In 1957, a black electrician in Cleveland, Ohio, was forced to sue Local 38 in an unsuccessful attempt to gain admittance. Unions aggressively removed black activists on the grounds that they were communists or subversives. In March 1952, UAW leader Walter Reuther, a liberal proponent of desegregation, purged five militant anti-racists from leadership of Detroit's Local 600 and barred them from seeking re-election. Several industrial unions, including the Communications Workers of America and the Steelworkers Union, concluded blatantly segregationist provisions in their contracts with many factories. A number of unions continued to exclude blacks from membership, such as the Brotherhood of Railroad Trainmen, or deliberately kept black participation to a minimum. In December 1958, NAACP leader Roy Wilkins issued an open memorandum to Meany, declaring that:

> Three years after the merger agreement there is clear evidence that many unions continue discriminatory practices. . . . [Some] AFL-CIO affiliates limit Negro membership to segregated or "auxiliary" locals. . . . Increasingly, we are receiving complaints against trade unions from our members and from Negro workers throughout the country charging racial discrimination and segregation. Careful investigation by our staff has in most instances sustained these individual charges and, in addition, has revealed a pattern of racial discrimination and segregation in many affiliate unions.[17]

Under considerable attack, Meany and other racist labor officials' actions became even more outrageous towards desegregation proponents within the unions. At the 1959 San Francisco convention of the AFL-CIO, Randolph urged that the Brotherhood of Railroad Trainmen and the Brotherhood of Locomotive Firemen Enginemen be ordered to remove their anti-black exclusion clauses from their constitutions. Randolph also demanded that the AFL-CIO expand the programs and effectiveness of their Civil

Rights Commission. These and other anti-discrimination measures were promptly defeated. During the debate, Meany was so enraged with Randolph that he shouted, "Who in hell appointed you as guardian of the Negro members in America?" Willie Baxter, vice president and director of civil rights of the Trade Union Leadership Conference of Detroit, responded, "Brother Randolph was accorded this position by the acclamation of the Negro people in recognition of his having devoted almost half a century of his life in freedom's cause."[16] Relations between Meany and Randolph, long sour, reached a new low two years later. On 12 October 1961, the Executive Council censured Randolph for creating a "gap that has developed between organized labor and the Negro community." In a classic instance of blaming-the-victim, Meany explained to the press that Randolph was too impatient, and that he had "gotten close to those militant groups." Roy Wilkins' response to Randolph's censure was shared by virtually every black American:

> The NAACP believes that the AFL-CIO's "censure" of A. Philip Randolph is an incredible cover up . . . a refusal to recognize the unassailable facts of racial discrimination and segregation inside organized labor, as well as an evasion on the part of the AFL-CIO leadership of its own responsibility in fighting racism within affiliate unions. . . . Meany and the AFLO-CIO Executive Council have not taken the required action to eliminate the broad national pattern of anti-Negro practices that continues to exist in many significant sections of the American labor movement, even after five and a half years of the merger and the endless promises to banish Jim Crow.[19]

The struggle of Randolph to uproot racism within organized labor assumed special significance in the 1950s, as the political economy of black America was being rapidly transformed. Between 1950–60, the black civilian labor force increased from 5.8 million to 6.7 million workers and 83 percent of all black males and 48 percent of black females over the age of 16 in 1960 were actively seeking jobs. Between 1940 and 1960, the percentage of blacks involved in farm labor had declined sharply, 32 percent to 8 percent: 38 percent of all black workers were classified as blue-collar workers, up 10 percent in twenty years. By 1960, 9 percent of all construction workers were black, as were 7 percent of all manufacturing workers and 34 percent of all employees engaged in personal services. Unions which practiced a deliberate policy of racial exclusion thwarted blacks' efforts to find employment suitable to their training and talents. Blacks in unions which excluded them from leadership positions had little incentive to support their unions during strikes.

Many rural black families had left the South during the decade with the expectation that their incomes and standard of living would improve dramatically. Incomes for blue-collar jobs were higher in northern states, to be sure, but membership and apprentice positions in many unions were not readily available to all black workers. In the early post-war years, black families nationwide experienced a rise in real incomes. Non-white median income in 1947 was $3,563; by 1952, the median income figure reached $4,344, 57 percent of white median income of $7,643. Between 1952 and 1959, the trend was towards greater income inequality. By that later year, the black median income of $5,156 was only 52 percent of the white median income level—roughly where it had been in 1948. In 1959, 19 percent of all white American families earned over $15,000 annually, compared to 4 percent of all non-white families: 51 percent of all white families earned $7,000 to $15,000 each year; for non-whites in that income range, only 29 percent. One-fifth of all non-white families earned a meager median income in 1959 of $1,207, and one-third of all black families earned less than $3,000 annually, compared to 7.5 percent for whites. Even as late as 1962, the median income of all non-white males was below the 1960 figure.

The AFL-CIO's refusal to desegregate unions contributed in some degree to the growing rates of unemployment among black workers in the North in these years. During the Truman Administration, non-white unemployment rates peaked at 9 percent in 1950, dropping to 5.4 percent by 1952. Under Eisenhower, the unemployment rates for non-whites reached new highs. In the 1958 recession, 12.6 percent of all non-white workers were unemployed, more than twice the level experienced by whites. In 1960, 24.4 percent of all non-white youth in the labor force were without jobs; 802,000 non-white workers were unemployed during the year, 30 percent of them being laid off for more than 15 weeks. A growing army of idle and desperate black men and women began to appear in the industrial centers of the nation, driven to the edge of poverty. In 1960 55.9 percent of all non-whites lived below the "poverty level," a federal government index which indicates a severe lack of the income necessary to provide food, clothing and shelter for any family. For the 1.5 million black families without a husband present, the situation was even more severe: 65.4 percent of such families in 1959 were below the poverty level. Of all black female-headed households in rural areas, 82.2 percent were also under the poverty level. Increasingly, as the economic situation worsened, blacks began to demand the inclusion of special economic reforms within the overall goals of the civil rights struggle. It was no victory for black men to be allowed to sit in a formerly white-only theater or to rent hotel accommodation which had been segregated, when they had no jobs. It was cruel to permit black children to sit in all-white schools, when their mothers had no money to provide their lunches.

V

For most historians, the struggle for Negro equality since the Civil War has been characterized as an attempt at cultural assimilation on the part of blacks into the great social mainstream of American life. Certainly part of the African-American struggle involved a fierce belief by many, particularly within the middle classes, that any form of racial separation was intolerable. But it would be a mistake to equate the battle against Jim Crow with a cultural affinity for the aesthetics and social norms of the Anglo-Saxon, Protestant majority. Almost every black person resisted segregation, because it was imposed upon him/her by a powerful white capitalist order. Beyond that, the black consensus for building alternative institutions which addressed the critical needs of black workers and the poor fell apart. Since the 1850s, a significant portion of the African-American people have tended to support the ideals of black nationalism, defined here, in part, as a rejection of racial integration; a desire to develop all-black socio-economic institutions; an affinity for the cultural and political heritage of black Africa; a commitment to create all-black political structures to fight against white racism; a deep reluctance to participate in coalitions which involved a white majority; the advocacy of armed self-defense of the black community; and in religion and culture, an ethos and spirituality which consciously rejected the imposition of white western dogmas. At certain historical moments, such as in the 1850s and the 1920s, a majority of the black working class, rural farmers and the poor were in their political and social behavior extremely nationalistic. Marcus Garvey was only one of a great tradition of black leaders who expressed that nationalistic tendency, and developed a political program which won the support of thousands and in some instances millions of advocates. By the 1950s, Garveyism had long since disappeared from the black urban North, except in a handful of ghetto communities. Yet the vision of Garveyites remained long after their institutions had crumbled. Many blacks could clearly separate the fight for desegregation from a NAACP-prompted policy which might lead to the eventual cultural and ethnic extinction of their national minority group. Black nationalists of the post-war era were both *anti-racist and anti-integrationist*, in the sense that they opposed Jim Crow laws and simultaneously advocated all-black economic, political and social institutions.

The Nation of Islam was the dominant black nationalist formation of the period. Born in Detroit's black neighborhoods during the Great Depression, its creator and first "divine" prophet was an obscure peddler of uncertain racial identity, W. D. Fard. After preaching for four years an eclectic mythology of Sunni Islam doctrine and black racial supremacy, Fard succeeded in recruiting 8,000 blacks. He established the Fruit of Islam, a paramilitary force; the Muslim Girls Training Class, a school specifically for women members of the Nation; and a University of Islam. After Fard's somewhat mysterious disappearance, his chief lieutenant Elijah Muhammad became the leader of the religious movement. During the 1930s, the Nation declined in membership, and by 1945 only four Muslim temples and about 1,000 adherents were still followers of Muhammad. At this point, an event intervened which greatly accelerated the growth of the Nation. Muhammad was convicted and imprisoned briefly during World War II for resisting the draft. While in a federal penitentiary, Muhammad recognized that black churches and civil rights organizations had no programs to recruit and to transform the most oppressed members of the race: convicts, dope addicts, pimps, young delinquents, prostitutes, criminals, and the permanently unemployed. During the post-war period, the efforts of the Nation shifted toward these lower-income strata. The results were astonishing: by 1960, the Nation's membership was between 65,000 to 100,000 nationwide. Under Muhammad's tight discipline and pro-black nationalist creed, thousands of drug addicts quit their dependence on narcotics; prostitutes in the Nation were transformed into so-called "respectable women." Educational and social programs directed at ghetto youth also produced similar results. By 1960, over three-fourths of the Nation's members were between 17 and 35 years old. Members donated one-quarter to one-third of their annual incomes to the Nation, and the money was used to construct Islamic schools, temples, and businesses. In Chicago alone, the Nation owned half a million dollars' worth of real estate by 1960. The political program of the group provided a striking contrast to that of the NAACP: racial separation; the ultimate creation of an all-black nation state; and capitalist economic development along racial lines.

The Nation's success during these years was also attributable to Muhammad's recruitment of a gifted and very charismatic spokesman named Malcolm Little. Converted to the Nation of Islam while in prison, Little had been a pimp and small-time criminal in the Boston and New York City ghettos. Leaving prison in 1952, Little was renamed Malcolm X—the "X" symbolically repudiating the "white man's name." Muhammad carefully nurtured Malcolm X's career upwards into the organization's hierarchy. By 1954 Malcolm X became the minister of Harlem's Temple No. 7. Travelling across the country, Malcolm X was the articulate mouthpiece, as Aaron was for Moses, in a sense, to deliver the "truth" to the race. Political leaders began to relate to the Muslims, recognizing that Muhammad's absolute control over so many thousands of voters represented an important political bloc. Adam Clayton Powell attended a "Leadership Conference" staged by Malcolm X in Harlem in January 1960. The leader of the Cuban revolution, Fidel Castro, met with Malcolm X in a private discussion during his travels to the U.S. that same year. Simultaneously, the FBI and state and local police began to infiltrate the Nation, keeping closer surveillance of its actions.

As the Nation of Islam prospered, white liberals and Negro integrationists alike became fearful of the movement's stunning success in attracting lower-class blacks. Scholars studied in the Nation, and drew parallels with the rise of fascism and anti-semitism in Europe. White sociologist Gordon W. Allport described the Nation as "the hate that hate produced," a racial supermacist cult similar to "Hitler [and] the White Citizens' Council." In C. Eric Lincoln's *The Black Muslims in America*, the black social philosopher expressed concern that "the Black Muslims' virulent attacks on the white man" might "threaten the security of the white majority and lead those in power to tighten the barriers which already divide America."[20] Civil rights leaders committed to racial assimilation were appalled by the Nation. In August 1959, Roy Wilkins of the NAACP declared that the Muslims had a "hate-white doctrine" which was "as dangerous as [any] group" of white racists. The Nation was clearly "furnishing ammunition for the use" of white supremacists. NAACP chief counsel Thurgood Marshall, speaking at Princeton University, stated that the Nation of Islam was "run by a bunch of thugs organized from prisons and jails, and financed, I am sure, by Nasser or some Arab group."[21] James Farmer of CORE denounced the Nation as "utterly impractical" and dangerous. "After the black culture was taken away from us, we had to adapt the culture that was here, adopt it, and adapt to it. By rejecting integration, Farmer reasoned, the Muslims were aiding Jim Crow. With a surer grasp of racial history, Malcolm X responded to these criticisms. "We who are Muslims, followers of the honorable Elijah Muhammad," he explained, "don't think that an integrated cup of coffee is sufficient payment for 310 years of slave labor." Malcolm X made the simple distinction between desegregation and integration which Farmer, Randolph, Wilkins, Marshall and other Negro leaders could never grasp. "It is not a case of [dark mankind] wanting integration or separation, it is a case of wanting freedom, justice, and equality. It is not integration that Negroes in America want, it is human dignity."[22]

The black nationalist current which Elijah Muhammad and Malcolm X had generated could not be contained in the Nation of Islam. Within a few local branches of the NAACP, similar tendencies developed. Robert Williams, an ex-marine and black militant, had become the leader of the Monroe, North Carolina, NAACP chapter. Viewing King's nonviolent campaigns as ineffectual, he preached that the racist order would have to be overthrown with force. Blacks must "convict their attackers on the spot. They must meet violence with violence," he told the press in May 1959. Within one month, the NAACP suspended Williams for six months for making statements which could "be used by segregationists to spread the false impression that the NAACP supported lynching and violence." Williams's response was that "negroes should have the right of armed self-defense against attack."[23] Eventually expelled by Wilkins from the NAACP, Williams organized a militant local group. He saved the lives of 17 passive demonstrators who were threatened at Monroe's county courthouse by armed gangs of white racists. After a series of confrontations, Williams and his family fled to Canada, and finally received political asylum in Cuba. For many young blacks, Williams's bitter denunciations of racism and the placid Negro middle-class leadership were inspirational and provocative. As Williams observed, "the forces with a vested interest in the equilibrium of the U.S. master-slave society . . . are more than willing to point out to our miserably exploited and dehumanized masses that violent resistance and self-defense will mean total annihilation and extermination. This is in itself an unwitting admission of the beastly nature of the oppressor."[24] The NAACP could banish Williams, but they could not silence him; neither could they stop the escalation of nationalist sentiment within the black rural South and urban North. With every white racist atrocity, the black nationalists' supporters grew; for every failure of the federal government in protecting blacks' lives and liberties, the black reaction to white authority became more refined; with every press statement of Wilkins and Randolph calling for black passivism and restraint, more blacks were recruited into the Nation of Islam.

VI

It is not an historical accident that the demand for racial reform in the late 1950s paralleled the temporary decline of the Cold War. Civil rights workers in the South were constantly "red-baited," but by Eisenhower's second presidential term in office (1957–61) the international climate of superpower confrontation had diminished to a degree. Desegregation advocates were not generally anti-capitalists, and the fierce anti-communism of Wilkins, Randolph and other Negro spokespersons made their views somewhat more acceptable to corporate and political power brokers. The Red Scare had silenced the black left, and had made the NAACP and Urban League less "relevant," to use the expression current at the time, to many younger black activists. Eisenhower had done little to advance the cause of desegregation, activists argued, and moderate civil rights organizations had indirectly contributed to the reaction against racial justice by failing to advance a more "direct-action" oriented program.

One issue on which all major tendencies of the black movement could agree was the importance of the forthcoming presidential election of 1960. The two major candidates, Republican vice president Richard M. Nixon of California and Democratic senator John F. Kennedy of Massachusetts, were both remarkably alike. Elected to Congress in 1946, both became militant red-baiters on the House Committee on Education and Labor, chaired by McCarthyite Fred Hartley. Nixon excelled Kennedy in his opportunistic denouncement of the red menace, and as a result, rose to political power much more rapidly than the Cold War Democrat. In his successful bid for a California senate seat in 1950, Nixon pilloried liberal Democratic congresswoman Helen Gahagan Douglass as a Communist Party sympathizer. From 1953 to 1961 he served as vice president under Eisenhower. During his fourteen years in national politics, he acquired the popular epithet "Tricky Dick" for his endless attacks against liberals, leftists, and the trade unions. In his central position at HUAC, for example, he fumed at one point that one suspected "red" ought to be "boiled in oil." [25] Kennedy was only marginally to the left of Nixon on most issues, and in his actual international policies was more of an anti-communist.

Most political observers in the fall of 1960 thought that Nixon, who was the more widely known, should defeat the two-term Democratic senator. Kennedy was "a member of an emergent Irish upper class in America." A Catholic, he was close to certain eastern corporate interests, including the influential Committee for Economic Development, and the "Ivy League"–trained intelligentsia.[26] The white South was traditionally anti-Catholic, and Kennedy's failure to protest against the Civil Rights Acts of 1957 and 1960 undermined traditional Democratic support he would have received in the region.

Black staff workers in Kennedy's campaign urged the senator to assume Truman's strategy of 1948 by appealing directly to black voters. The senator attacked the Republicans for perpetuating segregation in public housing, although as president, Kennedy would not pursue this issue for almost two years. He campaigned in urban areas with heavy concentrations of black voters. As in 1948, most civil rights leaders favored the Democratic candidate, and the NAACP actively registered thousands of black voters. Several weeks before the election took place, King was sentenced to four months in prison for leading a nonviolent protest in downtown Atlanta. Kennedy wisely telephoned King's wife, Coretta, and offered his support. Robert F. Kennedy, the senator's chief strategist, used his influence to obtain King's release. This event, more than anything else, won the presidency for Kennedy. In most cities and states, three-fourths of all black votes went to the Democratic nominee. In Mobile, Alabama, 72.2 percent of the blacks voted for Kennedy, while only 36.2 percent of upper-income whites had supported him. In Houston, 85.3 percent of all blacks and 50.8 percent of the low-income whites favored Kennedy, compared to only 16.7 percent of the suburban white voters. In several states, the overwhelming black mandate made the difference in the electoral vote. In Illinois, for example, with black voters casting 250,000 ballots for Kennedy, the Democrat carried the state by merely 9,000 votes. Since Kennedy's popular margin over Nixon was only 100,000 votes out of 68.8 million total votes, it seemed clear that the new administration would have to commit itself aggressively to the cause of desegregation.

Given America's racist history, it is not surprising that Kennedy fell far short of blacks' expectations. Kennedy pleased the black élite by nominating Thurgood Marshall to the New York Circuit Court. Black journalist Carl Rowan was named deputy assistant secretary of state. Other blacks in the new administration included Robert Weaver, director of the Housing and Home Finance Agency; Mercer Cook, ambassador to Norway; and George L. P. Weaver, assistant secretary of labor. Publicly, Kennedy supported the gradual desegregation of American society, but he took few concrete steps at first to promote civil rights. Indeed, almost all of Kennedy's initial appointments to federal district courts in the southern states were either uniformly hard-line racists or quiet proponents of Massive Resistance. This action made it difficult if not impossible for southern blacks and civil rights activists to appeal to the federal courts for prompt justice. The administration did little to attack the South's opposition to blacks voting or registering. Cold War liberalism, under Truman and later Kennedy, offered blacks only token concessions in the battle with Jim Crow. This recognition, by 1960, led to a new and more militant campaign to end racist hegemony over black people.

4. We Shall Overcome, 1960–1965

We will soon wear you down by our capacity to suffer, and in winning our freedom we will so appeal to your heart and conscience that we will win you in the process.

Martin Luther King, Jr.

Ain't gonna let nobody turn me 'round
turn me 'round, turn me 'round,
Ain't gonna let nobody turn me 'round
I'm gonna keep on walkin', keep on a-talkin'
Marching up to freedom land.

SNCC workers' song, summer, 1962

When the Constitution said all men are created equal, it wasn't talking about niggers.

J. B. Stoner, white racist leader

I

The Second Reconstruction actually began in earnest on the afternoon of 1 February 1960. Four young black students from North Carolina Agricultural and Technical College, Joseph McNeil, David Richmond, Franklin McCain and Izell Blair, sat at a drugstore lunchcounter in the "whites only" section. Politely, but firmly, they refused to move until the store was closed. The next day about 30 students joined the desegregation protest, in what would become known as a "sit-in." On 3 February, over 50 black students and 3 white students participated in the demonstration. News of this form of nonviolent, direct-action protest spread quickly across North Carolina, and then over the country. Within a week, sit-ins were being staged or planned in High Point, Charlotte, Winston-Salem, Elizabeth City, Concord and other North Carolina cities and towns. By the last week of February black students held sit-ins in Richmond, Virginia; Tallahassee, Florida; Baltimore, Maryland; Nashville and Chattanooga, Tennessee, and in two dozen or more cities in southern and border states. The student revolt of February 1960 was, for the NAACP leadership, a completely unpredicted event. As historians August Meier and Elliott Rudwick observed, the early sit-ins

> speeded up in calculably the rate of social change in the sphere of race relations; broke decisively the NAACP's hegemony in the civil rights arena and inaugurated a period of unprecedented rivalry among the racial advancement groups; and made nonviolent direct action the dominant strategy in the struggle for racial equality during the next half-decade.[1]

With the spring of the year, the number of sit-ins rapidly increased. New forms of nonviolent, direct-action protests using the Greensboro strategy developed: stand-ins at theatres refusing to sell tickets to blacks; wade-ins at municipal pools and segregated beaches; pray-ins at Jim Crow churches. By April 1960, 50,000 black and white students had joined the sit-in movement. A core of new activists emerged from the campuses in the process. The son of a noted black educator, Julian Bond, co-ordinated a major sit-in action by closing down ten of Atlanta's major restaurants on 15 March. A Harvard graduate student majoring in mathematical logic, Bob Moses, travelled south to become part of the demonstrations in Newport News, Virginia. Ruby Doris Smith, a 17-year-old undergraduate at Spelman College in Atlanta, quickly assumed a leadership role among her peers. Marion Barry, Paul LePrad, Diane Nash and John Lewis left Fisk University's campus to lead the desegregation campaign in Nashville. Other prominent student leaders included Charles Jones of Charlotte, North Carolina; Charles Sherrod of Virginia Union University, Richmond, Virginia; and Chuck McDew of South Carolina State College, Orangeburg, South Carolina. Northern students responded favorably to the demonstrations by holding sympathy rallies. The students who engaged in the protests evoked different kinds of responses from local whites. In some cities, whites offered little or no direct resistance, and after a period of demonstrations, agreed to modify or abolish segregation practices in public accommodations. In many other instances, however, whites were bewildered and outraged. Nonviolent black protestors were beaten and cut with razors and knives; hot cigarettes and cigars were burned into their arms and faces; they were spat upon and kicked to the floor; policemen locked them by the thousands into cramped, unsanitary jails. What is truly astonishing, given the white South's near-universal commitment to Massive Resistance, is that the number of students who were permanently injured or crippled was comparatively small.

It was inevitable that the leaders of the growing student movement would attempt to co-ordinate strategies and tactics on a national scale. Ella Baker, the perceptive and courageous executive director of King's Southern Christian Leadership Conference (SCLC), sponsored the founding meeting of what became the Student Nonviolent Coordinating Committee (SNCC) on 16–18 April 1960, in Raleigh, North Carolina. Barry was elected chairman of the new group, and in the next four months, Moses, Bond, and the other Fisk student leaders became dominant figures in SNCC. Like most of the NAACP and Urban League leaders, SNCC members were afflicted with an anti-leftist political bias which influenced them to resist any aid from socialists or radicals. At the 14–16 October SNCC conference in Atlanta, for instance, Bayard Rustin's "radical" identification with social democracy so worried key student organizers that his invitation to speak there was rescinded. It was only in mid-1961 that SNCC accepted a grant of $5,000 from the progressive Southern Conference Educational Fund through the intervention of socialist southern activist Anne Braden. Coming of political age ten years after the silencing of DuBois and Robeson, the mostly lower-to-middle-class black students in SNCC had no identification with traditional black working-class struggles. They could not comprehend the meaning of the Cold War, the capitulation of the NAACP to the anti-communist Red Scare, and the devastation of legitimate black activism during the 1950s. They were, at this point, militant reformers and not revolutionaries, much like the black freedmen and politicians of the First Reconstruction. As participant Debbie Louis writes, "their perspective was toward ending segregation. Their involvement from the very beginning was based on a decision that this equality was important enough to suffer heavily for. . . ." The students "were motivated by a determination to secure the means for their own economic and social mobility, which in the circumstance clearly necessitated a direct assault on the tradition and law which limited them absolutely."[2]

From other quarters, the NAACP was also challenged into action by the renaissance of CORE. At the high point of Cold War, CORE had almost ceased to exist. Gradually, local chapters began to be restructured, new members were recruited, and some level of activism developed. CORE's Los Angeles chapter, which contained only ten members in 1955, initiated a modest but successful local effort to win jobs for black barbers and clerks. In 1958 Nashville's CORE provided leadership in the city's school desegregation efforts. In 1959 CORE co-sponsored a nonviolent protest in Richmond, Virginia. Small CORE chapters in South Carolina had staged boycotts against racist local merchants. In St. Louis, CORE activist William Clay led the black community's efforts to win desegregation in public accommodations. From 1958 to 1960 the number of CORE locals increased from 8 to 19, and the number of individuals providing financial support to the organization had grown from 4,500 to 12,000. When the sit-in movement began, therefore, CORE was in a position to provide immediate support and direction. On 12 February, just twelve days after the first Greensboro demonstration, every CORE chapter across the country picketed drug and retail stores who allowed segregated services in their southern-based facilities. North Carolina CORE activist Floyd McKissick led nonviolent workshops across the state. Unrestrained by the gradualistic directives of the NAACP, Tallahassee CORE leaders led local blacks to wage the first "jail-in"—filling the city's jails with large numbers of black and white demonstrators, during February 1960.

CORE's next move was to revise its tactics of 1948 to the 1960s—the "Freedom Rides." In December 1960, the Supreme Court ruled in *Boynton v. Virginia* that racial segregation was illegal on all interstate buses and trains, and in transportation terminals. James Farmer assumed the post as CORE's national director in February 1961, and soon began to plan for another "journey of reconciliation." Thirteen persons, including Farmer and SNCC activist John Lewis, travelled into the South, leaving Washington, D.C. on 4 May 1961. Predictably, the biracial group encountered violent resistance. Lewis and another Freedom Rider were assaulted in Rock Hill, South Carolina on 9 May. White mobs in Anniston, Alabama, attacked and burned one bus. In Montgomery, Alabama, white racists pulled Freedom Riders off the bus and administered a brutal beating. In Jackson, Mississippi, Farmer and a group of 26 other Freedom Riders representing SNCC and SCLC were given 67-day jail sentences for sitting in the whites-only sections of the city's bus depot. Farmer's jail term served to mobilize every CORE chapter; hundreds made the journey south to join the Freedom Rides. By July, CORE had spent almost $140,000 on bail and legal fees. Despite the legal burden, the Freedom Rides established CORE's credentials as a militant force for desegregation, winning for the group the enthusiastic support of SNCC and the grudging respect of the NAACP. From fiscal 1960–61 to 1961–62, CORE's national income soared from $240,000 to over $600,000; membership climbed from 26,000 in May 1961 to 52,000 in December 1962. By late 1961, CORE had established chapters in the most segregated counties of the Deep South, and the organization was mounting a series of nonviolent protests, pickets and activities in dozens of rural areas.

The desegregation battles of the early 1960s were conceived, planned, and carried out by young people—and all the impatience and idealism which characterize youth were an organic and integral aspect of this campaign for racial justice. Farmer, 41 years old when the Freedom Rides began, was viewed by black students as a veritable sage and "distinguished elder." King was only 31, but even he seemed rather remote from the mind and mood that simmered across the black college campuses. The vast majority of black youth who were arrested, imprisoned and beaten were teenagers, or scarcely into their twenties. They viewed the legalistic maneuvers of the NAACP with a politely hidden contempt, and judged the Urban League as being in the "enemy's camp." They knew little, if anything, of DuBois, the National Negro Congress, the 1941 March on Washington Movement, or Randolph's futile battles in the AFL-CIO. Many young whites who joined the sit-ins came from parents who had been members of the Socialist and Communist parties. Others came from upper-class suburban homes, and had turned against the pampered affluence which their parents had showered upon them as children. They saw what blacks had always understood: the hypocrisy, the contradiction of America's democracy which was based upon the continued subjugation of the Negro. "They captured and held on to the traditional democratic ideals they had been taught, eliminating the inconsistencies between doctrine and reality that they felt had crept into the preceding generation's practical values in relation to those ideals."[3] Thus, racial reform in the South was not an aberration of bourgeois democracy; it was its fulfillment. Sit-ins were no rejection of the American Dream; they were the necessary although ambiguous steps taken towards it culmination. Historian Vincent Harding writes of this generation in the following manner:

> They were believers. When they sang in jail, in mass meetings, in front of policemen and state troopers, "We Shall Overcome," they meant it. Few were certain about details, but they *would* overcome. Vaguely, overcoming meant "freedom" and "rights" and "dignity" and "justice," and black and white together, and many other things that people in a movement feel more than they define. But they knew they were part of a revolution, and they believed that if they only persisted in courage, determination, and willingness to suffer, they would make it over.[4]

II

If the movement seemed at times to be a modern great awakening, or revival of the spirit, this was due in part to the religious character of its leadership. At every level of organization, and in almost every small town where sit-ins or jail-ins occurred, black ministers were at the very center of the struggle. In Tallahassee, the Reverend C. K. Steele had founded the Inter-Civic Council, a desegregation coalition which was designed after King's original Montgomery Improvement Association. Black minister and historian Vincent Harding led a prayer vigil at Atlanta's City Hall to protest against the vicious beating of Mrs. Coretta Scott King, which resulted in her miscarriage. The Reverend C. T. Vivian of Chattanooga was a prominent SCLC organizer across Tennessee. The Reverend Walter Fauntroy supported desegregation activities by directing SCLC's Washington, D.C. bureau office. The Reverend Wyatt Tee Walker, the articulate black Baptist leader of Petersburg, Virginia, served as SCLC's executive director for a time, and was a constant thorn in the sides of his state's racist politicians. Fred Shuttlesworth of Birmingham; William Holmes Borders of Atlanta; Ralph David Abernathy of Montgomery and Atlanta, Kelly Miller Smith of Nashville; and Matthew McCollum of Orangeburg, South Carolina, were only a small part of the hundreds of black preachers and divinity students who repeatedly, sometimes daily, risked their lives in the concerted effort to destroy Jim Crow.

Despite the vital contributions of the black clergy, SNCC stood alone in its unselfish determination to confront the segregationist power structure. By the early summer of 1960, at the suggestion of Rustin, Bob Moses led the development of a voter registration project in Pike County, Alabama. In 1961–62 SNCC joined forces with the NAACP, SCLC and other black groups in Albany, Georgia, to create the Albany Movement for desegregation. Despite the prominent participation of King, Abernathy and other SCLC leaders, the young SNCC workers—James Forman, Norman Collins, Bill Hansen, Charles Sherrod, Cordell Reagan, and many others—distinguished themselves by their willingness to defy the segregation laws, to mobilize poor and working-class blacks in nonviolent demonstrations and to go to jail for their principles. It is very difficult, in retrospect, to comprehend the sheer courage of these black teenagers and young adults. Veterans of the Freedom Rides and the bloody Albany campaign, tested repeatedly, freely acknowledged the preeminent will to resist that fashioned SNCC members into the "True Believers" of the struggle. Let two examples illustrate this. On 30 April 1962, Diane Nash Bevel, who had married activist James Bevel the year before, stood before a Mississippi court on charges of contributing to "juvenile delinquency"—she had taught black teenagers in McComb, Mississippi, techniques needed for nonviolent demonstrations. Deliberately, she sat in the "whites-only" section of the courtroom. The angry judge sentenced the pregnant woman to serve ten days in the local jail for that single act of defiance. Nash responded, "I believe that if I go to jail now it may help hasten that day when my child and all children will be free—not only on the day of their birth but for all of their lives."[5] Deep in the heart of Mississippi, Bob Moses helped to create the Council of Federated Organizations (COFO), a coalition of CORE, NAACP and SNCC organizers. Tirelessly, Moses organized voter registration drives in the face of tremendous white resistance. As one black Mississippi resident stated: "Poor Bob took a lot of beatings, I just couldn't understand what Bob Moses was. Sometimes I think he was Moses in the Bible. He pio-

neered the way for black people. . . . He had more guts than any one man
I've ever known."[6]

After Albany and the Freedom Rides, the focus of political struggle
shifted back toward implementing desegregation in the universities. Black
Mississippi resident James Meredith was refused admission into the segregated University of Mississippi in January 1961. Supported by NAACP attorneys, Meredith managed to overturn the state's segregation restrictions
in the federal court of appeals. Supreme Court justice Hugo L. Black, a
native of Alabama, ordered Mississippi governor Ross Barnett and the
state courts to allow Meredith to enroll. On 24 September 1962, Barnett
declared to the press that any federal officers attempting to assist Meredith
would be arrested by state police. The next day, the governor personally
blocked Meredith from gaining admission to register in the university.
The Kennedy Administration was finally compelled, in the light of this
blatant defiance of federal authority, to call 320 federal marshals into Oxford, Mississippi, to gain Meredith's enrollment. On Sunday afternoon, 1
October, the marshals escorted Meredith into a dormitory hall on the campus. Within hours, several thousand racists attacked the federal marshals
with shotguns, clubs, broken glass, and homemade bombs. Kennedy had
seriously underestimated the brutality of the South, and that night he
commanded 1,400 troops at Fort Dix and Fort Bragg to disperse the white
vigilantes. By dawn, almost 2,500 soldiers were stationed in Oxford, but
the damage done by the mob was considerable. Two people were killed,
166 marshals and 210 demonstrators were injured, and dozens of automobiles had been destroyed. To ensure the peace, 300 soldiers were stationed at "Ole Miss" for a year. Meredith was finally allowed to attend the
institution. To white southerners, the "Battle of Oxford" was a grievous
insult and a gross example of federal intervention over the states' traditional rights to segregate "niggers" from their institutions of higher learning. They blamed King, SNCC, and other so-called "Communist-inspired"
groups for the violence. Northern Democrats and many liberal Republicans were now more repulsed by the South's Massive Resistance, and
urged the Kennedy Administration to develop legislation which would
force the South to accept desegregation. After the Battle of Oxford, it was
clear that Kennedy, who had at first tried to placate both the racists and
the desegregationists simultaneously, had to make a decision which side to
support.

Meanwhile, the successes achieved by the civil rights forces spawned
new types of protest maneuvers in the North as well as the South, and in
turn, generated serious disagreements over strategies and tactics necessary
to win desegregation. In the South, CORE locals co-operated closely with
SNCC in mounting voter education and registration campaigns. In New

Haven, Connecticut, CORE activists led by a 27-year-old worker, Blyden Jackson, staged the first "sit-outs"—demonstrations wherein blacks in dilapidated public residential units and slums blocked the city's sidewalks in efforts to obtain adequate housing reforms. Seattle, Washington, CORE members picketed a local supermarket in October 1961, and secured employment for five blacks. CORE locals in East St. Louis, Illinois, Kansas City, Missouri, Rochester, New York and other cities mobilized blacks to protest against police brutality in their cities. As the focus of CORE shifted toward "non Southern issues" such as housing and police violence in the North, many members began seriously to question the formation's long-held commitment to Gandhian nonviolence. CORE chapters in Cleveland, Ohio and Greensboro, North Carolina, rejected Farmer's protests by supporting a defense committee for Robert Williams. CORE chapters in Hartford, Connecticut, Baltimore, Maryland, New Orleans, Louisiana and at least four other major locals developed close organizational and programmatic links with the Nation of Islam and its fiery spokesperson, Malcolm X. San Francisco CORE held workshops discussing black nationalism in 1962, and many new black recruits of CORE were not sympathetic to the ideal of cultural integration with whites. Partially because of CORE's internal shift in priorities, it soon came under the criticism of the NAACP for being too aggressive and unwilling to compromise with white corporate and political leaders. With some desperation, Farmer admitted at the 1962 CORE convention: "We no longer are a tight fellowship of a few dedicated advocates of a brilliant new method of social change; we are now a large family spawned by the union of the method-oriented pioneers and the righteously indignant ends-oriented militants."[7] Black attorney Floyd McKissick was elected national chairman of CORE in 1963, and new CORE leaders Ruth Turner of Cleveland and Harold Brown of San Diego revealed clear sympathies toward a Malcolm X-type militancy and nationalism. The biracial pacifist collective was becoming rapidly more black in constituency and ideology.

SNCC also began to experience ideological and programmatic growing pains at this juncture. The essence of any social theory evolves from concrete practice. Since SNCC was, admittedly, the real vanguard of the gritty desegregation and voter registration efforts, it was inevitable that the most advanced theoretical positions would emerge from these young people. The idealism of the early years had worn away quickly. By mid-1962, some SCLC leaders in Albany, Georgia, were attempting to moderate SNCC's militant role in the town's desegregation actions. SNCC activists complained about the overwhelming television attention riveted in King, at the expense of local conditions and personalities. King was privately termed "De Lawd" at this time, a symbolic media figure who actually did little nuts-

and-bolts organizing at the constant risk of his own life. By 1963, SNCC activists had repeatedly been the targets for murder across the region. SNCC offices were firebombed; SNCC workers were attacked with shotgun blasts, pistols and chains; SNCC organizer Jimmy Travis was attacked by whites armed with machine guns in Greenwood, Mississippi. Southern legislators proclaimed wildly that SNCC was simply a Marxist revolutionary formation, determined to destroy American capitalism and the social institutions of order. Increasingly, Forman urged SNCC leaders to engage in the study of socialist texts, and to learn more about the Cuban revolution and the concurrent African liberation struggles. Rapidly, SNCC lost its initial reluctance to work with avowed Marxists, although few students had ever really read or understood socialist or communist doctrines. In 1963, when King dismissed a key white aide, Jack O'Dell, when the FBI discovered and publicized his previous connections with the Communist Party, many SNCC radicals were outraged. One rising SNCC activist, Stokely Carmichael, charged that King and other Negro moderates must "stop taking a defensive stand on communism."[8] Like CORE's militants, many blacks began to question the utility or even the necessity of white participation in their organization. SNCC's repeated attacks on the milktoast Kennedy Administration embarrassed and humiliated the older and more conservative civil rights leaders. As SNCC matured, it became clear that the students would have to confront their own theoretical and organizational dilemmas at some future point.

III

The dramatic highpoint of the desegregation movement was achieved in 1963. In three difficult years, the southern struggle had grown from a modest group of black students demonstrating peacefully at one lunchcounter to the largest mass movement for racial reform and civil rights in the twentieth century. Between autumn 1961 and the spring of 1963, 20,000 men, women and children had been arrested. In 1963 alone another 15,000 were imprisoned; 1,000 desegregation protests occurred across the region, in more than 100 cities. Above all else, two significant actions during that year stand out—the desegregation campaign in "America's Johannesburg," Birmingham, Alabama; and the March on Washington, D.C.

For decades, Birmingham had represented the citadel of white supremacy. No black resident was ever secure from the wide sweep of white terrorism—institutional and vigilante. White police officers in the city casually picked up black women pedestrians and raped them at gun-point. Throughout the 1950s, black homes and churches were bombed. In April

1959, a black Baptist preacher was kidnapped by the Klan and beaten senseless with tire chains. Every aspect of cultural, social and economic life in the town was strictly segregated. Birmingham itself "conjured up all the worst images of southern white urban racism," Vincent Harding notes. "Unyielding white supremacy, blatant segregation, brutal police, easily organized white mobs, and unresponsive elected officials. . . . Every black person seemed to know someone who had been beaten, bombed, raped, or murdered in Birmingham."⁹ For years, civil rights activists had conceived the plans for attacking Birmingham's Jim Crow laws. In May 1961, Freedom Riders had been threatened and arrested by the city's unrelenting, segregationist police chief, Eugene "Bull" Conner. Conditions had become even worse with the election of Wallace as the state's governor in 1962. Upon taking his oath of office, the populist-turned-white-supremacist vowed that the federal government would never dictate racial policies in his state. "I draw the line in the dust and toss the gauntlet before the feet of tyranny and I say segregation now, segregation tomorrow, segregation forever."¹⁰ In May 1962, the Reverend Fred Shuttlesworth convinced other SCLC leaders that the time to tackle the most segregated city in the nation had now arrived.

The first organizational tasks in preparing for the demonstrations were given to Wyatt Walker. In January and February, he took careful notes on almost every public building, commercial establishment, and street in the downtown area. Wyatt also recruited 250 persons who were committed to engage in nonviolent actions and to go to the city jail. On 3 April 1963, the desegregation campaign began. Sit-ins were held at department stores and restaurants. On 6 April, the Reverend A. D. King and 42 other marchers were arrested for holding a vigil at the town hall. "Bull" Conner attempted to undercut the actions by closing all public parks and playgrounds. On 10 April, four days before Easter, King, Abernathy and other leaders spoke to a massive church rally. King openly castigated the black preachers who had ignored the demonstrations. "I'm tired of preachers riding around in big cars, living in fine homes, but not willing to take their part in the fight. If you can't stand up with your people, you are not fit to be a leader!" King urged every black person to stand up for freedom now. "We are winning the struggle for which we have sacrificed, but we must even be ready to die to be free, if that is what's necessary. Birmingham must put its house in order," King declared. "It's better to go to jail in dignity than accept segregation in humility." Abernathy rose to his feet, asking the congregation, "Who'll volunteer to go to jail with me and Martin. . . ?"¹¹ Men, women and children surged forward, hands upraised, tears in their eyes, singing and praying. King and Abernathy were arrested on Good Friday; marchers on Easter Sunday were clubbed and taken into custody.

On 2 May, Bevel co-ordinated a children's march involving 6,000 black youngsters from the ages of 6 to 16. Before national television cameras, Birmingham police let loose vicious police dogs on children as they knelt to pray; 959 children were arrested and jailed. Police used firehoses, dogs and clubs against pregnant women, children, and the elderly. Across the world, humanity was repulsed by the sickening spectacle of American racism, the reality of white democracy.

In April, eight moderate white Birmingham ministers denounced King for what they perceived as his "impatience" with white segregationists. They went so far as to applaud "Bull" Conner and his armed thugs for employing "restraint in maintaining order." The ministers "strongly urged our own Negro community to withdraw support from these demonstrations."[12] King's response was one of the most eloquent essays written in American history, the famous "Letter from Birmingham Jail." Writing from his jail cell on 16 April, King observed that the ministers and other white moderates were contributing to segregation by their blind inertia. "The Negro's greatest stumbling block in the stride toward freedom is not the . . . Ku Klux Klanner, but the white moderate who is more devoted to "order" than to justice . . . who constantly says "I agree with you in the goal you seek, but I can't agree with your methods of direct action"; who paternalistically feels that he can set the timetable for another man's freedom," King declared. The purpose of nonviolent action was not to evade or to defy the law. "One who breaks an unjust law must do it "openly, lovingly," King insisted. "I submit then an individual who breaks a law that conscience tells him is unjust, and willingly accepts the penalty by staying in jail to arouse the conscience of the community over its injustice, is in reality expressing the very highest respect for law." Perhaps King's most effective criticism was his insistence that the Negro could no longer "wait" to be freed by benevolent whites:

We have waited for more than 340 years for our constitutional and God-given rights. The nations of Asia and Africa are moving with jetlike speed toward gaining political independence, but we still creep at horse-and-buggy pace toward gaining a cup of coffee at a lunch counter. Perhaps it is easy for those who have never felt the stinging darts of segregation to say, "Wait." But when you have seen vicious mobs lynch your mothers and fathers at will and drown your sisters and brothers at whim; when you have seen hate-filled policemen curse, kick and even kill your black brothers and sisters; when you see the vast majority of your twenty million Negro brothers smothering in an airtight cage of poverty in the midst of an affluent society; when you suddenly find your tongue twisted and your speech stammering as you seek to explain to your six-year-old daughter why she can't go to the public amusement park that has just been advertized on television, and see tears welling up in her eyes when she is told that Funtown is closed to colored children, and see ominous clouds of inferiority beginning to form in her little mental sky, and see her begin to distort her personality by an unconscious developing bitterness toward white people; when you have to concoct an answer for a five-year-old son who is asking "Daddy, why do white people treat colored people so mean?"; when you take a cross-country drive and find it necessary to sleep night after night in the uncomfortable corners of your automobile because no motel will accept you; when you are humiliated day in and day out by nagging signs reading "white" and "colored"; when your first name becomes "nigger," your middle name becomes "boy" (however old you are) and your last name becomes "John," and your wife and mother are never given the respected title "Mrs."; when you are harried by day and haunted by night by the fact that you are a Negro, living constantly at tiptoe stance never quite knowing what to expect next, and are plagued with inner fears and outer resentments; when you are forever fighting a degenerating sense of "nobodiness"—then you will understand why we find it difficult to wait. There comes a time when the cup of endurance runs over, and men are no longer willing to be plunged into the abyss of despair. I hope, sirs, you can understand our legitimate and unavoidable impatience.[13]

Protests were mounting across the country, demanding that the Kennedy Administration resolve the battle of Birmingham. A. D. King's home was bombed, and other bombs exploded in black-owned buildings in the city. Republican liberal senator Jacob Javits of New York and other members of Congress demanded that the Justice Department intervene in the crisis. 100,000 people marched in San Francisco and thousands more demonstrated in Detroit to express solidarity with Birmingham blacks. Tens of thousands of whites who had up to now stood outside the Civil Rights Movement—teachers, lawyers, laborers, elected officials, clergy—were recruited into the cause for justice. Thousands of telegrams were sent to the administration demanding action. Finally, after the brutal beatings and arrests of black children, the Kennedy Administration went into motion. On 10 May 1963, Assistant Attorney General Burke Marshall, Secretary of Defense Robert McNamara and Treasury Secretary C. Douglas Dillon reached an agreement with Burmingham's corporate leaders and elected officials. The terms included local hiring policies on a "nondiscriminatory basis" and the immediate release of all black prisoners. Kennedy warned Wallace that federal troops would be called in to enforce desegregation and civil order if necessary.

Despite the victory in Birmingham, the racist violence continued unabated. In Americus, Georgia, local police were using electric cattle prods and clubs against unarmed citizens; in Plaquemines, Louisiana, 900 marchers were tear-gassed and clubbed, 400 were arrested and 150 hospitalized. In June, Mississippi asserted its rightful place as the most racist state with particular vigor; in Biloxi, 72 blacks were arrested; in Tchula, activist Willie Joe Lovett, 23 years old, was killed; in Winona, civil rights leaders Fannie Lou Hamer and others were viciously beaten and imprisoned by police. On the night of 11 June, NAACP state leader Medgar Evers was executed by racists in front of his Jackson, Mississippi, home. Kennedy was not unmoved by the carnage and the ordeals of blacks, but the racial crisis alone would not have prompted him to act. Many corporate leaders, always looking at the social costs of doing business in the South, had concluded that desegregation was inevitable; that the federal government's appropriate role was to ensure the civil order which was essential to business expansion. For both moralistic and economic reasons, then, big business had come to accept the death of Jim Crow, and a number of corporate and financial leaders urged the administration to do the same. On 12 June, Kennedy announced that he would deliver to Congress a strong civil rights bill. Later, promoting its passage, the president defended it "not merely for reasons of economic efficiency, world diplomacy and domestic tranquility—but above all because it is right."[14] Kennedy instantly became recognized as a powerful friend of civil rights. In later years, millions of poor and working-class black families framed photos of the late president, alongside those of his brother Robert, and Martin Luther King, and displayed them proudly in their homes. It is critically important to understand Kennedy's motivations for embracing desegregation at this relatively late date. Like Lincoln before him, Kennedy personally felt no great discomfort with racial segregation. In 1956, many southern delegates to the Democratic national convention favored his nomination as the party's vice-presidential candidate over that of a rival southern senator, because of Kennedy's moderate reputation on race and his outspoken anti-communism. The Cold War had again accelerated in the early 1960s: communist forces were winning in Laos and Vietnam; Castro was in power in Havana; a bloody civil war raged in the Congo; and in October 1962, the Cuban Missile Crisis had threatened the total destruction of world civilization. Kennedy and his advisers, notably Robert Kennedy, had to view Birmingham in a worldwide context, within the greater struggle for hegemony with the Soviet Union over the Third World. The image of battered and bloody black children in the streets of the American South could not help but undermine the U.S. government's image in non-aligned countries. Kennedy's subsequent actions were directly influenced more by cold geopolitical facts than by warm idealism.

As the Birmingham struggle climaxed, another major protest was being planned. Among several leaders, the idea of reviving Randolph's 1941

March on Washington movement had been discussed. Randolph and Rustin assumed leadership in the planning stages, with the latter doing most of the actual co-ordination. SNCC and a few CORE militants insisted that the march should become a massive civil disobedience demonstration, which would paralyze the nation's capital. But white liberals from labor, religious and political groups would not tolerate this radical approach. The SCLC, the Urban League and the NAACP explained that the demonstration should be planned without any arrests, with the complete co-operation of the federal authorities. This conservative position, backed by Kennedy, eventually became the dominant theme of the march. Instead of a massive, nonviolent army of black students and workers—which ironically closely parallaled Randolph's 1941 project—the new march was almost a festive affair, used to promote the Kennedy civil rights bill pending before Congress. "To orchestrate and guarantee the civility of the new march on Washington, the movement spent tremendous amounts of manpower, energy and money—all of which were diverted from the thrusts of direct action and voter registration in the South and elsewhere." [15] The result was a biracial audience of 250,000 or more, standing before the Lincoln Memorial, on 28 August 1963. Many movement radicals who attended the gathering agreed with Malcolm X that the event was nothing but a "farce on Washington." But for whites and many Negro moderates, the ceremony was the highpoint of their lives.

Televised before a national audience, most of the speakers endeavored to strike a moderate tone. Shuttlesworth declared: "We came here because we love our country, because our country needs us and because we need our country." Randolph, as was his custom, represented black labor. "We are the advance guard of a massive moral revolution for jobs and freedom," the veteran socialist observed. "Our white allies know that they cannot be free while we are not." Roy Wilkins, who was introduced erroneously as "the acknowledged leader of the civil rights movement," gave vigorous support to the proposed civil rights bill. Whitney M. Young, director of the Urban League, Matthew Ahmann of the Catholic Conference for Interracial Justice, and others gave moderate and unsurprising testimony. Problems surfaced when the contents of John Lewis's speech became known prior to his address. The Catholic archbishop of Washington, Patrick A. O'Boyle, declared he would leave the podium unless others deleted and rearranged the SNCC leader's presentation. Protesting, but in the end acquiescing, Lewis delivered a "sanitized" speech which still expressed key elements of his organization's radical posture. "We are tired of being beaten by policemen. We are tired of seeing our people locked up in jail over and over again!" Lewis dismissed the Kennedy civil rights bill as "too little and too late." King came to the speaker's platform last, and gave what many in the audience declared was a rhetorical "miracle," his "I have a Dream" speech. King began by terming the march "the greatest demonstration of freedom" in American history. He illustrated in resounding oratory his vision of society: a land where freedom rang "from every mountainside," and where blacks and whites could join hands together to proclaim the words, "Free at last, free at last; thank God Almighty, we're free at last!" Historians of the movement were struck by the fact that a portion of King's speech was originally delivered in 1956, at the first anniversary ceremonies for the Montgomery Bus Boycott movement. Other parts were derived from political speeches and sermons he had given for over seven years.[16] Militants were bitterly disappointed that King had chosen not to include extensive critical remarks on the recent racist violence in the South, and the failure of most white liberals to respond concretely or adequately to the Negro's economic plight. But before a predominantly white viewing audience in the U.S., King represented a reasonable and even admirable spokesman for the cause of civil rights. The speech mirrored, in a sense, Booker T. Washington's Atlanta Compromise of September 1895: both were delivered to primarily white audiences; both were self-consciously restrained in their demands; both captured the dominant political trends in the white civil society at that point in American racial history. Washington of course championed "separation of the races," while King called for "integration" and "civil rights." Yet across the gulf of history, the two black men personified a body of public policies which dealt directly with the present and future status of the Negro. Both won the grateful support of their respective presidential administrations; both proposed the implementation of their racial policies in the South. King and Washington were catapulted after their respective speeches into international fame.

If the Negro moderates thought that a nonviolent celebration would pressure the Congress to adopt the civil rights proposals, they were sadly mistaken. Not a single vote changed in Congress after the march. If anything, the mood among grassroots blacks had swung towards greater defiance. In July 1963, one month before the march, writer Lerone Bennett argued that "the burning militance of the Birmingham leaders . . . pinpointed a revolutionary shift in the attitudes of blacks." CORE militants in San Francisco declared that "Birmingham brought a drastic revision in our thinking. You can nibble away at the surface for a thousand years and not get anywhere."[17] CORE chapters across the country began to set firm and short "deadlines" for white businesses to hire certain numbers of blacks, promising to disrupt commercial traffic and to protest repeatedly unless goals were reached. Many black nationalists targeted King and other more conservative Negro leaders with personal and even physical abuse. In Harlem, black separatists tossed eggs at King after his appearance in a local church. When A. D. King addressed a Harlem rally of 3,000 in May 1963, a section of the audience jeered: "We want Malcolm, we want Malcolm!"[18] Dissatisfied with the mildly reformist policies and practices of the Negro Old Guard, SNCC leaders increasingly looked overseas for ideological direction. In December 1963, staff members had a fruitful discussion with Kenya's socialist vice president, Oginga Odinga, when he visited Atlanta. Nine months later eleven SNCC leaders, including Fannie Lou Hamer, Julian Bond, Ruby Doris Robinson, John Lewis and James Forman travelled across Africa, and met with national leaders. In Africa the SNCC delegation met Malcolm X, and the beginning of an influential relationship was established. Domestically, SNCC moved closer to the organized left. In December 1963, Lewis urged Congress to abolish HUAC; the following year, SNCC accepted the legal assistance of the leftist National Lawyers Guild, over the vigorous objections of NAACP Legal Defense Fund director Jack Greenberg, a Cold War liberal.[19] Even the SCLC and NAACP experienced a bewildering sense of "What Next?" after the March on Washington. Rustin was disturbed by the "talk of violence" and growing sympathy for Malcolm X's nationalism. "We cannot get our freedom with guns," Rustin wrote in Ocrtober 1963. "You cannot integrate a school or get a job with a machine gun." But Rustin admitted that Kennedy still "reassures the segregationists" and privately "bows to the Dixiecrats and gives them Southern racist judges."[20]

Ever-present in the post-march discussions were certain questions: "once desegregation is legally won, what is the next objective?"; "what does freedom actually mean in terms of public policies?"; and "are integration and nonviolence the only possible methods to wage the Second Reconstruction?" Sadly, with the growing exceptions of SNCC and CORE, the majority of Negro leaders were poorly equipped theoretically even to grapple with these social and economic contradictions, for at their roots they signified the reality of America's racist and capitalist state. The one black theorist and activist who could have provided the answers had been banished from political discourse. In October 1961, DuBois applied for membership in the Communist Party, and late that year left the U.S. to relocate in Nkrumah's Ghana. He died at the age of 95, hours before the March on Washington. Yet before his final departure, in one of his last public addresses, delivered at Johnson C. Smith College in Charlotte, North Carolina, on 2 April 1960, DuBois predicted the dilemmas which would later confound and confront the civil rights leadership. Long before his critics, DuBois recognized that the struggle for desegregation would be victorious in the end, but that this effort to abolish Jim Crow would not destroy the economic prerogatives of private capital over black lives, which was the basis for all the exploitation and racism which existed in the

Further, he warned the sit-in demonstrators not to confuse deseg-
1 as a political goal with cultural assimilation into the white major-
: desegregation struggle in American should not force Negroes ever
t slavery and "the whole cultural history of Africans in the world.
1at I have been fighting for . . . is the possibility of black folk and
ltural patterns existing in American without discrimination, and
s of equality." Political equality with whites would eventually oc-
black scholar stated, but without an economic program of so-
and "the preservative of African history and culture" among Af-
nericans, a truly biracial democracy was impossible.[21] Few noted
for DuBois's remarks; but within five brief years, the words of his
ins would resound throughout the black movement in many ways.

IV

1962 and 1965, Martin Luther King was the acknowledged moral
tical leader of millions of Americans, black and white. After the
n Washington, King became one of the three or four most influen-
es in the world. His books and articles were read by millions; his
were memorized; he was honored with the 1964 Nobel Peace
? was celebrated by artists and poets of all races and cultures.
ersonal achievements and acclaim gave the domestic struggle for
lemocracy an international audience. For the historian, King rep-
series of paradoxes, each of which obscures the real meaning of
ness. Some commentators suggest that without King, the civil
use would have faltered, and certain major legislative victories—
rly the Civil Rights Act of 1964 and the Voting Rights Act of
rould not have been won. This idealist interpretation misses the
lationship between the individual and the dialectical evolution of
Other social movements throughout human history are often char-
l by the singular actions of one prominent figure: Cromwell in the
Civil War; Lenin, during the Russian Revolution of 1917; Mao in
Robespierre during the French Revolution. But history creates hu-
as well as the conscious choices which are possible for any political
o select. G. Plekhanov's *The Role of Individual in History* sheds
able light on this issue. If a social movement for reform or revolu-
broad enough, Plekhanov insisted, any series of individuals can
io can articulate the vision of that movement. "If the accidental fall
ck had killed [Robespierre] . . . his place would, of course, have
ken by someone else; and although that other person might have
iferior to him in every respect, events would have nevertheless
he same course as they did with Robespierre." A great politician

"sees farther than others and desires things more strongly than others," but he/she cannot overturn the basic direction of struggle.[22] Reconsidering the black movement from 1954 to 1965, King appears "indispensable" because in retrospect, his great gifts for oratory and his dynamic use of non-violent direct-action techniques appear to stand alone. But King did not create the Second Reconstructon; the movement made the young minister its own spokesperson, and could have done the same for others if he had not existed. Had King been killed in Montgomery in 1956, Abernathy was fully equipped to carry out the boycott. Randolph and Wilkins were far better known; Farmer of CORE was more willing to go to jail and to lead nonviolent actions; Shuttlesworth, C. T. Vivian and others would have created an organization like King's SCLC by the late 1950s; the sit-ins, Freedom Rides, and jail-ins had nothing directly to do with King, and they would have occurred without his input.

King's powerful influence must be explained, therefore, by factors other than his indispensability. First, and probably foremost among his credentials was his identity as a black preacher. Among his contemporaries in the black clergy, King had no peer as an orator. From small towns in the rural South to his father's Ebenezer Baptist Church in Atlanta, King delivered sermons with a grace, cadence and power unmatched since the great preachers of the A.M.E. church and other black denominations from the late nineteenth century. Author Luis Lomax describes a typical sermon:

"I got my marching shoes!" Martin would shout.
"Yes, Lord, me too,"the people answered back.
"I woke up this morning with my mind on freedom!"
"Preach, doctor, preach."
"I ain't going to let nobody turn me around!"
"Let's march, brother; we are with you. . . . ."
"The struggle is not between black and white!"
"No, no," the people confirmed.
"But between good and evil."
"That's it; that's it."
"For God is not dead; I know because I can feel him. . . . ."
"Deep in my soul!" the people shout completing the line from the Negro spiritual.
   Then, arm in arm with the local leader, Martin led the people into the street to face dogs, tear gas, firehoses, and, frequently, brutality and additional jailing.

Black novelist James Baldwin described King as a "great speaker" whose "secret lies in his intimate knowledge of the people he is addressing," by keeping "his hearers absolutely tense." On the church pulpit King personified their own best hopes, their desires for human equality their love of God, their will to resist. "Once he had accepted the place they had prepared for him, their struggle became absolutely indistinguishable from his own, and took over and controlled his life. He suffered with them and, thus, he helped them to suffer."[24]

King appealed to white liberals for other reasons. He had none of Lewis's or Carmichael's fiery political rhetoric; but this allowed him to be judged as a moderate and reasonable counselor in a time of racial crisis. He lacked Randolph's peerless credentials as a leader of black workers; but this gave the black minister access to corporate directors and many conservatives who still viewed Randolph with some suspicion. King's SCLC had none of the organizational clout or prestige of Wilkins's NAACP; yet this permitted King to be viewed not as a desegregation bureaucrat, but as a moral and spiritual leader. Writing in 1965, historian August Meier explained that King's religious terminology and the manipulation of the Christian symbols of love and nonresistance are responsible for his appeal among whites. To talk in terms of Christianity, love, nonviolence is reassuring to the mentality of white America." King made white liberals feel guilty every time they saw him lead a nonviolent prayer group or march that was assaulted by southern police, armed with firehoses, dogs and clubs. But King's faith in the essential humanity of even the worst white bigot gave other whites the sense that this black leader valued and respected law and order, tempered with justice. Whites could love King, because King had "faith that the white man will redeem himself."[25]

In politics, King tried to strike a balance between protest and accommodation. Inside his own closed coterie of supporters, he listened to the advice of radicals like Bevel and gradualists like Andrew Young. When President Kennedy was assassinated on 22 November 1963, King immediately issued a statement which blamed all American blacks and whites equally, for creating "a climate where men cannot disagree without being disagreeable, and where they express their disagreement through violence and murder." King was ready to support Lyndon Johnson as he assumed the presidency, in return for the former segregationist's vigorous endorsement of the Civil Rights bill. Congress passed the legislation on 2 July 1964; King repaid the new president by campaigning for his election throughout that year. In *Why We Can't Wait*, released in July 1964, King praised "Johnson's emotional and intellectual involvement" in the desegregation campaigns.[26] King urged civil rights leaders to diminish their protest actions during the campaign, in the fear that any black boycotts or jail-ins would undercut Johnson's chances for election. When black urban rebellions erupted in Rochester, Philadelphia, and Harlem—brought about by decades of economic exploitationand federal government apathy—King took a law-and-order posture. Travelling to New York City's burning ghettoes, even without contacting local black leaders in advance, King insisted that the black underclass should return quietly to their rat-infested slums. "Lawlessness, looting and violence cannot be condoned whether used by the racist or the reckless of any color."King declared, to the popular acclaim of white politicians and police.[27] Johnson was elected in November over right-wing challenger Barry Goldwater with a massive majority; indeed, had every black voter stayed home, or had voted for Goldwater, Johnson still would have triumphed. Nevertheless, even after the November 1964 elections, King attempted to moderate the activism of the movement in order to maintain the president's support.

King's compromised and contradictory politics were revealed tragically in Selma, Alabama, in 1965. SNCC workers had been organizing in that section of black-belt Alabama for two years. One black man, Jimmy Lee Jackson, was clubbed to death by police officers as he tried to protect his mother. SCLC and SNCC organizers agreed to schedule a march from Selma to Montgomery beginning on 7 March 1965, to protest against the Wallace regime's brutality. On the morning of the march, SNCC leaders were shocked that King was inexplicably absent. Walking across Selma's Pettus Bridge, the 2,000 nonviolent demonstrators were attacked and brutally beaten by hundreds of state troopers and local police. On 10 March, King agreed to lead a second group of 3,000 protestors across the bridge—but secretly made an agreement with Johnson's Attorney General, Nicholas Katzenbach, that the marchers would not confront the Alabama state police again. With King at the head of the march, the demonstrators sang and prayed as they walked over the bridge. As the police barricade approached, King ordered everyone immediately to retreat. In subdued anger, the amazed SNCC leaders and others walked back into Selma, singing "Ain't Gonna Let Nobody Turn Me 'Round." Later, after hard bargaining, the march to Montgomery was finally held; but the damage to King's reputation was incalculable. Harding expressed the sense of betrayal which characterized the moment:

> When the time came to assert their right to march for freedom, there is every evidence that King backed off. Listening to mediators from President Johnson, he refused to press the movement into so harsh and predictably bloody a confrontation. Many sagging spirits were finally broken with that act of retreat, and the distrust that had been building against King, SCLC, and the Johnson Administration poured out in deep anger and disgust. The powerful, forward thrust of the Southern civil rights struggle had now been finally broken, and that turned out to be the last traditional, major march of the Southern movement.[28]

For five difficult years, King had been the glue which kept the civil rights united front intact. Leaders to his right—Young, Randolph, Wilkins—could accept his activism without personally becoming involved in street demonstrations on a daily basis. He had been a mentor to the left wing of the movement: speaking at SNCC's founding conference, urging teenagers to be arrested for their ideals; writing a powerful fund-raising letter for CORE in 1956, which helped to subsidize its activities; joining CORE's Advisory Committee in 1957, and protecting and aiding Freedom Riders in Montgomery in 1961. Now the myth was shattered, and the politician was something far less than what many True Believers had hoped he was. Robert Allen bitterly denounced King as "a reluctant accomplice of the white power structure." King was manipulated by "the liberal establishment . . . to restrain the threatening rebelliousness of the black masses and the young militants."[29] Even before Selma, Meier levied the harshest criticisms:

> In a movement in which respect is accorded in direct proportion to the number of times one is arrested, King appears to keep the number of times he goes to jail to a minimum. In a movement in which successful leaders are those who share in the hardships of their followers, in the risks they take, in the beatings they receive, in the length of time they spend in jail, King tends to leave prison for other important engagements, rather than remaining there and suffering with his followers. In a movement in which leadership ordinarily devolves upon persons who mix democratically with their followers, King remains isolated and aloof. In a movement which prides itself on militancy and "no compromise" with racial discrimination. . . [King] seems amenable to compromises considered by some half a loaf or less, and often appears willing to postpone or avoid a direct confrontation in the streets.[30]

V

Reason and right seemed to triumph. NAACP activist Clarence Mitchell declared that Johnson had "made a greater contribution to giving a dignified and hopeful status to Negroes in the United States than any President including Lincoln, Roosevelt, and Kennedy."[31] Johnson committed his administration to the goal of "the full assimilation of more than twenty million Negroes into American life." The Civil Rights Bill of 1964 outlawed Jim Crow in public accommodations of every kind, in every city and state. The Voting Rights Act of 1965, prompted by events at Selma, had even greater scope. By votes of 328 to 74 in the House of Representatives, and 79 to 18 in the Senate, bill H.R. 6400 was signed into law by Johnson on 6 August 1965. "I pledge we will not delay or we will not hesitate, or will not turn aside until Americans of every race and color and origin in this country have the same rights as all others to share in the progress of democracy," Johnson declared. Federal examiners were sent into the South with the full powers of the government to safeguard the registration and voting of blacks. Within five years, the effects of the Voting Rights Act were apparent to all. Between 1964 and 1969, the percentage of black adults registered to vote in the South soared: Alabama, 19.3 percent to 61.3 percent; Georgia, 27.4 percent to 60.4 percent; Louisiana, 31.6 percent to 60.8 percent; Mississippi, 6.7 percent to 66.5 percent.[32] Older blacks, for the first time in their lives, were permitted to cast votes. Black children could shop in department stores, eat at restaurants, and even go to amusement parks which were once off-limits. The left wing of the Civil Rights Movement applauded these legislative achievements, but with a grain of cynicism born from hard experience. "The Civil Rights Bill was designed to answer three elements at once," Debbie Louis noted. White liberals were pleased with "the Administration [for] fulfilling its campaign promises. "The black community was placated and its "explosive" sentiment diffused. Most important of all, the 1964 bill pleased "the business community whose survival depended on quelling minority unrest and unprofitable white resistance to moderate black demands."[33]

If anything, the adoption of the 1964 Civil Rights Act increased the institutional, political and vigilante violence against blacks across the South. As Johnson swung the Democratic Party behind the moderate tendency of the desegregation movement, white Southern Democrats abandoned the party by the thousands. An opponent of the Civil Rights Act, Goldwater carried 54.6 percent of the black belt South's popular votes in 1964, and was the first Republican candidate to receive all the electoral votes of Mississippi, Alabama, Georgia, South Carolina and Louisiana. Dixiecrat Strom Thurmond campaigned for Goldwater, and joined the Republican Party in 1966. The new "racist-Republican" won seven additional House seats, elected three senators and two governors in 1966. Many southern politicians who remained Democrats shifted to the far right. In Georgia, a racist Atlanta restaurant owner, Lester Maddox, acquired a widespread following. Maddox was a leader of Georgians Unwilling to Surrender (GUTS) and the White Citizens' Councils. After the Civil Rights Bill was passed, Maddox threatened black would-be patrons with axe handles and physical threats. In 1966, this bizarre yet very American defender of "God, liberty, free enterprise, and states' rights" was elected governor of Georgia. No one, however, surpassed Wallace of Alabama in crude political ability, fiery demagoguery, or defense of white supremacy. Wallace recognized that the South could not defeat the federal government's racial policies alone; he knew that many northern white workers hated and feared blacks, and that this fear could be harnessed into a national political movement. Campaigning against Johnson in the Democratic Party primaries of early 1964, Wallace took his anti-communist, anti-black and quasi-fascist program to northern factories, churches and suburbs. In Indiana, he polled 30 percent of the Democratic popular vote, 34 percent in Wisconsin, and 43 percent in Maryland. Legally barred from running for re-election in Alabama, Wallace proposed that his apolitical wife, Lurleen, be elected governor in his place. On a campaign completely dominated by the racist rhetoric of her husband, Mrs. Wallace carried 54 percent of the Democratic primary vote, and subsequently became governor.[34] The startling success of the Wallaces and Maddoxes created the conditions for racist violence to continue unchecked. During the Mississippi Summer Project of 1964, a joint effort of the NAACP, CORE, SCLC and SNCC to register blacks, there were 6 blacks who were murdered and 1,000 arrested; 30 buildings were bombed and three dozen black churches were gutted by fire. Racist attacks still occurred in every southern city: in Birmingham, blacks at one restaurant were clubbed with baseball bats; in Gransville, Louisiana, the town's leader of the NAACP Youth Council was viciously beaten by white terrorists supervised by the local sheriff; in St. Augustine, Florida, black youths were assaulted by whites with chains and knives. SNCC and CORE activists began to protest that voting rights and desegregated public facilities were not enough. Somehow, the federal government must halt the racist violence against all blacks.

It was only then that some black activists recognized, at last, the limitations of reform. America's political economy was still profoundly racist, and Johnson's legislation had erased only the crudest manifestations of racial suppression. Beyond allowing the Negro the opportunity *not* to be restricted by color *per se*, Johnson and the Congress would not go. Even as Wallace was becoming a national voice for prejudice, bigotry and modern American fascism, white liberals expressed the view that blacks had no more obstacles to confront. Freedom, for them, was achieved by the Voting Rights Act. Woodward explains their joyful mood:

> American institutions were responding effectively to the most serious domestic problem the country faced. Jim Crow as a legal entity was dead. Congress had fulfilled its role, the courts were vindicated, and the executive furnished inspired leadership. Granted that discrimination and segregation still flourished in spite of the law, nevertheless the means were now at hand to deal with all these problems. . . . With the powerful new laws on the books, with public sentiment behind them, and an Administration thoroughly committed to the cause, a new era of progress was about to dawn.[35]

Virtually none of the black leaders, from left to right, shared this gross misconception. Even Whitney Young of the Urban League, a group distinguished by its conservatism and pro-corporate views, had to offer some dissent. "I think the white community makes a real mistake in reminding the Negro of the possibility of alienating white people because he pushes for his rights. A Negro mother whose husband is unemployed," Young noted, "whose children are bitten by rats, who are living in a house without heat, couldn't care less about alienating some white person."[36]

If the tepid Young could feel hostility toward white liberals, the anger of blacks to his left was ten fold. By the autumn of 1963, as we have seen, many CORE members had begun to re-evaluate their historic commitment to nonviolence. In 1964, many blacks were forcing white veterans of CORE to resign their posts as chairs of local chapters. Late that same year, CORE's national membership became, for the first time, predominantly black. Long Island CORE was seized by black nationalists under the direction of militant Lincoln Lynch. In 1965, a black men's caucus was created and led by the egotistical yet charismatic Roy Innis, with the specific political goal of black nationalism. Farmer was increasingly isolated and challenged. In mid-1964, he became fearful that Rustin would be named to replace him. McKissick denounced Farmer for mismanagement and lack of effective leadership. Farmer resigned in January 1966, and was replaced by McKissick. Politically, CORE was increasingly at odds with the Johnson Administration, especially with its policies in Vietnam. Many CORE chapter leaders were among the earliest critics of American involvement in Southeast Asia. McKissick and Farmer co-signed an official condemnation of the war, stating that U.S. money sent to the South Vietnamese regime could be better spent at home to end poverty and institutional racism. CORE had begun to redefine itself, into becoming an all-black formation, although still quite petty bourgeois, which promoted radical reforms and racial pride. Robert Allen described this metamorphosis from biracial pacifism to black militancy in CORE as an attempt to respond to and organize the new militancy which had infected certain parts of the black middle classes, as a result of the rebellions initiated by the black masses."[37]

SNCC was again at the vanguard of change. White liberals watched with horror and dismay as an assertive black nationalist trend became more pronounced in the group. The most articulate voice for nationalism was young Stokely Carmichael. Once a proponent of Rustin's form of gradualist socialism, Carmichael became a SNCC worker on a full-time basis after graduating from Howard University in 1964. Widely praised as a natural organizer of rural workers and farmers, Carmichael registered black voters in Mississippi. From the beginning, however, he could not accept the religious and nonviolent tenets of many SNCC activists. Jailed repeatedly with his co-workers, he refused to participate in the prayers with others in his cell. During organizing efforts in Lowndes County, Alabama, in 1965, Carmichael usually carried a loaded pistol for protection, and advised his friends to do the same. Carmichael and others organized a militant, all-

black political formation, the Lowndes County Freedom Organization—
better known in the state as the Black Panther Party—to oppose the Wallac-
ites electorally. Earlier than CORE, SNCC also publicly denounced Johnson's
war policies. Bob Moses spoke at an anti-war rally of 25,000 in Washington, D.C. on 17 April 1965. Other SNCC leaders, notably Bond, urged the
organization to emphasize the issue. By July 1965, SNCC members produced their first uncompromising statement of the war, declaring that
blacks should not "fight in Vietnam for the white man's freedom, until all
the Negro people are free in Mississippi."[38]

In the process of social transformation, there are always bitter seeds of
defeat hidden within the fruit of victory. Jim Crow was legally finished, yet
black workers and sharecroppers were still the victims of bombings, lynchings and rapes. Thousands had been imprisoned, and their jailers were
still at large; Wallace was now a dangerous national figure to be reckoned
with; white liberals were demanding that the Negro "quiet down" and
"accept" the gains that he/she had gained. Black southerners had the electoral franchise; but what of economic security, housing, child care, medical care, and the right to live without fear? So much had been won, but the
greatest expectations of the black poor and working class had not yet been
achieved. The "echoes from Paul Robeson and W. E. B. DuBois were
sounding in Mississippi," writes Harding. "Every movement forward had
been purchased at great cost. Bleeding ulcers, nervous breakdowns, mysterious, incurable ailments took their toll on young lives." Yet what of
freedom? Was this too simply an illusion? "Every time they smashed away
some obstacle to black freedom and equality, another larger, newly perceived hindrance loomed before them, challenging the last ounce of their
strength and their spirit."[39] The idealistic teenagers of 1960 had become
the steely veterans of racial reform. If white liberals blocked proposals for
gaining a decent material life for the masses of poor blacks, then they
would have to leave our organizations. If Johnson persisted in sending off
young black men to die in an Asian war, his administration would have to
be toppled. If nonviolence could not win the white racists to biracial democracy and justice, then their brutal terror would be met, blow for blow.
If equality was impossible within the political economy of American capitalism, that system which perpetuated black exploitation would have to be
overturned. No more compromises; no more betrayals by Negro moderates. Rebellion would supplant reform.

5. Black Power, 1965-1970

> We are living in an era of revolution, and the revolt of the American
> Negro is part of the rebellion against the oppression and colonialism
> which has characterized this era. . . . It is incorrect to classify the revolt
> of the Negro as simply a racial conflict of black against white, or as a
> purely American problem. Rather, we are today seeing a global rebel-
> lion of the oppressed against the oppressor, the exploited against the
> exploiter.
>
> Malcolm X, 1965

> If a man hasn't found something he will die for, he isn't fit to live.
>
> Martin Luther King

I

Walter Rodney, the noted Guyanese historian and political theorist, once
observed that the slave revolts in his native land "had taught the lesson
that slavery as a form of control over labor was proving uneconomical and
unstable."[1] The same can be said for the U.S. black nonviolent uprisings
of the early 1960s as they related to the Jim Crow system of American caste
and class oppression. Racial segregation had become an international em-
barrassment for the Kennedy and Johnson administrations. Every world
headline for George Wallace, and every citation of a fresh atrocity against
blacks in the South destroyed the credibility of the U.S. as a nation committed to democracy and human equality. Domestically, racial unrest was
costly to the private sector. Eastern U.S. capital and the multinational corporations had no direct historic commitment to the maintenance of rigid
caste divisions within the American working class. They viewed the mild
reforms proposed by Wilkins, Young and Randolph with no great anxiety.
If desegregation could provide the necessary civil order to maintain private
capital accumulation, why not ratify federal legislation to that effect? Racism itself—the systemic exploitation of black labor power and the political
and cultural hegemony of capital's interests over black labor—would still

remain intact. The fragile black middle strata could be absorbed into marginal levels of affluence in both the private sector and the government. This price was modest compared to the greater costs of permitting racial conflagration to continue as it had for five years and more. The rightist tendency of the desegregationist forces were amenable to this proposal. Dedicated anti-communists themselves, their goal had never been to overturn the political economy of capitalism. As integrationists, they simply desired an "equal opportunity" to compete within society and the labor force, without the debilitating restrictions of caste. They were opposed to the notions of black nationalists that blacks should concentrate their own numbers into a power bloc which would demand structural changes in the racist/capitalist order. Their dream of "freedom" was as American as Horatio Alger: social acceptance and upward mobility within the very centers of corporate power. Black radicals in SNCC had come to repudiate this dream; black nationalists had never shared it. As the civil rights united front gradually came unstuck, the only original voice which articulated an alternative vision for black Americans was that of Malcolm X.

It is difficult for historians to capture the vibrant essence of Malcolm X, his earthy and human character, his position as a revolutionary teacher for a generation of young militants, his total love for the dispossessed. Part of his greatness as a social figure was derived from his sordid urban origins. As we have seen, Malcolm rose from being a pimp, drug dealer and ghetto hustler into the most forceful proponent of nationalism since Garvey. His rhetoric, more so than even King's, was almost hypnotic upon black audiences. As the chief spokesperson for the Nation of Islam, he preached a militant message which changed the lives of thousands of poor and oppressed blacks. In any typical sermon, Malcolm might speak these words:

My beautiful, black brothers and sisters! Look at your skins! We're all black to the white man, but we're a thousand and one different colors. Turn around, look at each other! . . . During slavery it was a rare one of our black grandmothers who escaped the white rapist slavemaster. That rapist slavemaster who emasculated the black man with threats, with fear until even today the black man lives with fear of the white man in his heart!

Think of it—think of that black slave man filled with fear and dread, hearing the screams of his wife, his mother, his daughter being taken—in the barn, the kitchen, in the bushes! . . . And you were too filled with *fear* of the rapist to do anything about it! . . .

Every white man in America, when he looks into a black man's eyes, should fall to his knees and say "I'm sorry, I'm sorry—my kind has committed history's greatest crime against your kind; will you give me the chance to atone?" But do you brothers and sisters expect any white man to do that? *No, you know* better! . . .

Every time you see a white man, think about the devil you're seeing! Think of how it was on *your* slave foreparents' bloody, sweaty backs that he built this empire that's today the richest of all nations—where his evil and his greed cause him to be hated around the world![2]

As a devout organizer for the Nation of Islam, Malcolm had served in Detroit, Boston and Philadelphia before leading the powerful Temple Number Seven of Harlem. Word of his sermons brought in hundreds of "Southern migrant people" who in Malcolm's words "would go anywhere to hear what they called 'good preaching'." After hours on the speaking platform, Malcolm "would become so choked up sometimes I would walk in the streets until late into the night. Sometimes I would speak to no one for hours, thinking to myself about what the white man had done to our poor people here in America."[3] As Malcolm began to become better known outside the Nation of Islam, he became the object of bitter attacks from the media and many Negro leaders. His teachings were described in newspapers as "fascist," "violent," "racist," "anti-Christian," and surprisingly, even "Communist-inspired." When white interviewers asked Malcolm, "Why do you teach black supremacy, and hate," Malcolm's response was "to pour on pure fire in return": "For the white man to ask the black man if he hates him is just like the rapist asking the raped, or the wolf asking the sheep, 'Do you hate me?' The white man is in no moral position to accuse anyone else of hate!"[4] Even as a follower of Elijah Muhammad, Malcolm insisted at every opportunity that he opposed racial segregation "even more militantly" than the leaders of the NAACP and other integrationists. For the Muslims, segregation was a system which was "forced upon inferiors by superiors." Complete racial separation, however, would be a means for blacks to stop "begging" the system "for jobs, food, clothing and housing."[5]

In 1962 and 1963, Malcolm's personal prominence began to create tensions and organizational rivalries within the Nation of Islam. Malcolm began to speak out less on religious issues, and increasingly asserted himself on contemporary political questions. The Muslim newspaper he had founded, *Muhammad Speaks,* was ordered to print less about Malcolm. Muhammad's tight authoritarianism prohibited Malcolm and other more activist-oriented ministers from becoming involved in black political struggles. Finally, two events forced Malcolm to divorce himself from the Nation entirely. On 3 July 1963, two former secretaries of Muhammad filed paternity suits against him claiming that the 67-year-old patriarch had fathered their four children. Any other Muslim member or leader would have been promptly expelled for the crime of adultery, yet Muhammad maintained his high post, even after admitting that the charges were true. Malcolm interviewed the women, and learned that Muhammad had described him privately as a "dangerous" threat to his own position. When President Kennedy was assassinated, Malcolm commented to the press that his death was a case of "the chickens coming home to roost . . . that the hate in white men had not stopped with the killing of defenseless black people, but that hate, allowed to spread unchecked, finally had struck down this country's Chief of State."[6] Muhammad used this statement as a pretext to neutralize his chief spokesperson. Malcolm was ordered into "silence" for ninety days, not allowed to teach in his own mosque, nor to speak with the media. Returning to New York, Malcolm was shattered to discover that Muhammad might have authorized several Muslims to assassinate him. By March 1964, it was apparent that the Nation of Islam had no desire to reinstate Malcolm under any conditions of submission. Malcolm left the Nation, and announced the creation of a new organization on 8 March 1964, the Muslim Mosque, Inc. Malcolm informed the press that he was now "prepared to cooperate in local civil rights actions in the South and elsewhere and shall do so because every campaign for specific objectives can only heighten the political consciousness of the Negroes and intensify their identification against white society."[7]

In his last hectic year of life, Malcolm was attempting to develop a revolutionary ideology and program appropriate to the conditions confronting black Americans. In this search, Malcolm's greatest obstacle was his own earlier public image. "I was trying to turn a corner, into a new regard by the public, especially Negroes," he stated in his autobiography. "I was no less angry than I had been, but at the same time the true brotherhood I had seen" in a 1964 journey to the Middle East and Africa "had influenced me to recognize that anger can blind human vision."[8] Renamed El-Hajj-Malik El-Shabazz after his visit to Mecca, Malcolm adopted Sunni Islam as his personal faith, but carefully separated his religious tenets from the political work in which he was engaged. In the summer of 1964, Malcolm and his growing cadre of followers formed the Organization of Afro-American Unity (OAAU), a militant black nationalist force based primarily in New York City. During these months, Malcolm restructured many of his older ideas into a clearly uncompromising program which was both anti-racist and anti-capitalist. Like DuBois before him, Malcolm and the OAAU planned to submit a list of human rights violations and acts of genocide against U.S. blacks to the United Nations. He criticized blacks for endorsing Johnson's 1964 presidential candidacy, predicting with grim accuracy that Johnson would stop far short of providing a meaningful economic and social program which benefited minorities. Criticizing the Negro middle strata's commitment to private enterprise, Malcolm declared, "you can't have capitalism without racism. And if you find [anti-racists] usually they're socialists or their political philosophy is socialism."⁹ The actual program of the OAAU was reformist rather than revolutionary. Their program included the following: the election of independent black candidates for public office, voter registration drives, rent strikes to promote better housing conditions for blacks, the building of all-black community schools, the creation of cultural centers, and initiating black committees for community and neighborhood self-defense. At one point, Malcolm even suggested that his older apocalyptic vision of a race war was no longer viable. "America is the first country . . . that can actually have a bloodless revolution." Evoking some of the ideas of Henry Lee Moon, Malcolm stated, "the Negro holds the balance of power, and if the Negro in this country were given what the Constitution says he is supposed to have, the added power of the Negro in this country would sweep all of the racists and the segregationists out of office. It would change the entire political structure of the country."¹⁰

Malcolm's base of supporters cut deeply into the Civil Rights Movement. Robert Gore, the assistant community relations director of CORE, attended a debate between Malcolm and Bayard Rustin in 1962, with the intention of rooting "with Bayard all the way." Gore left the debate "applauding more for Malcolm X." Half-ashamed, he wrote that Malcolm's eloquence was so moving that "it did my heart a world of good to sit back and listen to [Malcolm X] list the sins of the white man."¹¹ By late 1963, Malcolm was having a direct impact upon many CORE chapters. While Farmer futilely attacked Malcolm, declaring that "we cannot leave the ghetto to the rabid nationalist," other local leaders in the organization championed his ideas.¹² In April 1964, Malcolm urged activists to start "rifle clubs" to defend the black community against police brutality and white vigilante violence. In a similar vein, Cleveland CORE activist Lewis Robinson initiated a proposal for creating a gun club. Malcolm's impact upon SNCC was even greater. White activist Howard Zinn urged SNCC members to repudiate revolutionary black nationalism. "Friendships, and love affairs, have crossed race lines in SNCC," Zinn wrote in early 1964. "Recent calls by Malcolm X and others for Negroes to use self-defense, and even retaliation, against acts of violence by whites," must not be condoned.¹³ Later that year, however, Hamer and SNCC's "Freedom Singers" attended an OAAU meeting in Harlem. In early February 1965, Malcolm was asked by SNCC to speak to black students and workers in Selma, Alabama. Malcolm's electrifying speech gave the radical nationalist tendency within SNCC another boost. Even John Lewis, now increasingly at odds with more radical SNCC members, commented that Malcolm "more than any single personality" was able to "articulate the aspirations, bitterness, and frustrations of the Negro people." [14]

On 21 February 1965, Malcolm was assassinated by gunmen as he rose to address a black Harlem audience. For over a year, he had been followed by the specter of death: in a Cairo visit, he was severely poisoned; on 14 February 1965, his home was fire-bombed. There is now substantial documentation indicating that Malcolm's assassination may have involved the FBI and other agencies of the federal government. [15] From the moment of his death, however, both the Nation of Islam and most of the mainstream civil rights leaders attempted to eradicate Malcolm's political influence among young blacks. Muhammad cynically attributed Malcolm's death to his advocacy of violence. "He seems to have taken weapons as his god. Therefore we couldn't tolerate a man like that. He preached war. We preach peace." Muhammad moved rapidly to isolate pro-Malcolm opponents and to win over key dissidents, including one of his own sons, the Islamic scholar Wallace D. Muhammad, who had briefly sided with Malcolm. Wilfred X and Philbert X, Malcolm's brothers, who had also become leading Muslim ministers, defended Muhammad. For every different reasons, some integrationist leaders quickly seized the opportunity to join the Nation's attacks on Malcolm. A prominent journalist and black appointee in the Johnson Administration, Carl Rowan, described him as "an ex-convict, ex-dope peddler who became a racial fanatic . . . a Negro who preached segregation and race hatred." The most vitriolic yet articulate assaults on Malcolm came from Rustin. "Now that he is dead, we must resist the temptation to idealize Malcolm X, to elevate charisma to greatness," Rustin noted in March 1965. "Malcolm is not a hero of the movement, he is a tragic victim of the ghetto." Rustin insisted that Malcolm was a political failure; that "having blown the trumpet, he could summon, even at the very end, only a handful of followers"; that Malcolm's "central error" was his dedication "to the preservation of the ghetto, which he thought could either be transformed from within or transplanted to a happier environment." Rustin argued, "the movement we build . . . must be dedicated to [the ghetto's] destruction. White America, not the Negro people, will determine Malcolm's role in history." [16]

These sad attempts at blunting Malcolm's influence were ineffectual. In death, the dynamic black activist carried a greater effect upon the mood of black Americans and other non-whites than anyone in a generation. Newspapers across the Third World hailed Malcolm as "the militant and most popular of Afro-American anti-segregationist leaders." Black psychologist Kenneth Clark praised Malcolm for trying "to find a place in the fight for civil rights"; author James Baldwin termed Malcolm's death "A major set-back for the Negro movement." Widely quoted and long remembered were the remarks of black actor Ossie Davis at Malcolm's funeral:

> Many will ask what Harlem finds to honor in this stormy, controversial and bold young captain—and we will smile. They will say that he is of hate— a fanatic, a racist. . . . And we will answer. . . . Did you ever talk to Brother Malcolm? Did you ever touch him or have him smile at you? Did you ever really listen to him? Did he ever do a mean thing? Was he ever himself associated with violence or any public disturbance? For if you did you would know him . . . Malcolm was our manhood, our living, black manhood! This was his meaning to his people. And, in honoring him, we honor the best in ourselves. And we will know him then for what he was and is—a Prince—our own black shining Prince!—who didn't hesitate to die, because he loved us so.

Dead at the age of 39, Malcolm quickly became the fountainhead of the modern renaissance of black nationalism in the late 1960s. His autobiography and published speeches were widely read; even millions of white radicals grew to respect and honor Malcolm's legacy. Black nationalist groups with very divergent political and economic programs all referred to Malcolm as their theoretical touchstone. Even among his bitterest opponents, Malcolm evoked a kind of grudging respect. Prophetically, Wilkins said of him, "Master spell-binder that he was, Malcolm X in death cast a spell more far-flung and more disturbing than any he cast in life." [17]

II

Even before the assassination of Malcolm, many social critics sensed that nonviolent direct action, a tactic of protest used effectively in the South, would have little appeal in the northern ghetto. Far more likely were a series of urban social upheavals which could not be controlled or channelled by the civil rights leadership. In 1963, James Baldwin predicted that race riots would soon "spread to every metropolitan center in the nation which has a significant Negro population." [18] In the spring and summer months of 1964, 1965, 1966, 1967 and 1968, massive black rebellions swept across almost every major U.S. city in the Northeast, Middle West and California. In Watts and Compton, the black districts of Los Angeles, black men and women took to the streets, attacking and burning white-owned property and institutions. The Watts rebellion left $40 million in private property damage and 34 persons killed. Federal authorities ordered 15,000 state police and National Guardsmen into Detroit to quell that city's uprising of 1967. In Detroit 43 residents were killed; almost 2,000 were injured; 2,700 white-owned ghetto businesses were broken into, and 50 percent of these were gutted by fire or completely destroyed; fourteen square miles of Detroit's inner city were torched; 5,000 black persons were left without homes. Combining the total weight of socio-economic destruction, the ghetto rebellions from 1964 to 1972 led to 250 deaths, 10,000 serious injuries, and 60,000 arrests, at a cost of police, troops, other coercive measures taken by the state and losses to business amounting to billions of dollars.

Sociologists and politicians alike were at a loss to explain the furor of these "twentieth century slave revolts." They tacitly had assumed that federal measures toward desegregation would lead to a lessening of racial tensions. Now they had to confront their own theoretical inadequacies. A few white liberals, reluctant as always to accept harsh realities, attempted to explain away the revolts, claiming that most blacks were satisfied with gradual, liberal reforms, and opposed the violence in their communities. Many others defined the rebellions as quasi-anarchistic "riots," which were grounded in an urban youth subculture of social deviance. Herbert J. Gans, a consultant to the National Advisory Commission on Civil Disorders, claimed: "No one knows exactly what sets off the spiraling process [of urban rebellion]. However, most of the rebellious . . . takes on the mood of a carnival. This is not because the participants are callous, but because they are happy at the sudden chance to exact revenge against those who have long exploited and harassed them. The rebellion becomes a community event."[19] Closer to the mark was black sociologist Kenneth Clark, author of *Dark Ghetto,* who suggested: "Human beings who are forced to live under ghetto conditions and whose daily experience tells them that almost nowhere in society are they respected and granted the ordinary dignity and courtesy accorded to others, will, as a matter of course, begin to doubt their own worth." The act of rebellion, the collective venting of long-held hostilities, was in a social and psychological sense a rejection of blacks' "pernicious self- and group-hatred" imposed by the white society.[20] Another important yet overlooked factor in understanding these rebellions was the growth of unfulfilled "rising expectations" among many blacks. In some respects, the 1960s brought an unprecedented improvement in the material, day-to-day conditions for the black working class. From 1964 to 1969, the median black family income in the U.S. increased from $5,921 to $8,074. The ratio between the median family incomes of blacks and whites narrowed from 54 percent to 61 percent. The percentage of black families below the U.S. poverty level declined from 48.1 in 1959 to 27.9 in 1969. Unemployment rates for non-white married males with families dropped from 7.2 percent in 1962, 4.3 percent in 1965, to a low 2.5 percent in 1969. But even these modest advances in jobs, civil rights, and other areas did not keep pace with the expectations of freedom which had awakened the black masses during the decade. Non-white youth unemployment actually increased in these years, from 24.4 percent in 1960 to 29.1 percent in 1970. The quality of black urban life—poor housing, rat infestation, crime, high infant mortality rates, disease, poor public education—continued to deteriorate.

Against this volative background of black urban rebellion, the Civil Rights Movement could not exist as it had in previous years. On 5 June 1966, the first black student to attend the University of Mississippi, James Meredith, began a march from Memphis to Jackson as an individualist act to assert all blacks' rights to move across the South unmolested. Within hours, Meredith was the victim of a shotgun attack. Promptly flying to Memphis, King, McKissick and Carmichael agreed to complete Meredith's symbolic march to Jackson. From the beginning, dissension filled the ranks. Charles Evers, the brother of the martyred NAACP leader, complained, "I don't see how walking up and down a hot highway helps: I'm for walking house to house and fence to fence to get Negroes registered." [21] King was having an increasingly difficult time trying to keep SNCC's black nationalists in check. Carmichael pressured King to accept the request of the Deacons of Defense, a militant southern black organization, to provide paramilitary protection during the protest. As the march progressed, SNCC activist Willie Ricks began to promote the slogan, "Black Power." As a political expression, Black Power was nothing new: novelist Richard Wright and politician Adam Clayton Powell had used it before, as well as others. But combined with Ricks's infectious contempt for Mississippi's white authorities, and in the context of the Meredith march, the slogan captured the mood of the majority of CORE and SNCC activists and most rural blacks as well. On 16 June, Carmichael and several others were arrested and held for six hours in Greenwood, Mississippi. After his release, Carmichael informed a rally of supporters: "This is the twenty-seventh time I have been arrested. I ain't going to jail no more. What we gonna start saying now is "black power." Ricks perceptively picked up the phrase, demanding, "What do you want?" Blacks from the rural community and SNCC activists alike chanted, "Black Power!" Later, King desperately tried to keep others from using the phrase, describing it as "an unfortunate choice of words." It was too late. [22] McKissick now sided firmly with Carmichael, explaining that "Black Power is not Black supremacy; it is a united Black Voice reflecting racial pride in the tradition of our heterogeneous nation. Black Power does not mean the exclusion of White Americans from the Negro Revolution; it means the inclusion of all men in a common moral and political struggle." [23] Within two weeks, "Black Power" sparked a national debate, dividing old friends and bringing to an abrupt halt the last vestiges of unity between the left and right wings of the desegregation movement.

Never had the Old Guard intergrationists moved so swiftly, even in battling the forces of racism. At the July 1966 NAACP convention, Wilkins led the assault. "No matter how endlessly they try to explain it, the term "black power" means anti-white power," he declared. "It is a reverse Mississippi, reverse Hitler, a reverse Ku Klux Klan." Black Power was a "quick, uncritical and highly emotional" slogan that would culminate in "black death." [24] Whitney Young warned that the Urban League would denounce ties with SNCC, CORE, or any group that "formally adopted black power" or attached issues of "domestic civil rights with the Vietnam conflict." Johnson and Vice President Hubert H. Humphrey also condemned Black Power, as did the rising leader of the Democratic Party's liberal wing, New York Senator Robert Kennedy. [25] After decades of pursuing the goal of black independent political power, NAACP leader Henry Lee Moon was repelled to confront his own logic. Black Power is a "naive expression, at worst diabolical, in the sense that at worst it's designed to create chaos," Moon stated defensively. The most articulate attack came from the Old Guard's most authoritative intellectual, Bayard Rustin. The former radical declared that Black Power had no real social program or coherent political philosophy (like Garveyism, it depended on simplistic "slogan" politics) and that it was "utopian and reactionary—the former for the by now obvious reason that one-tenth of the population cannot accomplish much by itself, the latter because [it] would remove Negroes from the main area of political struggle. . . . " National media painted Carmichael, McKissick and other defenders of Black Power as "racist demagogues" who were "inching dangerously toward a philosophy of black separatism." [26] King also had little choice except to denounce Black Power, but in doing so, he strived to maintain some personal link with the young people who had once idealized him. In his last book, *Where Do We Go From Here: Chaos or Community?*, King admitted that there were "positive aspects of Black Power, which are compatible with what we have sought to do in the civil rights movement. . . ." On balance, however, Black Power's "negative values prevent it from having the substance and program to become the basic strategy for the civil rights movement. Beneath all the satisfaction of a gratifying slogan, Black Power is a nihilistic philosophy born out of the conviction that the Negro can't win." [27]

In the movement's militant wing, Black Power simply completed the evolution from integrationist to black nationalist ideologies which had begun three years before. Setting the tone for CORE, McKissick announced, "1966 shall be remembered as the year we left our imposed status of negroes and became *Black Men* . . . when black men realized their full worth in society—their dignity and their beauty—and their power." CORE's 1966 convention was an inversion of the NAACP conference. Speaking at a CORE plenary session, Carmichael stated, "We don't need white liberals. . . .

We have to make integration irrelevant." Harlem leader Roy Innis pushed through a successful resolution which stated officially that CORE no longer favored integration. CORE proclaimed that nonviolent direct action was "a dying philosophy," and whites were told that they were no longer welcome in the formation.[28] As a result of the convention's actions, almost all white liberal patronage of CORE ceased. Several locals with white members vehemently opposed Black Power, and left the organization by the autumn of 1966. In two years, McKissick was replaced by the more militant nationalist, Innis. Inside SNCC, most white veterans had left, or were soon to resign. Lewis and SNCC's former field secretary Charles Sherrod quit the group in 1966. In public image, SNCC became more violent and revolutionary. When a Carmichael appearance at Vanderbilt University accidentally coincided with an urban rebellion in which 94 persons were jailed, Tennessee legislators demanded that Carmichael be deported from the U.S. Radical nationalists even attacked the much respected Fannie Lou Hamer for not accepting the necessity to expel whites, charging that she was "no longer relevant" to the cause of black liberation. SNCC activities in Houston were involved in a May 1967 campus demonstration in which two police and one student were shot and 481 were jailed. On 7 February 1968 former SNCC leader Cleveland Sellers organized a student demonstration at South Carolina State College which later culminated in a white police riot, leaving 3 students killed and 33 others wounded.

By 1967 and early 1968, Black Power had become the dominant ideological concept among a majority of black youth, and significant portions of the black working class and middle strata. But "Black Power" itself still remained as elusive and imprecise as it had been when Ricks chanted the phrase on a rural Mississippi highway. What was Black Power? Most radical blacks disagreed among themselves. In the 1967 book *Black Power*, coauthors Carmichael and political scientist Charles V. Hamilton declared that the concept was "a political framework and ideology which represents the last reasonable opportunity for this society to work out its racial problems short of prolonged destructive guerrilla warfare." Black Power would permit blacks to "exercise control over our lives, politically, economically and psychically. We will also contribute to the development of a viable larger society . . . there is nothing unilateral about the movement to free black people."[29] One militant CORE leader from Brooklyn, Robert Carson, related Black Power to a socialist transformation of the U.S. "I believe that capitalism has to be destroyed if black people are to be free," Carson told CORE's 1968 convention in Columbus, Ohio. "We don't want anything to do with the white power structure as it is now."[30] SNCC staff member Julius Lester wrote that Black Power was "only another manifestation of what is transpiring in Latin America, Asia, and Africa. People are reclaiming their lives on those three continents and blacks in America are reclaiming theirs. These liberation movements are not saying give us a share; they are saying we want it all!"[31] Further to the right, Julian Bond described Black Power as simply a natural extension of the work of the civil rights movement. . . . From the courtroom to the streets in favor of integrated facilities; from the streets on backwoods roads in quest of the right to vote; from the ballot box to the meat of politics, the organization of voters into self-interest units."[32] Perhaps the most radical interpretation of Black Power was made by black socialist theorist James Boggs, a former Detroit autoworker. The U.S. was a "fascist" state with a "master majority race," Boggs wrote in early 1967. Black Power was first the "scientific" recognition that "there is no historical basis for the promise, constantly made to blacks by American radicals, that the white workers will join with them against the capitalist enemy." As a political ideology, it represented

> the new revolutionary social force of the black population concentrated in the black belt of the South and in the urban ghettoes of the North—a revolutionary social force which must struggle not only against the capitalists but against the workers and middle classes who benefit by and support the system which has oppressed and exploited blacks. To expect the Black Power struggle to embrace white workers inside the black struggle is in fact to expect the revolution to welcome the enemy into its camp.

Other black radicals, in the Communist Party and elsewhere, tended to view Black Power as an anti-capitalist slogan.[33]

These lofty theoretical constructs had no direct impact upon African-American reality. For as the black left sought to reconstruct itself, after the harsh vacuum imposed by years of McCarthyism and Cold War liberalism, Black Power quickly became the cornerstone of conservative forces. The first major Black Power Conference was held in Newark, New Jersey, in July 1967, and was organized by a black Republican, Nathan Wright. The conference was housed in a plush, white-owned hotel, and a stiff registration fee ($25) held down the number of black poor peoples' activists and working-class progressives who wished to attend. The conference attracted 1,300 mostly middle-class black professionals, and concluded with a statement to the effect that Black Power connoted getting a "fair share" of American capitalism. The subsequent Black Power Conference, held in Philadelphia in June 1968, was formally co-sponsored by a white corporation, Clairol Company. Clairol's president spoke before the black gathering and gave a hearty endorsement for Black Power. The phrase in his words meant black "ownership of apartments, ownership of homes, ownership of businesses, as well as equitable treatment for all people." In short, Black Power was Black Capitalism. Quickly perceiving this, Richard

Nixon, who was running again for the presidency in 1968, took an aggressive pro–Black Power posture. As Nixon defined the term in a Milwaukee, Wisconsin, speech on 28 March 1968, Black Power was "the power that people should have over their own destinies, the power to affect their own communities, the power that comes from participation in the political and economic processes of society." Nixon spelled out his thesis at greater length in a subsequent address:

> . . . Much of the black militant talk these days is actually in terms far closer to the doctrines of free enterprise than to those of the welfarist thirties—terms of "pride," "ownership," "private enterprise," "capital," "self-assurrance," "self-respect." . . . What most of the militants are asking is not separation, but to be included in—not as supplicants, but as owners, as entrepreneurs—to have a share of the wealth and a piece of the action. And this is precisely what the Federal central target of the new approach ought to be. It ought to be oriented toward more black ownership, for from this can flow the rest—black pride, black jobs, black opportunity and yes, black power . . .[34]

Nixon's endorsement of Black Power as Black Capitalism was applauded by major corporations and the financial sector's chief organ, the *Wall Street Journal*. It was also supported and praised by McKissick and Innis.

The only major social theorist who understood the fundamentally pro-capitalist thrust of many Black Powerites by 1967 was Harold Cruse. Cruse drafted an essay "Behind the Black Power Slogan," which was prepared for a U.S. Socialist Scholars' Conference. In his characteristically abrasive style, Cruse argued with socialists that Black Power had absolutely nothing to do with revolutionary demands or Marxism:

> *Black Power is nothing but the economic and political philosophy of Booker T. Washington given a 1960's militant shot in the arm and brought up to date.* The curious fact about it is that the very last people to admit that Black Power is militant Booker T-ism are the Black Power theorists themselves. . . . The Black Power ideology is *not* at all revolutionary in terms of its economic and political ambitions; it is, in fact, a *social reformist* ideology. It is not meant to be a criticism of the Black Power movement to call it "reformist"; there is nothing wrong or detrimental about social reforms. But we must not fail to call reformism what it in fact is. The Black Power theorists who believe their slogan is in fact a revolutionary slogan are mistaken. . . . What *does* have a revolutionary implication about Black Power is the "defensive violence" upheld and practiced by its ultra-extremist-nationalist-urban guerrilla wing, which is a *revolutionary anarchist* tendency. Thus we have a unique American form of black revolutionary anarchism with a social reform economic and political "program."

Cruse also dismissed the socialists' now-popular interpretation of Malcolm as becoming a revolutionary "internationalist socialist" in the months before his assassination. Tracing his theoretical roots from the traditional black nationalism of Garvey, and then back into the political accommodationism of Washington, Cruse argued that Malcolm "was headed toward what became the Black Power position—which is *not* a revolutionary position. None of Malcolm's views on economics, politics, and self-defense was original with him. Malcolm X remained a militant black nationalist until the moment he died." [35]

Thus, from its origins, Black Power was not a coherent ideology, and never developed a unitary program which was commonly supported by a majority of its proponents. As the radical theoreticians and conservatives laid claims to the mantle of Malcolm, the notion of Black Power was transmitted to all strata of black society as a contradictory set of dogmas, platitudes, political beliefs, and cultural activities. Cruse noted with biting cynicism, "many of the rebellious urban youth think Black Power means 'Get the cops!' 'Burn, baby, burn!' 'Down with Whitey!' or 'Let's get the loot!'" [36] Debbie Louis explained that Black Power's popularity was a product of its inherent ambiguity. In the late 1960s, the "the black community stood as a conglomeration of often contradictory interests and directions, dubiously tied together by a common mood which combined centuries of anger with new hope, increasing desperation with new confidence." Black Power was diluted and expressed popularly in divergent ways: "black people were addressing each other as 'brother' when they passed in the streets; 'soul food' restaurants became a matter of community pride; 'black history' the all-consuming topic, Malcolm X the authoritative source. Even seven-year-old black children seemed to know a phrase or two of Swahili. Was this black power?" [37]

III

Black Power was not the only issue which divided black America in the mid- and late 1960s. Concurrent with the domestic unrest over the present and future position of the Negro was a growing public debate over the government's involvement in Southeast Asia. During the Cold War, the Eisenhower Administration assisted in the establishment of a corrupt, pro-U.S. dictatorship in South Vietnam. Under Kennedy, the number of U.S. military advisers increased steadily. In January 1965, 25,000 U.S. troops were stationed in Vietnam, and were actively fighting both communist North Vietnamese regulars and the popular organization of the South's workers and peasants, the National Liberation Front. In 1966, the U.S. forces in the country increased to 184,000; by January 1969, 536,000 U.S. troops were stationed in Vietnam. For black Americans, the war had a direct impact upon every community.

In the two decades after World War II, the number of blacks in all services almost tripled, from 107,000 in 1949 to 303,000 in 1967. Even after the desegregation of the armed services, blacks were poorly represented in the officers' ranks, and grossly over-represented among enlisted personnel. For example, in 1967, in the Marine Corps, 9.6 percent of all enlisted men were black, while only 0.7 percent were officers; in the army, 13.5 percent of all enlisted personnel were black, and only 3.4 percent of the army's officers were black. African Americans comprised one out of every seven U.S. soldiers stationed in Vietnam, and because blacks tended to be placed in "combat units" more often than middle-class whites, they also bore unfairly higher risks of being killed and wounded. From January to November 1966, 22.4 percent of all army casualties were black. Black leaders in the NAACP and Urban League viewed the Vietnam War as a tremendous opportunity to ingratiate themselves with the Johnson Administration. In one polemic against Black Power, drafted in November 1966, and signed by Rustin, Wilkins, Young, A.M.E. Church Bishop Carey A. Gibbs, Dorothy Height (leader of the National Council of Negro Women), and others, they reminded white Americans that most blacks eschewed domestic violence in favor of fighting abroad to protect U.S. interests. "For every Negro who tosses a Molotov cocktail, there are a thousand fighting and dying on the battlefields of Vietnam," they stated.[38] To their black critics, they warned that Vietnam had nothing to do with domestic politics and civil rights. Both the NAACP and the Urban League concluded that the mounting black casualty totals from Southeast Asia were irrelevant to the struggle to win racial reforms at home.

Malcolm X understood that the Old Guard's position was both politically stupid and morally bankrupt. Even before 3,000 black troops had been stationed in Vietnam, he analyzed the issue and had condemned both the Johnson Administration and the Negro élite. Malcolm argued that the French had not been able to defeat the Vietnamese nationalists, and that the U.S. would also have to admit failure within a few years. The war itself 'shows the real ignorance of those who control the American power structure . . . [their] ignorance and blindness."[39] SNCC was the first civil rights group to denounce the Vietnam War in uncompromising terms. In a press release of 6 January 1966, SNCC declared that the U.S. government "has been deceptive in its claims of concern for the freedom of the Vietnamese people." The Johnson Administration was "pursuing an aggressive policy in violation of international law. We maintain that our country's cry of "preserve freedom in the world" is a hypocritcal mask behind which it squashed liberation movements which are not bound and refuse to be bound by the expedience of the United States cold war policy."[40] The SNCC statement was bitterly attacked by Wilkins. Clifford Alexander, one of Johnson's chief black assistants, began to organize black U.S. representatives and others to blunt the effect of the statement. But SNCC continued its attack on Johnson's Vietnam policies. When SNCC decided to demonstrate in front of the White House during the wedding of Johnson's daughter, in symbolic protest against the Vietnam War, Wilkins, King, Randolph and Young pleaded with the group to cancel the action. SNCC activists challenged black youth to oppose the war. At Baltimore's Morgan State University, Carmichael insisted, "the war in Vietnam should interest you not only personally, but also because it is very political for black people." Black students were urged to resist the draft. "Either you go to the Leavenworth Federal penitentiary in Kansas or you become a killer. I will choose to suffer," Carmichael stated. "I will go to jail. To hell with this country." [41]

Black progressives in electoral politics began to speak in opposition to the war. Julian Bond, elected to the Georgia state House of Representatives, defended the right of "the Vietnamese peasants who . . . have expressed a real desire to govern themselves." The "gunboat diplomacy of the past" had little place in contemporary world affairs. [42] The most articulate opponent of the U.S. war effort, black or white, was U.S. Representative Ronald V. Dellums. From the floor of Congress, Dellums declared:

I consider our involvement in Indochina illegal, immoral, and insane. We are in a war which is the greatest human and economic drain on American resources in modern times—a war disproportionately waged on the backs of blacks and browns and reds and yellows and poor and working class whites, a war resulting in an untold number of deaths of the Vietnamese people, a war that is justified only by the notion that we, as a nation, must save face . . . the only way this nation can save face with respect to our involvement in Indochina is to stand up and admit to the world we made a tragic mistake in Southeast Asia and then to get out of Vietnam. . . . Millions of people in the country are no longer willing to engage in such folly and be cannon fodder, and go across the water to spill their blood on foreign soil in a cause many of them do not even understand. [43]

Black activists and intellectuals, who were part of the Black Power movement, had grave reservations about participating in anti-war organizations dominated by white liberals and leftists. But almost all of them, including CORE's proponents of Black Capitalism, had little to say in favor of black participation in the war effort. In April 1968, SNCC activist John Wilson organized a national anti-war conference in New York City which brought together hundreds of black nationalists and community militants. Baldwin lent his considerable talents as a polemicist to the anti-war cause. "Long, long before the Americans decided to liberate the Southeast Asians, they decided to liberate me: my ancestors carried these scars to the grave, and so will I," Baldwin wrote. "A racist society can't but fight a racist war—this is the bitter truth. The assumptions acted on at home are also acted on abroad, and every American Negro knows this, for he, after the American Indian, was the first 'Viet Cong' victim." Black literary critic Addison Gayle, Jr., praised the "large number of black men [who] would prefer to die fighting tyranny, oppression, hunger and disease in the black ghettoes of America than to die in the jungles of Vietnam." Black poets were also among the most effective critics of America's war. S. E. Anderson's "Junglegrave" was written as an ode to the black soldiers overseas:

> Send me no flowers, for they will die
> before they leave America
> Send me home, no matter how far strewn
> I am across this rice-filled land
> Send me home, man, send me home
> even if I am headless or faceless
> Keep my casket open and my grave uncovered . . .
> Vietnam: land of yellow and black genocide
> Send the President my flowers cremated and
> scented with the odors
> Of my brothers' napalmed flesh and my
> sisters' bombed out skulls
> Send me no flowers . . .

Robert Hayden's "Words in the Mourning Time" evoked echoes of Du-Bois's yearnings for peace a generation before:

> Vietnam bloodclotted name in my consciousness/
> recurring and recurring/ like the obsessive thought
> many midnights/ now of my own dying
> Vietnam and I think of the villages/
> mistakenly burning the schoolrooms
> devouring/ their children and I think
> of those who/ were my students/
> brutalized killing/ wasted by horror/
> in ultimate loneliness/ dying/
> Vietnam Vietnam.[44]

During the bitter national debate on Vietnam, all public leaders within black America were forced to choose sides. As a dedicated pacifist, King could not look upon the conflict benignly without taking some kind of public stand against the war. At the annual SCLC executive board meeting held in Baltimore on 1–2 April 1965, King expressed the need to criticize the Johnson Administration's policies in Southeast Asia. His old colleagues, fearful that King's support for the anti-war would hurt the SCLC financially and politically, voted to allow him to do so only as a private person, without organizational endorsement. Rustin, who still maintained close ties with King, tried to pressure the SCLC leader into a position of neutrality on Vietnam. On 10 September 1965, Rustin, King, and SCLC aides Andrew Young and Bernard Lee met with United Nations ambassador Arthur Goldberg. Goldberg convinced King, for the moment, that the Johnson Administration had every intention of bringing the conflict to a peaceful resolution. For several months, King watched patiently as the number of U.S. troops increased. Finally in January 1966, King published a strong attack on the Vietnam War. "Some of my friends of both races and others who do not consider themselves my friends have expressed disapproval because I have been voicing concern over the war in Vietnam," King stated. But as a Christian, he had no choice except to "declare that war is wrong." Black leaders could not become blind to the rest of the world's issues, while engaged solely in problems of domestic race relations. "The Negro must not allow himself to become a victim of the self-serving philosophy of those who manufacture war that the survival of the world is the white man's business alone."[45] The negative response to King's statement was swift. SCLC leaders in Chattanooga, Tennessee, severed relations with the organization in protest. Whitney Young replied that blacks were not interested in the issue. King lobbied hard among his allies in SCLC to back his position on Vietnam, and in the spring of 1966 the organization's executive board came out officially against the war.

The SCLC's primary national focus shifted to Chicago in 1966, in an effort to gain jobs and housing desegregation in a major northern city. Chicago's political machine, led by the city's tough and unscrupulous mayor Richard Daley, was more than a match for the SCLC. Unlike the southern segregationists, Daley had the full support of the Johnson Administration and the Democratic Party. The meager anti-racist concessions which King and other top aides, notably Jesse Jackson, James Bevel, and Andrew Young, were able to extract from the "Northern segregationists" did not justify the financial and personnel expenditures of the long and hard campaign. Increasingly, King's attention was drawn to the Vietnam issue, and also to the necessity for black Americans to devise a more radical strategy for domestic reforms. "For years I labored with the idea of reforming the existing institutions of society, a little change here, a little change there. Now I feel quite differently," King admitted in 1966.[46] Quietly, King was beginning to articulate a democratic socialist vision for American society: the nationalization of basic industries; massive federal expenditures to revive central cities and to provide jobs for ghetto residents; a guaranteed income for every adult American. King had concluded, like Malcolm X, that America's political economy of capitalism had to be transformed, that the Civil Rights Movement's old goals of voter education, registration, and desegregated public facilities were only a beginning step down the long road towards biracial democracy. And like DuBois, King recognized the correlation between his democratic socialist ideals and the peace issue. Massive U.S. military spending and the bloody war effort in Vietnam meant that the nation as a whole had less revenue to attack domestic poverty, illiteracy, and unemployment. These new ideas forced King to conclude that the Vietnam conflict had to end immediately. On 4 April 1967, speaking at New York City's Riverside Church, King announced: "It would be very inconsistent for me to teach and preach nonviolence in this situation and then applaud violence when thousands and thousands of people, both adults and children, are being maimed and mutilated and many killed in this way."[47] Eleven days later, in New York City's Central Park, King led a rally of 125,000 in protest against the war.

Just as the Truman Administration had sponsored a "political assassination" of DuBois's influence during the 1950s, another Democratic president was now ready and quite willing to take steps towards reducing King's reputation. Johnson's black epigones did whatever they could to destroy the image and popularity of King. Ralph Bunche urged King either to cease his attacks on the Johnson Administration, or to relinquish his role as a civil rights leader. Rustin, who was appointed director of the A. Philip Randolph Institute, vilified King's stance on the war. NAACP and Urban League officials privately and publicly attacked King and defended Johnson. Black Republican Edward Brooke, elected to the Senate from Massachusetts on an anti-war platform, swung behind the Vietnam War in 1967 and joined the anti-King chorus. Carl Rowan drafted a vicious, brutal essay against King which appeared in *Reader's Digest* magazine. King's response was identical with that of DuBois—he moved even further to the left. Defiantly, King announced an SCLC-sponsored campaign against poverty, the Poor Peoples' March, which would bring thousands of the unemployed and the oppressed of all races into Washington, D.C. in April 1968. Their demands for legislative action would include a federal guaranteed incomes policy. On 23 February 1968, the one-hundredth anniversary of the birth of DuBois, King gave the keynote address honoring him in New York City. "So many would like to ignore the fact that DuBois was a Communist in his last years," King noted. In an obvious reference to Vietnam, King added, "Our irrational, obsessive anti-Communism has led us into too many quagmires."[48] When black Memphis sanitation workers voted to strike on 12 February, to protest against low wages and the accidental deaths of two black garbage men twelve days before, they asked the SCLC for help. King and his closest associates—Abernathy, Young, Jackson, Bevel—arrived in the southern city to help mobilize popular support for the strike. The pacifist minister who once struggled for desegregated buses, was now, thirteen years after Montgomery, organizing militant black urban workers, building a national poor peoples' march, and defying a president. He had come a long way; so had his vision for reconstructing America.

Speaking before a black audience in Memphis on 3 April, King was predicting that their struggle would succeed. Then, abruptly and rather strangely, he began to talk about himself in the past tense:

> I don't know what will happen now. But it really doesn't matter to me now. Because I've been to the mountaintop. I won't mind. Like anybody, I would like to live a long life. Longevity has its place. But I'm not concerned about that now. I just want to do God's will. And He's allowed me to go up to the mountain. And I've looked over, and I've seen the promised land. . . . I may not get there with you, but I want you to know tonight that we as a people will get to the promised land. So I'm happy tonight. I'm not worried about anything. I'm not fearing any man. "Mine eyes have seen the glory of the coming of the Lord." [49]

King's assistants were bewildered and even a little angry with him. What was the meaning of the speech? Perhaps King sensed something that no one else could possibly know. At 6:08 P.M., that next day, he was assassinated by a white man, James Earl Ray, in Memphis. Strangely, the police who had been guarding King were absent at the time of his death. Blacks across the country, even the militant nationalists, felt a grievous loss to the cause for racial freedom. White anti-war activists had lost their most effective and prominent representative; poor people and the black working class had lost a major spokesperson. More than anyone else in the period 1945–82, King would come closest to bringing together a biracial coalition demanding peace, civil rights, and basic structural changes within the capitalist order. King's assassination meant that any linkages between these vital reform movements would be much more difficult to achieve. And in the light of subsequent congressional testimony and historical research on his death, King's unfinished search for more radical reforms in America may have been the central reason he was killed.

IV

King's assassination was only one more indication to black nationalists that white capitalist America had no intention of resolving racial conflicts "nonviolently." By 1968, the black nationalist renaissance had begun to inspire a tremendous outpouring of literary criticism, poetry, music and art, all of which served to reinforce Black Power and the uneven nationalist movement, in politics. In their myriad voices, the new black aestheticians played a critical role in forging a popular nationalist consciousness. Post–Harlem Renaissance poets Dudley Randall, Margaret Walker and Gwendolyn Brooks, all of whom were over 50 years old, acted informally as patrons and inspirations for the younger artists. Hoyt W. Fuller, editor of the *Black World*, used his magazine to introduce to black America a growing list of poets and playwrights: Etheridge Knight, author of *Poems From Prison* (1968); Naomi Madgett, author of *Star by Star* (1965); Carolyn M. Rodgers, whose poems appeared in *Paper Soul* (1968); and *Songs of a Blackbird* (1970); Mari Evans, author of *Where Is All the Music?* (1967) and *I Am A Black Woman* (1970); Sonia Sanchez, author of *Homecoming* (1969) and *We are a BaddDDD people* (1970); Don L. Lee, founder of the Institute of Positive Education in Chicago, Third World Press, and author of *Black Pride* (1968) *Think Black* (1969), *Don't Cry, Scream* (1969), and *We Walk the Way of the New World* (1970); and essayist June Jordan, whose collected poems appeared in *Some Changes* (1970). Perhaps the two most popular black poets of the period were LeRoi Jones (Imamu Amiri Baraka) and Nikki Giovanni. Born in 1934, Jones was first part of the "beat generation" of essayists and critics in America's version of the Left Bank, Greenwich Village, New York. In the mid-1960s he became actively involved as a nationalist in Harlem and nearby Newark, New Jersey. Changing his name, renouncing his white wife and liberal associates, Baraka established Spirit House, a center for the black arts and culture in Newark. Baraka won acclaim as a prolific nationalist writer: *Home: Social Essays* (1966); *Black Music* (1970); *Raise, Race, Rays, Race* (1971); *It's Nation Time* (1970); Kawaida Studies: *The New Nationalism* (1972); *Afrikan Revolution* (1973). His political poetry and plays were recited and performed by thousands of young blacks in secondary schools and colleges across the country. Ten years Baraka's junior, Giovanni's emergence was especially meteoric. In her popular poetry collection *Black Feeling, Black Talk, Black Judgment* (1970), Giovanni spoke uncompromisingly of the necessity for violence:

> Nigger
> Can you Kill
> Can you Kill
> Can a nigger kill
> Can a nigger kill a honkie . . .
> Can you shoot straight and
> Fire for good measure
> Can you splatter their brains in the street
> Can you kill them
> Can you lure them to bed to kill them
> We kill in Viet Nam for them . . .
> Can we learn to kill WHITE for BLACK
> Learn to kill niggers
> Learn to be Black men.[50]

Integration was a bogus illusion; the liberation of "the black nation" would not be achieved via the ballotbox:

> . . . this second reconstruction is being aborted as was the first . . .
> if we vote this season we ought to seek to make it effective
> the barrel of a gun is the best voting machine
> your best protest vote is a dead honkie. . . .[51]

The rejection of integration as a social and cultural ideal sparked the development of a new interest in Africa. The writings of Martinique's revolutionary social theorist Frantz Fanon, a psychiatrist who took part in the Algerian revolution of the 1950s, were popularly read by black Americans. Books by African socialists and leaders such as Tanzania's Julius Nyerere, Ghana's Kwame Nkrumah, and Guiné-Bissau theorist Amilcar Cabral became an integral part of the African-American revolutionary nationalists' lexicon. It is not altogether clear that black Americans adopted the insights of African and Caribbean revolutionaries in constructive and appropriate ways. West coast nationalist Maulana Ron Karenga developed a black cultural cathechism, the "nguzo saba," and a black holiday, "Kwanzaa," which employed the Swahili language and cultural imagery of Tanzanian traditional society. Karenga argued that black revolution was not a class struggle, but a battle to change "racist minds" and the patterns of black culture. "The international issue is racism, not economics," he suggested in 1967. "Race rules out economics because whites are racists, not just capitalists."[52] Yet Nyerere's *Ujamaa: Essays on Socialism*, make the point that "socialism and racialism are incompatible. The man or woman who hates 'Jews,' or 'Asians,' or 'Europeans,' or even 'West Europeans' and Americans, is not a socialist," Nyerere argued. "He is denying the equality and brotherhood of man. Those who stand for the interests of the workers and peasants, anywhere in the world, are our friends."[53] Carmichael declared that Fanon was one of his "patron saints," and after the summer rebellions of 1967, one radical editor declared that "every brother on a rooftop can quote Fanon." Militant nationalists praised Fanon's advocacy of revolutionary violence, and his polemical thrusts aimed at the Negro petty bourgeoisie in colonial Africa. But what did Fanon think about the African-American struggle? "The test cases of civil liberty whereby both whites and blacks in America try to drive back racial discrimination have very little in common in their principles and objectives" with African liberation efforts. For Fanon, the struggle to destroy white oppression was not in essence a racial dialectic, but an anti-racist movement that welcomed the participation of committed whites. In *Black Skin, White Masks* (1952), Fanon's most "nationalist-oriented" work, he explained that his ultimate vision for the U.S. was the liberation of all exploited people: "I can already see a white man and a black man hand in hand."⁵⁴ The question here is not so much that of intellectual dishonesty, but a failure of many Black Powerites to relate their eclectic versions of nationalism to the actual material needs and aspirations of the black working class and the poor. Addison Gayle characterized many of these dogmatic black separatists as "black fascists" in 1970:

> The Professional Nationalist [has] a "more militant than thou" attitude. He has read Fanon—although he does not understand him . . . and quotes Malcolm verbatim. This superficial machinery is designed to prove his militancy; yet, in effect, it allows him to serve as a liaison between the black community uptown and the [white] Man downtown. . . . The [black] fascist is not interested in persuading men to accept his point of view through reason and logic—since his point of view differs little from The Man's. Instead, he hopes to establish a totalitarian apparatus wherein all proposals will be subject to his authority. . . . If the fascists are allowed to take over a movement begun by sincere and honest people, then we will have not Black Power but Black Fascism, differing in no respect from the white fascism against which Blacks have fought and died throughout our history in this country.⁵⁵

Nationalists of every kind, from the nihilistic "cultural nationalists" or "black fascists" which Gayle described, to the socialist-oriented nationalists on the eft, to Black Capitalists, rapidly created institutions and groups which influenced electoral politics. In Michigan, many nationalists were involved in the Freedom Now Party, which in 1964 placed 39 black independent candidates on the ballot. In 1968, two black independents were presidential candidates, former prisoner and black revolutionary writer Eldridge Cleaver and social critic Dick Gregory. Cleaver, endorsed as the Peace and Freedom Party candidate, recieved 195,135 votes nationally, mostly from black revolutionary nationalists and white leftists. In a campaign marked more by political satire than actual political content, Gregory totalled 148,622 votes. At municipal levels, many black nationalists simply endorsed black middle-class candidates who ran independently from traditional, white-controlled business and political interests. Within the Democratic Party, middle-class Black Powerites supported the nominations of the Reverend Channing Phillips of Washington, D.C. for president and Julian Bond for vice president at the Chicago national convention in August 1968. In the South, nationalists and integrationists alike supported several independent electoral efforts, including the black National Democratic Party of Alabama and Georgia's Party of Christian Democracy, both formed in 1968.

The most provocative challenge to white liberal politics was generated by the Black Panther Party, founded in Oakland, California, in October 1966, by two black college students, Huey P. Newton and Bobby Seale.

Using the name of SNCC's formation from Lowndes County, Alabama, Newton and Seale developed a political cadre of militant young blacks. Their political philosophy, despite their revolutionary rhetoric, was basically that of radical reform. In their original "Ten Point Program," the Black Panthers demanded from the American state the following reforms:

1. We want freedom. We want power to determine the destiny of our black community.
2. We want full employment for our people.
3. We want an end to the robbery by the white man of our black community.
4. We want decent housing, fit shelter for human beings.
5. We want education for our people that exposes the true nature of this decadent American society. We want education that teaches us our true history and our role in the present day society.
6. We want all black men to be exempt from military service.
7. We want an immediate end to *police brutality* and *murder* of black people.
8. We want freedom for all black men held in federal, state, county, and city prisons and jails.
9. We want all black people when brought to trial to be tried in court by a jury of their peer group or people from their black communities, as defined by the Constitution of the United States.
10. We want land, bread, housing, education, clothing, justice and peace.[56]

The Panthers recruited from the black working-class and poverty-stricken districts of East Oakland, California, organizing armed patrols to defend the black community against police attacks. Newton, who had considerable knowledge of state and local laws, monitored police arrests of black inner city citizens, armed with a shotgun to ensure his own protection. In late 1967 the Panthers initiated a free breakfast program for black children, and offered free health services to ghetto residents. Many white critics viewed the Black Panthers as a dangerous ultra-leftist group and a threat to social order. But the Panthers pointedly affirmed their commitment to the American tradition of social change by quoting slaveholder Thomas Jefferson, the author of the Declaration of Independence, in their own program:

> Governments are instituted among men, deriving their just powers from the consent of the governed, [but] whenever any form of government becomes destructive . . . it is the right of people to alter or abolish it, and to institute new government, laying its foundation on such principles and organizing its powers in such form as to them shall seem most likely to effect their safety and happiness.

Unlike many nationalists, the Black Panthers quickly established organizational and programmatic relations with radical whites, and sought to lead a progressive coalition of Third World and white groups to battle the "Establishment."[57]

By the late 1960s, the Black Panthers had become the most influential revolutionary national organization in the U.S. Eldridge Cleaver joined the Panthers as their minister of information, and soon began to attract his own left tendency within the formation, oriented around his questionable thesis of "lumpenproletarian revolution." Cleaver married SNCC activist Kathleen Neal, who soon became the organization's communication secretary. By early 1968, other SNCC veterans had become Panthers. Bob Brown, a close ally and friend of Carmichael, became director of the Chicago branch of the Black Panther Party; SNCC leader Chico Neblett served as the Panther's "Field Marshal" for the western states of the U.S.; Forman briefly assisted the Panther's organizational efforts, and in February 1968, Carmichael was named the party's prime minister. By 1969, Carmichael and his successor as head of SNCC, Hubert "Rap" Brown, had broken with the Black Panthers because of Newton's and Cleaver's close ties with white leftists and the biracial Peace and Freedom Party. Other cultural nationalists viewed the Black Panther Party's emphasis on class struggle with great suspicion. Karenga's cultural nationalist formation, called US, bitterly opposed the Black Panthers' actions in California. Nationally, however, the Panthers succeeded in organizing chapters in several dozen states, and had at least 5,000 members by the end of 1968.

The black nationalist upsurgence was viewed by the American government with considerable alarm. Remarkably few black nationalists and Black Powerites had advocated violence against white-owned property, the subversion of authority, or the seizure of state power. Most Black Power spokespersons came from upwardly mobile working-class or middle-class backgrounds, were trained at universities, and had been groomed for ultimate assimilation into the existing system. Forman was an economics and management major at Chicago's Roosevelt University, president of his student body, and had done graduate work in African affairs at Boston University in the 1950s; Bevel was a ministerial student in Nashville's American Baptist Theological Seminary; Rap Brown was a student at Southern University; SNCC's Ralph Featherstone was an elementary school-teacher; Carmichael and Baraka were graduates of Howard University; Giovanni, Lester, Nash and Barry were trained at Fisk University; Karenga was the first black student body president at his junior college in Los Angeles, and was at work on a master's degree in politics at the University of California; Newton was the principal student leader at Oakland's Merrit College, and would later work towards a Ph.D. degree. Only one small fraction of the major proponents of Black Power had the gritty background of Malcolm X, whose actual ordeal as part of the ghetto underworld served as a crucible for his ultimate political trajectory. But federal and state authorities, after years of inaction or, at times, active co-operation with racists and white supremacists, could not listen to the rhetoric of blacks with anything except severe trepidation. Black Power defined as Black Capitalism seemed harmless enough. But black nationalism, either in its most radical tendency as expressed by the Black Panthers, or in its more inchoate and chauvinistic manifestation as cultural nationalism, was seen as a direct threat to the survival of the republic. It was not enough to buttress the Old Guard integrationists, for they had lost much of their respectability in the eyes of millions of blacks. A more effective means to thwart black nationalism was to employ illegal and covert methods of repression against its proponents.

SNCC was the first radical black group targeted by the Federal Bureau of Investigation (FBI) and the U.S. Justice Department for surveillance, disruption, and suppression. In late 1960, FBI agents began to monitor SNCC meetings. Johnson's attorney general, Nicholas Katzenbach, gave approval for the FBI to wiretap all SNCC leaders' telephones in 1965. In August 1967, FBI director J. Edgar Hoover ordered the extensive infiltration and disruption of SNCC, as well as other Black Power–oriented formations, such as the Militant Revolutionary Action Movements, the Deacons of Defense, and CORE. Hoover also included for federal scrutiny and repression nonrevolutionary nationalist groups, such as the SCLC and the Nation of Islam. FBI agents spread the rumor that Carmichael was an agent for the CIA, creating severe rifts between SNCC activists. FBI agents were sent to monitor Carmichael and Brown wherever they went, seeking to elicit evidence to imprison them. Brown was charged with inciting a race riot in Maryland, and was eventually sentenced to five years in a federal penitentiary for carrying a rifle across state lines while under criminal indictment. Featherstone and SNCC activist Ché Payne were murdered on 9 March 1970, when a bomb exploded in their automobile in Bel Air, Maryland. Sellers was indicted for organizing black students in South Carolina and for resisting the draft. Newton was shot in a 1967 confrontation in which one white police officer was killed, and was sentenced to prison for three years. Cleaver was forced to flee the U.S. in late 1968 for violating parole restrictions, and went into exile. Seale was tried with several white radicals for inciting a riot in Chicago, and in the courtroom the judge ordered that he be bound and gagged. Local police and federal marshals raided Black Panther offices across the country. By July 1969, the Panthers had been targeted by 233 separate actions under the FBI's COINTELPRO, or Counter Intelligence Program. In 1969 alone, 27 Black Panthers were killed by the police, and 749 were jailed or arrested. Whenever possible, the FBI provoked violence between cultural and revolutionary nationalists. In 1969, the FBI was directly or indirectly responsible for engineering several murders, shootings and bombing attacks between US and the Black Panther Party. In Hoover's words, any illegal acts of suppression were justified, because the Panthers were "the greatest threat to the internal security of the country." The federal authorites would resort to political assassinations and any other gross violations of civil liberties to "prevent a coalition of militant black nationalist groups" and to "prevent the rise of a messiah" who could lead the black masses.[58]

The possibility for greater political repression increased with the presidential election of 1968. The three major candidates did not inspire enthusiastic support among many blacks or progressive whites: George Wallace, running as an independent on a platform of "law-and-order" and racial bigotry; Democrat Hubert Humphrey, a Cold War liberal who had defended the Vietnam War during his undistinguished tenure as Johnson's vice president; and Republican nominee Richard Nixon. The assassination of Robert Kennedy in June 1968 left liberal Democrats bickering with unpopular Johnson's handpicked successor, Humphrey, and Wallace was able to mount a major effort, winning sizeable shares of the white working-class vote across the country. Blacks overwhelmingly supported Humphrey in the end, but by a margin of only one-half million votes out of 73.2 million cast, Nixon emerged as the winner with only 43.4 percent of the popular vote. Nixon sought to placate the black middle class by appointing Farmer to his administration as assistant secretary of Health, Education and Welfare, and by continuing his advocacy of Black Capitalism. Towards progressives in the black movement, however, Nixon was absolutely ruthless. Nixon's vice president, former Maryland governor Spiro T. Agnew, was well known for his orders for police to "shoot-to-kill" black urban rebels in Baltimore; for his statement that Rap Brown should be arrested—"pick him up soon, put him away and throw away the key"; and for his blatant racism—"when you've seen one ghetto, you've seen them all."[59] Nixon's attorney general, John Mitchell, co-operated with Hoover and the FBI to exterminate the Black Panthers and other militant black organizations. Nixon made it perfectly clear to the NAACP and other Negro moderate groups that he had no intention of pursuing desegregation goals. Within one year after taking office, Leon E. Panetta, the director of civil rights for the Department of Health, Education and Welfare, resigned to protest against Nixon's reinstatement of Jim Crow directives. In the spring of 1970, 125 staff members in the Office of Civil Rights sent an open letter to Nixon, declaring "bitter disappointment" over Panetta's departure and criticizing the president's lack of "strong moral leadership that we feel is now essential to avoid a reversal of the nation's long-standing commitment to equal opportunity." For openly expressing views favorable to desegregation, Nixon's U.S. commission of education, James A. Allen, was fired in 1970.[60]

The forces of racial inequality had won a major victory with the election of Richard Nixon. Yet the Black Power movement had not been checked. As the Black Panther Party was being destroyed as a national organization by the FBI, other lesser known black activist groups were arising from community centers and colleges across the country. As the militant defenders of Black Power were silenced—either through imprisonment, exile, or assassination—newer, younger voices were still being heard. The integrationist Old Guard had been temporarily forced into retreat, buffeted by the massive popularity of black nationalism and under attack by the racist policies of the Nixon Administration. The number of black elected officials in the U.S. had climbed from 100 in 1964 to 1,400 in 1970; many of these men and women were also sympathetic to one or more variants of the Black Power trend. Thus, after the assassinations of Malcolm and Martin, the modern black movement for biracial democracy had been crippled, to be sure, but it was by no means destroyed. Yet the absence of a widely shared theory and strategy for black liberation was still missing; the political goal of black equality was still murky and ill-defined; the opportunism and accommodation of many black militants and political leaders still raised unresolved questions for future struggles; and the programmatic relationship between democracy and racial justice, socialism and peace that DuBois and King had strived to attain was becoming ever more distant.

6. Black Rebellion: Zenith and Decline, 1970–1976

It is the worst thing that can happen to the leader of an extreme party when he is forced to seize power in an epoch which is not yet ripe for the rule of a class which he represents, and for the carrying-out of the measures which this class demands. What he *can* do does not depend upon his will, but upon the level of the conflict between the classes and of the development of the material conditions of existence. . . . What he *can* do contradicts all his previous positions, his principles and the immediate interest of his party; and what he *should* do cannot be done. He is, in a word, forced to represent, not his party, not his class, but that class for whose rule the time is ripe.

Friedrich Engels

Hurl me into the next existence the descent into hell won't turn me. I'll crawl back to dog his trail forever. They won't defeat my revenge, never, never. I'm part of a righteous people who anger slowly, but rage undamned. We'll gather at his door in such number that the rumbling of our feet will make the earth tremble.

George Jackson

The idea that Black people can have unity is the most dangerous idea we've ever let loose.

Bayard Rustin

I

Most historians fail to observe that the massive efforts waged for desegregation and, to a lesser extent, for Black Power, were basically black workers' movements. Black workers had comprised the great majority of those who had sacrificed during the local battles to uproot Jim Crow. They had been arrested, attacked by police with dogs and firehoses, intimidated, fired from their jobs, and even killed. King's gradual recognition that the civil rights campaigns needed to address the necessity of social guarantees for jobs, housing and health care pushed the movement clearly toward the premises of democratic socialism—the politics of much of the working class in other advanced capitalist nations. Gradually, the impetus toward racial reform which black workers pressed against the larger society began to be manifested within organized labor itself. By 1968, over two and a half million blacks were members of the AFL-CIO and the UAW. Most unions had abandoned their anti-black restrictions on membership, and a few of the more liberal unions had actively supported the desegregation actions in the South. Yet Randolph's original goals of creating an effective and powerful presence for blacks inside the House of Labor were not realized. Patterns of racist discrimination still existed, and black workers tended to occupy the most dangerous, lower-paid jobs inside the unions. Within the steelworkers' union, for example, not a single black leader served as an officer in its 30 districts, and less than 100 black employees were hired among the union's staff members. Less than 2 percent of the members of the carpenters' union and the largest construction union were black. Only 0.3 percent of the steel-metal workers were black in 1968. Even after the passage of the Civil Rights Act, segregated locals were still affiliated with the AFL-CIO: the all-white Brotherhood of Railway Clerks, Sulphite and Paper Mill Workers, United Papermakers and Paperworkers, International Association of Machinists, and the American Federation of Musicians. Thus, the struggle for biracial democracy and equality was still blocked by racist resistance and a deliberate policy of white supremacy fostered by most American trade union leaders.

Impatient with decades of AFL-CIO apathy and inaction, black workers influenced by the Black Power trend began to fight union racism through the creation of their own unions. In 1967, Detroit workers formed the Trades Union Local 124 to maneuver around white racists in that industrial city's union bureaucracy. Black nationalists and young workers at Ford Motor Company's major automobile plant in Mahwah, New Jersey, established the militant United Black Brothers that same year. In 1968, Boston black laborers formed the United Community Construction Workers of Boston; black steelworkers in Maryland created the Shipyard Workers for Job Equality to fight the racist practices of both the unions and the steel corporation where they were employed. Civil rights activists continued for a time the policy of relating desegregation efforts to the broader labor movement. In September 1968, Ralph Abernathy, Andrew Young and Hosea Williams were jailed for leading an action of black sanitation workers in Atlanta. The most militant black labor tendency to emerge out of the Black Power period, however, centered in Detroit. In September 1967, a group of revolutionary black nationalists and independent black Marxists launched a militant black workers' newspaper, *Inner City Voice*. The key activists behind the effort—Marxist attorney Ken Cockrel, theorist Mike Hamlin, General Baker, John Watson, and John Williams—soon developed extensive organizational ties with rank-and-file black autoworkers and Detroit's growing black working class. In the spring of 1968, these radical black workers and intellectuals created the Dodge Revolutionary Union Movement (DRUM), in response to Baker's expulsion from the Dodge Main automobile plant, along with six other workers. DRUM attacked the management's use of plant "speed-ups," racist hiring policies, the lack of adequate medical facilities in the factory, unequal pay between black and white laborers, and other long-standing grievances. DRUM coordinated pickets and "wildcat strikes" against Dodge, and criticized the UAW's leadership for bowing to capital's interests over those of all workers. Within a year, other black revolutionary labor organizations developed along DRUM's model: the Ford Revolutionary Union Movement (FRUM); the Eldron Avenue Revolutionary Union Movement (ELRUM); the Harvester Revolutionary Union Movement in Chicago (HARUM); the Black Panther Caucus of Fremont, California; the General Motors Revolutionary Union Movement (GRUM), and many others. In 1969, many of these militant formations coalesced into the League of Revolutionary Black Workers, which was co-ordinated by Hamlin, Baker and Cockrel. For a time, former SNCC leader James Forman aided the process, participating in the formation of the Black Workers' Congress.

The UAW's response to the black radicals was twofold: first, it attempted to characterize DRUM as anti-working class and fanatical; second, it tried to split off older black workers from independent movements through a combination of paternalistic measures and co-optation. UAW secretary-treasurer Emil Mazey attacked DRUM in March 1969, as "a handful of fanatics . . . black fascists whose actions are an attempt to destroy this union." Mazey declared that the "black peril" of Black Power was worse than the infamous "red peril" of earlier years.[1] A. Philip Randolph was also instrumental in AFL-CIO efforts to quiet the black militants. Throughout the 1960s, he had begun to move even further to the right politically, and he halted his criticisms of the labor bureaucracy. In December 1965, Randolph announced proudly at the AFL-CIO convention in San Francisco that racial bias was no longer a major problem within organized labor. The following year, he resigned his position as president of the Negro American Labor Council, and counselled his old colleagues to cease their stinging condemnations of white union officials. Randolph's demise as a representative of black labor militancy was quickly followed, if not directly encouraged, by that of Rustin. At the September 1972 convention of the

International Association of Machinists, Rustin declared that blacks themselves were the major reason for labor's record of blatant discrimination. "I want to say to our trade union Black brothers, nobody got anything because he was colored," Rustin stated. "That is a lot of bull. . . . Stop griping always that nobody has problems but you black people." The point must be made, however, that the Machinists whom Rustin had praised so vigorously had maintained for 60 years a mandatory policy excluding black membership.[2]

Rustin's and Randolph's accommodation to racism and betrayal of the black working class did not go unanswered. In September 1972, a progressive conference of 1,200 black workers was held in Chicago, co-ordinated by five black national spokespersons of labor: Cleveland Robinson of the Distributive Workers Union; William Lucy of the American Federation of State, County, and Municipal Employers; William Simons of the American Federation of Teachers; Charles Hayes, vice president of the Amalgamated Meatcutters and Butcher Workmen; and Nelson Jack Edwards, vice president of the UAW. The new organization formed at the conference, the Coalition of Black Trade Unionists, aggressively attacked the racism of the Nixon Administration and proposed meaningful social democratic reforms akin to those expressed by King shortly before his assassination. A statement of these five black unionists, made at the coalition's second convention in May 1973, expressed the view that:

> A free and progressive trade union movement should and must reflect greater participation of black trade unionists at every level of its decision-making process. As black trade unionists, we have an important role to fulfill, if the goals of the overall labor movement are to be achieved on behalf of all workers. . . . Today, blacks occupy key positions in the political machinery of the labor movement and hold the critical balance of political power in this nation . . . it is our challenge to make the labor movement more relevant to the needs and aspirations of black and poor workers. The CBTU will insist that black union officials become full partners in the leadership and decision-making of the American labor movement.[3]

Despite growing black opposition from the rank-and-file to top officials, many unions continued to fight attempts to bring racial equality and justice within their ranks. Black workers in the International Longshoreman's Association (ILA) protested to white union officials against a systemic pattern of segregated locals and racist job referral policies no avail. Using Title Seven of the Civil Rights Act, black ILA members in Philadelphia, Baltimore, and Galveston–Port Arthur, Texas, successfully sued their union in the federal court in the 1970s. Although ILA lawyers explained that their segregated locals were "separate but equal," the federal courts ruled that "the segregated unions . . . by their very nature deny equal employment opportunities." When the Johnson Administration established "Project Build," an apprenticeship program funded by the Department of Labor with the goal of increasing the number of blacks in the construction crafts unions, white unionists devised elaborate methods to circumvent the law. After ten years, only 25 percent of the minority workers had completed the program, those who did finish usually found themselves assigned by unions to tasks as low-paid laborers. Black graduates of the apprenticeship program of the Operating Engineers Union in Philadelphia, who were also excluded from full union membership and jobs commensurate with their training, filed suit against the union in August 1970. During their legal battle, white engineers physically assaulted black apprentice graduates at work sites and in their union hall. Ruling against the racism of the Operating Engineers Union, federal judge A. Leon Higginbotham, Jr., declared:

> Here we have a tragic situation where Black men going to the union hall looking for work are attacked by large numbers of white operating engineers without any justification. . . . By the laws and the Constitution of the United States the defendant union is not permitted to be a divisive and coercive force to retard Blacks from also seeking an open society with the usual rights of other men. . . . It is now too late in the corridors of history for a court to sanction defendant-labor union's attempt to turn back the swelling tides of equal racial justice which the federal law demands.[5]

White union opposition to racial equality continued to fester, much to the trade union movement's own detriment. A number of unions, especially the American Federation of Teachers—AFL-CIO, led by racist social democrat Al Shanker, fought to oppose the instatement of "affirmative action" policies designed to increase the percentages of racial minorities and women within the labor force. At local levels, many white trade unionists were prominent participants in protests to halt the desegregation of public schools. In Boston, for example, a former leader of the Sheet Metal Workers' Union, James Kelley, became affiliated with a white racist paramilitary group which terrorized black poor and working-class families. In electoral politics, the backlash of white workers against black equality was translated into support for anti-working-class conservatives. In southern cities with large white working-class populations in 1968, Wallace polled 33 percent of the popular vote in Little Rock, Arkansas; 23 percent in Greensboro, North Carolina; 36 percent in Jacksonville, Florida; and 38 percent in Nashville, Tennessee. In the Democratic Party primaries of 1972, working-class whites gave Wallace victories in Florida, Michigan, and Maryland. Nixon and Agnew also made direct appeals to the conservatism and racism of white trade unionists, and reaped similar gains. The AFL-CIO was part of this conservative strategy, and did little to halt the trend to the right. When the Democrats nominated a social democrat who opposed the Vietnam War, Senator George McGovern, as their presidential candidate against Nixon in 1972, Meany and other labor leaders declared their "neutrality" in the contest. As a result, at least two-thirds of white working-class voters supported the anti-labor candidate Nixon, whereas 85 percent or more black voters cast ballots for McGovern's losing effort.

The bitter irony of labor's racist and pro-corporate positions was that they crippled the overall trade union movement; they alienated minorities and women from taking part in unionization efforts; and they diminished the ability of the working class to affect meaningful federal and state legislation which would benefit all of labor. The fruits of these practices and policies meant a decline in labor's ability to organize American working people. Union membership as a percentage of the labor force, for instance, dropped from 36 percent in 1960 to 20.9 percent in 1980. From 1973 to 1978, unions actually lost over three-fourths of all certified workplace elections. During the Nixon and Ford administrations the absence of a unified, strong union movement was directly responsible for federal inaction to reduce unemployment rates. From 1969 to 1975, joblessness for married males increased from 1.4 percent to 4.8 percent for whites, and from 2.5 percent to 8.3 percent for non-whites. Overall unemployment rates during these years jumped from 3.1 percent to 7.8 percent for whites, and 6.4 percent to 13.9 percent for non-whites. Beyond all other factors, racism undermined the political strength of labor, and concurrently made the blacks' struggle for desegregation and biracial democracy much more difficult.

II

In electoral politics, Black Power was translated into a growing voting bloc which blacks exercised in several specific ways. Between 1964 and 1972, the number of black Americans of voting age increased from 10.3 million to 13.5 million. The Voting Rights Act of 1965, combined with the registration campaigns of SNCC, CORE and the NAACP, dramatically increased the numbers of black potential voters. Thus the number of black elected officials continued to climb at an unprecedented rate. In March 1969, there were 994 black men and 131 black women who held offices across the country. By May 1975, this figure had more than tripled, to 2,969 black men and 530 black women. In the latter year, there were 18 blacks in Congress; 281 serving as state legislators or executives; 135 mayors of cities, towns, or municipalities; 305 county executives; 387 judges and elected law enforcement officers; 939 elected to city or county boards of education; and another 1,438 elected to other positions of municipal government. The southern states contained slightly more than half of these new politicians: 82 of the 135 black mayors were in the South; 1,702 of the 3,069 county, municipal, educational, and law enforcement officers and judges were southerners. The growing list of black officials represented, to be sure, a victory for proponents of civil rights. Yet within that victory resided certain ambiguities. Many of these men and women were nominally members of some desegregationist organization, such as the NAACP, CORE, or locally based groups. Perhaps a majority of them, however, had no prior experience as activists within desegregation campaigns. Most tended to come from the black middle class—doctors, lawyers, entrepreneurs, college professors—and not directly from the black working class or poor. This is not to suggest that the new black élites did not retain empathy for the conditions and plight of black labor; yet their ideological outlook and basic political practices tended to align them more with other parvenu élites than with the black working class. Part of the reason for this is reflected in the class and educational composition of the national black electorate. Among the black poor, where levels of education tend to be much lower than among the black élite, voting participation levels are also much lower. In the presidential election of 1972, for example, only 35.9 percent of black adults with educational levels below 5 years actually voted. For black high school graduates, the voting rate was 46.9 percent; blacks with 1 to 3 years of college education, 63.5 percent; black college graduates, 80.3 percent. Thus the relative weight of the black middle classes and blacks with advanced education was, within the "electoral marketplace," almost twice that of the lower-income, poorly educated black workers. The result of this bias toward the élite was reflected in the types of black candidates who were invariably elected to office.

Most civil rights leaders and black nationalists agreed that any major electoral victories registered by blacks would occur in major cities. In 1972, there were 89 U.S. cities which had populations exceeding 50,000, in which 20 percent or more of the total population was black. Combined, the total adult population of these cities was 23.7 million, of which 6.7 million, or 28.3 percent, were blacks. In larger cities, blacks were represented in even greater numbers. In 1972, there were ten major U.S. cities with total populations of half a million or more in which blacks comprised over 31 percent of the voters. These included Baltimore, with 273,000 black potential voters, 43.7 percent of the electorate; Detroit, 423,000 black voters, and 39.4 percent; New Orleans, 164,000 black voters, and 39.7 percent; Atlanta, 168,000 black voters, and 47.3 percent; and St. Louis, 159,000 black voters, and 35.9 percent. Yet in 1972 none of these five major cities had black mayors. In most metropolitan centers, old and well-entrenched political machines, established in the late 1800s and early 1900s by white ethnics tied to the Democratic Party, systemically kept blacks from achieving elective offices at the local level. During the early 1970s, urban blacks recognized that the efforts toward desegregating the rural South had to be channelled into the cities. In Newark, New Jersey, where blacks totalled 54.2 percent of the city's total population, only one-third of the members of the city council were black. Memphis blacks held only 3 out of 13 city council posts in 1972. New Orleans blacks did not have a single city council position that year. Black Atlantans held only 2 of 9 city council chairs. In Oakland, Calfiornia, a city with a black voting age population of almost 30 percent, only 1 out of 8 council members were black. Despite the black gains in congressional representation since the 1960s, here too there was a pattern of relative powerlessness. In the 92nd Congress, for example, 12 congressional districts had black populations between 38.2 percent and 49.8 percent, yet only one of these seats was held by a black person, Dellums of California. In a few instances, such as Mississippi's arch-racist Thomas G. Abernathy, whose House district held a 46.2 percent black population, the U.S. representatives from these districts were adamantly opposed to civil rights legislation. It was clear to all blacks, therefore, that Black Power could only become relevant to the material interests of blacks if and when their newly won electoral power was transferred into a greater share of public offices.

In Congress, black representatives began to devise a national strategy to boost the number of black elected officials (BEOs). In 1969, Representative Charles Diggs of Detroit initiated the Democratic Select Committee, a council of all nine black congressmen, to lobby against the Nixon Administration's initiatives against black and poor people. Within a year, former CORE activist William Clay, elected as representative from St. Louis in 1968, began to push his colleagues toward a more formal organization. In 1971, after the election of three more black representatives—Dellums of Oakland, California, George Collins of Chicago, and Parren Mitchell of Baltimore—the Congressional Black Caucus (CBC) was formed. During 1971 and 1972, CBC attempted to represent a "united voice for Black America" in the Congress, and to an extent, across the nation.[6] CBC staff members supported local races of black candidates; lobbied for progressive reforms in job training, health care, welfare and social service programs; and attempted to fashion a national strategy to increase black political power from local to federal levels. The black nationalists at this point began a period of tactical co-operation with many CBC members, particularly Diggs, who was vice chairperson of the House Committee on African Relations, and Dellums, who was at the time the only avowed socialist in the Congress. Baraka began to discuss with them the idea of developing an all-black "pre-party formation" which could be used both as a means to mobilize black voters and as a structure which would force the Democratic Party's white leadership to become more compliant with blacks' interests. In short order, Detroit representative John Conyers and Percy Sutton, Malcolm X's former lawyer and a major political leader in New York City, promulgated the suggestion. A meeting was called by Richard Hatcher, newly elected mayor of Gary, Indiana, to determine a firm strategy. The Northlake, Illinois, conference of 24–25 September 1971, co-ordinated by Hatcher, was probably the only instance between 1965 and 1983 when representatives of virtually every major tendency of the black movement sat down together in the same room. At Northlake were Julian Bond; CBC members Walter Fauntroy of Washington, D.C., Augustus Hawkins of California, and Conyers; the new leader of the Urban League, Vernon Jordan; Roy Innis of CORE; Atlanta attorney Maynard Jackson; SCLC representative Andrew Young; Percy Sutton, recently elected as Manhattan Borough president; and Baraka. These diverse and often feuding representatives of both integrationist and nationalist tendencies came to terms by accepting Baraka's plans for holding a major black independent political convention in early 1972.

The result of Northlake was the Gary Convention of 10–11 March 1972, the largest black political convention in U.S. history. About 3,000 official delegates were in attendance, representing revolutionary nationalist, cultural nationalist, moderate integrationist, and Black Capitalist tendencies. In all, about 12,000 persons attended the proceedings, which were co-chaired by an intriguing troika: Baraka, Hatcher, and Diggs. Almost every faction of the black movement was there: Jesse Jackson, the SCLC leader who had recently launched his own Operation PUSH (People United to Save Humanity), Martin's widow, Coretta Scott King, and Dorothy Height during one moment of Black Power frenzy were heard to shout the black nationalists' slogan—"Nationtime! Nationtime! Nationtime!" The convention established a political formation, the National Black Political Assembly, which would help elect black mayors, congressional representatives, and other officials, as well as mobilize poor and working-class blacks at neighborhood levels around key issues of concern. What was particularly important about Gary was the political tone of black nationalism which filled the convention hall, and affected the policies and even the rhetoric of all BEOs and diehard integrationists. Among the Old Guard, only some NAACP leaders refused to take part in the convention. Indeed, Wilkins bitterly attacked the policy statements of the Gary meeting *before* the convention was actually held. No one at Gary really cared. For the moment, the nationalists were in control of the black movement, a fact of political life that many CBC members and black mayors like Hatcher astutely recognized. The National Black Political Assembly was a marriage of convenience between the aspiring and somewhat radicalized black petty bourgeoisie and the black nationalist movement. Gary represented, in retrospect, the zenith not only of black nationalism, but of the entire black movement during the Second Reconstruction. The collective vision of the convention represented a desire to seize electoral control of America's major cities, to move the black masses from the politics of desegregation to the politics of real empowerment, ultimately to create their own independent black political party.[7]

What almost no nationalists and only a very few BEOs recognized *before* maneuvering for political power were the many structural crises which confronted America's major cities. A decade before Black Power assumed an electoral form in the campaigns to win public offices for blacks, urban metropolitan centers were faced with a series of fiscal problems which white mayors and city councils had left unresolved. Millions of white upper-to-middle-class families had fled the central cities; of the 212 U.S. towns with populations exceeding 50,000, 60 had declined in total population between 1950 and 1960. Historian Carl Degler notes: "Between 1952 and 1959 expenditures by local governments rose almost twice as fast as the gross national product." One consequence of these expenditures was that "the public debt of localities rose 40 times as fast in the 1950s as did the federal debt. In 1960 alone, expenditures by local governments exceeded their total income by $18 billion." By the era of Black Power, most cities were in the Kafkaesque situation of "spending more on interest payments than they were on the fire department."[8] Thus the BEOs were faced with the task of providing immediate and tangible benefits to their black and liberal white constituencies, while the governmental terrain upon which they operated had become quicksand. Political scientists William E. Nelson, Jr., and Philip J. Meranto listed some of the "most vexing problems adversely affecting the leadership capabilities" of the new black mayors and local officials during this period:

(1) A declining tax base spawned by reliance on the property tax and the dispersal of large sectors of the white community—both citizens and business—into surrounding suburbs;

(2) the influx into central cities of high-cost citizens—especially poor blacks—in desperate need of governmental assistance for survival;

(3) racial conflict generated by competition between blacks and whites for dwindling job opportunities and access to decent schools, homes, and recreational facilities in the central cities;

(4) the emergence of a city bureaucracy protected by civil service . . . ;

(5) decentralization of power from strong party organizations over which the mayor exercised control to a plethora of governmental agencies and competing interest groups over which he had little effective control;
(6) the impact on the social, economic, and political life of cities of policies made by corporate élites in private sanctuaries beyond the effective scrutiny and influence of any public official, including mayors;
(7) insensitivity to central city needs by important state and national officials.[9]

With relatively few exceptions, the black mayors and councillors were caught in an unenviable position, between black constituents with high expectations, a massive fiscal debt, a deteriorating industrial and commercial base, and an alienated and fearful white constituency. Cleveland, Ohio, while only one example, displayed many of the problems in all such cities. By 1967, Cleveland's black population had reached 36 percent of the city's total. In the city bureaucracy, all of the lowest-paying jobs (transit workers, parks and recreation employees, and sanitation workers) were held disproportionately by blacks, while the highest-paying positions (police, administrators, firemen) were held almost exclusively by whites. Whites had for a generation fled the inner city—from 1930 to 1960 almost 300,000 whites had left Cleveland, and they were replaced by an addition of 204,000 blacks. Economically, conditions for blacks were every bit as bad as they had been in some southern, segregated towns. In 1965, black unemployment reached 8.9 percent vs. 2.4 percent among whites. Well-established trade unions continued to practice policies of Jim Crow. In 1966, for example, of Cleveland's 1,482 plumbers, only 3 were black; out of 1,786 members of the local ironworkers' union, none were black. Thousands of African-American families lived in rat-infested, dilapidated, and overcrowded housing. In this environment, Ohio state legislator Carl B. Stokes was elected mayor in November 1967, defeating a white Republican opponent by a margin of 1,679 votes. Stokes's election was clearly along racial lines: 95 percent of the black wards supported Stokes, while 78.5 percent of the white wards favored his conservative opponent. Stokes's slender victory was the result of a massive black voter turnout, 79.7 percent of all registered voters, and because one-fifth of all white voters decided to support him.

Almost the day after Stokes's election as mayor, he ran into a series of difficulties. Two important Stokes allies, his former campaign manager and the city's acting mayor, both resigned from his administration after less than six months, claiming that the mayor was unwilling to listen to their suggestions for municipal reform. Stokes's appointment of Benjamin O. Davis, Jr., a black former general, as director of public safety backfired. A political conservative, Davis publicly pursued the police suppression of local black nationalists; he failed "to aggressively pursue whites who regularly attacked blacks in white neighborhoods"; and he openly sided with racist white policemen by demanding the right for officers to use "'dum-dum' bullets (soft-core bullets that expand on impact)." Davis was forced to resign by 1970, but not before notifying the press that Stokes gave "continued support and comfort . . . to the enemies of law enforcement." Stokes's administration was plagued by almost endless scandals: one of his black aides was forced to leave when the press publicized her part-ownership of an illegal liquor establishment; his public relations assistant resigned when the media learned of his questionable financial dealings; two other top Stokes appointees resigned in a "civil service scandal." Scandals of this type are a recurring theme of U.S. big-city politics, but under the administration of a black mayor, these events became major racial crises. By 1969, relations between Stokes and white city employees had reached rock-bottom. At one point, during a racial disturbance, white police and firemen refused to answer dispatches and emergency calls. Requests for police services at fires or shootings were responded to by epithets such as, "Let Mayor Stokes go piss on it"; "Let 'em burn the damn place down"; "To hell with the mayor." [10] Local white supporters of George Wallace initiated a political move legally to separate the city's black districts from the rest of Cleveland. Stokes tried to resolve his political problems by soliciting large sums of federal aid for the city. In 1968, he received a $12 million federal grant for much-needed urban renewal. From 1968 to 1970, Stokes's "Cleveland Now" fund-raising effort collected $177 million for new jobs, improved health care delivery services, and public housing. Despite these fiscal successes, Stokes's relations with the white working class and even with many black voters continued to deteriorate. A transit workers' strike in 1970 crippled downtown businesses, as thousands of employees were unable to get to their jobs. A long sanitation workers' strike left Cleveland's inner city beneath tons of uncollected garbage. By 1971, the black community was thoroughly disoriented and frustrated with Stokes's inability to provide solutions to their festering socioeconomic problems. Stokes did not seek re-election, and a conservative white Republican, Ralph Perk, was elected mayor over two rival black candidates. Stokes resigned from politics altogether, and since 1971 Cleveland to date has not had another black mayor. After Perk's election, white Republicans dismissed most of the 270 black administrators that Stokes had elevated into the city's bureaucracy. Leading black Democrats, including Stokes's brother, Congressman Louis Stokes, feuded with one another to control what was left of the crumbling black political power base in Cleveland. Disillusioned, many blacks ceased voting at all, and between

1971 and 1975, total black registration dropped from 127,000 to 102,000 in the city. Black voter turnouts in general elections plummeted from 81.7 percent in 1967 to only 47.7 percent in 1979. Great expectations had been overtaken by great apathy and an omnipresent sense of failure. The experience in Cleveland and the collapse of independent black politics would be mirrored in other major cities in the 1980s.

III

Even before the flawed electoral strategies of black nationalists and the emerging black élite had been tested nationally, the Nixon Administration set about the task of systematically destroying the still powerful radical wing of the Black Power movement. Politically, this was accomplished through several means. It was clear that many white Americans had to be prepared ideologically to accept the massive violation of civil liberties, the denial of human rights, and the illegal executions which were necessary to blunt the rhetoric and reality of black militancy. By the late 1960s, Nixon and his conservative supporters, in both the Republican and Democratic parties, employed the rhetorical slogan "law-and-order" in their campaigns for office in order to instill reactionary anxieties among whites. They pointed out to nervous voters that the number of murders in the U.S. had doubled between 1965 and 1975. Reported incidents of rape per 100,000 jumped from 12 to 26, and aggravated assaults from 111 to 227, during the decade. They insisted that black urban unrest and the militancy of the more nationalistic Black Power groups were somehow connected with the breakdown in civil obedience and social peace. The conservative politicians did not usually add the fact, however, the most violent crimes committed were not black-against-white, but were intraracial; that black male homicide rates were between 600 to 800 percent higher than for white males. The political propaganda to increase the length of jail sentences, to silence militant blacks, produced a popular white political reaction. By 1972, 74 percent of all Americans believed that the U.S. criminal justice system "was not dealing harshly enough with criminals."[11] By 1978, this figure had reached 90 percent. Thus Nixon and other political reactionaries developed a popular mandate for expanding the activities of COINTELPRO, and for unleashing the Department of Justice, the FBI and state law enforcement agencies to eradicate the most militant tendencies of the black movement, all in the name of "law-and-order."

The arrests and executions of Black Panthers continued under Nixon, with the FBI in close co-operation with local law enforcement agencies. On 4 December 1969, Chicago leaders Mark Clark and Fred Hampton were murdered by police in a raid on the Black Panthers' headquarters. A federal grand jury ruled in May 1970, that "the police fired eighty-three shots into the apartment while only one shot was fired toward the police." The grand jury implied strongly that the police raid was used as a pretext to assassinate the black revolutionaries.[12] FBI directives to nine field offices in January 1970, ordered officials to "counteract any favorable support in publicity to the Black Panther Party" by placing anti-Panther propaganda in the media. In Los Angeles and San Francisco, the FBI drafted "editorials" and "news articles" for local television stations and newspapers which attacked the organization.[13] In August 1971, FBI agents and local police arrested two Black Panthers in Omaha, Nebraska, David Rice and Ed Poindexter, on charges of killing a local policeman. In subsequent investigations by Amnesty International and other human rights agencies, it was revealed that the FBI had collected over 2,000 pages of information on the Omaha chapter of the Black Panthers, and that the actual murderer of the police officer was a former drug addict who was soon released by authorities, and who subsequently "disappeared." Both Rice and Poindexter were convicted, however, and still remain in federal penitentiaries. Other black activists having no connection with the Black Panthers were similarly harassed, arrested and imprisoned. On 18 August 1971, FBI agents and 36 policemen armed with shotguns, machine guns and an armored car raided the headquarters of a black nationalist organization, the Republic of New Afrika (RNA), in Jackson, Mississippi. RNA leader Imari Obadele (Richard Henry) and ten others were arrested on charges of murder, assault, and "treason against the state of Mississippi!" Nine other RNA members were arrested on questionable charges such as "spitting and talking back to an officer." Three weeks later, 65 Detroit police raided that city's RNA headquarters and arrested group members at gunpoint. An FBI internal memo, dated 8 September 1971, reveals that the federal government wanted to imprison Obadele at all costs: "If Obadele can be kept off the streets, it may prevent further problems involving the RNA inasmuch as he completely dominates this organization and all members act under his instructions." In September 1973, Obadele and six other RNA leaders were "found guilty of conspiracy to assault federal officers, assault, and the use of firearms to commit a felony." Obadele was given a sentence of twelve years.[14]

Most instances of blatant injustice against black activists received little or no media attention. Three cases, however, ultimately became major international issues. The Reverend Benjamin Chavis, civil rights organizer for the United Church of Christ, led two nonviolent demonstrations in Wilmington, North Carolina, in pursuit of quality education for black children in the city. In March 1972, Chavis, eight black student leaders and one progressive white woman were arrested for burning a local grocery store. A jury of ten whites (some of whom admitted to membership in the Ku Klux Klan) and two elderly, intimidated blacks gave sentences to the "Wilmington Ten" which totalled 282 years. In order to ensure their convictions, the FBI and the Alcohol, Tobacco and Firearms (ATF) division of the U.S. Treasury Department secretly paid three witnesses, two convicted criminals and a 15-year-old boy, to testify against Chavis. From prison, Chavis wrote a stirring appeal to the 1977 Belgrade Conference on the Helsinki Accords guaranteeing the protection of human rights:

> From a torturous prison cell in the state of North Carolina I make to the world community . . . an urgent public appeal for human rights. As one of many victims, I shall not keep silent.
>
> . . . I wish in no manner to embarrass or criticize my country unduly. I love my country. It is because I love my country that I decry publicly the domestic exploitation, persecution and imprisonment of innocent citizens for political, economic and racist motives. No doubt I will face reprisals and retaliatory punishment for daring to write and speak these truths which are self-evident but I take the risk, accepting what may come with courage. In the United States the present reality for millions of Black Americans, Native American Indians, Puerto Ricans, Chicanos, Asian Americans and other oppressed national minorities is that violations of fundamental human rights and freedoms are commonplace. . . . We are the victims of racism and monopoly economic exploitation. And yes, we are the victims of governmental repression.[15]

Two other prominent victims of political repression were Angela Davis and George Jackson. In June 1969, Davis was dismissed from her position as philosophy professor at the University of California-Los Angeles by the order of California's ultra-conservative governor, Ronald Reagan, for her membership in the U.S. Communist Party. In August 1970, FBI agents charged her with involvement in a California shootout which led to several deaths, including one judge and a member of the Black Panthers, 17-year-old Jonathan Jackson. Davis immediately went "underground," and was arrested in New York City after FBI officials named her one of the country's "ten most wanted criminals."[16] Jailed at first in the same prison which once housed Claudia Jones, she was constantly harassed and supervised. On 4 June 1972, after a massive international campaign had been waged, a California jury declared her innocent of all charges. The older brother of Jonathan Jackson, George Jackson, had been sentenced at the age of 18 to serve a term of "one year-to-life" for stealing $70 from a store. Annually denied parole, Jackson was determined not to be dehumanized by his prison environment. By 1970, thousands of black and white prisoners in every federal penitentiary knew of his legendary regimen: 1,000 finger-tip push-up exercises each day; authoring two major works of political theory and dozens of essays; being named national "Field Marshal" of the Black Panther Party while behind bars. Prison officials determined to break Jackson, placed in solitary confinement for years, segregated him from other prisoners, and attempted to bribe convicts to kill him. Jackson's public following grew alarmingly after the publication of his book *Soledad Brother*. On 21 August 1971, Jackson was executed by guards in San Quentin prison. Officials justified Jackson's death with an unbelievable story: that Jackson's attorney smuggled a 32-ounce, 8-inch long pistol to him inside the prison during an interview, and that Jackson hid the gun "in his medium-sized Afro [hair], before he was searched in the nude, then walked approximately 100 yards with a guard before the pistol was detected." During the unrest after Jackson's death, 26 San Quentin prisoners were "stripped, beaten and tortured and forced to lie naked in the [prison's] outside yard for seven hours." [17] Blacks were shocked and outraged that the 29-year-old Black Panther had been murdered. The East Palo Alto, California, city council immediately passed a resolution, stating:

> It is utterly incredible that a prisoner in isolation in a maximum security facility could acquire and conceal possession of a gun as has been claimed by authorities. . . . We do hereby affirm our disgust and dismay at this atrocious act of genocide. We demand, full, complete, and fair investigation of George Jackson's murder and a redress of grievances including the conviction and execution of all parties to this cowardly and criminal act. [18]

Protests against Jackson's death assumed many forms, both outside and inside the nation's prisons. One black underground formation, the George Jackson Assault Squad, killed a California police officer with a shotgun blast on 30 August 1971, in an act of vengeance. Radical whites sympathetic with Jackson bombed police buildings in three California cities. One group set fire to the Bank of America's downtown offices in San Francisco. Prisoners in the Attica, New York, penitentiary staged a one-day fast on 27 August in tribute to Jackson. Prison officials retaliated by tightening restrictions. On 9 September, Attica's 1,300 inmates—black, Puerto Rican and white—seized control of the state facility, demanding "that all inmates be given adequate food, water, and shelter." Other demands included "complete amnesty from physical, mental, and legal reprisals"; "true religious freedom" inside prisons; "an effective drug treatment program for all inmates who request it"; the modernization of "the inmate education system which would include a Spanish language library and a criminal law library"; and the "end of all censorship of newspapers, magazines, and letters." In short, Attica prisoners wanted to be treated like human beings. New York governor Nelson Rockefeller consulted with Nixon and state law enforcement officials, and decided to retake the prison. Hundreds of armed National Guardsmen, local and state police, and Attica prison guards attacked, killing 29 prisoners and 10 guards who had been held hostage. Unarmed prisoners stood before the police unafraid: "Go ahead and shoot, you pig bastards!" one victim cried aloud before his death. Screaming, the police surged forward, yelling and shooting wildly, indiscriminately. One prisoner who survived the attack had a rifle pointed at his head by a police officer who shouted: "Get on your feet you dirty, black nigger bastard! I'll kill all you niggers!" Recapturing the prison, troopers wrote racist obscenities along walls: "black blood will flow freely; Angela Davis sucks Troopers dicks; the Black Panthers are pussys; die, Jackson, die; All Blacks are Niggers." Attica's convicts "didn't believe they'd come in with guns and grenades," one surviving prisoner wroter in the *Black Scholar*. In a situation in which a bloody massacre could have been prevented through reasonable negotiations, U.S. officials deliberately chose to employ the harshest methods possible to restore "law-and-order." On 21 December 1973, 60 of Attica's leaders were tried for "murder, kidnapping, and other assorted felonies." [19]

After the Attica uprising, white American politicians seized on the incident as an excuse to create even more repressive conditions. Annual government expenditures for prisons grew to exceed $4.6 billion in 1977, and local government expenditures for police forces more than doubled, reaching $8.8 billion. Between 1970 and 1975, the prison population in some states increased 100 percent. Over half a million mentally ill persons were arrested and jailed every year; about half of the U.S. prison population was black, and half were under the age of 29. Prison conditions became so miserable, with chronic overcrowding, that a few federal judges even ruled in state cases that imprisonment under inhumane situations constituted "cruel and unusual punishment." The consequences of the deterioration of prison life in the 1970s were not only greater unrest, but other manifestations of suffering. In 1973, the suicide rate for the U.S. penal population was 600 percent higher than that of the general population. Less than 10 percent of all prisoners were involved in vocational education programs, which would aid them in becoming productive citizens once released. Young black male prisoners were often the victims of homosexual gang rape. Black women prisoners, particularly in municipal and county jails, were habitually raped by guards and law enforcement officers. One notorious instance of sexual abuse occurred in Beaufort County, North Carolina, in which a black garment factory worker, Joan Little, was raped by her guard. On 27 August 1974, Little struggled in her cell with her rapist jailer, managed to kill him, and fled the jail. Surrendering herself on 3 September 1974, she was promptly charged with murder. After an extensive trial and litigation, Little was declared not guilty by reason of self-defense. Despite this solitary yet important victory for civil rights, thousands of "Joan Littles," the rape victims of police and penal authorities, remained unheard and unknown.

Given Nixon's massive electoral mandate of November 1972, it is entirely possible that even greater criminal acts against black nationalists, Marxists, community organizers, elected officials, and ministers would have transpired during his second term of office. What undermined the construction of an American majority for the right, at least temporarily, was the Watergate scandal. On 18 June 1972, five men directed by a former FBI agent were arrested while burgling the Democratic National Committee headquarters at the Watergate Hotel in Washington, D.C. A Senate special investigating committee learned that Attorney General John Mitchell not only

> had sanctioned the break-in but also revealed that the administration had taken punitive action against its political opponents, had ordered unwarranted Internal Revenue Service audits of their tax returns, had tapped the telephones of government officials and newspaper reporters without court approval, and had hired agents to break into a psychiatrist's office and ransack his files in an effort to embarrass Daniel Ellsberg, a critic of the Vietnam War who had consulted the doctor professionally.

Vice President Agnew was forced to resign in disgrace when a court ruled that he had accepted corporate bribes. Nixon took the offensive, claiming arrogantly in one press conference, "I am *not* a crook." Yet in April 1974, the public learned that the president had paid in 1971–72 only $800 in taxes on an annual salary exceeding $200,000 and that he owed the government $432,000 in taxes. Gradually, as the administration fought desperately to restore public confidence, Nixon's ability to pursue aggressive domestic and foreign policies diminished. On 28 March 1973, the last U.S. troops were withdrawn from Vietnam. In two years, North Vietnamese troops would enter Saigon as liberators. At home, COINTELPRO, officially ending operations in 1971, began to place the FBI and other federal agencies on the defensive. Liberal Democratic senator Frank Church, chairperson of the Senate Select Committee to Study Governmental Operations with respect to Intelligence Activities, later exposed a sickening pattern of illegal surveillance acts which victimized blacks with absolutely no credentials in the black liberation movement: Roy Wilkins, actress Eartha Kitt, heavyweight boxing champion Muhammad Ali; retired boxer Joe Louis; and actors Ossie Davis and Harry Belafonte.

Nixon's grandiose plan to unite "the likeminded, the forgotten Americans, the good, decent, taxpaying, law abiding people" against blacks, Latinos and liberals came crashing to an end with his resignation on 9 August 1974. Nixon was replaced by the former House Republican minority leader, Gerald R. Ford, a political functionary possessing all the charisma, it was said, of a sleepy clam. The significance of Watergate was not lost upon black nationalists and progressives. Political theorist William Strickland, a leader of a progressive black research center, the Institute of the Black World, suggested in December 1973, "Watergate is no mere accident of history":

> It is the natural consequence of a government faced with the problem of trying to preserve the façade of democracy before its citizens while waging imperialist war abroad, plundering the public treasury at home, and supporting reaction wherever it can be found. To maintain the myth of American righteousness, the government has no other recourse except to lie. Indeed, lying becomes the central political behavior of the state . . . white politics seems to prefer the known evil to the possible unknown good. In the face of the greatest mass of criminal evidence ever assembled against a political figure, white politics and white people sit doe-like, almost hypnotically subservient to Big Brother.[21]

The wheels of governmental repression did not grind entirely to a halt in the mid-1970s, however, and the massive damage accomplished in Nixon's five and a half years of rule against the black freedom movement would never be undone. The possibility of a conservative restoration, and the effective end of the Second Reconstruction, was set during the Nixon years. But this would not be fully realized until the election of 1980.

IV

For historian Vincent Harding, and many black scholars and activists, the Gary Convention and the founding of the National Black Political Assembly represented the culmination of the entire legacy of black struggles, from the Montgomery bus boycott and the Greensboro sit-ins, to Malcolm X and the Black Power rebellions. "When we all gathered at Gary, many persons instinctively seemed to sense something of the powerful meaning of the last words of the preamble to the convention's declaration: 'We stand on the edge of history. We cannot turn back'." The delegates may have wondered: "Is this what Malcolm and Martin had seen and felt before us? Was this the vision that so troubled each of them in the last churning months of their lives?" In the weeks following the convention, Harding recognized that for many, this illuminating vision of black liberation, the powerful responsibility to make new history, was too weighty to bear. "Instead, in response to the most fundamental challenging calls of the convention's black agenda, many persons turned back to politics-as-usual, turned aside to the demands of self-interest, or wandered off into unclear, necessarily solitary ways, searching for their own best responses to the new time.[22] The CBC was the first significant force, although not the last, to back away from the mandate of Gary. Two controversial resolutions passed at Gary caused the greatest concern. Delegates declared themselves, first, in favor of black-controlled community schools, and in opposition to federal court-ordered busing for school desegregation purposes. Second, the convention called for the political right to self-determination for all peoples of color, including the Palestinians. Mindful of U.S. Jewish organizational support for civil rights legislation, the CBC promptly declared "its friendship with the State of Israel," stating, "we vigorously oppose the efforts of any group that would seek to weaken or undermine Israel's right to exist."[23] This statement immediately alienated many nationalists, who were politically sympathetic with the Palestine Liberation Organization, and who opposed the obvious military and economic linkages between Israel and the racist regime of *apartheid* South Africa. Shirley Chisholm, who had already begun a campaign for the Democratic Party's presidential nomination, viewed Gary as a "personal rebuff to her." By May 1972, most CBC members had aligned themselves behind a white Democratic candidate. Representatives Clay and Fauntroy, along with Jesse Jackson, touted the merits of McGovern, while Charles Evers and Stokes's protégé Arnold Pinckney backed Humphrey. A few Black Powerites, notably McKissick, endorsed Nixon's re-election in 1972. Soon after the election, most of the black Democrats were firmly back into the fold. By the second major convention of the National Black Political Assembly, which was held in Little Rock, Arkansas, in 1974, only newly elected Atlanta mayor Maynard Jackson, Hatcher, and a paltry collection of BEOs were in attendance. Despite the election of Youngstown, Ohio, black nationalist leader Ronald Daniels to the chairman's spot, replacing Diggs, many observers felt that the Assembly was at a dead end. Cynical as always, Harold Cruse denounced the Little Rock gathering of 2,000 activists as "a betrayal of the Black militant potential built up during the struggles of the Sixties. It was a political retreat from the field of political battle on which the enemy itself was floundering with its flanks openly exposed to further ambush."[24]

At this time, the nationalists perpetuated a series of theoretical debates and organizational ruptures which effectively broke their short hegemony over the black movement as a whole. After Nixon's espousal of Black Power as Black Capitalism, most progressive nationalists and cultural nationalists ceased to use the term. Instead, they championed "the politics of Pan-Africanism," an eclectic political theory which called for the liberation of all peoples of African descent across the black diaspora, and within the continent. From the outset, Pan-Africanism retained all of the ambiguities and contradictions which Black Power had come to symbolize. In 1971, political theorist Ladun Anise warned activists,

> Pan-Africanism has always been an ideology of progressively enlarging levels of consciousness, meanings, interpretations, and socio-political goals which can be understood only in relation to the differing configurations of problems within changing historical periods. It is an inclusive and open-minded ideology that means different things to the same people at different periods and, in the same period different things to different people.[25]

In 1972–73, the popularity of Pan-Africanism among broad segments of the black population was manifested in the activities of the nationalists' African Liberation Support Committee (ALSC). The ALSC was instrumental in sponsoring a series of popular mass demonstrations in the U.S. which expressed support for African independence from colonial and *apartheid* rule, called the "African Liberation Day" (ALD). At the ALD in Washington, D.C. held in May 1972, 20,000 black youngsters, workers and activists crowded around "Patrice Lumumba Square"—what nationalists called the grounds surrounding the Washington Monument. Speakers at the ALD included poet Don L. Lee (Haki Madhubuti), Baraka, and CBC members Fauntroy and Diggs, who was particularly resplendent in his purple dashiki. In 1973, ALSC raised $40,000 for African nationalists engaged in armed struggle, and the ALD marches nationally attracted over 100,000 people. Dissent surfaced in late 1973, however, when ALSC's chief organizer Owusu Sadaukai (Howard Fuller) began to reevaluate his opposition to Marxist ideology, and shifted to the left. At a national ALSC meeting in Frogmore, South Carolina, Sadaukai and his supporters declared themselves as favoring Marxism-Leninism, and defined Pan-Africanism as the struggle against both "racism and imperialism." Subsequently, the various forces which had successfully established ALD as a major political event were splintered over the issue of Marxism.[26]

The "Great Debate" between black independent Marxist-Leninists and the narrow cultural nationalists from 1973–76 was a kind of replay of the Black Panthers–U.S. battle of the late 1960s. Nationalist college students in the Students Organized for Black Unity (SOBU) adopted a Leninist position, and renamed their formation Youth Organized for Black Unity (YOBU), to reflect a more class-conscious mentality. Fisk University professor Abd-al Hakimu Ibn Alkalimat (Gerald McWorter), one of the founders of the Institute of the Black World, had been among the most dogmatically narrow nationalists. By the early 1970s, Alkalimat had become a Leninist, establishing a Marxist institute, "Peoples College," in Nashville, and was decisive in moving many former cultural nationalists to the left.[27]

Baraka underwent a similar metamorphosis. Founding the Congress of Afrikan People (CAP) in 1970, Baraka and his cultural nationalist supporters
exercised a major role in the nationalists' hegemony over the BEOs. Influenced by Sadaukai's movement to the left, and Karenga's incorporation of
certain Marxian concepts into his own formation, Baraka revised his political posture accordingly. By late 1974, CAP had become Marxist-Leninist in
all but name, and Baraka's allies inside the National Black Political Assembly became increasingly at odds with Daniels and other nationalists. Cultural nationalists attacked Baraka, Alkalimat, Sadaukai and others for
"selling out" to the white man. Haki Madhubuti expressed their somewhat metaphysical view in September 1974:

> The ideology of white supremacy precedes the economic structure of capitalism
> and imperialism, the latter of which are falsely stated as the cause of racism. To
> believe that the white boy mis-used and manipulated us for centuries up until
> today for purely economic reasons is racist and void of any historical reality. . . .
> Chinese are for Chinese first (Yellow Power), Europeans are for Europeans first
> (White Power), and Afrikans should be for Afrikans first (Black Power). . . .
> The Capitalist West convincingly uses anti-communism as an ideological weapon
> to protect themselves and the Communist East uses anti-imperialism and anti-
> capitalism as ideological weapons to protect themselves. As far as we are con-
> cerned communism and capitalism are the left and right arms in the same white
> body. And *the highest stage of white supremacy is imperialism whether it's communist
> or capitalist.*[28]

The struggle between the competing tendencies of black nationalism became increasingly fratricidal. Organizations collapsed beneath the weight of
polemics; old friends turned against one another, marriages were broken
over which African liberation organization one chose to support; individuals lost their jobs inside black studies departments at universities, depending upon where they stood politically on the Leninist-cultural nationalist
debate. Each side put forward its own theoreticians in the confrontation.
Shawna Maglanbayan's *Garney, Lumumba, Malcolm: Black Nationalist Separatists* declared that all communists, "whether they go under the pseud-
onyms of trotskyism, castroism or marxist-leninism, have consistently
sought to sap the life-blood from Black political thinking and sidetrack the
struggle of Black mankind by undermining and sabotaging every Black
Nationalist-Separatist effort." Chairman of Howard University's political
science department and a leading theorist for the National Black Political
Assembly, Ronald Walters, argued that "imperialism is not the highest
stage of capitalism as some would have us believe, but is the highest stage
of white culture and development: therefore, Black people in the world are
oppressed not because we are workers but because we are Black."[29] Some

narrow nationalists even suggested that their former co-workers were being paid by Moscow or Peking; that the new black Marxist-Leninists had
turned "traitor" in order to receive sexual favors from their white female
"comrades." Black Marxists such as Mark Smith retorted that Madhubuti
and others suffered from an "idealist" perspective, that they viewed the
black working class with complete contempt, and that their bogus interpretation of Pan-Africanism was pro-imperialist and profoundly "petty
bourgeois." Smith argued, "the right-wing nationalists" standard line of
attack" against Marxism was just what "the State Department and the im-
perialists wanted to hear." [30] A few intellectuals tried to salvage the nationalists' unity by articulating a synthesis of the two positions. Hoyt Fuller,
editor of *Black World* magazine, argued forcefully in July 1974:

> . . . there is no disputing that class conflict is integral to the (Black) struggle.
> Nor is the persistence of Marxist analysis, in itself, such a negative thing to
> Blacks with a sense of history and some balance in their world view. It seems
> that where Marxism has the power to terrorize is in those Black enclaves which
> are wedded to the proposition that "the American way" is the best of all possible
> approaches to "the good life." . . . There is no certainty of a *solid* middle
> ground as refuge between the Marxists and those middle-class Black strivers
> whose selfishness and short-sightedness serves the Marxists' purposes. . . .
> What I deplore most, I think, is the [Marxists'] absence of originality in their
> new intellectual and theoretical stances. What I miss most in what they now are
> saying is organic thought, ideas which have grown naturally from the struggle
> they, themselves, have waged and which are directly applicable to the situation
> they have tried against such odds and with so little support to change for the
> better.

With some sadness, Fuller declared, "We have come to another fork in the
road . . . the NAACPs and the PUSHs may seem to have it all their way. . . ."[31]
   It would not be fair to say that the Old Guard had trounced the Pan-
Africanists, black Marxists and nationalists; rather, it was the black militants who defeated themselves. Theoretically obtuse and organizationally
fractious, nationalist groups took turns in purging various tendencies out of
their respective formations. After mapping out a detailed strategy, Daniels
and a former ally of Baraka's Mtangulizi Sanyika (Haywood Henry), managed to neutralize Baraka within the Assembly at a particularly bitter
brawl in Dayton, Ohio, in late 1975. ALD shrank significantly, down to
7,000 participants in Washington, D.C., in 1974, and less than 4,000 two
years later. The number of black studies departments dropped roughly by
half between 1971 and 1976, as feuding scholars and preoccupied polemi-
cists tended to take some blacks' attention away from white-sponsored reductions in minority staff and faculties, and other administrative attacks

against blacks on white campuses. Tragically, the rhetoric of many black radicals had less to do with Marxism than with a crude economic determinism and a simplistic adaptation of the ideas of Mao Tse Tung to the terrain of black America. Many black activists who *claimed* to be Marxists had never actually read Marx, and if they had, they had left undigested the rich corpus of modern socialist theory which concretely relates Marx to the unique conditions of social transformation under late capitalism—Antonio Gramsci, Walter Rodney, Amilcar Cabral, Louis Althusser, Nicos Poulantzas. Most cultural nationalists articulated a political praxis that was at best incoherent, profoundly ethnocentric and ideologically inert. Despite powerful sociological evidence from a variety of sources providing beyond any reasonable doubt the centrality of class and the emergence of a conservative black élite, the narrow nationalists preferred to damn material reality, and embrace sterile cultural mutterings and blind dogmas to the death. The Old Guard simply watched their critics bludgeon themselves into political oblivion. In March 1976, the National Black Political Assembly could barely muster 1,000 participants at its third national convention in Cincinnati, Ohio. Dellums and Bond rejected the convention's 1976 draft to initiate an independent black presidential candidacy, and by 1977 the Assembly had less than 300 members nationally. The vision of Gary was gone.

V

The inchoate black rebellion of 1965–75 also inspired and, to a profound degree, initiated similar revolts among other American people of color. In New York City, Puerto Rican workers had joined with progressives whites and blacks in a series of successful labor union efforts. An outstanding example of multiracial co-operation was in the militant Drug and Hospital Employees Local 1199. The union's activities won the support of King, Malcolm X, and Randolph, and brought a number of Puerto Rican rank-and-file organizers into positions of local political leadership. More decisive, however, was the emergence of militant nationalist formations which called for the independence of Puerto Rico from the U.S. In the early 1960s, the Movement for Puerto Rican Independence (MPI) arose from a political faction within the moderate Puerto Rican Independence Party. MPI shared many of the characteristics of the later SNCC and the Black Panther Party, with its commitment to street demonstrations, its opposition to the Vietnam War, and its ideological efforts to combine socialism with their own aggressive nationalist program. At the end of the decade, the Puerto Rican Socialist Party (PSP) developed from the MPI, as an even more doctrinaire Marxist formation. At its height in the early to mid-1970s, PSP "made some inroads in the labor movement, succeeding in organizing a labor federation independent of the AFL-CIO," radical sociologist Stanley Aronowitz observes. "In the United States PSP established a branch which, although primarily dedicated to the independence movement, also participated in anti-war and other political protests and became for a time an important force on the American left, particularly on the East Coast and in the Midwest." [32]

The political unrest among Indians was channelled largely outside traditional trade unionism and Marxist-Leninist politics. More reformist and conservative Indian leaders maintained their political support for the Association on American Indian Affairs, the National Congress of American Indians, and the Indian Rights Association. Young nationalist militants increasingly viewed such groups as black radicals saw the Urban League and the NAACP—as irrelevant social anachronisms which often did more harm than good. Indian activists frequently noted that their people held potential economic and political power which had not been co-ordinated collectively by conservative tribal leaders. On their meager land holdings still maintained as Indian reservations, Native Americans controlled about 3 percent of all U.S. oil and gas reserves, 15 percent of all coal, 55 percent of the U.S. supply of uranium, and about 11 percent of all uranium reserves in the world. Yet economic development programs promoted by private U.S. firms and the federal government usually stripped these mineral and natural resources from the reservations, still leaving the Indian people in a state of perpetual penury. U.S. courts generally refused to grant civil justice to Indians' land claims, and local and state courts and law enforcement officials often treated Indians as aliens. No effective social programs for housing, education and health care were maintained for urban Indians. As late as 1966, less than 2,000 Indians were in college or graduate school, out of a population of 710,000. Over one-half of all Indians could not read or write in English, and infant mortality among Indians still remained the highest in the country. [33]

The clearest manifestation of a renaissance in Indian nationalism first occurred in 1969, when advocates of "Red Power" took control of Alcatraz Island, a former prison set in San Francisco Bay. Maintaining the island for one and a half years, the militants announced to the media that the island was the property of Indian people. This symbolic act of resistance was repeated elsewhere. In 1971 Indian activists in New York City defaced a statue of George Washington, to bring greater public attention to the genocidal policies of the American government. Indian militants in Minneapolis–St. Paul, Minnesota, led by Chippewa Indian organizer Dennis Banks, launched the American Indian Movement (AIM) in 1968. Like the Black Panther Party in Oakland, AIM's first goal was to address police brutality against non-whites in their city. Patrolling Minneapolis and St. Paul streets after dark, Banks and AIM activists stopped police officers from harassing individual Indians, and promptly publicized incidences of police violence. AIM's direct intervention was responsible for reducing the number of weekend arrests of Indians from 200 down to nearly zero. From 1969 to 1972, AIM's program expanded to include a variety of public welfare and political training projects. Pressuring a major Minneapolis employer, Honeywell corporation, AIM increased the number of Indian workers at that firm by 450 persons. AIM pressured city officials in Minneapolis to establish a center for Indian culture, and after seven years of political effort, a $1.9 million public institute was opened. Creating their own housing corporation, AIM leaders initiated the construction of homes for Indians in Minneapolis. Funded by the federal government's Housing and Urban Development Department, AIM used a $4.3 million grant to build 241 homes. In Minnesota's public school systems, Indian militants fought to change the educational curriculum to reflect a more multicultural perspective. When local school boards ignored AIM's demands, the organization initiated urban Indian schools in Minneapolis, St. Paul, and later in Rapid City, South Dakota. Challenging the racism of the penal system, AIM backed an Indian candidate's successful election to the Minneapolis State Parole Board in 1972.

AIM's constructive successes in educational, economic and social welfare work among Indians brought the group into close political scrutiny by the FBI and local law enforcement agencies. Unlike more traditional Indian public interest organizations, AIM developed a vision of American society without oppression, a critique of the status quo which drew consciously both from their own resistance leaders of the nineteenth century, and from Malcolm X and Martin Luther King. In a 1976 interview, Dennis Banks observed that AIM was founded because of the "many deaths in this country of Native Americans," but added that a broad coalition of poor people and workers of different nationalities and races was essential in order to change American society:

> When Martin Luther King was standing we should have stood with him no matter what his beliefs because we know objectively he was also asking for social change in this country. . . . We have been divided. Indian people are being killed and we are the only ones fighting for Indian people. Blacks are being killed and only blacks are fighting for blacks. Poor whites are fighting for change in the poor white section. Asians and Chicanos are the same way. I think that inspired AIM to stand up finally and say look, we have got to pull it together, and that is where we are at right now, trying to bring non-Indians and the Indians together and bring about massive change in this society.[34]

Confrontation between AIM and federal authorities broke out into open warfare early in 1973. The Pine Ridge Sioux Oglala Civil Rights Organization asked AIM to assist them in removing the accommodationist Tribal

Council in their South Dakota reservation. Many of the Minnesota leaders of AIM had been originally from the Pine Ridge reservation, and they quickly joined forces with older, more experienced Indian elders who had been resisting federal authorities for three and four decades. When the Indian nationalists took control of the site, federal authorities and army personnel laid siege on Wounded Knee, South Dakota, from 27 February to 8 May 1973. During the siege, Indians across the nation were inspired to new levels of resistance. Dozens of militant organizers journeyed to Wounded Knee, and almost every civic club, political association, and cultural group run by Native American people became involved in the controversy. Two local Indian militants, Pedro Bissonette and Buddy LaMonte, were killed by federal officers, but a peaceful settlement was finally reached. Federal authorities under the Nixon Administration were determined at last to uproot and destroy AIM and to use the Pine Ridge reservation as a graphic example for other Indian nationalist organizations and leaders of what legal repression might hold for their own formations. Pine Ridge became an "occupied zone"; local Indians who participated in the Wounded Knee takeover were tried, imprisoned and assassinated. When two FBI agents at Pine Ridge were assassinated in 1975, Indian leader Leonard Peltier was legally framed for the murders and was ordered to serve a life sentence in a federal prison. Indian conservatives stuffed ballot boxes to keep AIM leader Russell Means from winning the Tribal Council's chairmanship in the Pine Ridge elections held in 1974. In three years, Indian "goon squads," local white officers and the FBI were responsible for the execution or disappearance of over 300 Indian women and men in Pine Ridge and across the country. In 1976 the FBI declared that AIM had replaced the Black Panther Party and other black nationalists formations as the "number one terrorist organization in the United States."[35] Dennis Banks was charged by federal authorities with "rioting while armed with intent to kill" in the aftermath of a courtroom disturbance in South Dakota.[36] An all-white jury promptly convicted Banks. Believing with some justifications that the FBI or penal authorities planned his assassination, Banks fled to California. The FBI initiated a massive nationwide manhunt, and finally captured the nationalist leader in California in early 1976.

As in its bloody suppression of the Black Panthers, the FBI was absolutely ruthless in its treatment of AIM activists. AIM leader Annie Mae Aquash disappeared and was found dead on the Pine Ridge reservation. FBI officials claimed that Aquash's death was due to exposure. Finally, an independent coroner was allowed to view her remains at the repeated insistence of her family. Aquash had been brutally shot in the brain, and her hands had been chopped off. AIM organizer Byron DeSersa was assassinated in South Dakota. Russell Means and John Thomas were wounded.

Local leader Raymond Yellow Thunder was murdered in Nebraska, which led Indian organizations across that state and in South Dakota to form a civil rights coalition which demanded an investigation. But even in the midst of repression, Indian advocates of Red Power fought back. In June 1974, thousands of AIM supporters and members created the International Treaty Council at the Standing Rock Sioux reservation. Indians called for the intervention of the United Nations and other "international forces necessary to obtain the recognition of our treaties." The new council expressed political solidarity with all Third World struggles for emancipation, giving special note of the "colonized Puerto Rican People in their struggle for Independence from the same United States of America."[37] One year later, Navajo factory workers and AIM activists expropriated an electronics firm on the Navajo reservation, which had exploited Indians with low wages and benefits. In 1976 Navajo refinery laborers and AIM took control of an oil refinery on the Navajo reservation. Dozens of Indian groups became more involved in militant union confrontation with corporations and industries which had traditionally underpaid Native Americans. The National Congress of American Indians became affiliated with the internationalist World Council of Indigenous Peoples, established in Canada in 1975. Other progressive resources for Indians which formed included the Indian Law Resource Center and the pan-Indian publication *Akwesasne Notes*. From February to August 1978, Indian activists staged the "Longest Walk" protest across the U.S. to demonstrate against discriminatory laws. AIM survived the Nixon-Ford administrations' repression, and the nationalist spirit among the Indian people continued to rise.

The recent history of the Chicano *movimiento* provides even more parallels with the rise and fall of black nationalism. Before 1960, there were almost five million Chicanos in the U.S. Although hundreds of thousands still provided cheap labor for the ranches, vegetable and fruit farms of California, Texas, and other southwestern states, many Mexican-American families flocked to urban areas in search of higher pay and a decent standard of living. San Diego, Los Angeles, Denver, Phoenix, Tucson, Albuquerque, El Paso, and San Antonio acquired large Chicano working- and middle-class populations. Smaller Chicano neighborhoods could be found in Chicago, Kansas City, and even New York. By 1950, two-thirds of all Chicanos lived in urban areas. In 1960, about four out of five Mexican-Americans were urban dwellers. Like blacks, Chicanos occupied the lowest level of industrial and commercial employment, and tended to be confined to manual and semi-skilled blue-collar and service jobs. In the southwestern states in 1960, the median family income of a Chicano family was $4,164, only 64.4 percent that of white median family income in the region. In 1970, national Chicano median family income was still only

$6,002. Over a half of all rural Chicano families were judged by federal authorities to exist below the poverty line, a much higher rate than that among rural whites and about the same level as that of rural blacks. Almost one out of three urban Mexican-American families were poor. The new stresses of urban life impacted upon the social and cultural traditions of Chicano households. By 1970, one out of six Mexican-American families was a single-parent home. Youth gangs became prevalent in the lower income barrios of Los Angeles and San Diego. Of all Chicanos, 85 percent had been born inside the U.S. but according to U.S. census records, 72 percent claimed Spanish as their principal language. Separated by culture, language, and socio-economic status, whites in the Southwest continued to view Chicanos as having only a "temporary or tentative" position within American political society. Anti-Mexican stereotypes and racist language were often tolerated within local political campaigns. In one five-year period during the 1950s, almost four million Mexican-Americans were seized and expelled from the country.[38]

In central California, a traditional vehicle for Chicano working-class opposition emerged in the early 1960s—the National Farm Workers Association of Cesar Chavez. Born in 1927 in Arizona, Chavez began to work as a migrant worker at the age of ten. In 1952 he became active in the Community Service Organization of California and gained experience registering thousands of Chicanos to vote. Ten years later he joined the National Farm Workers Association, and began the tedious and often dangerous process of organizing rural Mexican-American farm laborers. The objective material conditions which California plantation life imposed upon poor Chicanos was literally only a step above slavery. Most workers lived in "barracks-like labor camps," and were forced to accept "polluted drinking water, no toilet facilities, inadequate sanitation and health care, infestation by insects and rodents, and overcrowding." The typical hourly wage in 1969 was $1.33 and "due to the seasonal nature of the work, average annual wages were about $1,000."[39] White farm owners and businessmen routinely fired and harassed Chavez's supporters and organizers from the fields. When Filipino farmworkers began a 1965 strike against California grape-owners, Chavez quickly followed suit. For almost five years, Chavez conducted a massive nationwide boycott of all grapes from California produced by non-unionized laborers. Civil rights organizations, black nationalists, feminist organizations, organized labor and many church groups honored the grape boycott. Despite extraordinary pressure by the agricultural corporations, the union finally forced management to acquiesce to its demands. Chicanos and people of color across the nation were thrilled by the farmworkers' triumph. Chavez himself "emerged as a passionately charismatic leader, a spokesman for the Mexican-American's desire to reclaim his manhood, and a religious leader with the mystic qualities of a Gandhi."[40] Forming his laborers into the United Farm Workers (UFW) of America AFL-CIO, Chavez used his new political leverage in other struggles. In 1973, farmers signed a union contract with the Teamsters, a powerful U.S. union with strong links to organized crime, rather than with the UFW. A second field boycott was waged successfully until 1975, when the state government was forced to intervene. In spite of intimidation by the Teamsters, over two-thirds of all labor elections in 1976 determining the official representatives of the workers were won by the UFW. Chavez's influence grew within both the California and the national Democratic parties, as the UFW pursued national policies which addressed the economic and social needs of low-income whites and all national minorities.

The emergence of Cesar Chavez as a national labor and civil rights leader in the late 1960s marked the simultaneous rise of hundreds of Chicano political activists across the nation. A 1967 survey of five southwestern states indicated that of the 603 members of state legislatures "48 were Mexican-American: the New Mexico legislature having the greatest number—33; and Texas having 10. New Mexico was also represented in the United States Congress by a Mexican-American [senator]."[41] In Colorado, the Crusade for Justice was formed among Denver Chicanos by Rudolfo "Corky" Gonzales. Gonzales developed a political philosophy which paralleled that of Imamu Baraka in the early 1970s, or of Frantz Fanon a decade before, an uneven mixture of fiery nationalism and socialism. Chicano scholar Richard A. Garcia describes Gonzales's approach to politics:

> Gonzales's socialism was somewhat similar to Malcolm X's socialism: it emanated more from experience and emotions than from philosophy and reason. Gonzales's world view posited a society divided into two diametrically opposed categories: Chicanos and Anglos. For him the political and social struggle was always basically bipolar. The Chicano struggle was for equality and freedom, but it was not . . within the United States, but in the mythical Chicano nation of Aztlán. On occasions, for Gonzales, the myth blurred the reality. His basic goal was separation, not integration, and he fought a nationalist, not a workers', struggle. Gonzales's "nationalist heart" was always in conflict with his "socialist head"; he could not fully accept a fusion of socialism and nationalism.[42]

Perhaps the most articulate young proponent of Chicano nationalism was Reies Lopez Tijerina of New Mexico. Tijerina acquired a rural and poor peoples' following in the northern part of his state by campaigning for the return of all lands stolen by the Anglo settlers to their rightful owners, the Chicano peasantry and workers. Despite his militant language and provocative style, Tijerina was probably the most politically moderate of the new generation of leaders. Finally, the most complex and pragmatic activist was from Texas, José Angel Gutierrez. As leader of the Texas La Raza Unida Party, Gutierrez came to national attention by delivering a militant speech termed "Death to the Anglos" at a 1968 south Texas Chicano rally. Gutierrez built an electoral bloc of Chicano voters, and with some marginal degree of national support provided by the Trotskyist Socialist Workers Party and Chicano leftists, effectively challenged the state's Democratic Party from the left. Unlike Gonzales, however, Gutierrez was always a practical politician whose goals for the Chicano *movimiento* were a cultural pluralist society within the context of the U.S., and a greater share of economic and political power for the Chicano people.[43]

By the early 1970s, Chicano activism reached virtually every level of civil and political society in the southwestern U.S. Youth created the Brown Berets in California and Texas, patterned largely after the Black Panther Party cadre. In Texas, the Mexican-American Youth Organization emerged and created ties with Gonzalez's Crusade for Justice. Nationalist-oriented Chicano entrepreneurs joined the *movimiento*, calling for Brown Capitalism and the creation of federal programs which would promote capital formation among their own petty bourgeois strata. Chicano university students initiated MECHA (Movimiento Estudiantil Chicano de Aztlán). In Los Angeles, Marxist-Leninists within the Chicano community created the Center for Autonomous Social Action-General Brotherhood of Workers (CASA-HGT), which championed a Cuban-style socialist agenda.

This unprecedented social ferment impacted the more reformist Chicano associations, exactly as SNCC, the National Black Political Assembly, and the League of Revolutionary Black Workers had influenced the black political mainstream. LULAC was forced to assume a more activist orientation, and began to develop strategies to become involved in state and national politics. Chicano members of the Texas Democratic Party effectively pointed to their left at La Raza Unida, and gradually won substantial concessions from entrenched party conservatives who feared the specter of Gutierrez and the threat of Chicano political hegemony in that state. Despite the multiplicity of organizations and programs which were inspired by "el espiritú de La Raza," political observers concurred that there were four dominant activists who maintained a regional or national presence among Chicano nationalists: Chavez, Gutierrez, Gonzales, and Tijerina. "By 1972 these four chieftains had sectioned off the Southwest and, like the rebels of the Mexican Revolution, each distrusted, envied, and skirmished programmatically with the others," notes Garcia. "Each chieftain had his own personal ideological interpretation of nationalism."[44]

The 1972 El Paso, Texas, convention of the Raza Unida Party was, in critical respects, similar to the Gary Black Political Convention as a highpoint for Chicano nationalism. Delegates at the convention voted to adopt the nationalistic and socialist program of Gonzales, but elected Gutierrez to serve as party chairman. Bitterly disappointed, Gonzales returned to Denver, "beaten and hounded by left-leaning lieutenants." Local police officers stepped up their harassment of the Crusade's activities, and within several years his group fell into a narrow chauvinistic posture, turning "ideologically inward [and] politically and organizationally powerless."[45] Angered by his repudiation, Tijerina rejected the Raza Unida and any efforts to build an independent Chicano political party. Chavez left the convention with a firm commitment to build a Chicano presence in the left wing of the national Democratic Party, and by the late 1970s he exercised a major influence on the policies of the rather eccentric liberal Democratic governor of California, Edmund Brown, Jr. Gutierrez continued to exercise some influence in Texas politics, winning a county judgeship and electing his supporters to local office. But his political style and Machiavellian outlook bothered even his most dedicated followers. After cultivating a cozy relationship with white and Chicano Trotskyists, for example, he personally ordered the delegates from the Socialist Workers Party to be thrown out of the El Paso convention. After the Trotskyists ran a Chicano activist, Pedro Camejo, as their symbolic candidate for president in 1976, Gutierrez warmed toward them again. Taking advantage of the situation, LULAC and other liberal political and cultural groups were able to recover their losses, and recruited thousands of young militants who had become casualties of the fractious battles between various Chicano nationalist formations. One testament to the collapse of La Raza was represented by the July 1977 conference of "Mexican American Democrats" in El Paso. Of the 400 delegates, a majority were middle-class urban liberals, a smaller number of Chicano rural farmers and political conservatives, and some leaders from La Raza Unida Party. The expressed goal of the convention was "to organize Mexican Americans in Texas under a single political banner"—in short, within the populist and liberal flank of the Democratic Party.[46] Neither the Chicano nor the Black movements had collapsed without a trace, yet both had become part of a broader, non-socialist reform impulse which sought incremental change within the system. As the fringe elements of both nationalist movements fought each other, lurching deeper into theoretical confusion and cultural mysticism, the mainstream was able to incorporate the very valid social criticisms of the nationalists into a more realistic and limited series of socio-economic and political goals.

VI

For black and Chicano nationalists, the period of their respective ideological and cultural hegemony had come to an unceremonious end. Splintered, confused, weary of polemical debate, most had returned to their original neighborhoods, far from the national stage, leaving their reformist counterparts firmly in place to dictate the national minority agenda. As the presidential campaign of 1976 proceeded, both Chicano and African-American civil rights leaders prepared to build a solid base of support for whoever the Democratic Party decided to select as its nominee. In the state primaries, an obscure, one-term governor of Georgia began to emerge as the frontrunner, James E. (Jimmy) Carter. Bond was the first black leader to denounce Carter on the basis of principle. He observed that in Carter's primary electoral victory of 1970 in Georgia he polled less than 10 percent of the blacks' votes; that Carter's "running mate" that year was none other than Lester Maddox, the notorious bigot; that Carter did not believe in "traditionally liberal principles and humanistic values"; and that the former governor was a "liar," prone to "chameleon-like rhetoric." [47] Other black leaders, sensing Carter's momentum, ignored the southerner's contradictory background and campaigned vigorously for him. Some of the first to wear "Carter-for-President" buttons were the cultural nationalists, such as Nikki Giovanni. The black mayors, notably Maynard Jackson of Atlanta and Coleman Young of Detroit, were early Carter proponents. Martin's family, including Coretta Scott King and the Reverend Martin Luther King, Sr., campaigned for Carter. Carter's greatest supporter in the black community, and indeed his most valuable ally, was former King aide Andrew Young, then a two-term U.S. representative from Atlanta. After Carter's nomination, the Old Guard went to work to bring the black electorate to the polls. The NAACP and other groups initiated "Operation Big Vote," a campaign to register blacks in 36 major cities. Black supporters of Carter, especially Young, Mrs. King, former SNCC leader John Lewis, and Georgia state senator Ben Brown, travelled and spoke extensively for the Georgian. In November 1976, Carter defeated the incumbent president, Gerald Ford, by 40.3 million v. 38.5 million votes. Carter's electoral college victory was, however, much closer: 297 to 241 votes. As in 1960, blacks proved to be the decisive margin of victory for the Democratic candidate. In one industrial state, Ohio, out of 4 million votes cast, Carter carried the state by a slender margin of 7,600 votes: Ohio's blacks had cast roughly 280,000 ballots for Carter. In Mississippi, Carter polled an 11,500 vote edge over Ford; 59 percent of all whites had voted for Ford, but over 90 percent of the state's 187,000 black voters endorsed Carter. States where the black vote was decisive included Pennsylvania, Alabama, Texas, New York, and seven others. The Carter victory left BEOs and many black political scientists in rapture. Eddie N. Williams, president of the Joint Center of Political Studies in Washington, D.C., announced proudly that Carter's narrow victory had made "blacks full partners in the nation's policy making franchise." The new president should "start by integrating" civil rights leaders and BEOs into the upper hierarchy of the state's "apparatus."[48] Without hesitation, the president-elect notified the press that Young would become the new United Nations ambassador for the U.S. and a full member of Carter's presidential cabinet. Seemingly, a new phase in American race relations had begun; the Second Reconstruction would be renewed.

Many observers viewed Young's appointment as a dramatic vindication of the struggles and sacrifices of King and the entire Civil Rights Movement. Black mayors supported Carter with nervous anticipation, hoping that fresh federal funds would be poured into the major cities for economic development, to restore public schools, health delivery systems and necessary social services. Black desegregation activists such as John Lewis and Louisiana attorney Weldon Rougeau were appointed to power posts in the federal bureaucracy. Yet there were present, even then, troubling indications that Carter's election would not produce meaningful reforms. During Carter's primary campaign in Pennsylvania, he treated black local leaders with a kind of cautious contempt, what political scientist Chuck Stone described as "a veiled warning of retributive hostility."[49] Before the general election, Carter refused to attend national conferences held by the CBC, the black National Association of Media Women, and the National Negro Business League. There was also a larger question to consider. In the four years after the Gary convention, BEOs broke off all organizational ties with black nationalists, and along with the integrationist Old Guard, had reaffirmed their commitment to a bourgeois democratic road toward black freedom. King had died fighting a Democratic president; his protégés now rushed to embrace a Democratic president from a Deep South state, whose own credentials as a proponent of civil rights prior to 1970 were nonexistent. King was killed mobilizing sanitation workers in Memphis and antiwar demonstrators in the streets; his followers had joined with Martin's bitterest black opponents on the right in accepting posts in the new administration. The Civil Rights Movement was flushed with victory, yet in retrospect, it was a victory in defeat. COINTELPRO and the fratricidal struggles between leftists and dogmatic separatists had reduced the nationalist movement to a whimpering, self-flagellating set of marginal sects. The League of Revolutionary Black Workers, DRUM, the Black Workers' Congress and other revolutionary black labor organizations had disappeared. Nationally, black workers and the poor felt more powerless to elicit meaningful social change within the system, and large numbers simply stopped voting. The percentage of the black voting age population who actually voted declined from 57.6 in 1968, 52.1 in 1972, down to 49 in 1976. The black movement for biracial democracy had left the lunch counters and the streets and had moved squarely into the corridors of electoral politics—a process wherein, not coincidentally, millions of blacks became "depoliticised." Could freedom be won in concert with a former segregationist, and within the mechanics of the racist/capitalist state? Retreating from the vision of Gary, most black leaders were now determined to cast their lot with the system that they had for years denounced as racist, in order to gain goods and services for their constituents. Reform, once more, had supplanted rebellion.

7. Reaction: The Demise of the Second Reconstruction, 1976–1982

Without a new vision of ourselves and the world beyond the borders of our persons, many of the events of the 1970s became nothing more than frustrating repetitions of history, new signs of white racism or mystifying novelties and epiphenomena. . . . What kind of a society do we want, and are we willing to struggle for? Without a nationwide pressing of that question among blacks and whites, we surely would not recognize "integration" if we saw it.

Vincent Harding

Starvation is God's way of punishing those who have too little faith in capitalism.

John D. Rockefeller, Sr.

I

Nothing fails like success. By the mid-1970s, the black nationalist impulse had been effectively splintered, repressed, and removed from political discourse. The black élite was retrieved from its marginal and defensive stance within the black community and, with the election of Carter, had unprecedented access to middle-to-upper levels of the political bureaucracy. The BEOs, like the Old Guard of the NAACP and Urban League, viewed the 1976 election as a kind of public ratification for the body of its own politics. Radicalism and militancy were defeated. Wallace, Maddox and the most overtly racist white southern governors and representatives either had been removed from public offices or, at least, no longer postured defiantly against desegregation. Jim Crow signs had been removed

from public restaurants; federally sponsored "affirmative action" programs brought tens of thousands of blacks into middle-class jobs in both
the public and private sectors; blacks were allowed to participate without
restrictions within the political marketplace; urban riots had been quelled,
and ghetto blacks seemingly succumbed to the quiescence of the dominant
society. The general interpretation of the period was, at least for the black
élite, one of tremendous optimism. There was no longer a need to march
in the streets against the policies of big-city mayors, because blacks were
now in virtually every municipal administration across the nation. The
total number of blacks in the Congressional Black Caucus had doubled in
the eight years before Carter's victory; there was every reason to believe
that their numbers would double again in another decade, as more congressional districts became primarily non-white. Certainly, it was said, the
Second Reconstruction was on the verge of success. Black freedom would
become a reality through gradual yet meaningful reforms within the existing system.

The prime beneficiary of the gains from the Second Reconstruction was
the black élite. It is imperative here to describe in some detail the socio-
economic position of this stratum, in order to explain its basically optimistic and reformist outlook. First, and foremost, the black élite was
characterized by its relatively modest size. Only about 50,000 black men
and 200,000 black women were employed as elementary and secondary
schoolteachers in 1977. In that same year, the numbers of black medical
and health-care workers were approximately 50,000 men and 116,000
women; professional and technical white-collar workers, 315,000 men and
505,000 women, respectively; and salaried managers and administrators,
180,000 males and 78,000 females, respectively. In contrast with whites,
however, the actual presence of blacks in white-collar jobs was actually
quite low when compared to their numbers in the overall labor force. In
1977 again, the actual percentage of blacks to all races within the medical
and health-care professions was 3.9 for all men and 8.4 among all women.
Among all salaried administrators and managers, only 3.0 percent of the
men were black, and 5.0 percent of the women employees were black. The
figures decline still further when each white-collar category is analyzed by
specific vocation. Over 90 percent of all black women employed in health
care were nurses or more commonly paramedics and hospital workers. As
late as 1970, the number of black doctors in the U.S. was only 6,106, about
2 percent of the total number of all physicians and surgeons. In the mid-
1970s, there were fewer than 5,000 practicing black attorneys in the U.S.,
about 1 percent of all lawyers.

This élite was in many respects, however, markedly similar in its socio-
economic profile to other upwardly mobile white ethnic groups which had

advanced in previous decades. Many of these men and women had attended the newly desegregated colleges and universities during the 1960s and 1970s. The federal government's requirements for affirmative action forced the admission of large numbers of blacks into positions which they had long been denied, solely on the basis of race. Thus, in the early 1970s, the upper fraction of the black labor force experienced a real advance in its absolute incomes. Between 1969 and 1974, for example, the earnings of the top 5 percent of all non-white families increased from $17,238 to $24,267, about 74 percent of the level for that of white families of similar background. By 1977, 21 percent of all black families had incomes between $15,000 and $24,999, and another 9 percent earned above $25,000. Advances in income were more likely for those black families whose major "breadwinner" had a college education. The median income of black family heads 25 years old and over who had acquired one to three years of college training was $13,371 in 1974 and $15,027 in 1976. For black family heads who had graduated from college, median earnings jumped from $17,316 in 1974 to $20,733 in 1976. For one special group, black husband-wife families below the age of 35 who were both income earners, the income gap between themselves and other white families with a similar socio-cultural profile virtually disappeared. In the South, black husband-wife families in this group earned $14,563 in 1976, roughly 90 percent of the earnings received by white families with the same background. In the North and West, the incomes of young black husband-wife families actually exceeded that of white families, $16,715 to $16,691, in 1976. The traditional income margin of racial inequality, at least for many of the black élite, had been almost eliminated by the mid-1970s.

In other economic aspects, the status of the black élite was remarkably secure. In 1977, for instance, the overall black unemployment rate for civilian workers was 13.1 percent for men, 14.8 percent for women. Black professional and technical workers, however, experienced unemployment rates of 6.1 percent for males, 5.1 percent for females. Black salaried and self-employed managers and administrators had jobless rates of only 5.3 percent and 5.6 percent for males and females respectively. Conversely, in 1977 black males employed as service workers had an unemployment rate of 13.7 percent; black female blue-collar workers experienced a jobless rate of 16.9 percent; and 16.4 percent of all black men who worked as non-farm laborers were without jobs. In the fields of commerce and finance, black entrepreneurs were also registering notable gains. Between 1969 and 1977, the total number of black businesses increased from 163,073 to 231,195; gross receipts of these firms almost doubled, from $4.5 billion to $8.7 billion. Between 1970 and 1975, 24 black-owned banks were founded, compared to only 11 established between 1960 and 1969. Yet even here, the fragility of the economic foundations of the black élite were clearly visible to any researcher. Blacks owned few if any corporations or industries which were most profitable. Fewer than 2 percent of all U.S. construction firms and manufacturing industries were black-owned. Blacks acquired only a half of 1 percent of all wholesale trade firms, financial establishments, insurance companies, and real estate firms. Over 80 percent of all black-owned firms in 1980 did not have a single paid employee, and over one-third of all black-owned establishments failed within twelve months after beginning business. In 1977, only 113 black-owned businesses out of 231,195 had more than 100 paid employees, and another 230 retained only 50 to 99 workers. The upper 0.005 percent of all black firms hired most of the employees and earned 28.5 percent of all black businesses' gross receipts.

Considered as a socio-economic group, the black élite—in the fields of banking, commerce, law, education, and medicine—comprised only 7 to 10 percent of the total African-American population. They were set apart from the vast majority of working-class and impoverished blacks by their relative income parity with whites; their educational training and professional advancement; their political moderation and social conformity; their advocacy of the economics of capitalism and corporate upward mobility. In all critical respects, this group had every reason to applaud the gains of the previous years, the destruction of Jim Crow, and the acceptance of affirmative action within the white-collar workforce. This stratum controlled the NAACP, and the Urban League, as well as other civil rights organizations. It owned or influenced the 50 black-owned radio and television stations which reached into the predominantly black metropolitan areas; it had access to white politicians, corporate leaders and influential social institutions; its own leaders were appointed to President Carter's administration in a variety of capacities. The rise and institutionalization of the black élite during the 1970s had a profound impact upon white and black societies. For whites of all income levels, the emergence of thousands of welll-educated, articulate and aggressive black professionals seemed to require a political "white backlash." Whites assumed incorrectly that the great majority of black Americans were now firmly within the "middle class." In growing numbers, whites asked bitterly: "Why are blacks still demanding civil rights? Segregation has ended, and with affirmative action, partially-qualified blacks are now taking jobs which rightfully belong to better-qualified whites." Conveniently ignoring economic data on the burgeoning millions of black unemployed and the poor, many white liberals and civil rights proponents began to insist that "too much" had been given to all blacks, and that some of the political and economic reforms allotted to non-whites had to be rescinded.

Conversely, the social and economic profile of the black élite was significantly different from that of the white majority, so that the material basis for collective grievance against the system remained. For example, in the higher-status jobs of professionals, managers and the crafts, African-Americans were generally concentrated in the lower-income positions. The 1980 census indicated that nearly one-fifth of all "middle-income" blacks who held "professional jobs" actually had personal income below $6,000 annually. Eighteen percent of all black female managers and 13 percent of all black male managers in 1979 earned wages below the federal government's poverty line. Black household incomes were artificially inflated into middle-class status because of the high proportion of adult women in black two-parent families in the labor force. In the 1980 census, about three in five wives of black two-parent families were in the labor force, significantly higher than the 48 percent for similar white two-parent families. Younger black households displayed an even higher rate of labor force participation. Almost three-fourths of all black adult, married women between the ages of 25 and 34 worked full-time or part-time, compared to only 57 percent of their white counterparts. Working, married women made more decisive contributions to the overall income growth of black households than white households. One-earner black married families had only 50 percent of the median income of two-income-earner black families, while white one-income-earner families received three-fourths of the median income of white two-earner families. Statistically, almost the entire income gain registered by black households compared to that of white families in the 1970s and early 1980s was represented by black two-parent families, in which both spouses were in the workforce.

Yet the narrowing of the income gap even within these select groups of middle-class families did not indicate a convergence of actual wealth or capital resources by the black élite, compared to affluent whites. According to William P. O'Hare, as of 1979 the median wealth of black households was $24,608, well below the median wealth figure of $68,891 for white households. O'Hare observed critically: "The income of whites was about 1.7 times that of blacks, but the wealth of whites was almost three times that of blacks. Looked at another way, white households had a total wealth that was four times their income, while blacks had a total wealth of about 2.5 times their income." [1] As of 1979, the combined personal wealth held by all African-Americans was $211 billion, which amounted to only 4 percent of the more than $5 trillion owned by white Americans. Compared to working-class blacks, the black élite therefore had a relatively "privileged" position. But the middle class generally recognized that its own material status remained marginal, and that the great American "dream" of economic mobility and capital accumulation remained more of an illusion than reality. Economist Robert Hill observed that the attitudes of racial militancy of middle-income blacks were often stronger and more assertive than those expressed by lower-income blacks. Surveys taken in 1979 indicated that 83 percent of all middle-income African-Americans expressed the opinion that the struggle for racial equality was progressing "too slow," compared to a similar response among only 73 percent of poor blacks. Seventy percent of middle-income African-Americans expressed the view that "a great deal of racial discrimination against blacks" still existed in the United States. Hill noted: "Similar patterns of bias among middle-income and low-income black families were prevalent regarding getting credit, applying for loans, property vandalism and contacts with the police. . . . These data should help to explain why middle class blacks have traditionally been in the vanguard of the struggle for racial equality since slavery." [2] The data also illustrate the economic basis for middle-class protest, which would help to motivate the Jackson presidential campaigns of 1984 and 1988.

II

While the black élite advanced, the social and economic conditions for the majority of blacks remained the same and in some respects grew worse. Millions of blacks in the South and North lived in dilapidated, rat-infested dwellings. In 1970, 61 percent of all black families living in rural areas and 8 percent of black urban households lacked some or all plumbing facilities, compared to only 11 percent for rural whites and 2 percent of urban whites; 902,000 black families residing in the South lived in housing units which had either no toilets or incomplete plumbing facilities. Many black families lived in overcrowded apartments or rented houses in which their landlords, who usually were white, denied them adequate heat and other essentials. In urban renter-occupied dwellings, one-fifth of all black homes had a person-per-room ratio above 1.01 persons per room in 1970—a clear indication of overcrowded conditions. In rural areas and in the South, housing conditions were worse: 29 percent of all southern black renters and 19 percent of southern black homeowners lived in crowded housing. Among rural blacks who rented their dwellings, overcrowded conditions affected 40 percent of all families. Almost one-fourth of all rural black renters had an incredible person-per-room ratio above 1.5. Given these dire living conditions, it is not surprising that a disproportionately high number of blacks suffer from certain types of illnesses compared to whites. U.S. census statistics for 1974 revealed that blacks suffered much higher death rates than whites per 100,000 population in many categories: for tuberculosis, blacks had an annual death rate of 4.1 to the white death rate of

1.3; syphilis, 0.5 for blacks, 0.1 for whites; hypertension, 5.3 for blacks, 1.3 for whites; early infancy diseases, 29 for blacks, 11.3 for whites. Overall, by race and gender, blacks' life expectancies from birth were lower than those for whites. Using 1974 statistics, black males' life expectancy was 62.9 years; white males, 68.9 years; black females, 71.2 years; white females, 76.6 years. Black womens' mortality rates during childbirth were 600 percent higher than among white women in 1970. Out of every thousand, 16.8 black newborn infants died before reaching their first month, compared to only 10.4 white infants in 1975.

The most disturbing social characteristic within black America in the post-segregation period was the upward spiral in the rate of homicide. Trapped in the urban ghettoes of America's decaying inner cities, plagued with higher unemployment rates, disease, bad housing, poor public schools, and inadequate social services, young blacks were filled with a sense of anger, self-hatred, and bitterness. In the 1960s, this black rage lashed out against the symbols of white property, power and privilege. Black Power provided unemployed black youth with an opportunity to vent their collective anger into a political act of defiance. In the wake of the demise of militant black nationalism, and with the flight of the black élite into the safe havens of suburbia, the ghetto's black rage was unleashed against itself. In 1960, the homicide rate per 100,000 blacks was 21.9, slightly less than the black homicide figure of 1910 (22.3). By 1970, the black homicide rate reached 35.5 percent, compared to a 4.4 figure among American whites. During the Nixon, Ford and Carter administrations, black fratricidal violence soared. About 55 black males per thousand were the victims of violent crime during the 1970s. Of all black working-class and impoverished households 13 to 16 percent experienced robberies every year in the decade. Black male homicide rates were between 600 and 900 percent higher than those for whites by the late 1970s. And by 1980, 50 percent of all American homicides were black males killing other black males. The rise in urban violent crime allowed white politicians and corporate interests to increase the number of police and law enforcement officers within the black community. U.S. per capita police expenditures jumped 39 percent between 1970 and 1977. Federal government and local government expenditures for police in 1977 reached $1.4 billion and $8.8 billion, respectively. Despite sizeable increases in police spending, white Americans of all classes became terrified of the omnipresent specter of the "black criminal, rapist and burglar." By 1978, nine out of ten U.S. citizens were convinced that the courts were not attacking crime vigorously enough, and almost half were afraid to walk in their own neighborhoods. As a result, the urban centers of the nation were rapidly becoming permanently armed camps.

The social consequences of crime and fear were soon manifested in a more authoritarian treatment for blacks within the U.S. criminal justice system. By the late 1970s, over two million black Americans, a figure equalling 8 percent of the total black population, were arrested every year. Despite vast amounts of money spent to halt crime, almost nothing was done to improve the physical conditions of jails and prisons, or to initiate rehabilitation programs for persons convicted of crimes. In the state of Illinois, to cite one example, over $160 million was appropriated to the Illinois Department of Corrections in fiscal 1979. Of that sum, only $9,000 was spent on improving the facilities in the state's prisons. Many states abandoned "indeterminate sentencing" in favor of "mandatory sentences" for specific crimes. American critics of the prison system noted that "the trend is currently toward warehousing and punishment rather than toward rehabilitation, which is the professed goal of state prisons."[3] States passed "habitual offender laws," which ordered the life imprisonment of any person who had been sentenced a second time for certain crimes, including murder, treason, or "deviate sexual assault." To intimidate would-be felons, a few state governments experimented with novel methods. In May 1982, the state legislature of Georgia ordered the creation of a "mobile death wagon." Georgia's electric chair was literally placed on wheels, as it were, "so condemned criminals can be executed near the scene" of their alleged crimes."[4]

As the social environment continued to deteriorate, many black families began to splinter under the forces of oppression. The number of children born to unmarried black women increased significantly. In 1950, only 88,000 births among non-whites were outside wedlock. In 1975, the figure for blacks reached 250,000, 48.8 percent of all black births recorded that year. Birth rates, which had declined among blacks between 1900 and 1960, began to increase, especially among the uneducated and the poor. For black married women with an eighth-grade education or less, the average number of children increased from 3.6 in 1960 to 4.8 in 1975. Of all black married women between the ages of 35 and 39 years in 1975, 36 percent had five or more children, and another 46 percent had two to four children. As birth rates soared, the percentage of black children who lived with both parents dropped. Only 17 percent of all black children in 1975 lived with both parents in households where the total annual income was below $4,000. That same year 957,100 black children whose families earned between $4,000 and $5,900 annually lived with only one adult, while only 391,000 children in the same income group lived with both parents. Even for upper-income levels, the tendency for black children to live with only one adult was much greater among blacks than whites. Of all children from black families earning above $15,000, 86 percent lived in two-parent households, yet for whites of similar income the figure was 97 percent. Increasingly, some black women were having difficulty even finding males of marriageable age in certain metropolitan communities. Nationally, the percentage of black women 14 years old and over who were married declined from 60 in 1960 to 49 in 1975. The number of black women who were divorced doubled in this fifteen-year period; black households maintained by females with no husband present increased from 843,000 in 1960 to 1,940,000 in 1975.

By the late 1870s, American social scientists were struggling to develop new theoretical models to explain the destructive process of socio-economic disruption which was taking place in the ghetto. The most celebrated yet widely criticized effort was that of William Julius Wilson, author of the 1978 sociological study *The Declining Significance of Race*. Wilson's objective was to explain the evolution of race and class in American history, and the factors behind more recent economic problems within the urban black community. Wilson argued that the economy and the government had interacted in various historical periods to structure race relations, producing different contexts for racial antagonisms and divergent situations for racial group access to rewards, power and privilege. During the period of Jim Crow segregation, economic competition between the races over housing, jobs and political power had led to severe restrictions for blacks, including lynchings and electoral disfranchisement. The Civil Rights Movement, according to Wilson, marked a new historical phase in which "race declined in significance," as the government supported desegregation and African-Americans were integrated into the economic and social structure of the society as a whole. By the late 1970s, economic class had become "a more important factor than race in determining job placement for blacks," because most blacks had apparently made it into the middle class. Further governmental action was required "to attack inequality on a broad class front" with programs designed to uplift the urban "underclass," those who were stuck in poverty, illiteracy and unemployment.[5]

Wilson's thesis was disputed on several grounds. Sociologist Harry Edwards dismissed *The Declining Significance of Race* as a "mediocre work with a highly controversial title." Race, rather than class, continued to be central as the dominant factor of oppression, Edwards insisted. Critic Charles Payne raised other objections. Wilson was an "economic determinist of the narrower sort" who had lost "contact with the possibly independent effects of racial belief systems." He had ignored the social psychological impact of racism upon whites, minimizing the role of bigotry in contemporary conservative public policies. Wilson's assertion that continued racial antagonism in the cities was essentially between lower-income blacks and whites over economic issues underestimated white middle-class opposition to affirmative action, school desegregation and other manifestations of black group advancement. Harvard sociologist Charles Willie also blamed Wilson for the error of "particularism," perceiving racism by its individual "traits" rather than by its systemic, complex characteristics. This was the reason that Wilson ignored evidence that racism had actually increased for middle-income blacks, who were now coming more frequently into direct contact with whites because of legal desegregation.[6]

Wilson was angered and disappointed with the criticism surrounding *The Declining Significance of Race*, which he felt generally distorted his arguments. His critics "virtually ignored [his] more important arguments about the deteriorating conditions of the black underclass." Because he had urged civil rights leaders to shift from race-based remedies to class-oriented programs, the "erroneous perception" had developed "among some people that I am a black conservative," Wilson complained.[7] In his next work, *The Truly Disadvantaged* (1987), Wilson attempted to address his critics as well as provide the basis for a more enlightened urban policy. The basic question motivating Wilson's research was the troubling social class polarization between middle-income and lower-class blacks. His subsequent findings challenged both liberal and conservative assumptions and approaches to issues of poverty and race. Wilson openly rejected the liberals' refusal to employ terms such as "underclass," their emphasis on selective black achievement and denial of the existence of crime and social disruption, and their tendency to emphasize racism as the explanation for urban problems. He also rejected the white conservatives' thesis that economic success stemmed from cultural characteristics, or that the rise of female-headed households among blacks was caused by liberal social policies, welfare dependency or permissive attitudes. Instead, Wilson targeted black male joblessness, the economic disinvestment in central cities and other economic factors as the chief causes for "underclass" development. He concluded that "many of the problems plaguing the truly disadvantaged minorities in American society can be alleviated by a program of economic reform," a comprehensive social democratic agenda that would rebuild central cities and create new jobs and opportunities.[8] Wilson's book clearly indicated that, although he believed racial prejudice would inevitably disappear because it was a barrier to an expansive capitalist economy, affirmative action policies and other race-sensitive remedies would continue to be necessary so long as the work force was stratified into racial groups. These positions once again alienated critics on both the right and the left. Conservatives insisted that Wilson's empirical evidence illustrated the reasons why affirmative action policies were pernicious. The Association of Black Sociologists had previously condemned Wilson's thesis for obscuring "the problem of the persistent oppression of blacks" by promoting economistic, non-race based policies.[9] Such criticisms aside, Wilson's chief accomplishment was to force social scientists and policy makers alike to rethink old assumptions about the root causes of poverty and "underclass" development.

Theories of the black underclass began to be popularized in sociological literature by the early 1980s. For instance, Douglas G. Glasgow's *Black Underclass* (1981) outlined the development of a hard-core number of young blacks who had virtually no social or economic prospects for advancement. Unlike previous generations of impoverished blacks, the members of this new social strata "were jobless and lacked saleable skills and opportunities to get [jobs]; they had been rejected and labeled as social problems by the police, the schools, the employment and welfare agencies; they were victims of the new camouflaged racism." The urban society had become a social nightmare, in Glasgow's view, an environment in which black men "drank, gambled [and] fought," where "hustling, quasi-legitimate schemes, and outright deviant activity are also alternatives to work." [10] The principal weakness of the "underclass" sociological theses, whether advanced by Glasgow, Wilson or other social scientists, was a faulty theoretical understanding of both "class" and "race" as social constructions. Underclass theorists defined class purely as a function of income rather than of one's relationship to the means of production and the ownership of wealth and property. Consequently, they tended to be overly optimistic in their projections of middle-class development among blacks, and they underestimated the utility of the racial division of labor as a primary factor in the modern capitalist economy. If racism was not irrational but was a logical and systemic part of the political economy of American capitalism, then efforts to reform the system would never resolve the crisis of the underclass. And as the social scientists debated among themselves, the dimensions of the urban social crisis grew increasingly worse. City services, slipping badly in the 1960s, sharply diminished in the 1970s and 1980s. Uncollected garbage, sewage in open streets, rats and cockroaches, dilapidated apartments, buildings gutted by fire, police brutality, reductions in health care and welfare services—all of these social and economic characteristics had become increasingly familiar to millions of lower-income African-Americans.

III

In the mid-1970s, Vincent Harding notes, "everything seemed to change, the organic center fell apart." [11] In this environment of black upper-class success and black working-class poverty and repression, many blacks turned in large numbers to religion. With the overt suppression of revolutionary black nationalist groups, the Nation of Islam was in a position to recapture some of its former power. Most black radicals, influenced heavily by Malcolm X's public separation from and feud with the Nation in 1964–65, still viewed the organization with a great deal of skepticism. But Elijah Muhammad, the octogenarian who still reigned with an iron hand, was able to regain a degree of allegiance among new generations of urban black youth who were searching for spiritual and political direction. Simultaneously, Muhammad attempted to establish closer links with the U.S. government and other foreign interests in an effort to resolve his group's ongoing political and economic troubles. By making peace with Chicago's political boss, Richard Daley, the Nation was able to eliminate most of the police surveillance and harassment against the sect. Imitating the FBI, Nation of Islam members in Philadelphia destroyed that city's Black Panther Party headquarters in retaliation for the group's public advocacy of Malcolm X's ideas. In 1972, Muhammad negotiated a $3 million interest-free loan from Colonel Muamar Kadafi which was used to expand Black Muslim enterprises. Despite these gains, the Nation of Islam was still plagued by internal dissension. One of the Nation's most dynamic and powerful ministers, Hamaas Abdul Khaalis (Ernest McGhee) denounced the Nation as a corruption of the true faith, Sunni Islam, in 1972. Khaalis declared that Muhammad was "a lying deceiver" and stated that their leader "who inspired former dope addicts and prostitutes to monklike lives of sacrifice, discipline and hard work, was instead stealing his followers' money and leading them to hell."[12] For devout defenders of Muhammad, Khaalis's challenge could not remain unanswered. On 18 January 1973, at least five armed gunmen, all members of the Nation of Islam, entered Khaalis's Washington, D.C., home and butchered five members of his family.

With Muhammad's death in 1975, the leadership of the Nation of Islam passed to one of his sons, Wallace. Quickly and efficiently, Wallace Muhammad "Malcolmized" the organization within two years. The paramilitary formation, the Fruit of Islam, was disbanded; the mixture of racial mythology and religious dogma promulgated by Elijah Muhammad was abandoned in favor of the orthodox teachings of Islam; whites were permitted to attend services and in some instances even joined the group. The Nation was renamed the World Community of al-Islam in the West. In other matters, however, Wallace Muhammad did not abandon the overtures of his father toward Arab nations and the American government. In 1976 he obtained a gift of $16 million from Sheikh Sultan Ben Mohammad al-Qasimi, head of Sharjah, United Arab Emirates, to construct a new educational institution and a mosque. The World Community of al-Islam even succeeded in obtaining government contracts with the U.S. Army to package food and supplies for troops. Yet these dramatic changes did not occur without more dissension. Louis Farrakhan, perhaps the most charismatic minister in the Nation after the departure of Malcolm X, quietly left the Nation by 1978. In February 1981, Farrakhan announced the creation of the "old" Nation of Islam under his direction, following the tenets of Elijah Muhammad. Several thousand blacks soon flocked to Farrakhan's group, while many others simply withdrew from both versions of Islam, disillusioned and embittered. The decline and disintegration of the Nation represented in Harding's view the death of a "[corrupt] and dictatorial organization that had essentially separated itself from the day-to-day struggles of our people. It means the loss of a community that most blacks never formally joined, but which seemed to exist—sometimes romantically—on behalf of certain unspoken feelings and desires in millions of hearts and minds." [13]

Growing numbers of poor and dispossessed blacks turned to evangelical Christianity to find some comfort in their shattered lives. The great majority of itinerant preachers who were outside the old established churches in the black community were simply harmless rogues, plying their rhetorical craft in exchange for modest financial wealth, consoling the poor and the hopeless with a flair for drama and hokum. Others were more dangerous. One dynamic white preacher in Indianapolis, James Jones, developed his "People's Temple" with a predominantly black constituency. Moving his congregation to Ukiah, California, in the mid-1960s, Jones started a series of self-help institutions, an animal shelter, and a farm. Relocating to the black Fillmore district of San Francisco in 1970, Jones quickly established a popular following. Elderly and poor blacks joined People's Temple to benefit from the congregation's impressive array of social services. Almost 2,000 people were given free breakfasts and dinners every day at the Temple; young children were educated in the group's day-care program; teenagers were attracted to the social activities and the church's film workshop, printing press and carpentry workshop. Jones recruited social workers and counselors to assist members in completing forms to receive welfare benefits, and to aid them with other economic problems.

Within several years, Reverend Jones began to orient the church toward specific political struggles. His sermons and public statements became increasingly linked with other progressive organizations, from the radical American Indian Movement to black community activist groups. People's Temple members were organized into a political machine, registering black and other Third World people, and they mobilized thousands of inner city voters in support of liberal and socialist-leaning Democratic candidates. As a result, Jones became an influential figure in northern California politics and a political ally of two prominent black leaders, California lieutenant governor Mervyn Dymally and state assemblyman Willie Brown of San Francisco. For many white liberals and socialists, "the Temple was a remarkable institution—a mass political organization in the form of a revivalist church—and they praised it for bringing many poor blacks to demonstrations and involving them in the daily work of local campaigns."[14] Thousands of Bay Area residents read Jones's newspaper, the *Peoples Forum*, which claimed a circulation of 600,000. Democratic Party officials and civil rights leaders valued Jones's support, and praised the People's Temple's political activities. Glowing letters of endorsement and support for Jones were written by Wallace Muhammad, San Francisco mayor George Moscone, Roy Wilkins, Vice President Walter Mondale and the president's wife, Rosalynn Carter. Jones was appointed to a post in the San Francisco city administration, and was applauded for his members' outstanding and vigorous activities in community services and local politics. Beneath this façade of respectability, however, People's Temple was a veritable haven of fear and corruption: drugs, rape and aberrant sexual behavior, beatings and psychological torture of members.

In 1976–77 Jones ordered the movement of People's Temple to the South American nation of Guyana. Jones used his massive political credentials, his support from the U.S. vice president and other American dignitaries, to persuade the Guyanese government to allow the settlement to develop. By 1978 People's Temple had established a 3,000-acre estate in northwestern Guyana called "Jonestown," settled by 1,000 American citizens. The small town quickly cultivated crops, which were sold to Guyanese, Trinidadian, and Venezuelan markets. To secure his village, Jones and his followers purchased large amounts of arms and military equipment. In this secluded jungle haven, Jones's tendencies toward sexual brutality, paranoia and megalomania were increased tenfold. When an American congressman investigating rumors of Jones's enterprise visited Jonestown, he and his party were murdered. In desperation, Jones ordered his followers to commit suicide, along with himself and his wife: 912 bodies were recovered in Jonestown by Guyanese authorities; over two-thirds of the victims were African-Americans. The tragedy of Jonestown raised many still unresolved questions among U.S. blacks. U.S. medical services personnel performed no autopsies on the corpses; American government officials and politicians who had once been supporters of Jones offered no explanations or views on the mass suicides; rumors that Jones held up to $12 million in foreign banks were "suppressed." One black activist, Jitu Weusi, called on the United Nations to "perform an investigation into the imminent possibility" that Jonestown was a prelude to black "genocide. While the act physically occurred in Guyana," the Brooklyn, New York leader declared, "the architects for mass murder was a product of the decadent society of white, capitalist United States of America. . . . The questions and unexplained circumstances of the Jonestown massacre are entirely too numerous for us as a people to simply ignore and file as the actions of a religious fanatic and his misguided flock." [15] For white progressives, the entire fiasco called into question their "particular responsibility" for aiding an evangelical maniac to brutalize sexually, intimidate, and finally to murder innocent people. The editors of *Socialist Review* declared,

> No attempts to blame the Jonestown tragedy on the forces of anomic capitalism or on a paranoid leader who saw himself as the reincarnation of Christ and Lenin, or on the CIA, can free us of the need to explain why the Temple grew and why it was accepted as an ally of progressive movements in a region where the left is as strong as anywhere in the nation. . . . The damage done by Jonestown cannot be repaired; beyond the immediate horrors, it will remain for years a nightmarish vision of socialism as death, as passivity and escapism taken to their limits. [16]

IV

Throughout black political history in the twentieth century, most black activists, intellectuals and protest leaders have been preoccupied with the issue of "race," in an attempt to destroy the institutional barriers of inequality within society and the economic system. Relatively few of these leaders recognized the striking parallels between racial discrimination and institutions and policies of domination rooted in gender or sexual divisions. Women, like blacks, suffered from an absence of full political representation within the government. In the economy, they tended to occupy the lowest job categories and received less wages for comparable work done by males. They were generally denied supervisory or administrative positions, despite their educational abilities or technical qualifications. Property and productive resources were usually owned by males; business decisions were largely made in all-male confines, either at corporate headquarters or in country clubs segregated by sex. Culturally, male dominance was reinforced in the media, educational institutions and the arts. And as in racism, sexism was perpetuated by the ugly reality of violence— rape, sexual abuse, forced sterilization, and other forms of coercion. African-American women recognized the particularity of their oppression both as blacks and as women, even if the vast majority of black males were blind to this pervasive system of gender discrimination and exploitation.

In the previous period of the black power revolt, when the question of sexism was mentioned at all, black protest leaders and intellectuals generally dismissed the unique oppression of women as peripheral to the concerns of African-Americans as a group. Civil rights and black nationalist organizations had very few women within their leadership or policy-making positions. Racism was perceived as destroying the "manhood" of the Negro, a perception that denied the special reality of black womanhood in the struggle against racist dehumanization. Many examples can be cited for these sexist perspectives within the black movement. Stokely Carmichael and Eldridge Cleaver were only two flagrant models of discriminatory behavior toward women in general and black women in particular. In his lectures to college students, Carmichael had repeatedly declared: "Every Negro is a potential black man. We came to this country as black men and as Africans. It took us four hundred years to become Negroes." He accused black young women at Morgan State University of being responsible for defining "the criteria for black people concerning their beauty" and for failing to maintain black nationalist cultural and aesthetic standards.[17] Cleaver crudely equated black empowerment with the assertion of male sexuality and female subordination. Racism's greatest destructive crime, at least for Cleaver, was the imposition of "the naked abyss of negated masculinity upon the black man." The victim of psychological "castration," Cleaver declared, "my spirit was unwilling and my flesh was weak. . . . Instead of inciting the slaves to rebellion with eloquent oratory, I soothed their hurt and eloquently sang the Blues!"[18] Such anguish belonged to men alone, from this sexist vantage point. Black male social scientists generally reinforced such popular sexist stereotypes. Prominent sociologist Kenneth Clark, for example, insisted that the assertiveness and strength of African-American women was somehow directly responsible for "the weaker role of the Negro male." An aspect of black oppression was therefore perpetuated by "the prevalent idea" among young black males "that it is not masculine to sustain a stable father or husband relationship with a woman."[19]

Although black women activists for generations had challenged such perceptions of gender inferiority, an explicitly critical ideological current of black feminism did not develop until the 1970s. Initially, some black women attempted to distance themselves from the issues raised by the growing white feminist movement, arguing that blacks as a racial category were subjected to greater oppression than white females. Typical of this current was the observation of Linda LaRue in 1970: "Is there any logical comparison between the oppression of the black woman on welfare who has difficulty feeding her children and the discontent of the suburban mother who has the luxury to protest the washing of the dishes on which her family's full meal was consumed? . . . Can we really expect that white women, when put in direct competition for employment [with blacks], will be any more open-minded than their male counterparts?"[20] Others agreed with LaRue, but went further to outline the feature of sexist exploitation that affected the lives of African-American women. In 1978 Elizabeth Hood concurred that most middle-class white females had defined women's liberation as having "access to those thrones traditionally occupied by white men." But Hood also criticized the sexism of black male leaders as destructive to the goals of black liberation.[21]

The decisive turning point in black feminist criticism occurred in the years 1979–83, as a rich and intellectually diverse body of literature, social essays, and activist organizations developed. Certainly the most controversial black feminist writer to emerge was Michele Wallace. Before the age of thirty, Wallace authored a widely read manifesto condemning sexism within the black movement—*Black Macho and the Myth of the Superwoman*, published in 1980. Wallace denounced the "myth of the black man's castration" as a vehicle for justifying the exploitation of black women. She bitterly accused the contemporary black man of betraying black women's interests by perceiving them as "possessions . . . the black woman was a symbol of defeat, and therefore of little use to the revolution except as the performer of drudgery (not unlike her role in slavery)." Wallace argued that all political and economic power was based on a gender division, and that any racial tensions which separated black and white males were secondary to the more fundamental divisions of wealth, privilege and authority within the societal hierarchy. Even more damaging for Wallace were the black man's sexist delusions concerning himself and his place in the world. "The contemporary black man no longer exists for his people or even for himself," she stated. Her fatal flaw was that his "black perspective, like the white perspective, supported the notion that manhood is more valuable than anything else."[22] Wallace's polemic sparked lively debate and was the object of much political and even personal denunciation. In some quarters, she was accused of representing the interests of white feminists, devoted to the disruption of the black freedom movement. But despite her tendency to oversimplify the complexities of gender and racial issues, the concerns raised in *Black Macho* forced elements of the African-American community to confront the question of women's oppression for the first time.

A feminist social critic who raised similar concerns was Bell Hooks. Born in rural Kentucky and educated at the University of Wisconsin and the University of California-Santa Cruz in the 1970s, Hooks was trained in Afro-American literature. In her first important work, *Ain't I A Woman*, published in 1981, Hooks criticized the history of sexism within the black community. Writing without the harshness of Wallace, Hooks attempted to establish the foundations for creative and humanistic dialogue between African-American women and men. She identified social class exploitation as perpetuating the practices of elitism and prejudice within human inter-

action. In a subsequent work, *Feminist Theory: From Margin to Center,*
Hooks suggested that racial, gender and class oppression created a structure of domination, which the system's victims helped to perpetuate. She
criticized those feminists who argued with "dogmatic" certainty that all
males were "the enemy," and urged both sexes to "re-think and re-shape"
the direction of the social protest movement for women's emancipation.
"Our emphasis must be on cultural transformation," Hooks argued. "Any
effort to make feminist revolution here can be aided by the example of liberation struggle led by oppressed peoples globally who resist formidable
powers." [23] At the core of Hooks was a poetic humanist, a committed
writer and artist who sought to reconcile her ideals and values with strategies to transform oppressive institutions. Her insistence that social change
must, of necessity, involve a detailed and critical reevaluation of the self
and community challenged black activists, particularly males, who all too
frequently developed programs for empowerment that ignored the question of values.

Angela Davis had already acquired an international reputation for political activism as the most prominent American Communist. But with the
1981 publication of *Women, Race and Class,* Davis made a major contribution to the literature of black feminist history. Unlike Hooks, who gave
equal weight to gender, race and class components in the dynamics of oppression, Davis believed that class was fundamentally decisive in perpetuating social divisions. *Women, Race and Class* reinterpreted the black
past, suggesting that African-American women were active creators of
black history and were responsible for important manifestations of collective resistance. Davis noted the racial biases of many white suffragists in
the nineteenth century and of white, middle-class feminists in the twentieth century, biases which perpetuated the divisions between themselves
and women of color. She highlighted the singular political contributions of
Communist and radical women to the struggles against class, race and gender domination. Davis's emphasis on traditional Marxist categories seemed
to some critics to veer toward economic determinism. Her explanation for
rape, for instance, was to note that "the class structure of capitalism encour-
ages men who wield power in the economic and political realm to become
routine agents of sexual exploitation. . . . It is not a mere coincidence that
as the incidence of rape has arisen, the [economic] position of women workers has visibly worsened." In a harsh review, historian Nell Irvin Painter
attacked Davis for "growing wooden, conjuring up images of socialist real-
ism rather than a recognizable past." [24] Painter's characterization neglected
Davis's larger intellectual and political contribution to progressive protest
movements within the United States, and the theoretical advance which
Women, Race and Class represented to black feminist thought.

Even more challenging than the writings of Davis and Hooks were the insights of black radical lesbian theorists, who included homophobia, or the systematic discrimination against lesbians and gay males, as an issue which challenged the black movement. A pivotal intellectual figure was Barbara Smith, a literary critic, essayist and short story writer. As co-editor of the provocative *All the Women Are White, All the Blacks Are Men, But Some of Us Are Brave: Black Women's Studies*, published in 1982, and editor of *Home Girls: A Black Feminist Anthology*, released in 1983, Smith helped many to recognize at long last the organic "womanist" tradition which underscored African-American history. Smith defined this tradition as the black woman's "ability to function with dignity, independence, and imagination in the face of total adversity." Smith criticized the narrow race-based organizing of the black nationalists, and the dogmatic econo-mism of many Marxists, both of whom tended to ignore the central role of homophobia and sexism as factors in the general oppression of African-American people, women and men alike. Smith emphasized the necessity for activists to mobilize around issues cutting across gender, sexual iden-tity, class and race, such as sterilization abuse, health care, child care, rape, educational reform, and reproductive rights. "A Black feminist analysis has enabled us to understand that we are not hated and abused because there is something wrong with us," Smith observed, "but because our status and treatment is absolutely prescribed by the racist, misogy-nistic system under which we live." [25]

Other black feminist writers who influenced the directions of the black and progressive movements during these years included poet/essayists June Jordan and Audre Lorde. Born in 1936, Jordan first established her literary reputation as a talented and creative poet in *Some Changes* (1971), *New Day: Poems of Exile and Return* (1974), *Things That I Do in the Dark* (1977) and *Passion* (1980). But her political essays, collected in *Civil Wars* (1981) and *On Call* (1985) revealed an insightful and critical mind, linking the issues of social justice and peace in a variety of cultural and social con-texts, from Nicaragua to America's ghettos. The strengths of Lorde's po-etry were first recognized by Langston Hughes in the early 1960s, when the older poet included selections of her work in an edited anthology, *New Negro Poets* (1962). Lorde's perception, creative depth and passion were realized in a series of outstanding works: *Cables to Rage* (1970), *From a Land Where Other People Live* (1973), *Between Our Selves* (1976), *The Black Unicorn* (1978), and *Chosen Poems Old and New* (1982). But it was Lorde's courageous testament of her struggle with breast cancer and the personal agony of mastectomy, *The Cancer Journals* (1980), which chal-lenged other black writers to address the most intimate questions within a broader, socially responsible discourse. Lorde's short but influential 1978 essay, "Scratching the Surface: Some Notes on Barriers to Women and Loving," forced many within the black movement to question their latent or expressed homophobia.[26]

The majority of young black women found encouragement and reinforcement in the writings and public careers of such prominent feminists, who had raised issues with practical relevance to other women. By the early 1980s, it had become increasingly difficult for male leaders and intellectuals to dismiss the demands of women within their own formations, or to assert with smug confidence that gender oppression was irrelevant to the interests of the black community. The patriarchal illusion that only males should make policy decisions was shattered by the dynamic examples of black women, who consistently were at the forefront of political and social reforms. In the field of the socio-economic rights of children, for example, the most influential voice during the 1980s and 1990s was unquestionably Marian Wright Edelman. Born in South Carolina in 1939, Edelman had received her law degree from Yale University and had served briefly as NAACP Legal Defense Fund staff attorney. In the 1960s she served for several years as a member of the executive committee of SNCC, and subsequently worked as a congressional liaison for King's Poor People's Campaign. In 1973, Edelman became president and founder of the Children's Defense Fund, a formation designed to improve public sector policies regarding children, such as the extension of health care, housing, educational and social service reforms. In the 1980s Edelman was in the national forefront challenging the growing social conservatism of Congress and the executive branch. In 1983, the Children's Defense Fund initiated a nationwide campaign to reduce pregnancies among teenagers. Edelman's *Portrait of Inequality: Black and White Children in America* (1980) and *Families in Peril: An Agenda for Social Change* (1987) set the agenda for liberals and progressives regarding the rights of children.[27] Despite the escalating social class and political contradictions which generated a sense of malaise and disillusionment among many African-Americans during the demise of the Second Reconstruction, one of the singularly hopeful signs of creative resistance and intellectual innovation was represented by black women.

V

From the beginning, Jimmy Carter seemed an unlikely champion of blacks' rights and political reform. The Georgia peanut farmer was the first candidate to defeat an incumbent president since 1932; he was the first Democrat to be elected from the Deep South since the narrow victory of James K. Polk of Tennessee over Henry Clay in 1844. Carter's election was due to overwhelming black support, but also to his ability to obfuscate essential public policy issues. His entire campaign rested on three "chief slogans: 'I will never lie to you,' 'The Golden Rule [should] be applied in all public matters,' and 'It is now a time for healing'—[which] specifically repudiated the deception, rancor, and divisiveness associated with Watergate."[28] Repeatedly, Carter identified himself to black supporters with the racially egalitarian image of Southern Populism which had flourished three generations earlier. Populist historian Lawrence Goodwyn noted, however, that the president's "paternal forebears were credit merchants who, like their counterparts elsewhere in the South, managed to acquire title to much of the surrounding countryside. As such, from a Populist perspective, they were part of the problem, not part of the solution."[29] Indeed, a fuller examination of Carter's own rise to power indicated a close and cordial relationship with corporate interests whch had perpetuated world-wide racial oppression and, in earlier years, racial segregation. Carter was a prominent member of the Trilateral Commission, a private organization of Western European, Japanese and North American financial, corporate and political leaders established in 1973 by the head of the Chase-Manhattan Bank, David Rockefeller. Many of Carter's selections for his administration were drawn from the Trilateral Commission—Vice President Walter Mondale, Secretary of State Cyrus Vance, Secretary of the Treasury Michael Blumenthal, Secretary of Defense Harold Brown, and U.N. ambassador Andrew Young. Other Carter appointees came directly from two of the largest multinational corporations in the world, Coca Cola (based in Atlanta, Georgia) and International Business Machines (IBM): Coca Cola attorneys Griffin Bell, Attorney General, and Joseph Califano, Secretary of Health, Education, and Welfare; IBM board directors Vance, Brown and black attorney Patricia Harris, Secretary of Housing and Development.

For almost five decades, the American political party system, ostensibly characterized by the electoral competition between the Democratic and Republican parties, had actually become marked by three distinct points of view identified by particular social characteristics. They comprised political blocs which cut across orthodox party lines. The first, which comprised about one-quarter to one-third of the U.S. electorate, was "mass conservatism," which included most of the Republican Party, some conservative Southern Democrats, former segregationists, and most of the corporations and financial interests. In addition, this first bloc included reactionary populist groups which either opposed certain civil rights-type reforms (e.g. court-ordered busing to promote racially integrated public schools) or which advocated legislation to limit the rights of women, homosexuals and political dissidents. The second point of view, "centrist social liberalism," was slightly less than half of the general electorate. This very

broad political bloc included Republican liberals, Eastern corporate leaders and financial interests, the Cold War liberals in the Democratic Party
(Truman, Kennedy), white ethnic workers, moderate and anti-segregationist Southern Democrats (Carter), most trade union leaders, and the
more conservative representatives of civil rights groups. The smallest bloc,
the "democratic left," encompassed one-fifth to one-quarter of the vote.
This grouping included almost all black and Hispanic organizations, liberal and leftist labor leaders, feminist groups, environmentalists, socialists, and perhaps one-third of the Democratic Party's leaders.

From 1932 until 1980, every American president had been a part of the
great "centrist social liberalism" tendency.[30] Roosevelt and at times Johnson had been in the left wing of this eclectic grouping; Eisenhower and
Nixon were to the right, but neither could accurately be described as "true
conservatives." On a racial axis, the democratic left was a strong proponent of civil rights, extensive social democratic reforms in welfare, public
housing, education and social justice; the conservatives were vigorous proponents of racial inequality; the centrists were to be found unevenly distributed between these two poles. Since blacks were chiefly responsible for
electing Carter, there was the clear expectation that the new president
would embrace a program of progressive racial reforms and social democracy. This did not occur. If anything, blacks were dismayed to learn, as the
administration developed its agenda, that Carter was probably the most
conservative Democratic president since Woodrow Wilson, the arch-segre-
gationist of 1913–21. After a short time in office, corporate leaders drew
pleasant parallels between Carter and Roosevelt's immediate conservative
predecessor in the White House, Herbert Hoover. One aide to Eisenhower
suggested that Carter "ventured no notions in economic philosophy to
which [Hoover] could have taken serious exception." Patrick Caddell, a
Carter pollster and assistant, urged the new president "to co-opt many of
[the Republicans'] issue positions and to take away large chunks of their
presidential coalition by the right actions in government." A move to the
political right would "cause rumblings from the left of the Democratic
Party," but these could be safely ignored.[31] Thus, blacks and the broader
American democratic left had helped to elect a president who had absolutely no intention of carrying out key elements of their program. Once he
had assumed office, Carter began to rescind many of the basic achievements of the Second Reconstruction.

The first real indication that Carter was actually carrying out a "Nixon-
Republican"-style program came in May 1977, when administration officials declared that no new social welfare, health care or educational programs would be initiated. Carter protégé Bert Lance, the director of the
Office of Management and Budget, stated that inflation, not unemploy-

ment, was the chief economic dilemma confronting Americans. Carter's oft-repeated campaign promise to reduce defense expenditures was promptly abandoned, and the 1978 military budget soared to the highest level in U.S. history up to that point, $111.8 billion. Despite the appointments of Young, Harris, John Lewis, and Weldon Rougeau to high administrative posts, relatively few blacks received positions in the executive branch of government. In a fifteen-month period between April and June 1976 and July–September 1977, non-white unemployment rates edged upward, from 12.9 percent to 13.6 percent, and non-white youth unemployment increased from 35.5 percent to 39.2 percent. In Carter's first year in office, an additional 131,000 black families fell below the federal government's poverty level—yet the White House remained opposed to any extensive initiatives to address the crisis. Black leaders who had campaigned for the Southern Democrat were now ashamed to meet with their own constituents. In August 1977, a number of black leaders who had campaigned for Carter caucused at the national office of the Urban League in New York City. All of the key participants—including Jesse Jackson, Bayard Rustin, Baltimore congressperson Parren Mitchell, Urban League leader Vernon Jordan, and the newly elected head of the NAACP, Benjamin Hooks of Memphis, Tennessee—claimed that they had been "betrayed," and that Carter was practicing a policy of "callous neglect" towards blacks.[32]

Carter's relations with blacks deteriorated still further in 1978–79. On economic policy, the president did not battle aggressively for the Full Employment and Balanced Growth Act of 1976, more popularly termed the Humphrey-Hawkins bill. Denounced by conservatives as "socialistic," the proposal was a joint effort of blacks, democratic leftists, labor union leaders, and many Cold War liberals such as Senator Hubert Humphrey. In its original form, the act stated that "all adult Americans able and willing to work have the right to equal opportunities for useful paid employment at fair rates of compensation," and declared that the federal government should "meet human and national needs" such as day care, public housing, and public transportation. The act called for the creation of "Job Guarantee Office" which was "responsible for actually enforcing the right of all 'able and willing' adults to a job." Humphrey-Hawkins was accurately described by friends and opponents alike as "the most significant employment legislation to appear in the United States in thirty years."[33] The act was passed eventually in a radically diluted form, such that the basic social democratic thrust of its proposed reforms was eliminated. Civil rights proponents were disappointed that the president had not used the full weight of the administration to gain a credible piece of legislation. Even Coretta King, who described the new law as "an important first step in the struggle for full employment" recognized that "we did not get all of the provisions in the bill that we would have liked." [34] Carter's imposed reductions in federal spending for social programs, combined with a relaxation in laws on the private sector, led to higher corporate profits at the expense of the working class. In January–March 1979, for example, after-tax profits of 552 major U.S. corporations had risen 37 percent over the preceding year. In a series of blatant overtures to business interests, Carter urged the U.S. Federal Reserve Board "to raise interest rates and tighten the credit supply, so as to curtail economic expansion"; increased the U.S. military budget by 10 to 15 percent "combined with unprecedented slashes in benefits and services to the population"; pushed Congress to pass "measures to increase the prices of dairy products, grain, meat, and other products, and to "deregulate" transportation industries, fostering monopolization and unrestricted price increases"; and imposed "wage/price guidelines, aiming to limit wage and benefit increases to 7 percent, in the face of living cost increases exceeding 10 percent." Liberal, black, and socialist economists condemned the Carter agenda "for lowering living standards for much of the population" and "for wiping out many small property owners." [35] By January 1979, only 33 percent of all Democrats stated in a national poll that they wanted Carter to serve as their party's nominee in 1980. Political columnist Ken Bode described the president as having "consciously [moved] the Democratic party away from nearly a half-century of its own history." [36]

For black social institutions and local governments controlled by blacks, Carter represented an acceleration of the political reaction imposed by Nixon. Black colleges and universities, for example, had received three-fourths of their institutional support from the federal government's "Developing Institutions Program," under Title III of the Civil Rights Act during the Nixon–Ford Administrations. Under Carter, the level of black institutional support was slashed to 53 percent in 1977, and was down to 18 percent in 1980. Promises of financial aid to black college students and administrators were never kept. Black political columnist William Raspberry attacked Carter's Secretary of Health, Education and Welfare, Joseph Califano, for his callous disregard for "the historical rose" of black colleges, and for this "[indifference] to the vital service they perform." [37] The administration's "comprehensive national urban policy," which was announced in March 1978, allotted only $1 billion per year to create new public jobs for the ghetto's unemployed, and provided only $150 million for urban social services. Increasingly, black mayors were unable to reconcile their feeble defense of Carter's austerity budget with the economic demands of black working-class constituents. In 1977, Atlanta mayor Maynard Jackson fired 900 mostly black sanitation employees during a strike which was provoked by their lack of a pay increase for over three years. Many of these AFSCME union employees had campaigned extensively for

Jackson during his first successful race for mayor in 1973, and were devastated when the black leader swung behind local corporate and anti-working-class interests once he was in office. Detroit mayor Coleman Young, once a leftist and activist in the National Negro Labor Council, formed an active alliance with corporate leader Henry Ford of Ford Motor Company and other executives. Black Detroit residents' city services were reduced; public educational and social programs were cut; yet corporate property taxes were lowered, to foster a favorable climate for greater business investment. The majority of black mayors were forced to discipline the black public labor force, as a result of federal government reductions in urban support; the chief beneficiaries in the process were the corporations.

The failure of Carter (and his black élite allies) to resolve the "pervasive and intractable crisis" of the "American political system" produced three significant trends, all of which affected the present and future status of African-Americans in public life. First, as political theorists John Judis and Alan Wolfe noted, Cold-War liberalism and the old political coalition of Roosevelt had finally collapsed. There was an "estrangement of Americans from party politics and governmental authority, demonstrated in flagging turnout at the polls, growing independent registration at the expense of both major parties, and the distrust of politicians and government indicated in many opinion surveys and in declining voting rates."[38] Centrist social liberalism, as the political center of U.S. political discourse, was fractured on the left and right. Second, there was a growing and perceptible degree of alienation between the black élite, who still favored Carter, and the majority of black workers and the poor, who were either neutral or by now completely alienated from the political process. Black labor had once believed that the elevation of a black professional into high public office could resolve its pressing economic and social problems. In the aftermath of Jackson's, Coleman Young's and other black mayors' betrayals of their own constituents, a sobering sense of disillusionment pervaded the black community. Even the black élite was shocked and angered in 1979, however, when Carter pressured U.N. ambassador Andrew Young to resign after he had held an informal discussion with a representative of the Palestine Liberation Organization. Finally, there was among the urban underclass, or permanent reserve army of labor, a new degree of volatility, of hopelessness and rage. This became strikingly evident in May 1980, when the residents of Liberty City, Brownsville, and Coconut Grove, the black neighborhoods of Miami, Florida, rose up in rebellion against local authorities and police. In the most disruptive urban revolt since 1968, between $50 to $100 million worth of property damage occurred in several days. Sixty-seven buildings were damaged; 1,250 persons were arrested; 400 persons were injured, and 18 were killed; 3,600 National Guardsmen were called into Miami to restore order. When Miami officials asked members of the black élite, including Benjamin Hooks, Jesse Jackson, Andrew Young and Houston congressperson G. T. Leland, to "cool off" the black community, they were uniformly told by local black activists that they were viewed as unwelcome collaborators. Blacks in Liberty City, where unemployment among adults reached 50 percent, "resent[ed] the way they were called in," one black journalist noted. Hooks, Young, and others "came because people who had ignored our warnings could not tell us they didn't know what was brewing." [39] The specter of black urban rebellion once again had made national headlines. But unlike in the mid-to-late 1960s, the backers of racial inequality and white "mass conservatism" were infinitely stronger in 1980, and were prepared to repress the rights of all national minorities by whatever means at their disposal.

VI

For 100 years, American racists had looked back fondly upon the Ku Klux Klan's central role as the bulwark of white supremacy during "each and every phase of Radical Reconstruction." The reaction to the struggle for multicultural democracy in the 1970s now gave the historical opening for Klansmen to employ "intimidation by any effective means of violence conceivable" against the grandchildren of former slaves. [40] Between 1971 and 1980, the Klan almost tripled its national membership. In January 1977, 250 Klansmen held a public rally in Carter's hometown, Plains, Georgia. In 1978–79, Klansmen engaged in a bloody campaign against blacks. The racists fired shotguns into the homes of several NAACP leaders in the South; on 8 May 1979, Klansmen shot one black man in the face in Carbon Hill, Alabama; the group firebombed black homes, churches and schools in over 100 towns and rural areas. One Klansman, "Grand Dragon" Thomas Metzger, organized a fascist-oriented, black-uniformed security force in California, which led violent attacks against progressive and interracial groups. In 1980, Metzger's support among conservative, southern California white voters was registered in his victory in the Democratic Party primary in the state's forty-third congressional district. Metzger's program of "white rights" included promises to end school desegregation, affirmative action, and "a five-year moratorium on all foreign immigrants." [41] The most outrageous act of Klan violence took place in Greensboro, North Carolina, on 3 November 1979. Seventy-five Klansmen and Nazis attacked an antiracist rally, leaving five protestors killed and eleven others wounded. Only six of the murderers were tried, and an all-white jury acquitted the racists, despite television videotaped evidence which documented the killings in cold and unambiguous detail. A few black groups responded to Klan violence in the only language that racists understand. In November 1978, Klansmen and Okolona, Mississippi, police co-operated in an ambush of members of the United League, a black southern rights organization. In the shoot-out, one Klansman was killed, and five others were seriously wounded. United League leader Skip Robinson stated later, "Over 100 rounds [of ammunition] were fired. The Klan never said anything about it, the police never said anything about it, the press never said anything about it. But after that we never saw no more Klan in Okolona."[42]

Unfortunately, the Klan and Nazis were only a very small portion of the forces of racism which were unleashed against the black community. Police across the country descended into black neighborhoods, applying "excessive force" when making routine arrests, shooting first and asking questions later. During the Miami Rebellion of May 1980, a small gang of white police officers destroyed black suspects' automobiles with billy clubs, rifles and steel pipes. Automobiles were spray-painted with the words "Looter," "Thief," and "I am a Cheap No Good Looter."[43] In Oakland, California, police officers killed nine black males in 1979 alone, one of whom was a 15-year-old boy. One of the victims was a trade unionist, 37-year-old Charles Briscoe:

> On September 5, 1979, Briscoe was gunned down by a police officer who had been involved in four other fatal shootings. First the officer emptied his shotgun into Briscoe and then finished him off with his service revolver. There were no witnesses to collaborate the officer's story that . . . he had to shoot Briscoe a second time because, after being shot with the shotgun, Briscoe walked towards his van and reached for a weapon. The coroner's report, however, indicated the shotgun blasts had broken both of Briscoe's legs; he couldn't have walked to the van. Nevertheless the district attorney and the police department found the shooting justifiable; a civilian police review board was prohibited from looking into the Briscoe case.[44]

In August 1980, Philadelphia police "accidentally" killed a 17-year-old black suspect while he was being "pistol-whipped." In Detroit, during the summer of 1980, police officers fired on seven black suspects, critically wounding three. Detroit police routinely arrested black women on minor charges such as speeding and, once in the station house, subjected them to humiliating strip-searches and sexual abuse. In one controversial arrest, police strip-searched and harassed three black female relatives of Detroit mayor Coleman Young. In another Detroit case, "a young black man died after being tortured by a white officer using [an electric] cattle-prod."[45] When a white policeman was killed in New Orleans on 8 November 1980, white officers assassinated four blacks in five days, in order to intimidate the black urban community. By the early 1980s, "for every white person killed by the police" in the U.S. in any year, "22 black persons, are killed."[46] Surveying police atrocities, Washington, D.C. black activist Damu Smith drew a direct correlation between police repression and mass conservatism. "The police have very consciously begun to link up more with the racist right wing movement, organizing for the ruling class in its stepped up assault on the rights of the people," Smith suggested in 1981. "The police today are working to protect and serve those who are in power as well as those in the right wing movement who are organizing at the behest of those in power.[47]

The most prevalent form of American racist violence was lynching: hangings, castrations, shootings, and other acts of racially motivated random violence. In 1976, Mobile police harassed a young black businessman and community activist Glen Diamond (Casmarah Mani). After beating him, officers "placed a noose around his neck" and temporarily strangled him in a downtown public square.[48] A Cleveland, Ohio, white patent attorney shotgunned two 14-year-old black girls. Convicted of felonious assault, the attorney countersued the girls' parents and was awarded $5,000. One mother of the girls declared to the press, "My daughter still has 12 pellets from a 16 gauge shotgun in her neck. It's like telling this man he was within his rights shooting my daughter."[49] In Arizona, 300 black evangelical Christians purchased a farm to develop a religious retreat. In several months, local whites destroyed their recreation center and swimming pool. Black members were shot at and "almost run down by automobiles." In October 1981, a bomb was planted in their church van which exploded, killing one and injuring eight others.[50] Mississippi whites were responsible for at least twelve separate lynchings of blacks in 1980. On 12 October 1981, the body of Douglas McDonald was pulled from a lake in Eastover, Mississippi: the black man's ears had been removed and his sex organs hacked off. Black investigators "could get no information from the mortician, the police nor the family."[51] In Social Circle, Georgia, the cousin of my wife, Lynn Jackson, was discovered lynched on 8 December 1981. Several months later, Frederick York, a 38-year-old black man, was found hanging from a tree in downtown Atlanta. The two most publicized incidents of random violence against blacks occurred in Buffalo, New York, and Atlanta. In September–October 1980, one or more whites randomly selected black males in Buffalo for murder. Several blacks were executed on street corners; one was nearly choked to death as he sat in a hospital room recovering from surgery. Two black men, 71-year-old Parler W. Edwards and 40-year-old Ernest Jones, were savagely beaten to death and, amazingly, had their hearts removed from their corpses by the killer or killers. Twenty-eight black youths were methodically murdered in Atlanta between 1979 and 1982. A black man was arrested and convicted of killing two of the youths in 1981, but the remaining murders were left unsolved. After the initial arrest, the FBI refused to pursue new evidence in the other cases.

COINTELPRO-type repression of black radicals, revolutionary nationalists and Marxists also resurfaced during these years. RNA Deputy Minister of Defense Kamau Kambui was arrested by FBI agents in Mississippi. Charged *"with signing his name incorrectly while purchasing a shotgun,"* he was convicted and sentenced to five years in prison.[52] After the acquittal of the Nazis and Klansmen, local police arrested eight anti-racist demonstrators in Greensboro, North Carolina, charging them with "fire-bombing, attempted fire-bombing and conspiracy to fire-bomb." Black Marxist Nelson Johnson, who had received severe knife wounds during the 1979 attack, was charged with "felony riot" immediately after the incident. Johnson was later jailed for 20 days on "contempt" charges.[53] On 1 November 1980, black community activist Yulanda Ward was executed by four armed assailants in Washington, D.C. A powerful 0.357 magnum pistol had been fired against her head, and her body was left in the streets of the city. Rodney Johnson, a black communist and San Diego labor activist, was charged with two white workers with "conspiracy to bomb an electrical transformer" in the National Steel and Shipbuilding Company's shipyards, the largest in the U.S. Days before his arrest, Johnson had led the fight among black and white workers against hazardous working conditions and low wages.[54] In May 1982, California officials arrested a former Black Panther activist, Michael Zinzun, for statements he had made at a black protest gathering in front of a police station. Charging Zinzun with "feloniously threatening the lives of five Pasadena police officers," the district attorney cited a "rarely-used 110-year-old law" which made it a "felony to threaten a government worker." One official admitted that the obscure law was only "rarely" applied in threats made against tax collectors and federal marshals, but "the gravity of Mr. Zinzun's conduct" more than justified his arrest under any possible grounds. An American Civil Liberties Union lawyer argued that Zinzun's arrest was a blatant violation of the rights of free speech covered in the First Amendment to the U.S. Constitution. "The implications of this kind of law are fairly obvious," Zinzun's attorney complained. "You can risk a felony prosecution anytime you utter words that the police don't like."[55]

Even moderate black civil rights leaders were not immune to racist assaults and harassment. Vernon Jordan was shot in the back by a gunman in Fort Wayne, Indiana, on 29 May 1980. Police charged an "avowed racist," Joseph Paul Franklin, with shooting the Urban League leader. Franklin had previously been charged with shooting two Salt Lake City black men in August 1980, and was later sentenced to two life imprisonment terms in

the case. During the Jordan trial, one prisoner familiar with Franklin testified that the white racist "talked of the shooting and identified Jordan by
name." Another witness stated under oath that Franklin came into his Ft.
Wayne grocery store and graphically detailed his shooting of Jordan: "It
was about perfect. If it had been a little different it would have gotten him
just right." Franklin himself told the jury that he "hate[d] the [black] race
as a whole." But on 17 August 1982, an all-white jury declared that Franklin was innocent in Jordan's shooting.[56] Travelling to Anderson, Indiana,
on 20 November 1981, Benjamin Hooks discovered a burning cross—the
historic symbol of the Ku Klux Klan—at the entrance of a public hall
where the NAACP leader was scheduled to lecture. No persons were arrested by police. The incidents of violence, an almost endless list of brutalities which touched the lives of millions of blacks, appeared to many to
constitute a pattern of black genocide. "There is almost a hysteria in black
communities because of the belief that there is a [racist] conspiracy," Jesse
Jackson stated in November 1980. "Racism has become fashionable again
and feelings of guilt toward blacks have turned to feelings of hostility. This
country has taken a definite swing toward fascism." Former King aide
Hosea Williams charged that the Carter Administration was indirectly responsible for "the mounting KKK's violent activities against blacks all
across the country."[57] Carter's response to the outraged demands of blacks
and the democratic left that he should conduct vigorous federal measures
against black genocide paralleled his other initiatives on welfare, guaranteed employment for the poor, and public housing—virtually nothing.
After all, the blacks had been given too much in previous years.

VII

The rising tide of modern white supremacy on America's streets was also
manifested within the nation's high court and political institutions. During
Nixon's term in office, several liberal Supreme Court justices retired. Chief
Justice Warren was replaced by a Minnesota Republican, Warren Burger;
other doctrinaire conservatives were later appointed. As a result, throughout the 1970s the Supreme Court's decisions reflected an increasingly conservative and anti-black bias. By a narrow five to four margin, the Court
ruled against Brian F. Weber, a white steelworker who sued the Steelworkers Union and the Kaiser Aluminum and Chemical Corporation in
Gramercy, Louisiana, to halt the company's affirmative action program for
blacks. But in 1978, the Court overturned the affirmative action program
of the University of California-Davis Law School in the *Bakke* decision.
After *Bakke*, the number of blacks recruited and admitted to many professional schools dropped sharply. As political economist Michael Reich ob-

served, "many whites apparently felt that affirmative action programs had taken away educational opportunities, jobs, and income away from white families . . . and had given these advantages to undeserving blacks who had not worked for them. The publicity given to the Bakke Supreme Court case provided a highly distorted picture of undeserved black gains" to many whites, leading "to charges of 'racism in reverse'." [58] The logic of Bakke was applied to electoral politics as well. In 1980, the Court upheld an electoral arrangement which diluted the voting strength of blacks, the *City of Mobile vs. Bolden*. Potter Stewart, associate justice and an Eisenhower appointee, argued that the Fifteenth Amendment did not include the "right to have black candidates elected." Political scientists Twiley W. Barker, Jr., and Lucius J. Barker noted that the decision "in effect" validated "electoral arrangements that have a discriminatory impact where the more stringent requirement of intentional or purposeful discrimination cannot be established. . . . It appears that the Court will be satisfied as long as the scheme does not abridge or deny the blacks the right to vote." [59]

Against this background of political retreat and racist reaction, of social malaise and economic disorder, Ronald Reagan rose to public prominence. As discussed briefly in Chapter 5, Reagan had earned his credentials on the far-right during the 1960s as governor of California. In 1976 he had challenged the Republican incumbent, Gerald Ford, for their party's presidential nomination, and was only narrowly defeated. For over a decade, Reagan was the darling of mass conservatism. So much was his 1980 candidacy for the White House identified with the various movements against affirmative action, court-ordered busing, and civil rights for blacks, Latinos, women and others that the entire reactionary political phenomenon was termed "Reaganism." Reaganites observed that U.S. military spending had declined from 8.0 percent of the gross national product (GNP) in 1965–70 to 4.6 percent of the GNP during the Ford and Carter administrations. Social spending for food stamps, unemployment compensation, Social Security and other social democratic-type reforms during the same period had increased from 5.1 percent of the GNP to 8.6 percent. Thus, Reaganites blamed non-productive federal expenditures as the root cause of inflation, and charged the Democrats and liberal Republican opponents with being "weak on defense" and accommodationist toward the Soviets. Business profits, adjusted for inflation, had grown a meager 3.4 percent in ten years: therefore, conservatives sought to give massive tax reductions to the corporations, waiving certain environmental protection laws, at the expense of working-class and non-white Americans. The "ideological glue" of Reaganism was racism. The 69-year-old conservative made this clear in August 1980, at a speech delivered in Philadelphia, Mississippi. Before a cheering white crowd, Reagan pledged that his administration would defend the principle of "states' rights." [60] Given that the town was the site of the brutal murders of three desegregation workers in 1964, and that the phrase itself was equated by many southern whites to mean "white supremacy," the gravity of Reagan's speech could not be lost upon most blacks. Despite Reagan's overtly racist stance, he was able to attract a small number of black intellectuals and former civil rights leaders to his campaign. Dr. Nathan Wright, convenor of the 1968 Black Power conference, announced his support for the Republican. Other "Black Reaganites" included Thomas Sowell, a Marxist-turned-conservative who served as a fellow at the Hoover Institute at Stanford University, California; economist Walter E. Williams of George Mason University; Republican leader J. A. Y. Parker; and Wendell Wilkie Gunn, assistant treasurer of the Pepsi Cola corporation. The two most influential black converts were King's closest aide, Ralph David Abernathy, and SCLC activist Hosea Williams. Abernathy justified his endorsement of one of King's bitterest opponents by attacking the dismal record of the Carter Administration on economic and civil rights issues.

Most black leaders were positively frightened by Reagan's conservative economic rhetoric and covert appeals to racism, and were especially outraged with Abernathy's actions. Mrs. King declared that Reaganism represented the most "negative" and "even irrational elements in our society." One black newspaper called Abernathy a "modern Judas," a "senile" turncoat who had forgotten "the police dogs, Selmas, Birmingham, the marches, the sit-ins, the kneel-ins, the pray-ins, Bull Connor, the jails, the beatings, the bombings and the humiliation. . . ." [61] Historically, Reagan was the first national candidate from the mass conservative tendency of American politics to be nominated since Barry Goldwater, in 1964. This fact alone made the record of Carter seem remarkably enlightened. The overwhelming majority of black élite political organizations, from the NAACP to local civil rights groups, vigorously worked for Carter's re-election. But the black poor and the working class, in spite of their genuine revulsion against Reaganism, could not be mobilized sufficiently to accept a candidate who had done so little to protect, much less expand upon, the legislative gains of the Second Reconstruction. In November 1980, Reagan received 43.3 million popular votes and 489 electoral votes, to Carter's 35 million popular votes and 49 electoral votes. A liberal Republican, Illinois representative John Anderson, ran an independent race and captured 7 percent of the popular vote in the general election. Between 85 to 91 percent of the blacks voted for Carter, a percentage slightly below his 1976 black voter figure. Of 17 million black adults who were eligible to vote in 1980, only 7 million or 40 percent actually voted. The slippage in black votes for Carter allowed Reagan to carry several closely contested southern states. Furthermore, most of the other New Deal electoral coalition constituencies had been badly divided. A majority of white trade unionists did not vote for Carter; most of the Jewish vote was split between Anderson and Reagan; and only 54 percent of Puerto Rican and Mexican-American voters supported Carter. Conservative Republicans captured control of the U.S. Senate for the first time in a quarter-century. Carter was sent back to Plains, Georgia, as blacks and the democratic left pondered with some anxiety what the new administration would mean.

With the rapid legislative maneuvers reminiscent of Roosevelt's "Hundred Days" period of 1933, when the nation was faced with the Great Depression, the Reagan Administration sought to construct a conservative and unequal order. Within months, Reagan illustrated that his government, unlike Nixon's, would not tolerate even the slightest concessions to the poor, the dispossessed, racial minorities, and labor. The Occupational Safety and Health Administration (OSHA), founded in 1970 under Nixon, was a modest federal government initiative which attempted to improve workplace conditions, especially for laborers in industries with a record of dangerous and environmentally unsafe conditions. Reagan named a millionaire construction owner, Thorne Auchter, as OSHA director, and a former CIA employee as Auchter's chief assistant. Heading the administration's Task Force to eliminate federal regulations on corporations was J. C. Miller III, a former academic fellow at a right-wing research center, who had once "testified in opposition to the proposed OSHA coke-oven standard intended to limit exposure of coke-oven workers to deadly cancer-causing fumes." Before Congress, Miller had "argued that the benefits of protecting coke-oven workers were not worth the cost." [62] Included within Reagan's broad assault upon the legacy of social centrist liberalism were numerous proposals: the abandonment of the Comprehensive Employment and Training Act program, funded in 1981 for $3.1 billion, and the elimination of its 150,000 federally funded jobs; the closing of the National Consumer Co-operative Bank, which granted loans to small economic co-operatives; a $2 billion reduction in the federal Food Stamps Program by fiscal 1983; the elimination of the $2 billion Guaranteed Student Loan Program; the reduction of $1.7 billion from child nutrition programs sponsored by the federal government by fiscal 1983; the closing of the Neighborhood Self Help and Planning Assistance programs, which allotted $55 million in fiscal 1981 to aid inner cities. To bolster economic growth and corporate profits, Reagan ordered the severe reduction in federal enforcement of affirmative action regulations. Under Carter, employers with federal contracts had to submit written affirmative action plans if they had at least 50 employees and had a contract at $50,000 or above. Reagan proposed submission of plans "only for contractors with 250 or more workers and a government contract worth $1 million." Reagan also reduced "both eligibility and levels of support" for poor women to receive food stamps and Aid to Families with Dependent Children payments. By August 1981, Congress had ratified most of these proposals, and began to contemplate even more stringent restrictions in the areas of human needs. The New York-based Popular Economic Research Group declared: "While the nation's leading homemaker—Nancy Reagan—spent over $200,000 to replace the White House china, thousands of other mothers began to wonder not what they would serve dinner on, but whether they would serve it all all. . . . Women and people of color are being forced to bear the burden of Reagan's misguided and destructive economics."[63]

In the areas of defense foreign policy, Reaganism articulated a vision of white capitalist world supremacy. The president proposed the largest military expenditures in human history, $1.6 trillion over a five-year period. This inconceivable amount came to almost $11,000 for every U.S. citizen who paid taxes on 1979 income. Abandoning the previous administration's public commitment to human rights, Reagan's State Department forged closer relationships with fascist military juntas and racist regimes. During 1982, as black miners and workers staged a series of strikes in South Africa, Reagan authorized the opening of new honorary consulates in three U.S. cities, Seattle, Denver, and Cleveland, for the *apartheid* regime. Reagan asked Congress for $2.3 million to train black South Africans inside South Africa, thereby reinforcing the separate-and-unequal educational system. Export control regulations on such critical items as air ambulances, computers and helicopters were weakened to provide greater support for *apartheid*. The dispatch with which conservative and most centrist politicians passed Reagan's authoritarian military program was described by an outraged U.S. representative Dellums in a May 1982 interview:

Two weeks ago, in the midst of all these polls about people being concerned about the military budget, my colleagues, in four hours and 40 minutes, with time off for lunch in the middle, passed a $255.1 billion military budget. Now, you tell me anybody can intelligently debate a quarter of a trillion-dollar budget in four hours and 40 minutes? The vote was 40 to 3. . . . Do you think, on a ratio of 40 to 3 . . . that the American people want to spend a quarter of a trillion dollars on the military budget? But that's how far away my colleagues are from the American people. Maybe we've arrived at a point where this system does not serve us well. I don't see anything sacrosanct about the two-party system.[64]

The impact of Reaganism was felt across the black community as a series of devastating shocks. The Office of Federal Contracts Compliance Programs, one of the federal government's desegregation agencies, was ordered to reduce its enforcement activities. Under Reagan, the Civil Rights Division of the Justice Department filed only 5 lawsuits on racial discrimination issues in its first six months, compared to 17 suits under Carter and 24 suits under Nixon during their first six months' tenure. On 4 September 1981, the U.S. Department of Agriculture reduced the amount of food served to 26 million children in over 94,000 schools across the nation. Dietary allowances were distorted in order to reduce federal expenditures for children's lunches. For three weeks, before they were forced to retract, Reagan's nutrition experts even classified catsup and pickle relish as "vegetables." On 1 October 1981, more than 400,000 poor families were removed from federal and state welfare rolls. In one year, Reagan had succeeded where Nixon had failed: he actually expanded poverty in America. Between 1969 and 1974, the total number of black families below the poverty line rose from 1.3 million to 1.5 million. Poor white families in these years actually declined slightly, from 3.6 million to 3.5 million; the total number of persons below the poverty line remained roughly the same for the period, 24.1 million in 1969, 24.2 million in 1974. In Reagan's first year in office, the real median income of all black families declined by 5.2 percent compared to the 1980 figure. The number of poor Americans increased by 2.2 million in 1981, and the share of black families below the poverty line moved upward from 32.4 percent to 34.2 percent. In a single year, "much of the progress that had been made against poverty in the 1960s and 1970s" had been "wiped out," according to the *New York Times.*[65] In August 1982, Dr. James D. McGhee, the Urban League's director of research, warned that Reaganomics had blunted "the hopes and [dashed] the dreams of millions of the poor," and had serious threatened "the existence of an emerging, still fragile black middle-class as well. . . . Programs that accomplished so much are now being eliminated one after another for seemingly ideological rather than budgetary reasons, and America is defaulting on its commitment to assure equal opportunity for all its citizens."[66]

In a sense, the triumph of Reaganism represented a cruel and paradoxical conclusion to part of the rebellious impulse of the late 1960s. No one expressed this better than Eldridge Cleaver. After returning to the U.S. in 1974, Cleaver was incarcerated for less than a year in jail. By the early 1980s, Cleaver had not only repudiated his old Black Panther ties but actually had joined forces with racist mass conservatism. In a February 1982 interview, Cleaver declared:

. . . God came to France and tapped me on my shoulder and said, "Eldridge, follow me. . . ." [Americans] don't believe or even manifest any awareness of what makes our democratic form of government different from other forms of government. They don't understand and appreciate the great battles and triumphs and victories that were involved in creating this country. We are still the most free and the most democratic country in the world. I think America is the greatest country in the world. I really feel in my heart that America really needs to take control of the world. . . . Black people are notorious for sitting on the sidelines complaining, but they won't get off their butts and go vote and so they are taking no responsibility for what happens except they have full responsibility for not doing anything to make it happen differently. I believe that instead of black people hating the police department, I think they need to join the police department . . . and make it our own.[67]

In Cleaver's "most democratic country in the world," 23.4 million Americans, or about one out of every five workers, were unemployed in 1981. Of all black workers 30.5 percent were jobless at some point during the year. In June 1982, Congress voted to cut federal welfare programs by one-fifth and Medicaid spending by one-sixth, and reduced other domestic programs, including assistance to state and municipal governments, by a projected $45 billion by 1985. Congress's budgetary actions were aimed specifically to cripple blacks, Hispanics, low-income workers, and the unemployed. The 1982 budget "goes to the people who were bloodied last year and bloodies them and guts them some more," declared black Congressman Parren Mitchell.[68] Reaganism, racism, and political reaction has made a mockery of democracy.

8. The Paradox of Integration: Black Society and Politics in the Post-Reform Period, 1982-1990

> For one hundred years, 1865-1965, the fight [was] for civil rights; from 1965 to the present, the struggle to participate in the political structure. For the next ten years, 1990-2000, it will be to gain "silver rights," the fight for economic empowerment.
>
> Richard Hatcher, former mayor of Gary, Indiana
> April 1989

> The issue [is] not class or poverty. Martin Luther King appealed to justice, not to the class struggle.
>
> Andrew Young, January 1990

I

In the 1980s, American society became more thoroughly integrated in terms of race relations than at any previous point in its history. In the quarter century after the passage of the Civil Rights Act, the number of African-American elected officials increased from barely one hundred to nearly seven thousand. The number of African-Americans enrolled in colleges and universities quadrupled; the gross receipts of black-owned businesses and financial institutions increased more than eightfold; the size of the African-American middle class and number of professionals significantly expanded. Politically, blacks were elected mayors of the largest cities of the nation—Harold Washington in Chicago, David Dinkins in New York City, Andrew Young in Atlanta, Kurt Schmoke in Baltimore. Civil rights leader Jesse Jackson received millions of votes as a Democratic presidential candidate in 1984 and 1988. Perhaps the most striking changes in public

perceptions of race occurred in American popular culture, social institutions and the media, American musical theater, public education, the performing arts and both professional and collegiate athletics were heavily influenced by the participation and activities of blacks. Black images in
commercial advertisements became commonplace, and the most popular
television program of the 1980s starred an African-American, comedian
Bill Cosby. Blacks remained under-represented in the ownership and management of social and cultural institutions but were nearly omnipresent as
employees and public representatives, especially in the public sector.
Despite these obvious symbols of racial advancement, in many respects
the state of American race relations reached a new nadir in the late 1980s
and early 1990s. Hundreds of racially motivated acts of harassment and
violence occurred throughout the country. Thousands of black students
were victimized by intimidation, threats and even physical violence by
whites who were too young to remember racial segregation. Anonymous
hate notes, racist graffiti and pro-racist demonstrations took place at the
most elite private schools, such as Smith, Brown, and Colby, as well as at
larger, state-supported universities like Arizona State, Michigan, and Wisconsin. Surveys indicated that one-fifth to one-fourth of all minority students experienced at least one incident of racist harassment, intimidation
or physical abuse in any given year. At several institutions, white youths
formed "white student unions" to push back affirmative action and prefer-
ential recruitment of minorities as faculty and students. Civil rights organizations point to a disturbing pattern of legal indictments and political
harassment of black elected officials, and to the growth of violent incidents
aimed at black-owned property and individuals in urban areas. Racial tensions in cities such as New York culminated in a series of massive public
demonstrations by both African-Americans and whites, each side accusing
the other of "racism." Many measures of the social and economic status of
blacks began to deteriorate markedly. Black median incomes for families
dropped sharply in inflation-adjusted dollars during the 1980s. In higher
education, the number of African-American college students declined by
nearly one hundred thousand between 1980 and 1986; the number of black
doctorates granted annually plummeted from 1,166 in 1977 to only 765 in
1987, making it difficult to recruit productive or competitive black scholar/
teachers. Despite their gains, many blacks felt that the goal of racial harmony and integration into the American mainstream was more distant
than ever before.[1]
    What explains the modern racial paradox in American life, the emer-
gence of a successful black middle class and the acceptance of black participation in cultural, political and social institutions, within the context of a
deepening crisis in racial attitudes, behavior and relations? Any analysis of

the racial paradox at the end of the twentieth century must begin with an overview of the accomplishments and contradictions inherent within the Second Reconstruction, especially the movement's reformist stage between 1945 and 1965. The leaders of the modern Civil Rights Movement mobilized millions with one simple demand: freedom. In the context of the racially segregated society of the South in the post–World War II period, "freedom" meant the elimination of social, political, legal and economic barriers that forced black Americans into a subordinate status. Implicit in the demand for desegregation were several assumptions. Desegregation would increase opportunities for blacks in business, government and society overall. Desegregated educational institutions would promote greater racial harmony and understanding among young people from different ethnic communities, which in turn would promote residential integration. Affirmative action policies, the strategy of compensating for past discrimination against minorities, would gradually increase the numbers of African-Americans, Hispanics and other people of color in administrative and managerial positions. It was assumed that as African-Americans escaped the ghetto and were more broadly distributed across the social class structure and institutions of society, racial tensions and bigotry would decline in significance. As blacks became more thoroughly integrated into the economic system, the basis for racial confrontation would diminish.

The thesis above was fundamentally flawed in several key respects. First, desegregation did not benefit the entire black community uniformly. Black professionals and managers, those who had attended colleges and technical schools, were the principal beneficiaries. Working-class African-Americans also benefitted from income increases as new opportunities were created in upper-income levels of the labor force; their children for the first time had access to higher education. But opportunity in a capitalist society is always a function of social class position, which means ownership of capital, material resources, education and access to power. For the unemployed, the poor and those without marketable skills or resources, for those whose lives were circumscribed by illiteracy, disease and desperation, "race" continued to be a central factor in their marginal existence.

Legal desegregation had contributed to the popular illusion that the basis for racial discrimination and conflict no longer existed. The abolition of racially separate residential districts, hotels, schools, and other public institutions convinced many white Americans that the "Negro Question" had finally been firmly resolved. Black American leaders such as King had always insisted upon the achievement of a "color blind society." The passage of anti-discriminatory legislation had eliminated all basic impediments to the socio-economic and cultural advancement of African-Americans, according to this view. Thus, as many black leaders continued to speak out against more recent social injustices, or pointed to the growing economic disparities between blacks and the majority of middle-class whites, their complaints were easily dismissed as anachronistic, self-serving rhetoric. By raising the issue of racism, many whites now believed, blacks themselves had to be "racist."

Perhaps the most troublesome dilemma confounding any understanding of race relations in the post-reform period was an inability among Americans to distinguish between *ethnicity* and *race* and to apply these terms to the structural realities of American capital, political authority and social institutions. Throughout the period of slavery and Jim Crow segregation, blacks were treated both as an ethnic group and as a racial category. African-American ethnicity was derived from the cultural synthesis of the population's African heritage and its experiences in American society, first as slaves and subsequently as sharecroppers, as industrial laborers and, by the 1980s, as the core of the post-industrial urban workforce in the declining central cities of North America. As DuBois observed nearly a century ago, black Americans are both African and American, "two souls, two thoughts, two unreconciled strivings; two warring ideals in one dark body, whose dogged strength alone keeps it from being torn asunder."[2] This central duality is at the core of their ethnic consciousness, forming the fundamental matrix for all expressions of African-American music, art, language patterns, folklore, religious rituals, belief systems, family structure, and other cultural manifestations and social institutions. "Blackness" in the cultural context is the expression and affirmation of a set of traditional values, beliefs, rituals, and social patterns, rather than physical appearance or social class position.

Race is a totally different dynamic, rooted in the structures of exploitation, power and privilege. "Race" is an artificial social construction, which was deliberately imposed on various subordinated groups of people at the outset of the expansion of European capitalism into the western hemisphere five centuries ago. The "racial" consciousness and discourse of the West was forged above the bowels of slave ships, as they carted their human cargoes into the slave depots of the Caribbean and the Americas. The search for agricultural commodities and profits from the extreme exploitation or involuntary workers deemed less than human gave birth to the notion of racial inequality. In the United States, a "race" has been generally defined as a group of individuals who share certain physical or biological traits, particularly phenotype (skin color), body structure and facial features. But race has no scientific validity, as a meaningful biological or genetic concept. Beyond this, the meaning of race shifted according to the power relations between the racial groups. Even during the period of segregation in the South, "race" was frequently situational—a function not simply of physical appearance but also of explicit or implied power relations that connected any individual of color to his or her local surroundings. Thus in some segregated towns, African-Americans who owned property or who held respected professional positions as ministers, lawyers or physicians were occasionally granted social privileges normally granted solely to whites or had access to capital resources or, more rarely, voting rights, on a severely restricted basis.

Race, therefore, is not an abstraction but an unequal relationship between social aggregates, which is also historically specific. The subordinated racial group finds itself divorced from the levers of power and authority within the socio-economic order. The oppressed racial group's labor power, its ability to produce commodities, is systematically exploited, chiefly through abnormally low wage rates. It is denied ownership of the major means of production. It lacks full access to sources of capital and credit. The racial group's political status is marginal or peripheral, as full participation and legislative representation are blocked. Finally, racial categories are constantly reinforced in the behaviors and social expectations of all groups by the manipulation of social stereotypes and use of the legal system to carry out methods of coercion. The popular American myth of the Negro's sexual promiscuity and great physical prowess, for example, was constructed to denigrate the intellectual abilities and the scientific and cultural accomplishments of blacks. The racist stereotype of the black race's inclination toward extremely anti-social behavior, criminality and violence reinforced the series of discriminatory codes, employment patterns and legal harassment aimed at nonwhites. Institutional vigilante violence, including lynching, the death penalty, and the arrest of a disproportionately large number of African-Americans for crimes also committed by whites, helped to justify and reinforce the stereotypes.

Conversely, to be "white" in contemporary American society says nothing directly about an individual's cultural heritage, ethnicity or genetic background. "White culture" never existed, and does not exist today. White power, privileges and prerogatives within the capitalist economy and the political and social system do exist. Whiteness is fundamentally an index of the continued patterns of exploitation of subordinated racial groups which create economic surpluses for privileged groups. To be "white" in racial terms essentially means that one's life chances improve dramatically over those of nonwhites, in terms of access to credit, capital, quality housing, health care, political influence, and equitable treatment in the criminal justice system. People of African-American nationality, whose cultural patterns and social traditions were derived in part from Africa, were overdetermined externally as the subordinate racial category. Physical appearance and phenotype were convenient, if not always predictable, measures for isolating the members of the oppressed racial group, the "blacks." For white Americans, this racial ethnic overdetermination did not occur, for several reasons. White Americans originated from many different European countries and cultures, ethnic intermarriage was frequent, and the rigid economic and legal barriers that confined blacks behind the walls of the ghetto usually did not exist for whites. By the mid-twentieth century, millions of white Americans had no clear ethnic or cultural identity. Their sense of aesthetics was derived largely from the lowest cultural common denominator, the mass media and the entertainment industry. Their racial identity was ruptured from ethnicity, and was only politically or socially relevant as it affected issues of direct personal interest—whether Hispanic or African-American families intended to purchase homes in their neighborhoods, for example, or whether their employers planned to initiate affirmative action hiring programs for minorities. Whiteness was fundamentally a measure of personal privilege and power, not a cultural statement.

With the legal desegregation of America's cultural and social institutions after the 1960s, white Americans absorbed critical elements of African-American music, dance, literature, language, and artistic expression. They accepted black participation in professional athletics, and extended acclaim to African-American film stars and entertainers. But their affinity and tolerance for blackness were almost always cultural and ethnic, rather than racial. Young whites have learned to mimic African-American music and singing styles, but they might vote against a black candidate for public office solely on racial grounds or oppose an affirmative action program's adoption in their own businesses in order to avoid "reverse discrimination" against whites. In short, the dominant characteristic of American race relations at the end of the twentieth century is "interaction without understanding." White students might purchase the latest taped recordings of black performing artists or cheer the exploits of black athletes at their university, but also bitterly oppose the adoption of academic requirements mandating courses in African-American or ethnic history, politics or literature. White employers might encourage the recruitment of several black junior executives into their firms, but oppose tax increases to finance job training programs, public transportation or public housing projects in ghettos. Desegregation within the economic structures of capitalism created the symbols of racial progress and cultural interaction, without the transfer of power to blacks as a racial group or the deconstruction of many manifestations of vulgar racist ideology and discourse. Jim Crow no longer existed, but in its place stood a far more formidable system of racial domination, rooted within the political economy and employing a language of fairness and equality while simultaneously eroding the gains achieved by blacks during the Second Reconstruction.

Probably the greatest irony within the modern racial paradox is that African-Americans born after the apex of the Civil Rights Movement began to have difficulty identifying the realities of contemporary oppressive race/class structures, because of the transformation of white racial etiquette. No white politician, corporate executive or religious leader now uses the term "nigger" in public. African-Americans coming to maturity in the 1980s and 1990s have never personally experienced Jim Crow segregation. They could not express how it feels to be denied the right to vote, because their electoral rights are guaranteed by law. They have never personally participated in street demonstrations, boycotts, picket lines, and seizures of governmental and academic buildings. Few have tasted the pungent fumes of tear gas, or felt the fiery hatred of racist mobs. No black American could ever be "nostalgic" for Jim Crow. Nevertheless the absence of a personal background of struggle casts a troubled shadow over the current generation of black Americans who are poorly equipped to grapple with the present complexities of racial and class domination.

II

In the 1980s and early 1990s, the black community experienced two distinct crises which threatened to pull apart its social fabric. One crisis was external, generated by the federal government's retreat from equality and the consolidation of mass conservatism under the administration of Ronald Reagan, which was aggressively hostile to blacks' interests. The second crisis, far more devastating to the spirit and cultural consciousness of blacks, can be described as internal: the ordeal of the African-American family, neighborhood, cultural and social institutions, caught in the vise of violence, crime, social destruction and drugs. The internal crisis was generated in part by the paradox of desegregation itself. With the outlawing of Jim Crow segregation, a segment of the black middle class was able to escape the ghetto. Black attorneys who previously had only black clients could move into more lucrative white law firms. Black educators and administrators were hired at predominantly white colleges; black physicians joined the staffs of white hospitals; black engineers, architects, and other professionals went into white firms. This frequently meant the geographical as well as cultural separation of the black middle class from the working-class and low-income African-American population, which was still largely confined to the ghetto by the lack of educational and income mobility. As the black inner-city neighborhoods became less diverse in terms of socio-economic groups, the level of capital investment, financial resources and professional contracts available to lower-income blacks declined sharply. In large cities, where ghetto life had always retained a degree of vitality and an atmosphere of extended families at the neighborhood level, the environment turned increasingly ugly. The specter of violence and death became frighteningly familiar.

The most obvious manifestation of this internal crisis was the explosion of illegal drugs in black neighborhoods. Before the 1970s, drugs such as heroin and marijuana had been widely available within the black community. As cocaine was introduced and marketed, it evolved as the drug of choice for wealthier addicts, and also soon became widely popular within the white upper class. By the early 1980s, most researchers estimated the number of drug addicts in the United States at one-half million. As measured by a 1982 survey of more than 30,000 drug treatment centers across the country, over 40 percent of all reported addicts were black, and another 20 percent were Hispanic. Ninety per 100,000 white Americans were addicts, compared to 290 per 100,000 African-Americans. The narcotics problem intensified in subsequent years, however, with the introduction of a unique cocaine product called "crack." Crack cocaine was developed by the domestic and international drug cartels as a method to mass market narcotics to low- and middle-income people. It was smokable, efficient and inexpensive to obtain, usually less than five dollars per "rock." Physically, its impact upon consumers was immediate and intense, giving a sense of prowess and near-omnipotence. This "high" lasted only a few minutes, leading to a desire for renewed consumption. Habitual users tended to be hyperactive, paranoid, psychotic and extremely violent. Crack addicts neglected family responsibilities, would steal property and money from neighbors and friends, or would engage in overtly criminal activities simply to maintain their narcotics habit.[3]

The full social costs of the crack explosion remain difficult to measure. The majority of cocaine consumers were middle-class white Americans rather than racial minorities. However, the consequence of drug dependency for more privileged social classes were far less severe than for people of color and the poor. Health care programs for professionals routinely provided drug treatment facilities and programs, often on an out-patient basis, that permitted recovering addicts to maintain their regular employment. The legal system emphasized rehabilitation rather than punishment for white, middle-class first offenders. Conversely, this kind of elaborate, paternalistic social infrastructure was virtually nonexistent for the majority of blacks, Hispanics and lower-income people caught in the web of crack addiction. Addiction frequently meant unemployment, the loss of one's savings and personal property, and social alienation. In New York City alone, for example, there were only 35,000 residential treatment openings for an estimated 250,000 intravenous drug users. Between 1986 and 1988, the number of newborn infants testing positive for drugs increased 400 percent; moreover, the reported incidence of congenital syphilis soared 500 percent, primarily because poor and minority women were engaging in prostitution to purchase drugs. More than two-thirds of New York City's child neglect and abuse reports involved adults who were drug users.[4]

The most destructive by-product of the crack epidemic was violence. The marketing and distribution of crack cocaine was seized largely by urban youth gangs attracted by the high profitability of drug dealing. To ensure control over local markets, the gangs became aggressive—purchasing large numbers of weapons with substantial firepower, eliminating potential rivals, recruiting children and young adults to sell drugs in school grounds and local residences, harassing young people who refused to purchase drugs. Police infiltration within the gangs was particularly difficult, because recruitment of members was based frequently on kinship and/or relations with neighbors who had known each other for years. The federal government's Drug Enforcement Agency mounted a massive counter-offensive by the mid-1980s, arresting thousands of street-level drug dealers throughout American cities, seizing tons of narcotics illegally transported from Asia and Latin America into the United States. Despite these efforts, the drug crisis continued to grow. By 1989, the drug economy within the United States alone was estimated at $150 billion; the National Institute on Drug Abuse estimated the number of "serious" drug users—addicts who used any illegal drug two hundred or more times per year—at four million; and the total cost of lost productivity from employee abuse was approximately $120 billion annually. Despite billions of dollars spent on drug seizures and arrests, the amount of cocaine entering the United States more than doubled between 1981 and 1985, as street prices dropped 60 percent for consumers. In desperation many conservatives and even some liberals, including Kurt Schmoke, the black Democratic mayor of Baltimore, called for the legalization of drugs as a means of taking the profitability out of the traffic.[5]

The worst effects of violence occurred within the black community. In 1960, the homicide rate for black males was 37 per 100,000; two decades later, the rate reached 65 per 100,000, compared to a white male homicide rate of 10 per 100,000. Throughout the 1980s, murder was the fourth leading cause of death for all African-American males and the leading cause of death for black males aged 20 to 29. One graphic illustration of the violence is the comparison of murder rates by race and gender. In the 1980s, a typical white woman's statistical chances of becoming a murder victim anywhere in the United States were one in 606. For white male adults, the

odds narrowed to one chance in 186. For black females, the odds were reduced to one in 124. But for African-American males, the chances plummeted to one in 29. For black males in their twenties, living in major cities
such as Detroit, Los Angeles and New York, the odds for becoming murder victims were less than one in 20. In this environment, death at an early
age is a normative experience. Crack addiction, household violence, shoot-
outs between rival gangs, become part of the general ghetto milieu.[6]

   As the government sought unsuccessfully to check the cycle of illegal
drug proliferation and violence in America's urban centers, it was left to
the penal system to impose some degree of rudimentary order upon social
chaos. Increasingly in the 1980s, the federal and state prisons became a
means for resolving the social problems and deviance of the cities. By
1989, approximately 609,690 African-American males between ages 20
and 29 were either behind prison bars or on legal parole or probation. This
group represented 23 percent, or nearly one out of every four black American males in their twenties. By contrast, only one in 10 Hispanic males and
one in 16 white males were imprisoned, paroled or on probation. Black
women were also disproportionately represented within the prison population. The estimated cost for incarcerating and monitoring these young
African-American males as of 1986 exceeded $2.5 billion annually. The
Washington, D.C.-based Sentencing Project, a nonprofit agency, observed in a 1990 report on the problem: "For the black community in general, nearly one-fourth of its young men are under control of the criminal
justice system at a time when their peers are beginning families, learning
constructive life skills and starting careers. The consequences of this situation for family and community stability will be increasingly debilitating."[7]
When compared with the mounting penal population, the total number of
black males of all ages enrolled in higher education in 1989 was significantly smaller—436,000. African-Americans within the penal system generally received longer prison sentences for the same crimes committed by
whites and rarely were placed in meaningful rehabilitation programs before their release into society.

   Once the specter of the black criminal was popularized within the media
and the political arena, government leaders were pressured to adopt more
severe measures to ensure law and order. Chief among them was the widespread use of the death penalty. The Supreme Court moved gradually toward this objective in May 1986, with the decision to permit prosecutors to
eliminate jurors who opposed the death penalty in capital trials—a measure virtually assuring that defendants found guilty in such cases would be
executed. The Supreme Court's April 1987 decision concerning Warren
McCleskey, a black man convicted of killing a white police officer, was far
more critical. McCleskey's attorneys challenged the Georgia capital stat-

ute, under which African-Americans were more than four times more likely to be sentenced to death for killing whites than whites found guilty of murdering blacks. Studies submitted in the McCleskey case which reviewed over 2,400 murder cases in Georgia indicated that the administration of the death penalty was directly correlated with race. Nevertheless, despite the evidence, the Court ruled by a narrow five-to-four majority that "apparent discrepancies in sentencing are an inevitable part of our criminal justice system," according to the opinion of Associate Justice Lewis Powell. "If we accepted McCleskey's claim that racial bias has impermissibly tainted the capital sentencing decision, we would soon be faced with similar claims as to other types of penalty. . . . Studies already exist that allegedly demonstrate a racial disparity in the length of prison sentences."[8]

The McCleskey case was as significant to all cases regarding race and capital punishment as the famous Brown decision of 1954, which initiated the activist phase of the Second Reconstruction. After McCleskey, the Supreme Court became more aggressively restrictive and punitive in its legal interpretations. In June 1989, the Court declared that the Constitution permitted states to execute murderers who are mentally retarded and juveniles as young as sixteen. As of 1989, at least two dozen juveniles were death row inmates, and another three hundred prisoners awaiting execution were mentally retarded. Despite their youth or diminished mental capacity, they would now be eligible for execution. Liberals immediately denounced the decisions as "barbaric." "What a mockery these latest Supreme Court decisions make of this nation's pretensions to be the leading proponent of human rights!" observed journalist Tom Wicker of the *New York Times*. "Executing teenagers and individuals with the mental capacity of children, putting indigent persons to death without exhaustive attention to their appeals, speeding state killings by short-cutting long established rules. . . ."[9] As the rate of public executions increased, black inmates convicted of capital offenses found it increasingly difficult to obtain lawyers willing to supervise and direct their final appeals. Lawyers now cited the enormous financial costs and the high probability that, despite any discrepancies or evidence of racial bias within their cases, their clients were going to be executed eventually.[10]

The demand for more rigorous sentencing and retribution led to an explosion of the penal population. The number of inmates in federal and state prisons, for example, increased from 300,024 men and women in 1977 to 673,565 in 1989. Officials noted that the 1989 incarceration rates required the addition of nearly 1,800 new prison beds each week, simply to keep pace with current demand, and that 25,000 additional prison staff and officers would have to be hired by 1995. If the figures were expanded to include the inmate population of local and municipal jails, the number of Americans behind bars by December 1989 totaled approximately 1,055,800 men and women, or more than one out of every 250 citizens. The problem of warehousing this massive number of individuals was complicated by health care considerations. Officials admitted that about 3 percent of all federal prisoners tested positive for the AIDS virus; another 40 percent of all inmates who had entered federal prisons in 1988 were found to have a "moderate" or "serious substance abuse problem." [11] Despite ambitious prison construction programs—Florida alone added over 9,000 new cells at a cost of $118 million in 1989—states were unable to keep pace with the rate of inmate additions. In a move reminiscent of the late nineteenth-century convict-leasing system in the American South, or the Soviet Union's infamous network of forced labor camps, politicians began to initiate measures to extract inexpensive products from their prison populations. In Ohio, thousands of inmates were producing over three hundred different products, ranging from soap to computer equipment, at the rate of 31 cents per hour. [12]

The growth of the overcrowded prison and inefficient criminal justice establishment was increasingly difficult to reconcile with the traditional objectives of a political democracy, with its presumption of civil liberties, and the principle of a swift trial and due process. By the end of the 1980s, black Americans were incarcerated at a rate of over 700 per 100,000, nearly seven times the rate for whites. African-Americans surpassed South African blacks in achieving the highest prison population per capita in the world. Another way of viewing the destructive impact upon blacks was the reality that one out of every four black American males would go to prison at some point in his lifetime. [13] Despite these grim realities, the power incentive for this coercive apparatus was the continued epidemic of crime which affected the lives of millions of Americans. Between 1973 and 1987, the Bureau of Justice Statistics noted, there were 14.7 million robberies in the United States. One-third of the robbery victims were injured, two-thirds lost money or personal property, and one in twelve was raped, knifed or suffered gunshot wounds. The victims of this violence were disproportionately black. Black males were robbed at two-and-one-half times the rate of white males; black women had a 30 to 60 percent higher chance of being raped than white women; black children were far more likely to live in a household that was burglarized than whites. As of 1986, one out of every 25 African-Americans annually became the victim of a crime. The social and psychological consequences for blacks were profound. Writer Paul Ruffins observed that in most ghetto communities, crime destroyed the quality of life for all residents: "Crime is an ongoing source of the kind of physical and mental trauma that contributes to causing depression, family violence, and drug dependencies. . . . Robbery and shoplifting impact health by increasing food prices, making it harder to eat a healthy diet. Rampant crime also shuts down businesses and increases unemployment which fosters even more crime."[14] As the primary victims of violence, most working-class and poor African-Americans were inclined to support extreme legal measures promoted by the government to retard crime, despite the mounting evidence of violated civil liberties and the higher taxes required for constructing penal institutions. Given the distinctly distasteful alternatives of living in fear as opposed to tolerating expanded police surveillance and a prison system that incarcerated hundreds of thousands of blacks annually, the majority of African-Americans accepted the latter option with deep misgivings.

III

For black Americans, the central political characteristic of the 1980s was the conservative reaction to the legacy of the Civil Rights Movement, and the apparent capitulation of both political parties to a more conservative and repressive social order. No politician symbolized this reaction more than President Ronald Reagan, whose electoral victories in both 1980 and 1984 occurred with overwhelming white majorities and against nearly unanimous opposition from African-American voters. Two-thirds of all white voters, and more than 80 percent of all southern whites, supported Reagan in 1984. In purely racial terms, the Reagan Administration attempted to communicate its opposition to political reforms such as affirmative action, without employing vulgar racist rhetoric or programs that specifically discriminated against blacks, Hispanics or other racial minorities. The administration accomplished this feat through the manipulation of racial symbols, as well as by eliminating specific federal agencies that had been created to safeguard civil rights and equal opportunity. William Bradford Reynolds, the assistant attorney general in charge of the Justice Department's Civil Rights Division, failed to enforce aggressively violations of the 1965 Voting Rights Act, and was a sharp critic of affirmative action policies designed to increase employment opportunities for minorities. Attorney General Edwin Meese, a close personal friend of the president, refused to follow federal regulations which required his department to set minority hiring goals with the Equal Employment Opportunity Commission. The upper levels of the Justice Department held few women and virtually no blacks in positions of authority. To undermine civil rights enforcement still further, in 1983 Reagan dismissed three liberal members of the U.S. Commission on Civil Rights. In a subsequent compromise with Congress, a bipartisan commission with a conservative majority was formed. The once-proud agency was reduced to political mimicry, voicing Reagan's opposition to school desegregation and to the use of goals and timetables for the hiring of women and minorities. In late 1986, Ralph G. Neas, the executive director of the Leadership Conference on Civil Rights, a coalition of 185 groups, expressed with regret: "The commission has become a sham, a national disgrace, a perversion of what it was intended to be. It has abandoned its independence and has become a morass of mismanagement." Congress reduced the commission's budget from $11.8 million to $7.5 million; political acrimony and conservative tactics destroyed an important bulwark in the legal effort to uproot discrimination.[15]

It was in the federal courts, however, that the anti–civil rights philosophy of the Reagan Administration would achieve its most lasting results. Despite the negative impact of both the *Bakke* and *Weber* decisions of the 1970s, the Supreme Court still retained a working majority of moderate conservatives and liberals, who favored the expansion of civil rights, over the extreme conservatives led by Associate Justice William Rehnquist. In a series of high court decisions in 1985 and early 1986, for example, majority decisions in the Supreme Court repudiated the Reagan Administration on a number of cases. In *P. E. Basemore v. William C. Friday,* for example, the Supreme Court declared that minorities suing firms in discrimination cases had only to illustrate patterns of racism by statistical information rather than to prove intent to discriminate. Over the vigorous complaints of Justice Department officials of the Reagan Administration, the court refused in *Thornburg v. Gingles* to restrict the type of evidence used to prove voting rights violations. In *Wygant v. Jackson Board of Education,* the Supreme Court specifically upheld the use of racial goals and timetables to overcome patterns of discrimination in hiring policies.[16] Reagan's reelection in 1984 permitted him to reverse these trends by appointing several conservative members to the high court, tipping the balance to the right. The addition of Antonin Scalia and Anthony Kennedy as associate justices, and the nomination of Rehnquist as chief justice, consolidated an anti–civil rights majority. In his 1986 confirmation hearings, liberals were dismayed to learn that Rehnquist's political history was far more problematic than had been previously known. In 1952, for instance, as a young Supreme Court clerk Rehnquist drafted a memo declaring that the racist "separate but equal" doctrine was "right and should be reaffirmed." As a U.S. assistant attorney general, he had purchased a home carrying a deed requiring resale to "Caucasians only." As an Arizona Republican politician in the 1960s, he had harassed and intimidated African-American and Mexican-American voters. After being named to the Supreme Court by Nixon in 1972, Rehnquist voted against 82 out of 83 cases in which the court had focused on the rights of women, the elderly, the disabled and/or racial minority groups. Despite the record, Rehnquist was confirmed as the nation's sixteenth chief justice; he received the largest number of opposing votes against any confirmed high court nominee in the twentieth century.[17]

Rehnquist's ascension as chief justice marked a fundamental turning point in the history of civil rights. Despite the defeat of conservative legal scholar Robert H. Bork as associate justice in 1987, the liberal-to-moderate majority in the high court no longer existed. In a series of controversial decisions, the Supreme Court eroded or eliminated civil rights that had been taken for granted for more than a generation. In the *Patterson v. McLean Credit Union* decision of June 1989, sixty-six U.S. senators and 145 members of the House of Representatives had filed "friend of the court" briefs supporting the NAACP's contention that the Civil Rights Act of 1866 had prohibited discrimination in hiring policies. The court ruled, however, that the 1866 act did not cover on-the-job harassment. In the *Martin v. Wilkes* case, the Supreme Court ruled that no deadline applied to suits by white employees challenging affirmative action consent decrees which had been designed to halt discriminatory hiring patterns against minorities. The most controversial decision also occurred in 1989, *Atonio v. Wards Cove Packing Company. Atonio* declared that alleged victims of racism had to prove not only that a specific policy of their employers discriminated against women or minorities but also that such practice did not serve "legitimate business goals." Julius L. Chambers, the director-counsel of the NAACP Legal Defense and Education Fund, maintained the rulings demonstrated that "a majority of the Court is inclined to narrow significantly the statutory protections against racial and gender discrimination and to place nearly insurmountable obstacles before those who seek to vindicate their rights in court."[18] Most outspoken in his attacks on the Rehnquist majority was Associate Justice Thurgood Marshall. "It is difficult to characterize last term's decisions as the product of anything other than a deliberate retrenching of the civil rights agenda," Marshall declared in late 1989. Now as a participant in an embattled and aging liberal minority, Marshall denounced the Supreme Court for having "truly come full circle" on civil rights. "History teaches that when the Supreme Court has been willing to shortchange the equality rights of underrepresented ethnic groups, other basic personal civil liberties like the rights to free speech and to personal security against unreasonable searches and seizures are also threatened."[19]

As liberal criticism of the Reagan Administration's civil rights record mounted, conservatives astutely attempted to recruit African-American middle-class leaders to join the Republican Party. A core of black administrators and attorneys was appointed into the administration, including Thelma Duggin, the liaison of the Republican Party's National Committee to the National Black Voters Program; Presidential Assistant Melvin Bradley; Vice President George Bush's assistant Thaddeus Garret; and Arthur Teele, Jr., a wealthy Florida attorney named to administer a four-billion-dollar budget as director of the Urban Mass Transit Administration. More influential was Clarence Thomas, a conservative black attorney named in 1982 to direct the Equal Employment Opportunity Commission. The Democrat-turned-Republican was a caustic critic of affirmative action programs and timetables in 1985. Under Thomas, the Commission deliberately retarded its investigation of discrimination complaints, and the proportion of cases in which the agency ruled "no cause" for a lawsuit soared from 28.5 percent in 1980 to 56.6 percent in 1986.[20]

After Reagan's political landslide of 1984, upper-middle-class blacks became increasingly vocal about the limitations of supporting the Democratic Party. The majority of white Americans were becoming more conservative ideologically, they observed, and African-Americans had to align themselves with the more influential bloc. This political logic motivated Michigan politician William Lucas, a powerful black Democrat, to make a well-publicized switch to the Republicans in May 1985. Lucas's background—former New York City police officer, FBI agent, and county sheriff—appealed to the "law-and-order," conservative white constituency, and his fiscal conservatism and opposition to abortion rights placated white extremists who usually would oppose a black candidate purely on racial grounds. Lucas ran successfully for the Republican gubernatorial nomination in Michigan in 1986, with thousands of black Democrats crossing over to vote for him. Defeated in the general election by a white conservative Democrat, Lucas received only 31 percent of the vote but helped to reinforce the Republicans' public commitment to African-American candidates. Others followed Lucas's lead into the Republican Party. Also in 1986, blacks ran as Republican candidates for Congress in Arkansas, Massachusetts, Michigan, Illinois, Georgia, Ohio, and Maryland. In Maryland, attorney George Haley, the brother of black novelist/journalist Alex Haley, was the unsuccessful Senate candidate in the Republican Party primary. Moderate white Republicans who made earnest attempts to support civil rights issues found that they could garner impressive support from black voters, for the first time since the Great Depression. The best example came in New Jersey in 1985, when 60 percent of the African-American vote was cast for Republican governor Thomas Kean. His self-serving advice to blacks was to break their half-century commitment to the Democrats and to use their influence within both parties pragmatically. In 1986, when he was invited to deliver that message to the San Francisco convention of the National Urban League, he received a standing ovation.[21]

The most prominent black Reaganites to emerge were Samuel Pierce, secretary of the Department of Housing and Urban Development; Robert Woodson, president of the National Center for Neighborhood Enterprise; and a group of conservative black economists and social scientists, led by Hoover Institution scholar Thomas Sowell, Walter Williams of George Mason University, and Harvard University professor Glenn Loury. Almost without exception, the black Reaganites rejected the traditional civil rights agenda of affirmative action, government-sponsored social welfare programs, and coalitions with trade unions and white liberal constituencies. Pierce served in the Reagan Administration for eight years, but was known as "Silent Sam" because he avoided publicity. Behind the scenes, however, Pierce and his lieutenants actively allocated federal funds for low-income housing to Republican consultants and corporate interests. Pierce's successor as secretary of Housing and Urban Development, Jack Kemp, estimated in 1990 that the cost of fraud, official graft and influence-peddling under Pierce totalled two to four billion dollars. Developers paid millions of dollars to Reagan Administration officials in order to obtain scarce federal housing funds, in direct violation of the law.[22]

The new black conservatives argued that African-Americans had to conform to the new reactionary political realities, and become active participants in the new social order of entrepreneurial capitalism. Williams aggressively condemned what he termed the "use of racial quotas for the purposes of redressing historical grievances" and urged the creation of a sub-minimum wage to promote black employment. Sowell, a former Marxist, articulated the rejection of the alliance with the Democratic Party: "Camelot seems unlikely to return and we cannot bet the future of twenty million blacks on its return. We have to recognize that many [liberal] methods were failing before they even lost public support." Woodson offered a more creative but equally conservative critique of the strategic shortcomings of the civil rights organizations and black liberal Democratic leaders. "Most groups in this society didn't start off trying to achieve political equity," he argued in 1986. "They went into business. Blacks, unfortunately, have focused almost exclusively on civil rights for the past twenty years or so, as if applying civil rights solutions would somehow translate into economic equity. It does not." Woodson's basic argument of economic power leading ultimately to political influence was an over-simplification, not validated by black history. It was a restructuring of Booker T. Washington's black capitalist strategy of acquiescence to racial segregation laws, in return for expanded opportunities for black entrepreneurs to control the Negro consumer market within the context of Jim Crowed society. Moreover, the juxtaposition of the struggle for equal rights with black economic empowerment was equally false. For example, the March on Washington in 1963 had called for a comprehensive jobs program. Affirmative action, a central tenet of the civil rights agenda, had created hundreds of thousands of new jobs for minorities throughout the 1970s. Despite the historical record, however, Woodson insisted that civil rights leaders had ignored economic issues. "If you have economic power," Woodson advised, "you vote every day with your money. If you have political power, you vote only once every two years."[23]

Inspired by the ideological offensive against the black liberal establishment, extreme conservative groups began to target the black community, recruiting African-American ministers, community leaders and even former militants to advocate far-right interests. Eldridge Cleaver was persuaded to challenge Ron Dellums for his congressional seat in 1986, and CORE leader Roy Innis ran against Representative Major Owens for central Brooklyn's congressional seat. Although both Cleaver and Innis were defeated by substantial margins, they succeeded in mobilizing a segment of the black community for conservative causes. More effective was the far right political cult of Lyndon LaRouche. In 1984 LaRouche's organization established the Schiller Institute, whose assistant director, Allan Salsbury, was an African-American. The Schiller Institute was designed to recruit unsuspecting black leaders to rally behind conservative causes. In January 1985, the Institute sponsored a march and rally in Washington, D.C. for the "Inalienable Rights of Man," which attracted as many as ten thousand African-Americans. Theoretically the mobilization was designed to honor the memory of King, and to support American relief efforts to address famine in Africa; but the march's program combined these liberal positions with support of the Reagan Administration's Strategic Defense Initiative, popularly termed "Star Wars," which would allocate billions of dollars to nuclear weaponry. Dozens of prominent black ministers and local leaders, including veterans of the Civil Rights Movement, participated in the Schiller-sponsored rally. One busload of African-American participants travelled from Tuskegee, Alabama, to attend the gathering. The rally's slogan captured the contradictory purposes of the mobilization: "I Have a Dream, Feed Africa, and Build the Beam." LaRouche followed this effort by fielding a number of African-American candidates, running on far-right platforms, against black officeholders. In Michigan, a black retired autoworker, Henry Wilson, received 6 percent of the vote as the LaRouche-backed candidate for governor. In Baltimore, LaRouche-supported candidate Hazel Judd, a black woman, received about 2 percent of the vote for a congressional seat. The net impact of LaRouche's intervention was to fragment the black community and to weaken its traditional leaders.[24]

Despite these efforts to create a political base for conservatism within

the African-American community, the vast majority of blacks from all social classes continued to reject Reaganism. One extensive black opinion
poll commissioned by the *Washington Post* in January 1986, indicated that
40 percent of all blacks believed that Reagan's policies had "held them
back," 33 percent stated that his policies had "made no difference," while
only 11 percent claimed that they had "helped." Fifty-six percent of all
blacks agreed with the statement that "Ronald Reagan was a racist."
African-Americans, by a substantial 80 percent to 16 percent margin, stated
that they desired a "larger government with many services"; while a majority of white Americans, 54 percent to 40 percent, favored the Reagan-
inspired philosophy of "smaller government with fewer services." In 1988
African-Americans indicated their preference for the Democratic Party
over the Republican by a margin of 86 percent to 11 percent; conversely,
among white Americans the Republicans held a slight edge over the Democrats in partisan affiliation, 49 percent to 44 percent. Consequently, when
Vice President George Bush organized his campaign for the presidency in
1988, he relied on many of the racially motivated methods of his predecessor, Ronald Reagan. Bush's campaign director Lee Atwater attempted to
associate the Democratic presidential candidate, Massachusetts governor
Michael S. Dukakis, with the image of tolerating black criminality. Bush
himself publicly aligned his campaign with local white political leaders,
such as former Philadelphia mayor Frank Rizzo, who had polarized racial
constituencies. By manipulating racial stereotypes, though more subtly
than Reagan, Bush successfully benefitted from conservative and racist
sentiment against blacks—a strategy that contributed to his electoral victory over Dukakis.[25]

Bush strategists recognized that the Republican Party would never
wrest control of the House of Representatives and many state legislatures
from the Democrats unless a substantial number of minorities defected
from their traditional allies. This defection would require a tactical shift in
racial rhetoric and, to a lesser extent, substantial programmatic support
for interests favored by the civil rights community. Consequently, as president Bush quickly attempted to distinguish himself from Reagan by being
sympathetic to blacks' concerns. In Reagan's eight years as president, for
example, he had met briefly and testily with black leaders only eight times;
by contrast, Bush caucused with African-American political, business and
educational representatives more than forty times during his first two years
in office. Bush publicly praised South African leader Nelson Mandela, and
endorsed the continuation of economic sanctions to pressure the apartheid
regime of South Africa to negotiate with black leaders. Bush increased the
budget of the Equal Employment Opportunity Commission to $185 mil-
lion, its largest fiscal allocation in history, in order to "ensure that the

agency maintains a productive workforce in its enforcement of laws prohibiting employment discrimination." [26] The Bush Administration launched an
"Initiative on Historically Black Colleges and Universities," designed to
direct more federal funds to black higher educational institutions. The administration encouraged black colleges to form consortia to work with federal agencies and promoted the creation of minority-owned enterprises
which could stimulate economic resources for these institutions. One
black Bush aide in charge of the program, Robert K. Goodwin, even became involved in Hampton University's attempt to assume control over
two failed savings and loan establishments. Black educators were impressed with the Bush Administration's sensitivity to their economic plight.
Speaking for many peers, Tougaloo College president Adib A. Shakir declared: "I'm glad to see they are realizing how pivotal strategic planning is
to the survival of historically black colleges." [27] Similarly, when in late
1989 several racist mail bombings killed a civil rights attorney in Georgia
and a federal judge in Alabama, Bush denounced these murders as "hide-
ous" and vowed publicly to bring these "bigots" to justice. "This administration will not let up in the fight against racism," Bush declared. "We
will work to bring the perpetrators of these crimes to justice." Bush also
repeatedly praised the political legacy of Martin Luther King, Jr., but astutely ignored the final five years of the civil rights leader's public career as
a critic of the Vietnam War, domestic poverty and capitalism. "Like President Lincoln, Martin Luther King, Jr., knew that the United States could
not remain a free and great nation so long as the rights of any individual
are denied." Bush stated in his proclamation declaring King's birthday a
federal holiday. "This event celebrates the greatness of a man whose life
and legacy helped set America free." [28]

The net impact of Bush's verbal and political overtures to black America
reaped impressive political gains. Bush's approval ratings among African-
Americans in public opinion polls exceeded 50 percent, substantially
lower than white public support for the president but nevertheless much
higher than any previous Republican chief executive's ratings among
blacks. Bush furthered his moderate image among blacks by nominating
liberal Republican Arthur A. Fletcher, the former executive director of
the United Negro College Fund, as chairman of the Civil Rights Commission. Fletcher's selection was an indication, according to Bush administration officials, that "the concerns of minorities" should be more "forcefully
represented." [29] Compared to the undisguised racial antipathy of Reagan,
Bush's rather modest response to blacks' concerns appeared almost liberal
and politically enlightened. In terms of actual economic and social policy,
however, Bush represented a continuation of the Reagan agenda of austerity for urban problems and reductions in human services and in federal

initiatives for employment. The Education Department's Office for Civil Rights stopped its staff members from conducting compliance investigations or reviewing universities that had already been found in violation of civil rights laws. In 1989, Bush unsuccessfully attempted to make William Lucas head of the Justice Department's civil rights division. Lucas's lack of experience in civil rights law, and his toleration of severe police brutality against blacks during his tenure as Wayne County sheriff in Michigan, led the NAACP and other liberal groups to oppose the nomination. After Lucas failed to win Senate confirmation, Bush nominated a White Republican politician, John Dunne, who had been described as "invisible" on civil rights issues. Bush also nominated Reaganite ideologue Clarence Thomas for a seat on the United States Court of Appeals for the District of Columbia. Thomas's appointment was widely interpreted as positioning the black conservative to replace the elderly Thurgood Marshall upon his retirement from the Supreme Court.[30]

The overt hostility toward African-Americans manifested by the Reagan Administration, and Bush's lukewarm embrace of civil rights, created a political culture among broad sections of the white public that was scarcely sympathetic to blacks' interests. Although the upsurge of random racist violence characteristic of the early 1980s subsided slightly in the following years, public officials felt more comfortable expressing racist opinions openly and without reservation. In New Orleans in 1986, for example, Jefferson Parish sheriff Harry Lee announced that local police would target probable criminals who have "no business in the neighborhood. If there are some young blacks driving a car late at night in a predominantly white area, they will be stopped." After Lee's statement was criticized by local civil rights groups, opinion polls indicated that whites overwhelmingly supported Lee's blatant violation of civil liberties.[31] Conservative Republican governor Evan Mecham of Arizona moved to rescind a state holiday honoring King, repudiating the civil rights leader's legacy.[32] The Ku Klux Klan operated with little federal pressure. Klansmen rallied in Oxford, Ohio, High Point, North Carolina, and dozens of U.S. towns and cities each year. In Atlanta in January 1990, Klansmen held a racist demonstration near King's gravesite, protected from outraged blacks by more than 2,500 law enforcement officers. Racist attorney Richard Barrett, speaking at the anti-King rally, voiced the opinion of many who had voted for both Reagan and Bush: "My fellow Americans, that grave is not a throne. That corpse is not a king."[33] In Florida, Klan groups announced that they intended to "join the battle against illegal drugs" by becoming "the eyes and ears of the police." Klansmen vowed specifically to "capture black drug dealers" and also to "target black prostitutes."[34] More sophisticated was the approach of former Klansman and Nazi David Duke.

Elected to the Louisiana House as a Republican, Duke ran openly as a white supremacist within the established political process. Duke's success prompted similar efforts elsewhere: in Memphis, white supremacist Scott Sheppard ran for the Tennessee state legislature; in Knoxville, neo-Nazi Gary Gallo announced his candidacy for Congress in 1990; in North Carolina, Harold Convington, leader of the Confederate Knights of America, declared his intention to run "white supremacist candidates as Republicans, Democrats and Independents" across the state.[35]

Racist violence still occurred throughout the 1980s, however, promoted by the government's hostility to affirmative action and legislation favorable to African-Americans. In the span of three months in the summer of 1985, for instance, a series of incidents occurred throughout the United States: in Mount Lebanon, Pennsylvania, in May and July, crosses were burned on the lawn of a black family; two crosses were burned at blacks' houses in Nashville; in Boston, white teenagers attacked three Vietnamese youths, and one Asian-American male was murdered in a racist attack; in Elizabeth, New Jersey, on 17 August, a cross was torched at the home of an African-American family in an upper-income neighborhood, with the words "No Niggers" painted on the driveway; and in Iowa City, two young black males were gang-attacked and sexually raped by white racists.[36] Although neither the Reagan Administration nor Republican officials condoned this type of racist violence, the example of Reagan himself inspired and perpetuated these manifestations of racial hatred. After Reagan's election, for example, one white male teacher was overheard confiding to his colleagues: "Now that Reagan is president, I guess we can say 'nigger' without going to court."[37]

IV

Behind the Civil Rights Movement was the concept of equality, the principle that every American should exercise certain political rights, such as the electoral franchise and the freedom to run for public office. But equality in social and material terms goes far beyond the confines of the political process, to the very heart of social-class divisions embedded within the fabric of the social order. Egalitarianism implies that a fairer and more democratic society can only be achieved through the deliberate intervention of the state, promoting more equal distribution of income, wealth and ownership of productive resources. In the 1980s, more than anything else, Reaganism represented a break with the half-century-old notion among both Democrats and Republicans that the state had a political and ethical obligation to reduce the vast chasm separating the society's wealthiest classes from the poor and the unemployed. Within the Reagan Administration, inequality as a political concept was defended as absolutely essential to continued economic growth and productivity. The unequal distribution of wealth was part of the natural order of humanity and, like plagues and droughts, would always be with us.

The consequences of social and economic policies that favored accelerating inequality were profound and long lasting. A generation ago, during the Republican administration of Dwight Eisenhower, the wealthiest Americans were taxed at the rate of 91 percent; under Reagan's tax reforms of 1986, the highest tax rate was only 28 percent. Corporate taxes fell sharply, and many major businesses paid absolutely no taxes. The burden of government fell disproportionately on the poor and working class. This shift in economic inequality can now be measured. According to the Economic Policy Institute of Washington, D.C., the "share of the nation's wealth owned by the top 10 percent of its households rose from 67.5 percent to 73.1 percent between 1979 and 1988." The after-tax family incomes of the wealthiest 10 percent of all Americans rose from 29.5 percent to 34.5 percent. Conversely, the income percentage for the poorest 10 percent declined from 1.7 percent to 1.4 percent during the same period. Between 1981 and 1989, the real value of the minimum wage in inflation-adjusted dollars declined 44 percent. The size of the middle class shrank significantly, and the numbers of working poor increased dramatically.[38] By the end of Reagan's second term in office, the number of Americans living below the official poverty level was 32 million. The poverty rates by race were 10.1 percent for whites, 26.8 percent for Hispanics, and 31.6 percent for African-Americans. According to Robert Greenstein of the Center on Budget and Policy Priorities, "the increasing prosperity of high wage earners and the statistically insignificant gains made by middle- and lower-income Americans widened the gap between the nation's richest and poorest Americans to an all-time level."[39] As the number of homeless Americans more than doubled to a figure between two and three million by 1988, the federal government and the private sector withdrew critical support to the disadvantaged. Federal government allocations of surplus food to charitable organizations fell sharply in the late 1980s, as the problem of hunger became a serious health issue for millions of poor people.[40]

For the African-American community, there were very practical consequences from the federal government's deliberate policies of social inequality. In terms of health care, federal resources for minorities were sharply curtailed. Hundreds of hospitals of inner-city areas were forced to reduce personnel; in 1988 alone, 81 community-based hospitals closed. By 1990, at least 31.5 million Americans were not covered by any health insurance or government programs such as Medicaid or Medicare. Poverty and the lack of federal health programs compounded a variety of health problems experienced by blacks. According to surveys of the Johns Hopkins Wilmer Eye Institute in 1990, for example, African-Americans are nearly twice as likely to be legally blind or to suffer impaired vision than whites, largely because they are unable to afford regular eye examinations and corrective lenses. About 1.5 percent of all blacks over 40 years of age are legally blind, compared to only 0.9 percent of all white Americans.[41] Between 1979 and 1986, asthma deaths among African-Americans increased by 50 percent, due in part to "poor medical care, heavier concentrations of pollution in the inner cities, and cockroach dust." The asthma death rate for blacks by 1990 was three times that for whites.[42] Diabetes also strikes blacks disproportionately. Between 1963 and 1985, diagnosed cases of diabetes among African-Americans increased nearly 400 percent, to one million cases. Blacks are 50 to 60 percent more likely to contract the disease than whites; one-fourth of all black women over 55 years have diabetes.[43] Cancer is particularly devastating to blacks, who have the highest rate of incidence for all types of cancers combined. About 373 per 100,000 blacks contracted cancer annually between 1978 and 1981, and the mortality rates for blacks were one-quarter to one-third higher than those for whites. Part of the heavy incidence of cancer among blacks could be attributed to the high expenditures for billboard advertising in black communities ($5.8 million in 1985), and the heavy promotion of tobacco-related products in black-oriented publications and media. Consequently, blacks smoke one-third more than whites. The absence of public health information on both smoking and dietary practices also contributed to the abnormally high death rates among African-Americans.[44]

Blacks are also particularly vulnerable to other treatable diseases. In the late 1980s, the most rapid increase in victims of Acquired Immune Deficiency Syndrome was among black and Hispanic males, many of whom contracted the disease through intravenous drug use. For years public health officials did little to provide safe sex information in poor neighborhoods. Poor blacks with AIDS survived on average half as long as whites with the disease, because of late treatment and lack of access to the latest experimental drugs. By 1990, 27 percent of all AIDS sufferers were African-American; more than half of all women with AIDS were black.[45] Reductions in public health expenditures contributed to problems of infant mortality and to the decline in black life expectancies as well. In 1987, the infant mortality rate for black babies was 17.9 deaths per thousand live births, more than twice the rate for whites. In the mid-1980s, black male life expectancies began to decline slightly in relation to those for whites; by 1987, black males had an average life expectancy of 65 years—seven years less than white males and thirteen years less than white women. The overall state of black health care was perhaps best illustrated by the *New England*

Journal of Medicine 1990 report, "Excess Mortality in Harlem." The report indicated that the "life expectancy for a black male born and living in Harlem is shorter than that of a male born in Bangladesh." Socio-economic factors contributing to what the authors termed the "excess deaths" of Harlem blacks included "poverty, inadequate housing, psychological stress, malnutrition, and inadequate access to medical care."[46]

Inequality of social conditions was also expressed in housing statistics. As of 1985, 40 percent of Hispanic and 37 percent of African-American households with incomes below the poverty line spent at least 70 percent of their disposable income solely on housing costs. More than half of all black households below the poverty line (nearly two million) and about 60 percent of all Hispanic households below the poverty line paid at least one-half their income to cover housing costs. Less than 44 percent of all black families owned homes in 1985, and only 28 percent of all low-income African-American households held mortgages.[47] Despite federal laws prohibiting racial bias in the lending of capital for home mortgages, blacks at all income levels found it extremely difficult to obtain adequate funds to purchase adequate housing. Between 1982 and 1987, according to a report by the Federal Reserve Bank of Boston, the city's African-American neighborhoods obtained 24 percent fewer home mortgage loans than white communities. Real estate agents, developers and bankers collaborated to deny blacks the capital for home purchases. Similarly, in Denver, according to a 1989 study, local whites received twice as many home mortgage loans as blacks and Hispanics, and local banks and savings and loan institutions gave three times more money to white neighborhoods than to minority areas in the city. Investigators observed that "race—not income—appeared to determine home-lending patterns at Denver's banking and savings institutions."[48] University of Chicago researchers also found that blacks were forced to live in neighborhoods of much poorer quality than whites with identical educational backgrounds and family incomes. Statistically, an Asian-American or Hispanic with a third-grade education is more likely to live in a racially integrated neighborhood than an African-American with a doctorate. A black American earning above $50,000 annually in 1989 was less likely to live in an integrated community than a Hispanic or Asian making under $2,500 per year.[49]

Under the Reagan Administration, federal housing allocations fell sharply, from $30 billion in fiscal year 1981 to barely $8 billion in fiscal year 1986. Reductions in federal expenditures curtailed the overall number of housing units available to the working poor, the unemployed and households receiving Aid to Families with Dependent Children. By 1986, the Department of Housing and Urban Development (HUD) admitted that over 70,000 housing units annually were "boarded up" and another

1,000 units were destroyed because the "repair costs exceed the units' worth." Between 1981 and 1986, the number of public housing units in minority neighborhoods dropped severely: from 3,500 to 2,622 in Indianapolis; from 7,000 to 6,400 in San Francisco. Simultaneously, under Samuel Pierce, scarce funds which should have been allocated for the housing of the urban poor were funneled to wealthy real estate developers and Republican Party donors. In Columbus, Ohio, for example, between 1987 and 1989, 2,500 minority families were denied public housing because HUD claimed that funds were not available. But during the same years, HUD gave local developers tens of millions of dollars directly from housing funds to build putting greens, whirlpool baths, and luxury penthouse suites worth $1,795 per month. So many luxury apartments were built in nearby Cincinnati with HUD funds that the market was oversupplied, and only one-third were even rented. Public losses from the Cincinnati project in 1987–89 exceeded $21 million, enough to pay two years' rent for 5,400 low-income and minority families.[50]

Even when federal and state funds were allocated for the construction of housing for low-income families and the homeless, the money frequently was misdirected or even unspent. In 1988, the New York state legislature set aside $85 million to build shelter for homeless families in New York City. After two years, city officials were unable to provide abandoned buildings or vacant properties for the construction of new housing.[51] Meanwhile, the crisis of urban homelessness continued to worsen. By 1987, it was estimated that Dallas had only one thousand beds at emergency shelters for an estimated homeless population totalling 14,000. Only several thousand of Los Angeles's 35,000 homeless people found shelter provided by government agencies or private sources. Most lived in city parks, under highway bridges, or in abandoned buildings and automobiles. More than one-half million children below the age of sixteen were homeless. More than one-quarter of the homeless population was black. The national shame of homelessness was symbolized in December 1986, when a homeless man in Boston burned to death attempting to stay warm.[52]

As urban society increasingly acquired Hobbesian characteristics, with daily life characteristically "nasty" and "brutish" and life spans frequently "short," there was an inevitable erosion of social institutions and traditional leadership within the African-American community. Despite difficulty in obtaining mortgages, many middle-class blacks found the resources to leave the central cities for the suburbs. Between 1970 and 1986, the black population in suburbia increased from 3.6 million to 7.1 million, representing one-quarter of all black homes. Black suburban households on average had significantly higher incomes and higher levels of education than their urban counterparts. In 1980, the black suburban household's average income of $20,063 was appreciably higher than the average black city household's figure of $13,362. Approximately two-thirds of all black suburban families whose chief income earner had four or more years of college lived in neighborhoods with less than 10 percent black population.[53] In some cities, the exodus of the black middle class was partially the product of deliberate government policy. In Washington, D.C., for instance, the share of the federal government's contribution to the city's budget declined from 20 to barely 14 percent in the 1980s. In compensation, local tax burdens sharply increased to $3,339 per capita in 1988, in order to cover the costs of city services, health and housing. As the city's economic and social problems multiplied, African-American middle-income households increasingly moved outside the District of Columbia's boundaries, in search of better property values and superior public schools. Washington, D.C.'s population lost nearly 30,000 residents between 1986 and 1989; by the end of the decade, more African-Americans lived in the suburbs than inside the city.[54]

For those blacks who were left behind in the ghetto, the influence of traditional social institutions deteriorated, or was distorted by the impact of violence, poverty and drugs. In New York City, burglaries and robberies of black churches became a serious problem. In October 1989, the Reverend Irving Wilson was murdered by robbers in the sanctuary of his black Baptist church in Brooklyn's Bedford-Stuyvesant neighborhood. After shooting him twice, the assailants dragged the minister's body to the front of his altar, leaving him in the position of a crucified Christ. Terrified, other black ministers began to arm themselves with guns and baseball bats. Many black churches installed elaborate security systems, booby traps, and electrical wires to protect their property. Increasingly, black citizens took the law into their own hands, refusing to trust the police or the courts to provide justice. In late December 1989, a so-called "Subway Samaritan" knifed and killed one black mugger and never surrendered to police, despite offers by one newspaper to pay his entire legal costs. Several weeks later Rodney Sumter, an unemployed Harlem plumber travelling on a subway, was assaulted by a homeless man. Sumter knocked the man down, battering his head against the concrete platform and killing him. After surrendering voluntarily, Sumter was exonerated by the New York grand jury. The "justification" for vigilante violence was drug-related crime, which in New York City totalled 93,377 robberies and 1,905 homicides in 1989 alone. In disproportionate numbers, African-Americans were the chief victims of such crimes.[55]

The social institution most deeply scarred was the minority family. By 1989, roughly 55 percent of the nation's 9.8 million African-American children and approximately one-third of the 7 million Hispanic children lived with only one parent. Thirteen percent of all black children lived in their grandparents' homes, compared to only 3 percent of all white children. The married, two-parent family became increasingly atypical among blacks. As of 1986, the Census Bureau projected that about one-tenth of all black males and 16 percent of black females currently at the age of fifteen would statistically never be married. Curiously, the Bureau noted that 21 percent of all black women with five or more years of college would likely remain unmarried. Black women with children by absent fathers were far less likely than white women to receive child support payments; moreover, payments to white mothers were much higher than those to blacks. The destructive sociological trends which had become evident in the 1970s were being fully realized, with devastating results.[56]

The social and economic problems confronting the African-American community seemed so overwhelming that traditional liberal remedies of government intervention appeared insufficient. In early 1990, the National Urban League revived a thirty-year-old proposal calling for a domestic version of the Marshall Plan, which would provide $50 billion to "ensure that our neglected minority population gets the education, housing, health care and job skills they need to help America compete successfully in a global economy," declared League president John Jacob. Many other liberal black leaders, recognizing the diminished probability in the Reagan-Bush era of receiving any significant support from the federal government, began to crusade for increased "self-help" efforts. Marian Wright Edelman, president of the Children's Defense Fund, argued in 1986 that "for most of the history of black America, the government has been our opponent, not our ally. The black community knows in its bones that without its strong leadership now, as in the past, little help can be expected from government or other institutions." Similar sentiments were advanced by Jesse Jackson: "Black Americans must begin to accept a larger share of responsibility for their lives. For too many years we have been crying that racism and oppression have to be fought on every front. . . . [We must stop] moaning about what the enemy has done to us."[57] Other blacks darkly suspected that the terrible ravages of crime, drugs and poverty were a conscious product of government and corporate policy, which by the early 1990s was popularly termed "The Plan." Millions were convinced that a "white-supremacist" strategy existed to jail and discredit African-American leadership, to deliberately increase joblessness and, in the words of journalist Clarence Page, "to cut down the nation's black population through massive doses of drugs, AIDS, booze, cigarettes and other alleged tools of black genocide." In April 1990, when black psychiatrist Frances Cress Welsing declared on national television that a "genocidal 'plan'" existed in which firearms and illegal drugs were deliberately placed in the ghetto "so blacks could destroy themselves," she received an ovation from other blacks. Even the National Urban League's 1990 report on the *State of Black America* suggested: "There is at least one concept that must be recognized if one is to see the pervasive and insidious nature of the drug problem for the African-American community. Though difficult to accept, that is the concept of genocide."[58] White social scientists and government officials dismissed blacks' ruminations on "The Plan" as an example of African-American paranoia. But as the casualty figures mounted, and as the post-industrial cities of the Northeast and Midwest became socially dysfunctional war zones, even cautious observers began to wonder. The black community's dysphoria was the product of calculated government policy, economic divestment and social irresponsibility, rooted in the preservation of the ideal of human inequality.

V

Black Americans could never forget that the demise of the rigid racial segregation laws throughout the United States during the first six decades of the twentieth century was not the result of a moral metamorphosis by white politicians, corporate executives, and philanthropists. Four pivotal factors explained the rapid collapse of the Jim Crow system during the 1950s and 1960s: (1) the outbreak of the Cold War between the United States and the Soviet Union, which resulted in international pressures for American governments to abandon support for their undemocratic and irrational policies of racial domination; (2) the independence from European colonial rule of Caribbean and African states whose people were connected with Americans of African descent by ethnicity, culture, and a common heritage of political and economic struggle against systems of exploitation; (3) the great migration of five million African-American sharecroppers and working people from the South into the urban ghettoes of the Midwest and Northeast between 1940 and 1970, a migration that transformed the political character of urban society and deeply influenced the patterns of American popular culture, sports, education and social relations; and (4) most important, the growth of popular democratic resistance movements, led by King and thousands of local activists, that used the nonviolent, direct-action protest techniques of Mohandas Gandhi's *satyagraha*. The definition of politics within the tradition of black political culture was radically different from that of the white majority, which perceived questions of governance and power within the context of electoral participation. The ordeals of black America, in the process of struggling for full rights, created a collective memory of resistance, which continued to motivate many African-Americans to search for innovative methods of challenging entrenched white elites in government and corporations.

The 1980s provided two outstanding examples of black political resistance. Following Reagan's reelection in 1984, a core of black progressive activists mapped out a strategy to attack the administration's links with apartheid South Africa. The group was led by Randall Robinson, executive director of Transafrica, a Washington, D.C.–based foreign policy lobbying group; civil rights commissioner Mary Frances Berry; and District of Columbia representative Walter Fauntroy. Robinson, Berry and Fauntroy staged a small symbolic demonstration in front of the South African embassy in late November 1984, and they were "pleasantly surprised" when officials panicked and called police. Thir arrests sparked a series of nonviolent demonstrations across the United States. Within two weeks, protests were staged at South African consulates in more than one dozen cities, including Salt Lake City, Boston, Chicago and Houston. The arrested leaders represented a range of liberal to moderate politicians, religious groups, labor leaders and minorities. In New York City, for example, those arrested for blocking the consulate entrance included the Reverend Herbert Daughtry, chairperson of the National Black United Front; Roman Catholic bishop Emerson J. Moore; Hazel Dukes, state chairperson of the NAACP; and New York City clerk David Dinkins. In Washington, D.C., among those arrested were Joslyn Williams, president of the Greater Washington, D.C. Central Labor Council; Congressman Parren Mitchell; and liberal Republican senator Lowell Weicker. Activists attacked the Reagan administration's policy of "constructive engagement" was apartheid, noting that the government had supported the extension of international monetary funds to the regime, had established offices in Johannesburg to promote U.S. investment inside the country, and had even sent apartheid police 2,500 electric shock batons which were used to torture prisoners. Jesse Jackson pressured the Democratic Party's leadership to demand immediate freedom for Nelson Mandela, the political spokesperson for the African National Congress who had been imprisoned for more than two decades, and freedom for other political prisoners as well. Black congressman George Crockett secured a nonbinding congressional resolution urging President Reagan to "use his good offices" to secure Mandela's release.[59]

On college campuses, thousands of students demonstrated against university investments in firms that did business inside South Africa. Divestment legislation amounting to $400 million in public funds was secured in Massachusetts, Connecticut, Michigan, Maryland, Philadelphia, Washington, D.C., and dozens of smaller cities. The mobilization had the positive effect of reviving the lagging coalition between civil rights leaders, liberal whites, labor and the Jewish community. Although some orthodox and conservative Jewish groups refused to demonstrate against apartheid, because of Israel's extensive economic and military connections with South Africa, the vast majority of Jewish leaders expressed solidarity with the mobilization. Members of the Union of American Hebrew Congregations and the American Jewish Congress organized protests. In San Francisco, members of the International Longshoremen's and Warehousemen's Union refused to unload cargo from South Africa, and more than five hundred dockworkers and community leaders staged daily demonstrations. As M. Carl Holman, the executive director of the National Urban Coalition observed, the renaissance of "sit-ins" was useful in bringing together progressive and anti-Reagan constituencies. "This kind of action will probably result in a spurt of action in other areas," Holman predicted.[60] The net result was congressional action in 1986 requiring strict economic sanctions against South Africa, passed over Reagan's fierce opposition. The economic and political disruption created by worldwide sanctions pressured the apartheid regime to release Mandela and other prominent critics in early 1990, to legalize the African National Congress, and to initiate discussions toward a multi-racial democracy in the near future. Black American protests against South African apartheid helped to accelerate the struggle for racial equality and human freedom.

The second manifestation of political militancy was represented by the 1984 and 1988 presidential campaigns of civil rights leader Jesse Jackson. Jackson had been widely viewed as a symbolic protest candidate in the fall of 1983, a representative of African-American unrest against the Democratic Party's failure to oppose the Reagan socio-economic and anti-civil rights agenda. The majority of black elected officials remained at arms length from Jackson, endorsing former vice president Walter Mondale, a moderate Democrat with cordial relations with civil rights groups. Jackson surprised his critics, however, by mobilizing the majority of the African-American clergy behind his candidacy. The National Baptist Convention, with a total membership of 6.5 million blacks, was the first endorser. Black nationalists, including the Black United Front's Daughtry, Los Angeles leader Maulana Karenga, and Nation of Islam leader Louis Farrakhan, backed Jackson's effort. Much of the white left, including socialists, feminists and community activists, joined the mobilization. Jackson advanced a social policy program which in international political terms could be described as "left social democratic": twenty- to twenty-five-percent reductions in military expenditures; a bilateral nuclear arms freeze with the Soviet Union; unconditional opposition to American military intervention in Central America, the Caribbean and southern Africa; the reallocation of billions of dollars in domestic spending to job training programs, health care, public housing, transportation, and urban renewal programs. Despite several major gaffes, including a regrettable offhand remark which smacked of anti-Semitism, Jackson was able to attract 3.5 million popular votes, winning several state primaries and caucuses. In a number of states without significant black populations, Jackson received respectable totals; for example, Arizona, a state with an African-American population of only 3 percent, gave Jackson 14 percent of the Democratic vote in 1984, and 35 percent in 1988. Jackson's electoral effort in 1988 was even more dramatic: more than seven million popular votes, and victories in one hundred congressional districts. Jackson again won victories in several states, notably Alaska and Vermont, with virtually no African-American populations. Three million voters supporting Jackson in 1988 were whites and non-black minorities. Following Jackson's triumph, his 1988 campaign manager, Ronald Brown, was named leader of the Democratic Party's National Committee.[61]

The problem with Jackson's strategy was that it had little impact upon the political agenda of the national Democratic Party. In 1988, Democratic nominee Dukakis refused to select the primaries' second-highest vote recipient, Jackson, as his vice-presidential running mate, choosing instead a conservative Democrat, Texas senator Lloyd Bentsen. Dukakis recognized that he had to win a larger percentage of the white middle-class electorate than either Mondale or Carter if he was to capture the White House. To do this, Dukakis distanced himself from the most loyal constituency of his own party, African-Americans. He didn't campaign in a black church or a major black community until weeks before the election. He casually assumed that African-Americans would vote for him, because with Vice President George Bush as the alternative they had nowhere else to go. It never occurred to Dukakis that another option was indeed available—staying home. Black disaffection with Dukakis was so profound that in the general election only 44 percent of the black electorate voted. Conversely, Dukakis's truncated liberalism alienated most white, upper-middle-class voters as well. His campaign rhetoric suggested a collection of "permissive" social programs and economic redistribution schemes designed for the poor, which from the perspective of elite white voters, connoted a tolerance of criminality and destructive behavior. As real incomes for the white middle class shrank during the 1980s, its members became less altruistic regarding the use of tax revenues to address the problems of the poor and the homeless. Whites earning more than $50,000 annually chose Bush overwhelmingly over Dukakis, because they consciously favored public policies reinforcing racial and class inequality, which benefitted their communities and themselves. Liberalism was sacrificed upon the high altar of narrow self-interest, and Bush defeated Dukakis by a substantial margin. Jackson's impressive constituency was abused by Bush, and all but ignored by Dukakis.[62]

Throughout the 1980s, the racial polarization in America's political system crystallized into a quasi-apartheid, two-tiered structure. Blacks, as a racial group, would frequently vote for white liberal candidates over African-American politicians, if in their judgment the former's agenda was more progressive on public policy issues. But the majority of white Americans, considered as a racial group, found it difficult if not impossible to vote in large numbers for any African-American candidate, regardless of his/her qualifications, education or previous political experience. When white Democrats were forced to choose between a black Democrat, who clearly articulated their class and political interests, and a white Republican who favored corporate interests, the clear majority of whites consistently defected to the white conservative. In the Chicago municipal elections of 1983, for example, black congressman Harold Washington shocked the city's white corporate and political establishment by winning the Democratic mayoral primary. Even though he ran against an unknown Republican state legislator, Bernard Epton, Washington received less than 20 percent of the white regular Democratic vote in the general election and won only by a narrow margin with critical support from Puerto Rican and Mexican-American voters. Through the election of 1988, almost no African-American candidates for statewide office had ever received more than one-third of any white electorate's support, even in solidly Democratic areas. No African-American candidate for mayor of any American city had ever received more than 35 percent of the white vote during his or her initial campaign.

This electoral drift to the ideological right eventually influenced the behavior of a growing number of black politicians, who for nearly two decades had been confined behind this electoral barrier of race—a barrier that kept them from competing for more powerful positions such as governor or United States senator. Positioning themselves further to the right to capture the support of upper-class white voters, they began advancing policy positions that were alien to the tradition of the black freedom struggle. Andrew Young, for example, was elected mayor of Atlanta in 1983 and pursued a conservative economic agenda in office. Running for governor of Georgia in 1990, Young embraced the death penalty, a position which his mentor King would have found repugnant. More influential was Douglas Wilder, a prominent attorney and Virginia state legislator with liberal political credentials. In the early 1980s Wilder began to remake himself, moving to the right of the political spectrum. Winning the lieutenant governorship of Virginia in 1985, Wilder was elected Virginia's first black governor four years later. Wilder's 1989 campaign largely ignored the state's black electorate, and concentrated exclusively on winning about one-third of the state's white vote. This percentage, combined with a strong black turnout, would guarantee victory over his Republican opponent. To achieve these figures, Wilder reversed himself almost completely, endorsing the death penalty, opposing the extension of statehood status to the District of Columbia, and supporting anti-union "right to work" laws. Wilder's victory was widely celebrated among black Americans, but at a cost. The triumph was symbolic, rather than substantive. The African-American community lacked the structures of accountability to modify or effectively check the public or political behavior of its own elected officials, as was apparent in Wilder's case. In the future growing numbers of black politicians could follow the Wilder model, attempting to transcend their own racial designation as "black," for the goal of furthering their personal political objectives. The result could be a vast sense of alienation and frustration with the political process among millions of African-American poor, working-class and unemployed people still trapped in the ghetto, who see little real significance in the elevation of a Wilder to high office. Black representation in government has rarely improved the quality of blacks' lives, and their actual material conditions have become markedly worse since the early 1980s. The new "post-black politicians" such as Wilder, Philadelphia congressman William Gray, Ronald Brown and others have little connection with the militancy and activism of previous leaders.[63]

As the decade of the 1990s begins, the challenges of race, class and power that confront black Americans are far more complicated than King ever anticipated when he stood on the steps of the Lincoln Memorial in August 1963, during the March on Washington. King dreamed of a color-blind society, in which his "four little children" would be judged not "by the color of their skin but by the content of their character." He could not have imagined that this colorblind philosophy would be manipulated to justify the demise of affirmative action programs, civil rights enforcement, and other social reforms designed to provide compensatory justice to the disadvantaged. King cautioned African-Americans not to "seek to satisfy our thirst for freedom by drinking from the cup of bitterness and hatred. . . . We must not allow our creative protest to degenerate into physical violence."[64] King could not have known that the violence engendered would be largely black against black, promoted by drugs and poverty; that the bitterness would be directed against unaccountable black officials and neo-conservative black apologists for the conservative corporate and governmental order. The objectives of the Civil Rights Movement require redefinition, to realize two interrelated goals: the extension of democratic principles from the political system into the structures of the economy and social order, making a job a human right and creating a network of public health care facilities, decent housing and access to free education from elementary school through university training for all social classes; and the distinct separation of ethnicity from race, to preserve America's diverse ethnic cultures while abolishing all forms of institutional discrimination based on genetic or biological factors. America's system of Jim Crow no longer exists, yet an elaborate system of race and class domination remains. The challenge for the future is to destroy and uproot "race" without negating African-Americans' ethnic and cultural heritage. The new foundations for progressive black politics would not be "race" as previously understood, but the elimination of social class inequality and privilege, which continues to perpetuate the inferior condition of black Americans and millions of other Americans on the other side of the color line.

9. Epilogue: The Vision and the Power

Because I do not hope to know again
The infirm glory of the positive hour . . .
Because I know that time is always time
And place is always and only place
And what is actual is actual only for one time
And only for one place
I rejoice that things are as they are . . .
Because I cannot hope to turn again
Consequently I rejoice, having to construct something
Upon which to rejoice.

T. S. Eliot, 1930

Let us not forget that in the Negro people, there sleep and are now
awakening passions of a violence exceeding . . . anything among the
tremendous forces that capitalism has created. Anyone who knows
them, who knows their history, is able to talk with them intimately . . .
watches them in their churches, reads their press with a discerning eye,
must recognize . . . the hatred of bourgeois society and the readiness to
destroy it when the opportunity should present itself, rests among them
to a degree greater than in any other section of the population in the
United States.

C. L. R. James, 1948

I

American history has repeated itself, in regard to its interpretation of the
pursuit of multicultural democracy: the first time as "tragedy," the second
time as "catastrophe."[1] In the aftermath of the First Reconstruction,
white American historians attempted to portray the democratic experiment of 1865–77 as a complete disaster. Writing in 1935, DuBois ex-

plained that "the facts" of the Reconstruction period "have in the last half century been falsified because the nation was ashamed. The South was ashamed because it fought to perpetuate human slavery. The North was ashamed because it had to call in the black men to save the Union, abolish slavery and establish democracy."[2] As the Second Reconstruction receded, a similar process of historical obfuscation occurred. In the 1980s, the pivotal role of rewriting the public's memory on race relations was played by President Ronald Reagan. In a controversial address before the NAACP's national convention in July 1981, for example, Reagan had declared that his program of severe budgetary reductions and economic austerity for minorities and the poor was "the surest, most equitable way to ease the pressures on all the segments of our society." African-Americans had to cease looking to the federal government to resolve their economic and social problems. "Just as the Emancipation Proclamation freed black people 118 years ago, today we need to declare an economic emancipation," the president argued. To the amazement of blacks, Reagan justified his draconian program by invoking the mantle of anti-slavery activist Harriet Tubman. "Tubman's glory was the glory of the American experience," Reagan observed. "It was a glory which had no color or religious preference or nationality."[3] Reagan's excursions into African-American social history continued. At a September 1982 meeting of the National Black Republican Council, the president declared that blacks "would be appreciably better off today" if Lyndon Johnson's Great Society—a series of social democratic reforms in housing, health care, education, vocational training, and the expansion of civil rights—had never been initiated: "With the coming of the Great Society, Government began eating away at the underpinnings of the private enterprise system. . . . By the time the full weight of Great Society programs was felt, economic progress for America's poor had come to a tragic halt. The poor and disadvantaged are better off today than if we had allowed runaway Government spending, interest rates and inflation to continue ravaging the American economy."[4]

By the end of the twentieth century, blacks and middle-class white Americans not only lived in two largely separate political worlds but also perceived their collective historical experiences of the Second Reconstruction in radically different terms. For several generations, the political mainstream of African-Americans was consistently and sharply to the left of white America. The black electorate had traditionally supported a progressive policy agenda which most European labor party activists might recognize instantly as their own: increased programs for the unemployed, expanded public housing, national health care programs, major reductions in military expenditures, criticism of U.S. intervention in Central America, and opposition to a confrontationist policy toward the Soviet Union.

Despite all of its internal weaknesses, the black freedom movement represented in practice the strongest and most articulate force for what in Europe might be termed leftist social democracy. Because of the absence of a strong democratic socialist or labor party within the American political system, African-Americans had no choice except to bring their agenda into the Democratic Party during the Great Depression and the Second World War. Gradually, alliances for civil rights legislation were formed with organized labor. At the zenith of the Second Reconstruction, in the brief period between the Birmingham desegregation campaign and the Meredith march in Mississippi, the liberal coalition secured passage of the Civil Rights Act and the Voting Rights Act, as well as the key legislative elements of the Great Society. Shifts in demography and political culture, the rise of Black Power and the devisive debate over the Vietnam War, slowly fragmented this grand coalition of reform. Two decades after the legal desegregation of America society, the AFL-CIO commanded less than 18 percent of the American working class, and more than half of all white trade unionists voted for Reagan in 1984. From 1968 through the 1988 presidential election, no Democratic candidates received more than 46 percent of the white vote. Walter Mondale and Michael Dukakis, for example, received 34 and 40 percent, respectively. Thus the black social democratic constituency perceived itself as increasingly isolated from the political mainstream, because by the 1980s it had no really effective allies.

African-Americans exercised their political weight strategically, and at times were decisive in halting the nation's conservative drift. Most important were the congressional elections of 1986, which returned the control of the U.S. Senate to the Democrats and constrained the authority of the Reagan Administration during its final two years in office. Between 86 and 89 percent of the national black electorate supported Democratic congressional candidates, according to polls. The only other significant constituencies that had favored Democratic candidates were Hispanics, with an estimated voter-support level of 75 percent; Jewish voters, 70 percent; and members of union households and government employees, 63 percent. By contrast, non-Jewish whites had supported Republican over Democratic candidates by approximately 53 to 47 percent. In five crucial states, African-American voters had provided the margin of victory for white Democratic senatorial candidates. In Alabama, for example, Reaganite Republican Jeremiah Denton was firmly ahead of conservative Democrat Richard C. Shelby among whites, by a substantial 61 to 39 percent margin. But local black voters, who comprised 21 percent of the electorate, gave Shelby 88 percent. With this crucial bloc, Shelby narrowly defeated Denton by less than seven thousand votes. In Louisiana, Democrat John B. Breaux defeated Republican Henson Moore for the Senate by winning 85 percent of the black vote. Moore had received 60 percent of the white vote, but it was insufficient to overcome the margin provided by African-Americans.[5] The limitations of this electoral strategy are also obvious. When whites vote overwhelmingly as an electoral bloc, as they did in endorsing Reagan by a 66 percent mandate in 1984, by sheer numbers they overwhelm the remnants of the liberal reform coalition. Similarly, when Republicans make earnest efforts to recruit sections of the black and Hispanic middle class and to cultivate conservative ideologues and entrepreneurs, as in the maneuvers of President Bush during 1989–90, they may succeed in fragmenting the minority electorate's support for Democratic candidates.

Three great challenges or crises confront the African-American community: the crisis of politics, the crisis of theory, and the crisis of historical imagination or consciousness. The political crisis, as previously outlined, is the chasm separating the black community from the majority of white Americans in the electoral arena. Yet this political crisis is also a failure of leadership. Throughout the First and Second Reconstruction, and within the social protest movements during other periods, one central weakness—what can be termed "the messiah complex"—undermined the power, impact and longevity of black political organizations. The messiah complex probably stemmed from a political reading of the Old Testament stories of Moses, who led the oppressed Hebrews out of Egyptian bondage, and of Joshua, who brought them into the Promised Land. The political style and discourse of black America were heavily identified with the church, and it was no accident that the vast majority of black political leaders were Christian ministers or religious figures. An articulate, religious-oriented, charismatic black male leader was able to build around himself a protest organization and lead the fight to advance the interests of the oppressed, racial minorities, labor and other exploited constituencies.

Most of the great black political activists of the twentieth century fit the model of the messiah complex. Garvey's Universal Negro Improvement Association during the 1920s was held together by the sheer power of its leaders's charismatic and dogmatic personality. A leadership cult developed around Martin Luther King, Jr., well beyond the boundaries of the Southern Christian Leadership Conference. Malcolm X, the most gifted and visionary black nationalist of his era, inspired millions after his assassination to pursue militant and sometimes contradictory goals of Black Power. But with the political demise or death of these individuals, their formations suffered and the social protest movements that had projected them onto the national stage were diminished. In the case of Malcolm X, none of the other prominent black nationalists who emerged in his aftermath—Maulana Karenga, Stokely Carmichael, Huey Newton, or Imamu

Baraka—were able to exercise his political weight. Malcolm X's Organization of African-American Unity disappeared after his assassination. The group was too heavily identified with the leadership and vision of a single individual, and without his guidance and remaining members were denied their ideological and political compass.

The messiah complex has created numerous problems throughout African-American history. The political formations led by charismatic messiahs usually reflect a pyramidic, top-down organizational structure. The leader and his coterie of political lieutenants make most of the decisions regarding policy, tactics and strategy. The branches or local organizations recruit new members in large measure on the popularity and charismatic appeal of the national spokesperson, rather than on the basis of a coherent agenda or a commonly perceived social problem requiring collective action. Eventually, a second tier of local leaders emerges—men and women who have talent, yet whose original ideas are muted by the demands issued from above by the national leader. They soon learn that loyalty is prized above political creativity and ability. The greatest single weakness in this structure of political leadership is manifested when the leader dies or is removed from power. The death or arrest of the leader freezes his organizational lieutenants, who can no longer think independently. It disorients most loyal rank-and-file members, and creates a pessimistic feeling that no one could possibly replace the fallen leader. In the wake of King's assassination, for example, Ralph Abernathy, Andrew Young, Hosea Williams and other prominent SCLC leaders could not accept a young, relatively inexperienced, yet charismatic newcomer, Jesse Jackson, as the heir to Martin's legacy. Even two decades after King's murder, there was deep bitterness between Martin's widow, Coretta Scott King, and Jackson. In 1984, both Mrs. King and Andrew Young refused to endorse Jackson's insurgent presidential candidacy, and publicly campaigned for Mondale in the Democratic primaries. The idea that the self-proclaimed "Country Preacher," Jackson, could possibly be the equal of the pivotal spokesperson for the Second Reconstruction was an absurdity to them.

In the void left by King's death, his followers travelled in different, sometimes conflicting directions. Abernathy was unable to keep up the SCLC's momentum, and he was quickly overshadowed by Jackson, who initiated a schism within the SCLC to create Operation PUSH in 1971. Abernathy and another King lieutenant, James Bevel, subsequently ran unsuccessfully for Congress. In the search to recapture his former political glory, Abernathy endorsed Reagan in 1980 but failed to obtain a government appointment or public influence from his controversial action. Both leaders drifted even further to the right as the 1980s progressed. Bevel became a Republican Party leader in Chicago's black community and soon earned a reputation as a right-wing extremist. Abernathy and Bevel were drawn into the political orbit of CAUSA, an anti-communist front established by conservative evangelical leader Reverend Sun Myung Moon. In April 1985, Abernathy joined Eldridge Cleaver as a prominent spokesperson at a CAUSA conference in Los Angeles. The following month Bevel and Abernathy were the key participants in a two-day "Freedom Rally and Convention" sponsored by CAUSA and held in the impoverished Lawndale section of Chicago's westside. Formed by Moon's Unification Church in 1980 as a vehicle to attract educators, civil rights leaders and clergy to conservative causes, CAUSA contributed to the perception that the African-American political leadership was in ideological and organizational disarray. This perception was particularly underscored by the connections with Moon, whose earlier public statements on blacks and race relations in general had much more in common with Lester Maddox or George Wallace than with Martin Luther King. In 1974, for example, Moon had articulated his reactionary ideas on racial characteristics: "Orientals can contribute in the spiritual aspect, white people can contribute in the analytical, scientific aspect, while black people can contribute in the physical area."[6] Because of their search to fulfill the messiah model of political leadership, these and other former black activists had become unwitting pawns in the strategy to impose conservative and even reactionary politics upon the African-American community.

Jackson continued to follow King's ideological trajectory, while pursuing his own destiny within the messiah tradition. The 1984 presidential campaign was for Jackson an extension of his career as a civil rights activist, an advocate of democratic social change. Four years later, as Jackson matured into the Democratic Party's leading critic on its liberal wing, it began to occur to him that he could actually become the party's presidential candidate in the general election. Jackson began to moderate his public policy positions slightly, muting his insurgent rhetoric and placing more moderate operatives in positions of authority in the campaign. After his defeat, Jackson pursued the Democratic Party's vice presidential nomination with singleminded determination, rather than demanding that pivotal elements of his program be incorporated into the party's agenda. Similarly, after Bush's victory in the general election, Jackson agreed to caucus with the president-elect in a well-publicized photo session. But Jackson had failed to consult adequately with his colleagues within his "Rainbow Coalition," and he made no demands on the Republican leader. Throughout 1989, Jackson flirted with the possibility of running for mayor of Washington, D.C., an office which he could easily have won, but finally withdrew in fear that the municipal post would not provide the national focus required for his type of charismatic leadership. Jackson refused to expand the political base of the Rainbow Coalition by extending political authority to local activists, failed to establish regional offices and field organizers, and provided no financial support for a national newspaper. In brief, he nurtured an autocratic, charismatic political formation, which lacked the capacity to provide effective leadership to address the contemporary problems within the ghetto or the society as a whole.

The crisis of political leadership is directly linked to the crisis of ideology. The dominant ideas that have motivated the political activities of black organizations have generally been the product of the African-American élite. In the post-reform period, critical elements of this élite have acquired a completely material interest in defending the economic and political status quo. The representatives of the middle class may, upon occasion, offer a stinging rebuke to representatives of mass conservatism, advocating affirmative action and an extension of progressive public policies. The black élite does in fact comprehend that its marginal influence upon government can best be exerted only when elements of the old liberal coalition or more centrist Republicans and Democrats control Congress and the executive branch. The problem with the élite's perspective, however, is an unthinking acceptance of the ideological limitations impressed on national political culture during the Cold War. The black élite is prepared to promulgate an economic program mirroring the moderate tendencies of European social democracy, but beyond that invisible boundary separating capitalism from socialism it is not prepared to go. The collapse of the communist system in eastern Europe and the process of democratization inside the Soviet Union itself in the late 1980s and early 1990s further devalued the alternative of democratic socialism in the minds of this group. African-American leaders are thus prepared to call for increased federal initiatives to provide employment for poor and working-class people, but they will not advocate a militantly egalitarian agenda that severely restricts the prerogatives of large corporations. The élite has no long-term solutions to the growth of the permanent reserve army of black labor, the crisis of drugs in the central cities, or the deterioration of the quality of life in urban areas.

The black middle class's failure, in brief, has been one of ideology and historical imagination. The élite constantly maneuvers, responding to minor political crises, but it is unable to project a constructive program for transforming society as a whole. It is a failure within a qualified and truncated success. As the century moves toward its conclusion, the élite's limited capacity for creative vision or historical consciousness has clearly generated a barrier between its own political objectives and the material needs and aspirations of the exploited black majority. With DuBois, I must agree that many critical failures of both reconstructions were the result of the blacks' leadership "by the blind. We fell under the leadership of those who would compromise with truth in the past in order to make peace in the present and guide policy in the future."[7] Such a judgment may seem excessively harsh. But as an African-American and a democratic socialist, I cannot investigate the patterns of the black past without a belief in the humanity and dignity of my own people and their culture, without some degree of political commitment to justice and a more equitable life for those on the edge of poverty, unemployment and despair. Yet as DuBois also reminds us, "as a student of science, I want to be fair, objective and judicial; to let no searing of the memory by intolerable insult and cruelty make me fail to sympathize with human frailties and contradiction, in the eternal paradox of good and evil."[8] Throughout the history of oppressed humanity, there has been a moral arch spanning the diverse political and social experiences of millions of people. This arch symbolizes the faith that, despite failures and defeats of every kind, oppressed and exploited people will not remain oppressed forever. What has sustained black courage in the face of adversity is this ethical and moral belief, fueling the dynamics of black political activism.

II

The impasse within the black freedom movement during the post-reform era will not be transcended unless a new, more creative leadership emerges to raise fundamental questions concerning ideology, politics and the future of African-American consciousness and identity. The prevailing attitude among most black leaders during the First and Second Reconstruction was a belief in the essential applicability of the American democratic system to the plight of the African-American. The U.S. Constitution was perceived as being "color-blind," despite the corpus of laws which had validated and perpetuated black inferiority for centuries. The majority of black activists fighting for desegregation desired to incorporate the Negro into the existing system. It rarely occured to them that a multicultural democracy was impossible to achieve without a structural re-positioning of the nonwhite labor force into jobs of authority and power in the production process. In 1945, DuBois suggested that any government which described itself as a genuine democracy must have, among its guiding objectives, "the abolition of poverty, the education of the masses, protection from disease, and the scientific treatment of crime." A democratic state should express in its public policies "the right and the capacity" for peoples of color to "share in human progress" equally, without artificial barriers. It must outlaw any and all restrictions based on race, gender, religious preference, physical handicap and other variables that have historically been used to perpetuate human inequality. Within these criteria, no real democracy had ever existed in the United States. DuBois was more specific some years later, in a series of articles on the subject of democracy for the *National Guardian*. Democracy in the U.S. was not "obsolete"; it had never been tried because of racism and the powerful control of corporate capital over the lives of common working people. Democracy for blacks and other oppressed national minorities would await the socialization of the economy, a massive restructuring of power, privilege and wealth. If African-Americans would choose to reject decisively the model of private enterprise and forge coalitions with the laboring classes, other people of color, and the unemployed, they might "loose for future civilization the vast energy and potentialities of the mass of human beings now being held in thrall by poverty, ignorance and disease."[9] Given the oppressive nature of the capitalist economic system throughout its historical relationship with blacks, no truly antiracist, democratic state could be developed unless its economic foundations involved to some extent a socialist pattern.

The goal of equality was certainly an integral theme of the Second Reconstruction. But in the minds of many leaders, equality meant parity, or equal opportunity to assume positions of political, social and economic power and privilege in America. However, the demand for racial parity within a state apparatus and economy based on institutional racism and private capital accumulation at the expense of the working-class majority was fatally flawed. Racism and capitalist exploitation have been, and remain, the logical and consistent by-products of the American political economy. Thus, reviewing the modest gains of the black élite in the post-reform era, one observes that a racist/capitalist state can easily co-opt a small number of representatives from the minority community and manipulate them for their own narrow purposes. The black freedom movement will have to recognize that the demand for equal opportunity or affirmative action is inherently limited, and that further steps will have to be taken to create a multicultural democratic order within society. Real equality occurs with the abolition of class divisions, and the transferral of power to those members of society who generate all wealth. Adding numbers of blacks to the government, in other words, will not create a less racist structure unless the vast majority of working-class and poor African-Americans themselves are empowered through this process. The problem of police brutality and excessive force within ghettos will not be resolved simply by hiring additional numbers of African-American police officers, or by black control of municipal governments that direct criminal justice investigations. It will cease only when black working people, the unemployed and the powerless have in their own hands the effective ability to control institutions within their own neighborhoods and communities.[10]

In the post-reform era, during the late 1980s and early 1990s, millions of blacks began to refer to themselves as "African-Americans," a term that provided a greater sense of cultural identity and political consciousness, perhaps even prefiguring an inclination to social protest and activism. The shift in language was supported by Jesse Jackson: "Black tells you about skin color and what side of town you live on. . . . African-American evokes a discussion of the world."[11] But the issue of collective terminology, and the unresolved transition from "colored" to "Negro" to "black" and finally to "African-American," speaks to a much deeper search for group consciousness. What has it meant to be identified as "black" within American society? During slavery, blacks were of course described by their oppressors chiefly by the color of their skin—negro, or black in Spanish. To be "black," or more commonly a "nigger," in a social order built upon exploitation was to be a prisoner of one's skin color and also of the idea of immutable inferiority conveyed by an entire nation of people. Well into the twentieth century, most white Americans continued to identify their national collective interests with those of European geopolitics, culture, philosophy and values, and perceived "blackness" through the destructive and false social construction of "race," implying permanent inferiority and domination for African-Americans. Yet the histories of the First and Second Reconstruction reveal that the slaves and their descendants never accepted the definitions of their oppressors. They saw themselves as a people to whom history had given a terrible burden—and a tremendous opportunity. They always looked backward, recalling their African roots, which were expressed in their language, syntax, verb tenses and idiomatic expressions. They forged within this bitter crucible a deep sense of cultural commonality and national identity as Americans of African descent.

Within this turbulent historical process, as the African-American people experienced war and segregation, death and disfranchisement, there has also existed a nearly unbridgeable gap between American democratic theory and political practice by the white majority. Yet against all reason and collective experience, millions of blacks harbored a deep vision, a dream of a democratic social order with unfettered access to political, economic and social rights, regardless of race, gender and class. Black Americans have given this dream a name: freedom. It is this unyielding belief in human freedom, more than any other single factor, which has sustained and nourished the American identity of the African-American. But every dream has its limitations. Historically, whenever the majority of white American institutions and political parties has turned sharply against the vision of equality for blacks, the African-American community has experienced periods of pessimism and inward soul searching. Shortly before the First Reconstruction, after the Compromise of 1850 and the passage of a strict fugitive slave law, northern free blacks became militantly nationalistic and explored methods to leave the United States for Central America or Africa. Similarly, in the 1960s, the rise of Black Power was partially created by the white political backlash against the gains of the civil rights movement. The post-reform period of the 1980s and early 1990s was in many respects similarly bleak, creating a sense of isolation and pessimism among contemporary African-Americans. The combination of destructive socio-economic forces and political conservatism from without, and the social chaos and urban decay from within, has created a sense of doubt and fragmentation, as well as a rethinking of black mission and purpose within the context of capitalist American society.

This crisis of consciousness can only be resolved by pursuing two goals simultaneously: the reinforcing of cultural, group identity through development of institutions that reclaim human resources and reactivate latent potentialities within the African-American community; and the redefinition of "freedom" to mean increased restrictions on the freedom of capital over the rights of working people, regardless of race. As the perpetual bottom of the American labor market, blacks, Hispanics and other people of color have traditionally been caught in a never-ending economic vise—the last hired during economic upturns, and the first fired during cyclical recessions. Freedom for black working people must mean the guarantee of a job as an absolute human right; the community's control over factory closings or relocations; freedom from the fear created by poor medical facilities in inner cities and rural areas; the right to free public education from preschool through university levels; and the right to decent housing. Such a definition of freedom is emancipatory, not simply in the economic sense but in the creative sense as well—the dedication to art, music, and other cultural pursuits. As long as unemployment, fear, and poverty dwell in half the black households of America, the potential for cultural genius and creative development will remain restricted. Such a humanistic and egalitarian definition of freedom is alien to the traditions of America's political system. But Martin and Malcolm, DuBois and Robeson, each in his own manner, came to this realization. There could be no peaceful and productive race relations within American society unless economic justice and cultural integrity for blacks also existed. Their historical imaginations had gleaned the vision of a society freed from bigotry and hunger, from unemployment and racial violence. This type of freedom will be realized only through a Third Reconstruction, which seeks to empower all people of color, working people and others experiencing discrimination, poverty, and oppression. This freedom of capital must be restricted to achieve freedom for the majority.

A Third Reconstruction will inevitably arise in the future, to fulfill the lost promises and broken dreams of the first and second social protest movements. Its vision even now is quite clear to many Americans. It is only a question of power.

Notes

1. PROLOGUE: THE LEGACY OF THE FIRST RECONSTRUCTION

1. W. E. B. DuBois, *Black Reconstruction in America, 1860–1880* (New York: Atheneum, 1971), 59.
2. Ibid., 378.
3. Lawrence Goodwyn, *The Populist Moment: A Short History of the Agrarian Revolt in America* (New York: Oxford University Press, 1978), 5–6.
4. C. Vann Woodward, *The Strange Career of Jim Crow* (New York: Oxford University Press, 1974), 118.
5. DuBois, *Black Reconstruction*, 703.

2. THE COLD WAR IN BLACK AMERICA, 1945–1954

1. Harold Cruse, *Rebellion or Revolution?* (New York: William Morrow, 1968), 12.
2. Philip S. Foner, *Organized Labor and the Black Worker, 1619–1973* (New York: International Publishers, 1974), 270.
3. Henry Lee Moon, *Balance of Power: The Negro Vote* (New York: Doubleday, 1948), 9, 18.
4. Isaac Deutscher, *Stalin: A Political Biography* (New York: Oxford University Press, 1949), 573, 575.
5. David Caute, *The Great Fear: The Anti-Communist Purge Under Truman and Eisenhower* (New York: Simon and Schuster, 1979), 539–40.
6. Richard Polenberg, *One Nation Divisible: Class, Race, and Ethnicity in the United States Since 1938* (New York: Penguin Books, 1980), 87–8.
7. Lillian Hellman, *Scoundrel Time* (Boston: Little, Brown, 1976).
8. Polenberg, *One Nation Divisible*, 106.
9. Caute, *The Great Fear*, 15.
10. Ibid., 11.
11. Foner, *Organized Labor and the Black Worker*, 279.
12. On Randolph's political career, see William H. Harris, *Keeping the Faith: A. Philip Randolph, Milton P. Webster, and the Brotherhood of Sleeping Car Porters* (Urbana, Illinois: University of Illinois Press, 1977); Theodore Kornweibel, "The Messenger Magazine, 1917–1928" (Ph.D. dissertation, Yale University, 1971); Manning Marable, *From the Grassroots: Social and Political Essays Towards Afro-American Liberation* (Boston: South End Press, 1980), 59–85.
13. Polenberg, *One Nation Divisible*, 112.
14. Hanes Walton, Jr., *Black Politics: A Theoretical and Structural Analysis* (Philadelphia: J. B. Lippincott, 1972), 66.

15. Foner, *Organized Labor and the Black Worker*, 280.

16. W. E. B. DuBois, *The Autobiography of W. E. B. DuBois* (New York: International Publishers, 1968), 293.

17. Ibid., 334. The shift in the NAACP's position on the Soviet Union and the American left in general can be observed by analyzing the attitudes of James Weldon Johnson. Johnson, who was not a leftist, wrote this passage in 1934:

> Soviet Russia [is] a land in which there is absolutely no prejudice against Negroes. . . . I hold no brief against Communism as a theory of government. I hope that the Soviet experiment will be completely successful. . . . If America should turn truly Communistic, . . . if the capitalistic system should be abolished and the dictatorship of the proletariat established, with the Negro aligned, as he naturally ought to be, with the proletariat, race discriminations would be officially banned and the reasons and feelings back of them would finally disappear.

See Johnson, *Negro Americans, What Now?* (New York: Viking Press, 1962).

18. W. E. B. DuBois, "The Negro and Radical Thought," *Crisis* 22 (July 1921): 204.

19. W. E. B. DuBois, "My Evolving Program for Negro Freedom," in Rayford Logan (ed.), *What the Negro Wants* (Chapel Hill, North Carolina: University of North Carolina Press, 1944), 31–70.

20. Polenberg, *One Nation Divisible*, 112–13.

21. Woodward, *The Strange Career of Jim Crow*, 136. Once out of office, Truman was absolutely candid about his opposition to blacks' civil rights. At a Cornell University lecture in 1960, Truman charged that "Communists" were "engineering the student sit-downs at lunch counters in the South." King and Wilkins deplored the former president's statement, and demanded that he provide details. Truman replied that he had no proof: "But I know that usually when trouble hits the country the Kremlin is behind it." Caute, *The Great Fear*, 35.

22. August Meier and Elliott Rudwick, CORE: *A Study in the Civil Rights Movement, 1942–1968* (New York: Oxford University Press, 1973), 35.

23. Woodward, *The Strange Career of Jim Crow*, 142.

24. Jessie Parkhurst Guzman (ed.), *Negro Year Book: A Review of Events Affecting Negro Life, 1941–1946* (Tuskegee Institute, Alabama: Tuskegee Institute, Department of Records and Research, 1947), 270–1.

25. Polenberg, *One Nation Divisible*, 159.

26. V. O. Key, Jr., *Southern Politics in State and Nation* (New York: Vintage, 1949), 649.

27. Meier and Rudwick, CORE, 64–5.

28. Polenberg, *One Nation Divisible*, 113.

29. DuBois, *Autobiography*, 369.

30. Ibid., 370.

31. Caute, *The Great Fear*, 418.

32. Ibid., 120, 128–9, 190, 193.

33. Foner, *Organized Labor and the Black Worker*, 293–311.

34. Caute, *The Great Fear*, 192, 198–9, 209–10.

35. W. A. Swanberg, *Norman Thomas: The Last Idealist* (New York: Charles Scribner's Sons, 1976), 353–5, 479–80.

36. Thomas Sowell, *Race and Economics* (New York: Longman, 1975), 94.

37. Mario T. Garcia, "On Mexican Immigration, the United States, and Chicano History," *Journal of Ethnic Studies* 7 (Spring 1979): 85.

38. Key, *Southern Politics in State and Nation*, 272–5.

39. Stan Steiner, *La Raza: The Mexican-Americans* (New York: Harper and Row, 1970), 232–3.

40. Roxanne Dunbar Ortiz, "Land and Nationhood: The American Indian Struggle for Self-Determination and Survival," *Socialist Review* 12 (May–August 1982): 109.
41. William Loren Katz, *The Black West* (Garden City, New York: Anchor Books, 1973), 201–14.
42. S. J. Makielski, Jr., *Beleaguered Minorities: Cultural Politics in America* (San Francisco: W. H. Freeman, 1973), 56.
43. Ortiz, "Land and Nationhood," 116.
44. Makielski, *Beleaguered Minorities*, 57.
45. Richard A. Garcia, "The Chicano Movement and the Mexican-American Community, 1972–1978: An Interpretative Essay," *Socialist Review* 8 (July–October 1978): 123.
46. Guzman (ed.), *Negro Year Book*, 182–3.

3. THE DEMAND FOR REFORM, 1954–1960

1. Woodward, *The Strange Career of Jim Crow*, 146–7.
2. Ibid., 144; Carl N. Degler, *Affluence and Anxiety, 1945–Present* (Glenview, Illinois: Scott, Foresman, 1968), 96.
3. Numan V. Bartley and Hugh D. Graham, *Southern Politics and the Second Reconstruction* (Baltimore: Johns Hopkins Press, 1975), 67. Wallace's metamorphosis as a racist demagogue merits serious examination, because it helps to explain the relationship between racism and American politics. When Wallace began his political career, he urged friends not to oppress local blacks. "You know, we just can't keep the colored folks down like we been doin' around here for years and years," he argued in 1946. "We got to quit. We got to start treatin' 'em right. They just like everybody else." On economic issues. Wallace was a progressive populist, a supporter of extensive state programs for public schools, medical clinics, and welfare. In 1958, Wallace's opponent for governor accepted the public support of the Klan. Wallace promptly issued a denunciation of the Klan. After that, he won the support of "the substantial Jewish minority in Alabama [and] the NAACP." Wallace's defeat in 1958, losing by 65,000 votes, made him into the South's most notorious bigot. In 1962, 1970 and 1974 Wallace was elected governor of Alabama on a racist program. In 1982, as huge numbers of blacks were now voters, and a black man, Richard Arrington, served as mayor of Alabama's largest city, Birmingham, Wallace ran successfully for governor for a fourth term—this time, as an economic liberal and racial moderate. In doing so, he managed to attract about one-third of the black voters in the state's Democratic primary race. See Marshall Frady, *Wallace* (New York: New American Library, 1976), 126–7, 137, 141.
4. Woodward, *The Strange Career of Jim Crow*, 156–8.
5. Ibid., 165–6.
6. Richard Wright, "A Blueprint for Negro Writing," *New Challenge* 11 (1937): 53–65.
7. Richard Wright, *The Outsider* (New York: Harper and Row, 1953), 366.
8. Langston Hughes, "Un-American Investigators," in Dudley Randall (ed.), *The Black Poets* (New York: Bantam, 1972), 79–80.
9. Harold Cruse, *The Crisis of the Negro Intellectual* (New York: William Morrow, 1967), 267–84.
10. LeRoi Jones, *Black Music* (New York: William Morrow, 1970), 21, 37–40, 56–57, 69–73.
11. Martin Luther King, quoted in Cruse, *Rebellion or Revolution?* 60–1.
12. DuBois, *Autobiography*, 399–401.
13. Herbert Hill, "Race and Labor: The AFL-CIO and the Black Worker Twenty-Five Years After the Merger," *Journal of Intergroup Relations* 10 (Spring 1982): 14.
14. Philip S. Foner, *Organized Labor and the Black Worker*, 314–15.

15. Gus Tyler, "Contemporary Labor's Attitude Toward the Negro," in Julius Jacobson (ed.), *The Negro and the American Labor Movement* (Garden City, New York: Anchor, 1968), 367.

16. Ibid., 363.

17. Hill, "Race and Labor," 20.

18. Foner, *Organized Labor and the Black Worker,* 330–1.

19. Hill, "Race and Labor," 25.

20. C. Eric Lincoln, *The Black Muslims in America* (Boston: Beacon Press, 1961), x, 251.

21. Ibid., 147–8.

22. Malcolm X and James Farmer, "Separation or Integration: A Debate," *Dialogue Magazine* 2 (May 1962): 14–18.

23. Cruse, *The Crisis of the Negro Intellectual,* 352.

24. Robert F. Williams, "USA: The Potential of a Minority Revolution," *The Crusader Monthly Newsletter* 5 (May–June 1964): 1–7.

25. David Caute, *The Great Fear* 59.

26. G. William Danhoff, *Who Rules America?* (Englewood Cliffs, New Jersey: Prentice-Hall, 1967), 74–86.

4. WE SHALL OVERCOME, 1960–1965

1. Meier and Rudwick, CORE 101.

2. Debbie Louis, *And We Are Not Saved: A History of the Movement as People* (Garden City, New York: Anchor, 1970), 51.

3. Ibid., 32.

4. Vincent Harding, *The Other American Revolution* (Los Angeles: Center for Afro-American Studies, 1980), 159.

5. Clayborne Carson, *In Struggle: SNCC and the Black Awakening of the 1960s* (Cambridge, Mass.: Harvard University Press, 1981), 68.

6. Ibid., 78.

7. Meier and Rudwick, *CORE:* 209.

8. Carson, *In Struggle,* 105.

10. Woodward, *The Strange Career of Jim Crow,* 175–6.

11. William Robert Miller, *Martin Luther King, Jr.: His Life, Martyrdom and Meaning for the World* (New York: Avon Books, 1968), 147.

12. Ibid., 150.

13. Martin Luther King, Jr., *Why We Can't Wait* (New York: Harper and Row, 1964), chapter 5.

14. Woodward, *The Strange Career of Jim Crow,* 181.

15. Harding, *The Other American Revolution,* 172.

16. Miller, *Martin Luther King, Jr.,* 67, 173–8.

17. Meier and Rudwick, CORE, 214.

18. Miller, *Martin Luther King, Jr.,* 161–2.

19. Carson, *In Struggle,* 106–7, 136–7.

20. Bayard Rustin, "The Meaning of the March on Washington," *Liberation* 8 (October 1963): 11–13.

21. W. E. B. DuBois, *The Education of Black People: Ten Critiques, 1906–1960* (New York: Monthly Review Press, 1973), 149–58.

22. G. Plekhanov, quoted in Isaac Deutscher, *The Prophet Outcast: Trotsky: 1929–1940* (New York: Vintage, 1963), 242–3.

23. Louis Lomax, *To Kill a Black Man* (Los Angeles: Holloway House, 1968), 113–18.

24. James Baldwin, "The Dangerous Road Before Martin Luther King," *Harper's Magazine* (February 1961).

25. August Meier, "On the Role of Martin Luther King," *New Politics* 4 (Winter 1965): 52–9.

26. Marable, *From the Grassroots*, 53–4.

27. Miller, *Martin Luther King, Jr.*, 206.

28. Harding, *The Other American Revolution*, 181.

29. Robert L. Allen, *Black Awakening in Capitalist America: An Analytic History* (Garden City, New York: Anchor, 1969), 111.

30. Meier, "On the Role of Martin Luther King," 52–3.

31. Steven F. Lawson, *Black Ballots: Voting Rights in the South, 1944–1969* (New York: Columbia University Press, 1976), 300.

32. Ibid., 321, 329, 331; Woodward, *The Strange Career of Jim Crow*, 182–3.

33. Louis, *And We Are Not Saved*, 132–3.

34. Bartley and Graham, *Southern Politics and the Second Reconstruction*, 106–7, 112–13, 117, 123, 126.

35. Woodward, *The Strange Career of Jim Crow*, 186–7.

36. Louis, *And We Are Not Saved*, 173.

37. Allen, *Black Awakening in Capitalist America*, 70.

38. Carson, *In Struggle*, 185–6.

39. Harding, *The Other American Revolution*, 183, 185.

5. BLACK POWER, 1965–1970

1. Walter Rodney, "Guyana: The making of the labour force," *Race and Class* 22 (Spring 1981): 331.

2. Malcolm X, *The Autobiography of Malcolm X* (New York: Grove Press, 1965), 201–2, 204, 213.

3. Ibid., 202, 219.

4. Ibid., 240–1.

5. Ibid., 246.

6. Ibid., 301.

7. George Breitman, *The Last Year of Malcolm X: The Evolution of a Revolutionary* (New York: Schocken, 1968), 19.

8. Malcolm X, *The Autobiography of Malcolm X*, 375.

9. Breitman, *The Last Year of Malcolm X*, 33.

10. Ibid., 57.

11. Meier and Rudwick: *CORE*, 206.

12. Ibid., 331.

13. Carson, *In Struggle*, 100.

14. Ibid., 136.

15. There is a great amount of evidence which indicates that the U.S. government may have had direct responsibility for the slaying of Malcolm X, and in the two-decade-long "cover up" about the identity of his killers. See George Breitman, Herman Porter and Baxter Smith (eds.), *The Assassination of Malcolm X* (New York: Pathfinder Press, 1976); Peter L. Goldman, *The Death and Life of Malcolm X* (New York: Harper and Row, 1973); William Seraile, "The Assassination of Malcolm X: The View From Home and Abroad," *Afro-Americans in New York Life and History* 5 (January 1981): 43–58.

16. Breitman, *The Last of Malcolm X*, 83, 87, 93–4; Malcolm X, *The Autobiography of Malcolm X*, 443, 444, 447, 454.

17. Malcolm X, *The Autobiography of Malcolm X*, 443, 444, 447, 454.

18. Baldwin, quoted in Stokely Carmichael and Charles V. Hamilton, *Black Power: The Politics of Liberation in America* (New York: Vintage, 1967), 155.

19. Herbert J. Gans, "The Ghetto Rebellions and Urban Class Conflict," in Robert H. Connery (ed.), *Urban Riots: Violence and Social Change* (New York: Vintage, 1969), 45–54.

20. Kenneth Clark, *Dark Ghetto* (New York: Harper and Row, 1965), 63–4.

21. David Lewis, *King: A Critical Biography* (Baltimore: Penguin, 1969), 323.

22. Carson, *In Struggle*, 209–10.

23. Meier and Rudwick, CORE, 417.

24. Roy Wilkins, "Whither 'Black Power'?." *Crisis* (August–September 1966) : 354.

25. Carson, *In Struggle*, 220.

26. Ibid., 220–1; Cruse, *Rebellion or Revolution?*, 200.

27. Martin Luther King, *Where Do We Go from Here: Chaos or Community* (New York: Harper and Row, 1967), 51–2.

28. Meier and Rudwick, CORE, 412, 414–15.

29. Carmichael and Hamilton, *Black Power*, vi, vii. Cruse's comments on Carmichael and Hamilton's *Black Power* are quite critical. Cruse argued that by 1965

the urban militants who had listened with rapt attention to the message of Malcolm X realized that militant-protest integrationism had reaped the last dregs of the rewards of diminishing returns. The moment the slogan "Black Power" was sounded, it signalled a turning inward, a reversal of self-motivated aims in the direction of "Black Economic and Political Control" of Black communities. . . . That [*Black Power*] failed to present anything so advanced . . . was only a very real reflection of the collective state of Black consciousness in force at the "Black Power" juncture of the Sixties. . . . Whatever occurred after publication of *Black Power* was simply anti-climactic. The book's analysis was not of the quality that it could have lent meaningful guidance to the movements which were visibly running out of steam in the late Sixties. These movements were infused with the methodology of militant pragmatism, and rife with the competing clash of varying consensuses. There was no general consensus as to where the competing factions of the Black militant *élites* wanted to lead the Black masses.

Cruse, "The Little Rock National Black Political Convention," *Black World* 23 (October 1974): 10–17, 82–8.

30. Meier and Rudwick, CORE, 423.

31. Allen, *Black Awakening in Capitalist America*, 59.

32. Cruse, *Rebellion or Revolution?*, 198.

33. James Boggs, *Racism and the Class Struggle: Further Pages from a Black Worker's Notebook* (New York: Monthly Review Press, 1970), 54–8. Even the American Communist Party, what was left of it following years of governmental suppression and the departure of thousands of members due to the reaction against the Soviet Union's intervention into Hungary in 1956, was generally favorable towards Black Power. Black Communist leader Claude Lightfoot recognized in early 1968 that the phrase "means many things to different people. . . . But the central reason why the slogan has been embraced by most people is the recognition of the necessity for black people to have a greater share of economic and political power." Black Power was "not only violence in the streets in response to provocations, but a revolt at the polls, a revolt to change the composition of government and to enforce the laws involving the rights of black people." In general, Lightfoot, like Boggs and other black socialists, tended to underestimate the capitalist thrust of many Black Powerites. Claude M. Lightfoot, *Ghetto Rebellion to Black Liberation* (New York: International Publishers, 1968), 17, 19.

34. Allen, *Black Awakening in Capitalist America*, 163–4, 228–9.

35. Cruse, *Rebellion or Revolution?*, 201, 206–7, 213–14. Cruse adds that "the conference steering committee refused to allow the paper to be presented, so I had no real motivation for attending in any event. It all added up to another of a long series of misadventures with the Marxists, with whom I am forever at odds" (p. 25).

36. Ibid., 197.

37. Louis, *And We Are Not Saved*, 296–7.

38. "Crisis and Commitment," *Crisis* (November 1966): 474–9.

39. George Breitman (ed.), *By Any Means Necessary: Speeches, Interviews and a Letter by Malcolm X* (New York: Merit, 1970), 162.

40. "SNCC press release: Statement on Vietnam," in Clyde Taylor (ed.), *Vietnam and Black America: An Anthology of Protest and Resistance* (Garden City, New York: Anchor, 1973), 258–9.

41. Stokley Carmichael, "At Morgan State," in Taylor, *Vietnam and Black America*," 271.

42. Julian Bond, "The Roots of Racism and War," in Taylor, *Vietnam and Black America*, 108–9.

43. Ronald Dellums, "Involvement in Indochina is Number One Priority," in Taylor, *Vietnam and Black America*, 103–4.

44. Addison Gayle, Jr., "Hell, No, Black Men Won't Go!"; James Baldwin, "The War Crimes Tribunal"; S. E. Anderson, "Junglegrave"; and Robert Hayden, "Words in the Mourning Time," in Taylor, *Vietnam and Black America*, 45, 101–2, 139, 143.

45. Lewis, *King*, 310–11.

46. Ibid., 354.

47. Ibid., 360.

48. Ibid., 376.

49. Ibid., 387. The great tragedy of monumental historical figures is that their legacy is left to their followers, many of whom often have no real insights into their political praxis. King provides a fitting example of this phenomenon. Vincent Harding cites an interview with one of King's closest advisers, given several years after the 1968 assassination. The adviser stated, "In a way, it was probably best for many of us who worked with Martin that he was killed when he was, because he was moving into some radical directions that few of us had been prepared for. And I don't think that many of us would have been ready to take the risks of life, possessions, security, and status that such a move would have involved. I'm pretty sure I wouldn't have been willing." Harding, *The Other American Revolution*, 212.

50. Nikki Giovanni, *Black Feeling, Black Talk, Black Judgment* (New York: William Morrow, 1970), 19–20.

51. Ibid., 83.

52. Allen, *Black Awakening in Capitalist America*, 166.

53. Julius Nyerere, *Ujamaa—Essays on Socialism* (New York: Oxford University Press, 1968), 39, 42.

54. David Caute, *Frantz Fanon* (New York: Viking Press, 1970), 104–5.

55. Addison Gayle, Jr., *The Black Situation* (New York: Delta, 1970), 84–7.

56. "What we want now! What we Believe," in John H. Bracey, Jr., August Meier and Elliott Rudwick (eds.), *Black Nationalism in America* (Indianapolis: Bobbs-Merrill, 1970), 526.

57. Ibid., 528. Relations between the Black Panthers and the "New Left" of the 1960s were not always harmonious. The largest white left formation, the Students for a Democratic Society (SDS), opposed the Panthers' claims that they represented the true "vanguard" of the socialist movement. At the National Conference for a United Front Against Fascism, held in

Oakland in July 1969, Bobby Seale declared sternly that the Panthers would administer "disciplinary actions" against "those little bourgeois, snooty nose SDS's" if they got "out of order." See John P. Diggins, *The American Left in the Twentieth Century* (New York: Harcourt, Brace, Jovanovich, 1973), 175–6.

58. Lennox S. Hinds, *Illusions of Justice: Human Rights Violations in the United States* (Iowa City, Iowa: School of Social Work, University of Iowa, 1978), 88.

59. Carson, *In Struggle*, 256.

60. Donald McDonald, "Nixon's Record Revealed," in Melvin Steinfield (ed.), *Our Racist Presidents* (San Ramon, California: Consensus Publishers, 1972), 283–96.

6. BLACK REBELLION: ZENITH AND DECLINE, 1970–1976

1. Foner, *Organized Labor and the Black Worker*, 418–19.

2. Ibid., 431.

3. Ibid., 435.

4. Herbert Hill, "Race and Labor," 40–41.

5. Ibid., 47.

6. Marguerite Ross Barnett, "The Congressional Black Caucus: Illusions and Realities of Power," in Michael B. Preston, Lenneal J. Henderson, Jr., and Paul Puryear (eds.), *The New Black Politics: The Search For Political Power* (New York: Longman, 1982), 35.

7. William Strickland, "The Gary Convention and the Crisis of American Politics," *Black World* 21 (October 1972): 18–26; and Imamu Amiri Baraka, "Toward the Creation of Political Institutions for all African Peoples," *Black World* 21 (October 1972): 54–78. The Gary Convention's statement was one of the most politically advanced statements produced by black Americans in history:

> We come to Gary in an hour of great crisis and tremendous promise for Black America. While the white nation hovers on the brink of chaos, while its politicians offer no hope of real change, we stand on the edge of history and are faced with an amazing and frightening choice: We may choose in 1972 to slip back into the decadent white politics of American life, or we may press forward, moving relentlessly from Gary to the creation of our own Black life. The choice is large, but the time is very short. . . . If we have never faced it before, let us face it at Gary: The profound crisis of Black people and the disaster of America are not caused by men nor will they be solved by men alone. These crises are the crises of basically flawed economics and politics, and of cultural degradation. None of the Democratic candidates and none of the Republican candidates—regardless of their vague promises to us or to their white constituencies—can solve our problems or the problems of this country without radically changing the systems by which it operates.

See Strickland, "The Gary Convention and the Crisis of American Politics," 20, 24.

8. Degler, *Affluence and Anxiety*, 192.

9. William E. Nelson, Jr., and Philip J. Meranto, *Electing Black Mayors: Political Action in the Black Community* (Columbus, Ohio: Ohio State University Press, 1977), 336.

10. Ibid., 343–51.

11. Bureau of the Census, *Social Indicators III: Selected data on social conditions and trends in the United States* (Washington, D.C.: U.S. Government Printing Office, 1980), 237.

12. Mary F. Berry, *Black Resistance, White Law: A History of Constitutional Racism in America* (Englewood Cliffs, New Jersey: Prentice-Hall, 1971), 228.

13. Hinds, *Illusions of Justice*, 119–22.

14. Ibid., 258–63.

15. Ibid., 168.

16. Angela Davis, *With My Mind on Freedom: An Autobiography* (New York: Bantam, 1975), 15.

17. Robert Chrisman, "George Jackson," *Black Scholar* 3 (October 1971): 2–4.

18. Eric Mann, *Comrade George: An Investigation into the Life, Political Thought, and Assassination of George Jackson* (New York: Harper and Row, 1972), 144.

19. Ibid., 28, 146–9; anonymous "Episodes From The Attica Massacre," *Black Scholar* 4 (October 1972): 34–9.

20. Polenberg, *One Nation Divisible*, 252–3.

21. William Strickland, "Watergate: Its Meaning For Black America," *Black World* 23 (December 1973): 4–14.

22. Harding, *The Other American Revolution*, 216–17.

23. Barnett, "The Congressional Black Caucus," 35.

24. Cruse, "The Little Rock National Black Political Convention," 13.

25. Ladun Anise, "The Tyranny of a Purist Ideology," *Black World* 24 (May 1975): 18–27. Anise added with emphasis:

> The argument that a collective identity of over 300 million Black people is a parochial identity fit for the zoo constitutes an intolerable misreading of history. Oppression wears many faces under many hats. No single, variable explanatory theory or model will ever provide a reasonable functional analysis of the problem. The constant proclivity toward extreme polarities is nothing more than a sophisticated escapism born of either a distorted view of history, ignorance or insecurity projected as power or tough-mindedness (p. 24).

26. Kalamu Ya Salaam, "Tell No Lies, Claim No Easy Victories," *Black World* 23 (October 1974): 18–34.

27. Alkalimat wrote in November 1969:

> The ofay has sinned against God. We are God's righteous warriors and must rise as Gods ourselves. The Black revolution must burn the earth rid of the white boys' curse so that love can reign and we can become who we were really meant to be . . . When we rebel and become our true African selves we will then have started acting out our true role in the post-American future of the world.

In stark contrast, in September 1974, Alkalimat declared that capitalism was

> the fundamental cause of the problems facing black people. . . . The imperialism which exploits and oppresses Africa is rooted in the system of U.S. monopoly capitalism. . . . Thus, while the black working class must of necessity lead the black liberation struggle— because of its unwavering militancy and because it has the firmest grip of the levers of social change of any sector of the black community—all progressive forces truly interested in the liberation of black people have a definite and important role to play.

See Alkalimat, "What Lies Ahead for Black Americans?" *Negro Digest* 19 (November 1969): 21; Peoples College, "Imperialism and Black Liberation," *Black Scholar* 6 (September 1974): 38–42.

28. Haki Madhubuti, "The Latest Purge: The Attack on Black Nationalism and Pan-Afrikanism by the New Left, the sons and daughters of the Old Left," *Black Scholar* 6 (September 1974): 43–56.

29. Maglanbayan and Walters quoted in Haki Madhubuti, "Enemy: From the White Left, White Right and In-Between," *Black World* 23 (October 1974): 36–47.

30. Mark Smith, "A Response to Haki Madhubuti," *Black Scholar* 6 (January–February, 1975) 45–52.

31. Hoyt Fuller, "Another Fork in the Road," *Black World* 23 (October 1974) 49–50, 97.

32. Stanley Aronowitz, "Remaking the American Left, Part One: Currents in American Radicalism," *Socialist Review* 13 (January–February 1983): 20.

33. Among a large number of recent texts which document the economic and political plight of the American Indian since the 1950s are Wilcomb E. Washburn, *The Indian in America* (New York: Harper and Row, 1975); Stan Steiner, *The New Indians* (New York: Harper and Row, 1968), and a book which reached a more popular audience, Vine DeLoria's *Custer Died for Your Sins: An Indian Manifesto* (New York: Macmillan, 1969).

34. Dennis Banks, "Interview," *Black Scholar* 7 (June 1976): 33.

35. Ortiz, "Land and Nationhood," 11.

36. Banks, "Interview," 29.

37. Ortiz, "Land and Nationhood," 111–12.

38. Sowell, *Race and Economics*, 111–13. For a detailed analysis of the political economy of Chicanos, see Mario T. Garcia, "Radial Dualism in the El Paso Labor Market, 1880–1920," *Atzlán* 6 (Fall 1975): 197–218; Tomás Almaguer, "Historical Notes on Chicano Oppression: The Dialectics of Racial and Class Oppression in North America," *Atzlán* 5 (Spring and Fall 1974): 27–56; Marietta Morrisey, "Ethnic Stratification and the Study of Chicanos," *Journal of Ethnic Studies* 10 (Winter 1983): 71–99; and Mario Barrera, *Race and Class in the Southwest* (Notre Dame, Indiana: University of Notre Dame Press, 1979).

39. Cesar Chavez, "The California Farm Workers' Struggle," *Black Scholar* 7 (June 1976): 16.

40. Makielski, *Beleaguered Minorities*, 68.

41. Ibid., 70.

42. Garcia, "The Chicano Movement and the Mexican-American Community," 120–1.

43. Gutierrez's political coup in Crystal City, Texas, is documented in a study by John Shockley, *Chicano Revolt in a Texas Town* (Notre Dame, Indiana: University of Notre Dame Press, 1974). Other general studies which explore modern Chicano nationalism are Rodolfo Acuna, *Occupied America: The Chicano's Struggle toward Liberation* (San Francisco: Canfield Press, 1972); and Richard A. Garcia's sweeping account, *The Chicanos in America, 1540–1974* (Dobbs Ferry, New York: Oceana Press, 1977).

44. Garcia, "The Chicano Movement and the Mexican-American Community," 119.

45. Ibid., 121.

46. Ibid., 131, 135.

47. Chuck Stone, "Black Political Power in the Carter Era," *Black Scholar* 8 (January–February 1977): 6–15.

48. Eddie N. Williams, "Black Impact on the 1976 Elections," *Focus* 4 (November 1976).

49. Stone, "Black Political Power in the Carter Era," 9.

7. REACTION: THE DEMISE OF THE SECOND RECONSTRUCTION, 1976–1982

1. William P. O'Hare, "Wealth and Economic Status," *Crisis* 91 (December 1984): 6–7.

2. Robert B. Hill, "The Black Middle Class: Past, Present and Future," in James D. Williams (ed.), *The State of Black America, 1986* (Washington, D.C.: National Urban League, 1986), 43–64.

3. Jim Thomas, David Stribling, Ra Rabb Chaka, Edmond Clemons, Charlie Secret and Alex Neal, "Prison Conditions and Penal Trends," *Crime and Social Justice* 15 (Summer 1981): 49–50.

4. Franklin H. Williams, "On Death Cars," *Milwaukee Courier* (12 June 1982).

5. William Julius Wilson, *The Declining Significance of Race: Blacks and Changing American Institutions* (Chicago: University of Chicago Press, 1978), passim.

6. See Harry Edwards, "Camouflaging the Color Line: A Critique," 98–103; Charles Payne, "On the Declining—And Increasing—Significance of Race," 117–39; Charles V. Willie, "The Inclining Significance of Race," 145–58; and William Julius Wilson, "The Declining Significance of Race: Revisited But Not Revised," 159–76, in Charles V. Willie (ed.), *The Caste and Class Controversy* (Bayside, New York: General Hall, 1979).

7. William Julius Wilson, *The Truly Disadvantaged: The Inner City, the Underclass, and Public Policy* (Chicago: University of Chicago Press, 1987), vii.

8. Ibid., 6–12, 15–16, 76.

9. The Association of Black Sociologists issued a statement denouncing *The Declining Significance of Race* as a "misrepresentation of the black experience." It declared: "In the past reactionary groups have seized upon inappropriate analyses as a basis for the futher suppression of blacks. We would hope that this is not the intent of the recent recognition that has been given to Professor Wilson's book. It must be underscored that the life chances of blacks (e.g., employment, housing, health care, education, etc.) are shocking and that discrimination in some areas is so pervasive that the income and employment gaps between blacks and whites have widened." See Willie, *Caste and Class Controversy*, 177–8.

10. Douglas G. Glasgow, *The Black Underclass: Poverty, Unemployment and the Entrapment of Ghetto Youth* (New York: Vintage, 1981), 1–9.

11. Harding, *The Other American Revolution*, 221.

12. Askia Muhammad, "Civil War in Islamic America," *Nation* 224 (11 June 1977): 721.

13. Harding, *The Other American Revolution*, 222.

14. Barbara Easton, Michael Kazin and David Plotke, "Desperate Times: The Peoples Temple and the Left," *Socialist Review* 9 (March–April 1979): 64.

15. Jitu Weusi, "Jonestown Massacre—An Act of Genocide?" *Black Thoughts* 10 (May–June 1979): 1, 30–1.

16. Easton, Kazin and Plotke, "Desperate Times: The Peoples Temple and the Left," 63, 74.

17. Stokely Carmichael, *Stokely Speaks: Black Power Back to Pan-Africanism* (New York: Vintage, 1971), 73, 114.

18. Eldridge Cleaver, *Soul on Ice* (New York: Delta, 1968), 206.

19. Clark, *Dark Ghetto*, 67–74.

20. Linda LaRue, "The Black Movement and Women's Liberation," *Black Scholar* 1 (May 1970): 36–42.

21. Elizabeth Hood, "Black Women, White Women: Separate Paths to Liberation," *Black Scholar* 9 (April 1978): 45–56.

22. Michele Wallace, *Black Macho and the Myth of the Superwoman* (New York: Warner, 1980), 42–3, 118. Typical of Wallace's acerbity was the following comment: "Come 1966, the black man had two pressing tasks before him: a white woman in every bed and a black woman under every heel. Out of his sense of urgency came a struggle called the Black Movement, which was nothing more or less than the black man's struggle to attain his presumably lost 'manhood'" (pp. 52–3).

23. Bell Hooks, *Feminist Theory: From Margin to Center* (Boston: South End Press, 1984), 161, 163. Also see Bell Hooks, *Ain't I A Woman* (Boston: South End Press, 1981).

24. Angela Y. Davis, *Women, Race and Class* (New York: Random House, 1981) 220. Other works by Davis include *Violence Against Women and the Ongoing Challenge to Resistance* (New York: Kitchen Table/Women of Color Press, 1985), and *Women, Culture and Politics* (New York: Random House, 1989). More aggressive and disjointed than Painter was reviewer Sheila Sinclair, who argued that Davis's "Marxist logic" and other theoretical transgressions illustrated that "the mind's reach exceeds the ideology's grasp." See review by

Sheila Sinclair, *Black Enterprise* (May 1982): 18; and review by Nell Irvin Painter in *Ms. Magazine* (April 1982): 99.

25. Barbara Smith (ed.), *Home Girls: A Black Feminist Anthology* (New York: Kitchen Table/Women of Color Press, 1983), xxiv, xxxiv–xxxv.

26. See Audre Lorde, "Scratching the Surface: Some Notes on Barriers to Women and Loving," *Black Scholar* 9 (April 1978): 31–5.

27. Influential articles by Edelman include "Southern School Desegregation, 1954–1973: A Judicial-Political Overview," *Annals of the American Academy of Political and Social Science* 407 (May 1973): 32–42; "On Mounting Effective Child Advocacy," *Proceedings of the American Philosophical Society* 119 (December 1975): 470–7; "Death by Poverty, Arms or Moral Numbness," *American Journal of Orthopsychiatry* 53 (October 1983): 593–601; "Defending America's Children," *Educational Leadership* 46 (May 1989): 77–80; and "Economic Issues Related to Child Care and Early Childhood Education," *Teachers College Record* 90 (Spring 1989): 342–51.

28. Polenberg, *One Nation Divisible*, 258–9.

29. Lawrence Goodwyn, "Jimmy Carter and 'Populism'," *Southern Exposure* 5 (Spring 1977): 45.

30. David Plotke, "The Politics of Transition: The United States in Transition," *Socialist Review* 11 (January–February 1981): 21–72.

31. Ken Bode, "Carter's Chosen Path," *New Republic* 180 (27 January 1979): 13.

32. Marable, *From The Grassroots*, 30.

33. Elliott Currie, "The Politics of Jobs: Humphrey—Hawkins and the Dilemmas of Full Employment," *Socialist Review* 7 (March–April 1977): 93–4, 103–4.

34. Barnett, "The Congressional Black Caucus," 45.

35. Victor Perlo, "Carter's Economic Prescription: Bitter Medicine for the People," *Political Affairs* 58 (January 1979): 1.

36. Ken Bode, "Carter's Chosen Path," *New Republic* 180 (27 January 1979): 12–14.

37. Manning Marable, *Blackwater: Historical Studies in Race, Class Consciousness, and Revolution* (Dayton, Ohio: Black Praxis Press, 1981), 151–2.

38. John Judis and Alan Wolfe, "American Politics at the Crossroads: The Collapse of Cold-War Liberalism," *Socialist Review* 7 (March–April 1977): 9.

39. Marable, *Blackwater*, 133.

40. John Hope Franklin, *Reconstruction After the Civil War* (Chicago: University of Chicago Press, 1961), 155, 157.

41. Baxter Smith, "The Resurgence of the KKK," *Black Scholar* 12 (January–February 1981): 29.

42. Andrew Marx and Tom Tuthill, "Resisting the Klan: Mississippi Organizes," *Southern Exposure* 8 (Summer 1980): 27.

43. Marable, *Blackwater*, 130.

44. Brenda Payton, "Police Use of Deadly Force in Oakland," *Black Scholar* 12 (January–February 1981): 62.

45. Herb Boyd, "Blacks and the Police State: A Case Study of Detroit," *Black Scholar* 12 (January–February 1981): 60.

46. Payton, "Police Use of Deadly Force in Oakland," 64.

47. Damu Smith, "The Upsurge of Police Repression: An Analysis," *Black Scholar* 12 (January–February 1981): 43.

48. Leonard Sykes, Jr., Jim Crow, Lynchings and a Return to Business As Usual," *Black Books Bulletin* 7 (Fall 1981): 20.

49. Joe Gilyard, "White Man Who Shot Two Black Girls Is Awarded $5,000 For His Trouble," *Cleveland Call and Post* (17 October 1981).

50. Chinta Strausberg, "White Sheriff Denies Rights to Black Religious Group," *Chicago Defender* (22 September 1981).

51. Demetri Brown, "Black Man Found Near Lake Stirs Rumors," *Jackson Advocate* (15–21 October 1981).

52. Chokwe Lumumba, "Short History of the U.S. War on the R.N.A.," *Black Scholar* 12 (January–February 1981): 77.

53. Janice Bevien, "Notes on Current Struggles Against Repression," *Black Scholar* 12 (January–February 1981): 82; Manning Marable, "Justice is on Trial in Greensboro," *San Francisco Sun Reporter* (10 September 1981).

54. Bevien, "Notes on Current Struggles Against Repression," 84.

55. John L. Marshall, "1872 Law Used to Prosecute Police Gadfly: Ex-Black Panther Accused of Trying to Turn Crowd Against Police," *Los Angeles Times* (6 May 1982).

56. Marable, *Blackwater*, 149, 157.

57. Ibid., 149, 157.

58. Michael Reich, *Racial Inequality: A Political-Economic Analysis* (Princeton, New Jersey: Princeton University Press, 1981), 5–6.

59. Twiley W. Barker, Jr. and Lucius J. Barker, "The Courts, Section 5 of the Voting Rights Act, and the Future of Black Politics," in Preston, Henderson, and Puryear (eds.), *The New Black Politics*, 62–3.

60. Marable, *Blackwater*, 155.

61. Ibid., 157.

62. Frank Carroll, "OSHA Under the Gun," *Political Affairs* 60 (September 1981): 28–9.

63. Popular Economics Research Group, "Barefoot and Pregnant Women and Reaganomics," *WIN* magazine 18 (15 April 1982): 12–14.

64. Ronald V. Dellums, interview, "Peace, Justice, and Politics," *Plain Speaking* (16–31 May 1982).

65. John Herbers, "Poverty Rate, 7.4%, Termed Highest Since '67," *New York Times* (26 July 1982).

66. Sheila Rule, "Black Middle Class Slipping, Study by Urban League Says," *New York Times* (4 August 1982).

67. Earl Anthony, "Interview: Eldridge Cleaver," *Players* 8 (February 1982): 27–35.

68. Sam Zuckerman, "House backs 'soak-the-poor' budget," *Guardian* (23 June 1982).

8. THE PARADOX OF INTEGRATION: BLACK SOCIETY AND POLITICS IN THE POST-REFORM PERIOD, 1982–1990

1. Joseph Berger, "Campus Racial Strains Show Two Perspectives on Inequality," *New York Times* (22 May 1989); and Manning Marable, "Beyond Academic Apartheid: A Strategy for a Culturally Pluralistic University," *Black Issues in Higher Education* 6 (7 December 1989): 24–25.

2. W. E. B. DuBois, *The Souls of Black Folk* (Chicago: A. C. McClurg and Company, 1903), 3.

3. Juliet Ucelli and Dennis O'Neil, "The Cost of Drugs," *Forward Motion* 9 (May 1990): 3–4; and Manning Marable, "Toward Black American Empowerment: Violence and Resistance in the African-American Community in the 1990s," *African Commentary* 2 (May 1990): 18.

4. Ucelli and O'Neil, "The Cost of Drugs," 4–5.

5. Ibid., 5–7.

6. Marable, "Toward Black American Empowerment," 19–21.

7. Marc Mauer, *Young Black Men and the Criminal Justice System: A Growing National*

Problem (Washington, D.C.: The Sentencing Project, 1990), pp. 1–11. Also see David E. Anderson, "Large Share of Young Blacks Afoul of Law," *New Pittsburgh Courier* (28 February 1990); and "Blacks in Jail," *Sacramento Observer* (1–7 March 1990).

8. Jonathan A. Bennett, "Report Finds Executions 'Arbitrary, Biased,'" *Guardian* (25 February 1987); Anthony Lewis, "Bowing to Racism," *New York Times* (28 April 1987); Jonathan A. Bennett, "Court fears 'too much justice,'" *Guardian* (6 May 1987); and Akinshiju C. Ola, "Supreme Court Votes for Death," *Guardian* (28 May 1986).

9. Linda Greenhouse, "Death Sentences Against Retarded and Young Upheld," *New York Times* (27 June 1989); Editorial, "The Supreme Court's Cruel 'Consensus,'" *New York Times* (3 July 1989); Peter Applebome, "Executions of Retarded Men Set in the South Stir Debate," *New York Times* (13 July 1989); and Tom Wicker, "Death and Mockery," *New York Times* (27 June 1989).

10. Robert Reinhold, "Lawyers Shunning Death Row Cases," *New York Times* (22 September 1986).

11. "A Record Prison Census," *New York Times* (17 May 1987); Janet Bass, "Unprecedented Prison Overcrowding," *New Pittsburgh Courier* (6 January 1990); Tom Wicker, "An Ungrand Total," *New York Times* (13 October 1989); and "Prison Population Sets a Year's Record, Early," *New York Times* (11 September 1989).

12. Douglas Martin, "Violence Grows as Crowding Worsens in New York City Jails," *New York Times* (15 April 1987); Andrew H. Malcolm, "Florida's Jammed Prisons: More In Means More Out," *New York Times* (3 July 1989); and "Ohio Curb Sought in Prison Products," *New York Times* (8 March 1987).

13. Khalid Fattah Griggs, "Courts order end to prison overcrowding," *Carolina Peacemaker* (18 July 1987).

14. "Of 1.2 Million Robberies a Year, A third of the Victims are Injured," *New York Times* (20 April 1987); and Paul Ruffins, "Crime," *Point of View* (Spring 1987), 10.

15. "Perception and Reality and Reagan's Civil Rights Policies," *New York Times* (4 January 1987); Robert Pear, "Reagan Man, Citing 'Credibility,' To Leave Civil Rights Commission," *New York Times* (30 November 1986); Howard Kurtz, "Meese Has Met Every One of His Minority Hiring Goals: None," *Washington Post National Weekly* (15 December 1986); and Editorial, "Don't Decommission Civil Rights," *New York Times* (30 November 1986).

16. Mary Frances Berry, "Affirmative Action and the Court," *Point of View* 1 (Fall 1986): 3–4.

17. William M. Kunstler, "The Deeper They Dig, the Dirtier Rehnquist Gets," *Guardian* (20 August 1986); Akinshiju C. Ola, "Will Rehnquist's new gown have a hood on it?" *Guardian* (17 September 1986); and Akinshiju C. Ola, "Justice: Where has the 'mainstream' gone?" *Guardian* (1 October 1986).

18. William T. Coleman, Jr., "Why Judge Bork Is Unacceptable," *New York Times* (15 September 1987); "Supreme Court deals setback to civil rights," *Westside Gazette* (22 June 1989); and "Blatant Racial, Ethnic Discrimination No Longer Prohibited," *New Pittsburgh Courier* (31 March 1990).

19. "Justice Marshall says Court Risks Civil Rights of All Americans," *Beacon Digest* (15 September 1989); and published "Remarks of Thurgood Marshall, associate justice of the Supreme Court, at the Second Court Judicial Conference," dated September 1989.

20. "Teele considering mayoral candidacy," *Westside Gazette* (18 December 1986); and Lena Williams, "Head of Rights Agency Harnesses the Horses Against Job Bias," *New York Times* (8 February 1987).

21. Manning Marable, "Black Politics in Crisis," *Progressive* 51 (January 1987): 20.

22. Dan Carmichael, "Prosecutor Named for Pierce Case," *New Pittsburgh Courier* (7 March 1990).

23. Marable, "Black Politics in Crisis," 20–21.

24. Benjamin F. Chavis, Jr., "LaRouche Invades Black Community," *Omaha Star* (7 August 1986); Simon Anekwe, "Innis Trounced in Election Bid," *Charleston Chronicle* (20 September 1986); Christopher J. Bille, "Owens Resists Invasion," *Guardian* (10 September 1986); and Clarence Lusane, "The Far Right Goes After Black Support," *Covert Action Information Bulletin* 27 (Spring 1987): 50–51.

25. Manning Marable, "Conservatism vs. Liberalism Among Black Voters in 1988," *Black Issues in Higher Education* 5 (15 June 1988): 48; and Thomas B. Edsall, "Race Continues to be a Wild Card in American Politics," *Washington Post National Weekly* (8–14 August 1988).

26. "President Requests Highest Budget Ever for EEOC to continue Record of Anti-Discrimination Enforcement," *Omaha Star* (8 February 1990).

27. Scott Jaschik, "Bush Aides Change Plan for Black-College Aid, Concentrate on Individual Institutions' Needs," *Chronicle of Higher Education* 36 (8 April 1990).

28. "Bush Says Racism Won't Be Tolerated," *New Pittsburgh Courier* (10 January 1990).

29. Maureen Dowd, "Bush Picks a Chief to 'Reinvigorate' Civil Rights Panel," *New York Times* (24 February 1990).

30. "Civil Rights Nominee 'Invisible' on Civil Rights Issues," *Beacon Digest* (2 February 1990); Lori Santos, "Bush Nominates New Civil Rights Chief," *New Pittsburgh Courier* (27 January 1990); and Steve Gerstel, "Senate Confirms Thomas for D.C. Appeals Court," *New Pittsburgh Courier* (7 March 1990).

31. Frances Frank Marcus, "Sheriff is Backed in Racism Dispute," *New York Times* (23 December 1986).

32. "A Holiday Dispute," *New York Times* (28 December 1986).

33. Ken Sugar, "Supremacist Group Holds Demonstration Near Dr. King Crypt," *New Pittsburgh Courier* (29 January 1990); Jim McNamara, "Columbus residents join thousands to counter Klan rally in Oxford," *Columbus Free Press* (May 1990); and Patrik Henry Bass, "Klan Entertains High Point," *Carolina Peacemaker* (22–28 March 1990).

34. "Ku Klux Klan Says It Will Fight Drugs," *Toledo Journal* (3–9 January 1990).

35. William Loren Katz, "The Ku Klux Klan: Update 1989," *Toledo Journal* (3–9 January 1990).

36. "Klan/Nazi and Hate/Violence Incidents from Around the Nation," *Klanwatch Intelligence Report* 1 (October 1985): 4.

37. Henry Duvall, "Snag in American race relations?" *Charleston Chronicle* (20 December 1986).

38. E. J. Dionne, Jr., "The Idea of Equality is Proving Unequal to the Demands of Today," *Washington Post National Weekly* (7–13 May 1990).

39. Felicity Barringer, "32 Million Lived in Poverty in '88, a Figure Unchanged," *New York Times* (19 October 1989).

40. "As Demands of Needy Rise, Source of Help is Shrinking," *New York Times* (24 November 1989).

41. "Blacks Twice as Likely to Have Vision Problems," *New Pittsburgh Courier* (10 February 1990).

42. "Asthma deaths up among Blacks," *Norfolk Journal and Guide* (18–24 April 1990).

43. "Rate of Diabetes Among Blacks Rises," *Southside Virginia Star* (3–9 May 1990).

44. Ronald L. Fletcher, "Cancer Among Blacks and Minorities," *Toledo Journal* (30 May–5 June 1990); and "The Impact: Black Men, Women and Youth Are Among the Most 'At Risk' Groups," *Sacramento Observer* (14–20 June 1990).

45. "Doctors Discuss Spread of AIDS Among Nation's Blacks," *Toledo Journal* (31 January–6 February 1990); "Facts on Black Men and AIDS," *Sacramento Observer* (14–20 June 1990); and "Blacks and the AIDS Epidemic," *Sacramento Observer* (10–16 May 1990).

46. Barbara Day, "Harlem healthcare worse than in Bangladesh," *Guardian* (31 January

1990); and "Health Disparity Between Blacks and Whites," *Sacramento Observer* (12-18 April 1990).

47. Edward B. Lazere and Paul A. Leonard, *The Crisis in Housing for the Poor: A Special Report on Hispanics and Blacks* (Washington, D.C.: Center on Budget and Policy Priorities, 1989), 1-5.

48. Allan R. Gold, "Racial Pattern is Found in Boston Mortgages," *New York Times* (1 September 1989); "African-Americans Face Tough Mortgage Road," *Buffalo Challenger* (20 September 1989); and Steven Wilmsen, "Minorities get short shrift on home loans," *Denver Post* (1 October 1989).

49. "Integrated housing still elusive for blacks," *Columbus Dispatch* (8 February 1989).

50. William Celis III, "Public Housing Units Are Rapidly Decaying, Causing Many to Close," *Wall Street Journal* (15 December 1986); and Roger Snell, "HUD left some of Columbus' poor out in cold," *Columbus Dispatch* (17 July 1989).

51. Alan Finder, "Aid to New York Homeless Not Spent," *New York Times* (6 June 1990).

52. James Barron, "Scratching to Find Shelter for Nation's Homeless Families," *New York Times* (12 July 1987); and "Boston Mayor Deplores Plight of the Homeless," *New York Times* (29 December 1986).

53. Gary Blonston, "Black Flight," *Detroit Free Press* (18 May 1986).

54. Felicity Barringer, "Two Worlds of Washington: Turmoil and Growth," *New York Times* (12 July 1990).

55. Stephanie Strom, "Ministers in Some Poor Areas of New York Are Arming Themselves," *New York Times* (23 April 1990); and Howard Kurtz, "When Citizens Jury-Rig Their Own Brand of Justice," *Washington Post National Weekly* (14-20 May 1990).

56. "Black Men More Likely to marry than Black Women, Census Bureau Study Shows," Bureau of the Census, Commerce News, February 1987; "Two-Thirds of Black Mothers Not Awarded Child Support Payments, Census Bureau Says," Bureau of the Census, *Commerce News*, August 1987; and Tamar Lewin, "Black Children Living With One Parent Put at 55 Percent," *New York Times* (15 July 1990).

57. David E. Anderson, "Urban League Proposes $50 Billion Domestic Marshall Plan," *New Pittsburgh Courier* (10 January 1990); Marian Wright Edelman, "Self-Help in the Eighties: Blacks Cannot Rely on Government Alone," *Sacramento Observer* (27 August- 3 September 1986); and quotation by Jesse Jackson, *Charleston Chronicle* (6 September 1986).

58. Clarence Page, "'The Plan': A Paranoid View of Black Problems," *Dover Herald* (23 February 1990).

59. Manning Marable, "Africa, Black America connect on Apartheid," *Witness* 68 (February 1985): 9-31.

60. Ibid., 11; also see Manning Marable, "Race and Realignment in American Politics," in Michael Davis, Fred Pfeil, and Michael Sprinker (eds.), *The Year Left* (London: Verso, 1985), 1-11.

61. See Manning Marable, *Black American Politics* (London: Verso, 1985), 247-305.

62. See Manning Marable, "Race and the Demise of Liberalism: The 1988 Presidential Campaign Reconsidered," *Black Issues in Higher Education* 5 (22 December 1988): 76.

63. See Manning Marable, "Black Politics and the Challenges for the Left," *Monthly Review* 41 (April 1990): 22-31.

64. Thomas Gentile, *March on Washington: August 28, 1963* (Washington, D.C.: New Day Publications, 1983), 244, 247.

9. EPILOGUE: THE VISION AND THE POWER

1. Boyd, "Blacks and the Police State," 61.

2. W. E. B. DuBois, *Black Reconstruction in America, 1860-1880* (New York: Atheneum,

1971), 711. DuBois's reflections on the First Reconstruction include "Reconstruction and Its Benefits," *American Historical Review* 15 (July 1910): 781–99; "A History of the Negro Vote," *Crisis* 40 (June 1933): 128–9; "Reconstruction, Seventy-Five Years After," *Phylon* 4 (1943): 205–12; "Civil Rights Legislation Before and After the Passage of the Fourteenth Amendment," *Lawyers' Guild Review* 6 (November–December 1946): 640–2; and "The Thirteenth, Fourteenth and Fifteenth Amendments," *Lawyers' Guild Review* 9 (Spring 1949): 92–5.

3. Manning Marable, "Reagan and the NAACP: Confrontation or Cooptation?" *Fort Lauderdale Westside Gazette* (6 August 1981).

4. Steven R. Weisman, "Reagan Says Blacks Were Hurt by Works of the Great Society" and "Excerpts from Text of Reagan Speech to Blacks," *New York Times* (16 September 1982).

5. Marable, "Black Politics in Crisis," 22.

6. Ibid., 22.

7. DuBois, *Black Reconstruction in America*, 727.

8. Ibid., 725.

9. W. E. B. DuBois, "There Must Come a Vast Social Change in the United States," *National Guardian* (11 July 1951); DuBois, "The Choice That Confronts America's Negroes," *National Guardian* (13 February 1952); and DuBois, "The Negro in America Today," five-part essay, *National Guardian* (16, 23, 30 January, 15 February, and 5 March 1956).

10. DuBois makes a similar point in "Bound by the Color Line," *New Masses* 58 (12 February 1946): 8; and "Negroes and the Crisis of Capitalism in the United States," *Monthly Review* 4 (April 1953): 479–85.

11. Manning Marable, "African American or Black? The Politics of Cultural Identity," *Black Issues in Higher Education* 6 (13 April 1989): 72.

Bibliographical Essay: Black Leaders in the Second Reconstruction

The social protest movement that attempted to uproot racial inequality within American society produced many gifted and capable women and men, whose writings, ideas and actions helped to reshape contemporary history. This volume presents only an outline of the various labor unions, youth and students' organizations, women's groups, black nationalist formations, socialist and radical parties and other agencies developed by such leaders. For further study, it would be important to review in greater detail the specific writings by and about these individuals. Their theoretical and political strengths, weaknesses and insights provide a necessary perspective on the reasons why the Second Reconstruction simultaneously succeeded and failed.

The African-American leaders who emerged in the years after the Great Depression developed a strategic alliance with the Democratic Party and the administration of Franklin Roosevelt, which oriented the black electorate's behavior for the remainder of the century. Two pivotal figures who were architects of this alliance were Walter White, national secretary of the NAACP, and educator Mary McLeod Bethune. White had been instrumental in the creation of the Fair Employment Practices Committee during World War II, and was responsible for the NAACP's legalistic and gradualistic approach to achieve desegregation. Sources on White include Charles F. Cooney, "Walter White and the Harlem Renaissance," *Journal of Negro History* 57 (April 1972): 231–40; and Darlene Clark Hine, "The NAACP and the Supreme Court: Walter F. White and the Defeat of Judge John J. Parker, 1930," *Negro History Bulletin* 40 (July/August 1977): 753–7. Another excellent source is Nathaniel P. Tillman, Jr.'s unpublished doctoral dissertation, "Walter Francis White, A Study in Intergroup Leadership" (University of Wisconsin, 1961). Bethune served from 1936 until 1944 as director of the Division of Negro Affairs for the National Youth Administration under Roosevelt and was founder and president, from 1935 until 1949, of the National Council of Negro Women. Biographies of Bethune include LaVere Anderson, *Mary McLeod Bethune: Teacher With a Dream* (Champaign, Illinois: Garrard Publishing Company, 1976); Ella K. Carruth, *She Wanted to Read: The Story of Mary McLeod Bethune* (New York: Abbingdon Press, 1966); Eloise Greenfield, *Mary McLeod Bethune* (New York: Crowell, 1977); Rackham Holt, *Mary McLeod Bethune* (New York: Doubleday, 1974); Ruby Lorraine Radford, *Mary McLeod Bethune* (New York: Putnam, 1973); Catherine O. Peare, *Mary McLeod Bethune* (New York: Vanguard Press, 1951); and Emma Gelders Sterne, *Mary McLeod Bethune* (New York: Knopf, 1957).

Further to the left were A. Philip Randolph and Paul Robeson. Founder of the Brotherhood of Sleeping Car Porters in 1925, and initiator of the 1941 March on Washington movement, Randolph was in many respects the first "modern" African-American protest leader. Randolph believed in a democratic socialist restructuring of the American economy, and argued forcefully that racial discrimination was a barrier to all working people in the achievement of economic as well as political rights. See William H. Harris, *Keeping the Faith: A. Philip Randolph, Milton P. Webster, and the Brotherhood of Sleeping Car Porters* (Urbana: University of Illinois Press, 1977); and Brailsford R. Brazeal, *The Brotherhood of Sleeping Car Porters* (New York: Harper and Brothers, 1946). Robeson was the century's Renaissance man: football All-American, actor, outstanding singer, political activist. Robeson's opposition to the Cold War led to his political harassment by the U.S. government, which illegally seized his passport. Barred from concert halls for years, Robeson sacrificed his entire career for his political beliefs, displaying a personal integrity lacking in some leaders. Robeson's account of his ordeal is presented in *Here I Stand* (Boston: Beacon Press, 1971). See also Philip S. Foner, ed., *Paul Robeson Speaks: Writings, Speeches, Interviews, 1918–1974* (Larchmont, New York: Brunner/Mazel, 1978); Ron Ramdin, *Paul Robeson: The Man and His Mission* (London: Peter Owen, 1987); and Joseph Nazel, *Paul Robeson* (Los Angeles: Holloway, 1980).

The desegregation movement relied upon challenges in federal courts wich incrementally eroded the legality of Jim Crow. The key figure in the NAACP's long assault on segregation before 1950 was Charles Hamilton Houston. In a short but productive life, Houston served as vice dean of Howard University's law school, special counsel for the NAACP (1935–40), general counsel of the Association of Colored Railway Trainmen, and vice president of the American Council on Race Relations. Two of Houston's pivotal legal victories were *Hollins v. Oklahoma* (1935), which overturned the conviction of African-American defendants due to the deliberate exclusion of blacks as members of the jury; and the *University of Maryland v. Murray* (1936), which forced the state's law school to admit blacks. See

William H. Hastie, "Charles Hamilton Houston," *Crisis* (June/July, 1979): 274–5; and Charles H. Houston and John P. Davis, "TVA: Lily-White Reconstruction," *Crisis* (October 1934): 290–1, 311. More influential was Houston's protégé, Thurgood Marshall, the NAACP's outstanding chief legal counsel and the first African-American appointed to the Supreme Court. As the NAACP's legal strategist, Marshall argued thirty-two cases before the Supreme Court on desegregation issues and won twenty-nine, the most famous being the 1954 *Brown* decision outlawing racially separate schools. Sources by and about Marshall include "Portrait of a Leader: Thurgood Marshall," *Negro History Bulletin* 19 (November 1955): 26–7; Marshall, "The Rise and Collapse of the 'White Democratic Primary,'" *Journal of Negro Education* 26 (Summer 1957): 249–54; Marshall, "An Evaluation of Recent Efforts to Achieve Racial Integration in Education through Resort to the Courts," *Journal of Negro Education* 21 (Summer 1952): 316–27; and Manning Marable, "Thurgood Marshall: The Continuing Struggle for Equality," *Black Collegian* 20 (January/February 1990): 72–8.

The field of African-American literature produced many novelists, poets, playwrights and social critics, who exercised influence in the movement against racism. Langston Hughes was unquestionably the most popular black poet of the first half of the twentieth century, the author of numerous volumes of verse, several novels and plays. Various essays capture aspects of Hughes's creative genius, artistic influence, and political views: Arthur P. Davis, "The Harlem of Langston Hughes' Poetry," *Phylon* 13 (1952): 276–83; Davis, "Langston Hughes: Cool Poet," *College Language Association Journal* 11 (June 1968): 280–96; Darwin Turner, "Langston Hughes," *College Language Association Journal* 11 (June 1968): 297–309; and James Presley, "The American Dream of Langston Hughes," *Southwest Review* 48 (Autumn 1963): 380–6. The definitive biography of Hughes is Arnold Rampersad's excellent study, *The Life of Langston Hughes: Volume I, 1902–1941* (New York: Oxford University Press, 1986). The most powerful black novelist of the 1930s and 1940s was Richard Wright. Author of the controversial *Native Son* (1940), Wright was for several years the Communist Party's outstanding artist. Breaking with Marxism in 1944 and subsequently turning bitterly anti-communist, Wright continued to produce challenging works, including *Black Boy* (1945), *The Outsider* (1953) and *The Long Dream* (1958). Wright's political polemic *Black Power* (1954), recounting his journeys through Africa, prefigured the emergence of militant Pan-Africanism and black nationalism in the United States a decade later. Wright's tradition as a social critic was continued into the 1960s and 1970s by James Baldwin. Born in New York City in 1925, Baldwin's penetrating social essays, such as *Notes of a Native Son* (1955) and

Nobody Knows My Name (1962), were more influential than most of his novels, including *Giovanni's Room* (1958) and *Another Country* (1963). Baldwin also wrote *Going to Meet the Man* (1965), *Blues for Mr. Charlie* (1964), *If Beale Street Could Talk* (1975), *The Fire Next Time* (1970), *No Name in The Street* (1973), *The Devil Finds Work* (1976), and *The Evidence of Things Unseen* (1985). For essays and books on Baldwin, see Fern Eckman, *The Furious Passage of James Baldwin* (New York: Evans, 1986); Keneth Kinnamon, *James Baldwin: A Collection of Critical Essays* (Englewood Cliffs, New Jersey: Prentice Hall, 1974); Therman B. O'Daniel, *James Baldwin: A Critical Evaluation* (Washington, D.C.: Howard University Press, 1977); Louis H. Pratt, *James Baldwin* (Boston: Twayne, 1978); Carolyn W. Sylvander, *James Baldwin* (New York: Frederick Ungar, 1980); and Fred L. Standley and Nancy V. Burt, *Critical Essays on James Baldwin* (Boston: G. K. Hall, 1988). See also two dissertations on Baldwin: Rosa Mae Bobia, "James Baldwin and His Francophone Critics" (Vanderbilt University, 1984); and Barbara S. Bayne, "The Role and Rhetoric of Female Characters in James Baldwin's Fiction" (Indiana University of Pennsylvania, 1983).

With the Montgomery bus boycott of 1955–56 and the eruption of the sit-in desegregation movement in the winter of 1960, new political leaders emerged at the head of protest organizations. Adam Fairclough's comprehensive study of the Southern Christian Leadership Conference, *To Redeem the Soul of America* (Athens: University of Georgia Press, 1987), provides important information on Ralph Abernathy, James Bevel, Ella Baker, James Lawson, Andrew Young, Fred Shuttlesworth, and other important political figures. Earlier sources charted the origins, development and demise of the Student Nonviolent Coordinating Committee: Allen J. Matusow, "From Civil Rights to Black Power: The Case of SNCC, 1960–1966," in *Twentieth Century America: Recent Interpretations*, ed. Barton J. Bernstein and Allen J. Matusow (New York: Harcourt, Brace and World, 1969), pp. 531–66; Howard Zinn, *SNCC: The New Abolitionists* (Boston: Beacon Press, 1964); and Emily Schottenfeld Stoper, "The Student Nonviolent Coordinating Committee" (Ph.D. dissertation, Harvard University, 1968). The definitive study of SNCC is Clayborne Carson, *In Struggle: SNCC and the Black Awakening of the 1960s* (Cambridge: Harvard University Press, 1981). Studies on the Congress of Racial Equality include Inge Powell Bell, *CORE and the Strategy of Nonviolence* (New York: Random House, 1968); William Gellerman, *My CORE Program Experience* (Ithaca: Cornell University Press, 1965); and August Meier and Elliott Rudwick, *CORE: A Study in the Civil Rights Movement, 1942–1968* (New York: Oxford University Press, 1973). Wilson Record's *Race and Radicalism: The NAACP and the Communist Party in Conflict* (Ithaca: Cornell University

Press, 1966) represents the worst form of ideological apologetics for the Association's capitulation to anti-communism during the Cold War,—capitulation that meant the sacrifice of a decade in the resistance movement to racism. Other more standard treatments of the NAACP's political history during these years are Charles Flint Kellogg, *NAACP: A History of the National Association for the Advancement of Colored People* (Baltimore: Johns Hopkins Press, 1967); and Langston Hughes, *Flight for Freedom: The Story of the NAACP* (New York: Norton, 1962). Sources by civil rights leaders of this period include Bayard Rustin, *Down the Line* (Chicago: Quadrangle Books, 1971); Floyd McKissick, *Three-Fifths of a Man* (New York: Macmillan, 1969); James Farmer, *Freedom, When?* (New York: Random House, 1966); Rustin, *Strategies for Freedom: The Changing Patterns of Black Protest* (New York: Columbia University Press, 1976); Rustin, "The Meaning of the March on Washington," *Liberator* 8 (October 1963): 11–13; Cleveland Sellers, with Robert Terrell, *The River of No Return: The Autobiography of a Black Militant and the Life and Death of SNCC* (New York: William Morrow, 1973); James Forman, *The Making of Black Revolutionaries* (New York: Macmillan, 1972); and Benjamin E. Mays, *Born to Rebel: An Autobiography* (Athens: University of Georgia Press, 1987).

The two fundamental black leaders for the entire Second Reconstruction period were Martin Luther King, Jr., and Malcolm X. Although generally presented as diametrically opposed on issues of nonviolence, coalitions with whites, and other issues, King and Malcolm represented two aspects of the same racial equation: the historical struggle for African-American people to overturn the structures of domination and exploitation, and the concomitant effort to empower the oppressed. The literature on King is already massive. Clayborne Carson is currently at work organizing King's personal papers. The best introduction to King's life and thought is provided by a series of biographies: David L. Lewis, *King: A Critical Biography* (New York: Praeger, 1970); Rolf Italigander, *Martin Luther King* (Berlin: Colloquium Verlag, 1968); James Alonzo Bishop, *The Days of Martin Luther King, Jr.* (New York: Putnam, 1971); Lerone Bennett, *What Manner of Man: A Biography of Martin Luther King, Jr.* (Chicago: Johnson Publishing Company, 1964); Laurence Dunbar Reddick, *Crusader Without Violence: A Biography of Martin Luther King, Jr.* (New York: Harper and Row, 1959); and Lee Augustus McGriggs, *The Odyssey of Martin Luther King, Jr.* (Washington, D.C.: University Press of America, 1978).

Malcolm X characterized his life as a series of rapid "changes"—from his marginal existence as a ghetto hustler, to national spokesperson for the black nationalist Nation of Islam, and finally to his status as the preeminent advocate of Pan-Africanism, Third World Liberation and African-American political militancy. Because Malcolm X's political perspectives and public statements were frequently subject to misinterpretation and even gross distortion by his critics, it is crucial to encounter this important figure first through his own voice. The Trotskyist Socialist Workers Party was responsible for publishing several important collections of Malcolm X's speeches: George Breitman, ed., *Malcolm X Speaks* (New York: Grove Press, 1966) and *By Any Means Necessary* (New York: Pathfinder Press, 1970); Malcolm X, *Malcolm X Talks to Young People* (New York: Young Socialist Alliance, 1969) and *Malcolm X on Afro-American History* (New York: Pathfinder Press, 1970). With the renaissance of black nationalism in the late 1960s, Malcolm X was elevated to the position of cultural and political icon, as various ideological tendencies contested for his mantle of uncompromising leadership. This change in status is amply reflected in the literature of the period: see Peter L. Goldman, *The Death and Life of Malcolm X* (New York: Harper and Row, 1973); George Breitman, *The Last Year of Malcolm X: The Evolution of a Revolutionary* (New York: Merit Publishers, 1965); Ossie Davis, "Why I Eulogized Malcolm X," *Negro Digest* 15 (February 1966): 64–66; Colin Macinnes, "Malcolm, The Lost Hero," *Negro Digest* 16 (May 1967): 4–5; William Keorapetse Kgositsile, "Brother Malcolm and the Black Revolution," *Negro Digest* 18 (November 1968): 4–10; C. Eric Lincoln, "Meaning of Malcolm X," *Christian Century* 82 (7 April 1965): 431–3; Marcus H. Boulware, "Minister Malcolm, Orator Profundo," *Negro History Bulletin* 30 (November 1967): 12–14; Tom Kahn and Bayard Rustin, "The Ambiguous Legacy of Malcolm X," *Dissent* 12 (Spring 1965): 188–92; and Jigs Gardner, "The Murder of Malcolm X," *Monthly Review* 16 (April 1965): 802–5.

In the period of Black Power, black leadership reflected a rejection of the goals of integration and nonviolence. The most important theoreticians of black nationalism to influence the directions of the black protest movement were Maulana Karenga, Harold Cruse, and Amiri Baraka. Karenga was the founder of "Kwanzaa," a black cultural holiday that reinforced an awareness of African history and consciousness among African-Americans. Viewed as the pivotal advocate of black cultural nationalism, Karenga was influential as a social and political critic beyond his own circles. His writings include "Prisons and Law," *Black Collegian* 6 (January–February 1976): 27; "Afro-American Nationalism: Beyond Mystification and Misconception," *Black Books Bulletin* 6 (Spring 1978): 7–12; "Black Art," *Negro Digest* 17 (January 1968): 5–9; "Ideology and Struggle: Some Preliminary Notes," *Black Scholar* 6 (January–February 1975): 23–30; and *Essays on Struggle: Position and Analysis* (San Diego: Kawaida Publications, 1978). Cruse was a freelance essayist based in New York, who joined the Communist Party briefly after World War II. Breaking sharply with Marxism-Leninism, Cruse adopted the perspective that the fundamental conflicts within American society were not rooted in class but in ethnic rivalries. His greatest single work, *The Crisis of the Negro Intellectual* (New York: William Morrow, 1967), was the most complex theoretical work produced in the Black Power period. Other works by Cruse include *Rebellion or Revolution?* (New York: William Morrow, 1968); *Plural but Equal: A Critical Study of Blacks and Minorities* (New York: William Morrow, 1987); and "Stalled Out in History: The Past and Future of Integration," *Sojourners* 19 (August/September 1990): 22–25.

Baraka first established his artistic reputation as a "beat" poet and music critic during the late 1950s and early 1960s in Greenwich Village. Radicalized under the influence of Malcolm X and resurgent black nationalism, he became a central force in the black literary and artistic renaissance of the late 1960s and 1970s. Baraka's turn to Marxism-Leninism in 1974 confounded his friends and critics alike. Representative samples of his works include: *Blues People* (New York: William Morrow, 1963); *Dutchman and the Slave* (New York: William Morrow, 1964); *Home: Social Essays* (New York: William Morrow, 1966); *It's Nation Time* (Chicago: Third World Press, 1970); *Raise, Race, Rays, Raze: Essays Since 1965* (New York: Random House, 1971); and *The Autobiography of LeRoi Jones/Amiri Baraka* (New York: Freundlich, 1984). For discussions of Baraka's influence as a radical author, see Mary Diane Dippold, "LeRoi Jones: Tramp with Connections" (Ph.D. dissertation, University of Maryland, 1971); Madelyn E. Hart, "Analysis of the Rhetoric of LeRoi Jones (Imamu Amiri Baraka) in his Campaign to Promote Cultural Black Nationalism" (M.A. thesis, North Texas State University, 1976); William Joseph Harris, "Jones/Baraka: The Evolution of a Black Poet" (Ph.D. dissertation, Stanford University, 1973); and Theodore R. Hudson, *From LeRoi Jones to Amiri Baraka: The Literary Works* (Durham, North Carolina: Duke University Press, 1973).

As rebellion gave way again to incremental reforms within the system, and as political conservatism gained ascendancy, leaders from the traditional civil rights organizations and from the political arena began to reassert their authority and influence. In the 1980s and early 1990s, the most dynamic political leader within the black community was the Reverend Jesse Jackson. As protégé to King, Jackson formed his own organization, People United to Serve Humanity, in 1971. Sources on Jackson's public life and thought include Eddie Stone, *Jesse Jackson: Biography of an Ambitious Man* (Los Angeles: Holloway House, 1979); Barbara A. Reynolds, *Jesse Jackson: The Man, The Movement, The Myth* (Chicago: Nelson-Hall, 1975); and Sheila D. Collins, *The Rainbow Challenge: The Jackson Campaign and the Future of U.S. Politics* (New York: Monthly Review Press, 1986).

All people generally receive the leadership they demand. The quality and commitment of black leadership has varied greatly over time, depending upon the collective consciousness of African-Americans, their recognition of grievances and their desire for social change. As the social crisis in America's urban centers deepens, it seems likely that new protest figures will emerge.

Select Bibliography

BOOKS (including books not mentioned in the Notes)

Rodolfo Acuna, *Occupied America: The Chicano's Struggle toward Liberation* (San Francisco: Canfield Press, 1972).

Robert L. Allen, *Black Awakening in Capitalist America: An Analytic History* (Garden City, New York: Anchor, 1969).

Rob Backus, *Fire Music: A Political History of Jazz* (Chicago: Vanguard Books, 1978).

Imamu Amiri Baraka (LeRoi Jones), *Black Music* (New York: William Morrow, 1970).

———, *Three Books by Imamu Amiri Baraka: The System of Dante's Hell; Tales; The Dead Lecturer* (New York: Grove Press, 1975).

E. D. Barbour (ed.), *The Black Power Revolt* (Boston: Sargent Press, 1968).

Mario Barrera, *Race and Class in the Southwest* (Notre Dame, Indiana: University of Notre Dame Press, 1979).

Numan V. Bartley and Hugh D. Graham, *Southern Politics and the Second Reconstruction* (Baltimore: Johns Hopkins Press, 1975).

Derrick Bell, *Race, Racism and American Law* (Boston: Little, Brown, 1973).

Lerone Bennett, Jr., *Confrontation Black and White* (Baltimore: Penguin Books, 1965).

Robert F. Berkhofer, Jr., *The White Man's Indian: Images of the American Indian From Columbus to the Present* (New York: Alfred A. Knopf, 1978).

Mary F. Berry, *Black Resistance, White Law: A History of Constitutional Racism in America* (Englewood Cliffs, New Jersey: Prentice-Hall, 1971).

Nelson Blackstock, *COINTELPRO: The FBI's Secret War Against Political Freedom* (New York: Random House, 1976).

James Boggs, *Racism and the Class Struggle: Further Pages from a Black Worker's Notebook* (New York: Monthly Review Press, 1970).

John H. Bracey, Jr., August Meier and Elliott Rudwick (eds.), *Black Nationalism in America* (Indianapolis: Bobbs-Merrill, 1970).

George Breitman, *The Last Year of Malcolm X: The Evolution of a Revolutionary* (New York: Schocken, 1968).

——— (ed.), *By Any Means Necessary: Speeches, Interviews and a Letter by Malcolm X* (New York: Merit, 1970).

George Breitman, Herman Porter and Baxter Smith (eds.), *The Assassination of Malcolm X* (New York: Pathfinder Press, 1976).

Thomas R. Brooks, *Toil and Trouble: A History of American Labor* (New York: Delta, 1971).

Bureau of the Census, "Selected Characteristics of Persons and Families of Mexican, Puerto Rican and Other Spanish Origins, March, 1971." *Current Population Reports* (Washington, D.C.: U.S. Government Printing Office, 1971).

———, *Social Indicators III: Selected data on social conditions and trends in the United States* (Washington, D.C.: U.S. Government Printing Office, 1980).

———, *The Social and Economic Status of the Black Population in the United States: An Historical View, 1790–1978* (Washington, D.C.: Government Printing Office, 1980).

Peter Camejo, *Racism, Revolution, Reaction, 1861–1877: The Rise and Fall of Radical Reconstruction* (New York: Pathfinder Press, 1976).

Clayborne Carson, *In Struggle:* SNCC *and the Black Awakening of the 1960s* (Cambridge: Harvard University Press, 1981).

Wilfred Cartey and Martin Kilson (eds.), *The Africa Reader: Colonial Africa* (New York: Vintage, 1970).

David Caute, *Frantz Fanon* (New York: Viking Press, 1970).

———, *The Great Fear: The Anti-Communist Purge Under Truman and Eisenhower* (New York: Simon and Schuster, 1979).

Barbara Christian, *Black Women Novelists: The Development of a Tradition, 1892–1976* (Westport, Connecticut: Greenwood Press, 1980).

Kenneth B. Clark, *Dark Ghetto* (New York: Harper and Row, 1965).

——— (ed.), *The Negro Protest: James Baldwin, Malcolm X, Martin Luther King Talk with Kenneth B. Clark* (Boston: Beacon Press, 1963).

Ramsey Clark and Roy Wilkins, *Search and Destroy* (New York: Harper and Row, 1973).

Eldridge Cleaver, *Post-Prison Writings and Speeches* (New York: Vintage, 1969).

Dick Cluster (ed.), *They Should Have Served That Cup of Coffee: Seven Radicals Remember the Sixties* (Boston: South End Press, 1979).

John Collier, *The Indians of the Americas* (New York: Norton, 1947).

Robert H. Connery (ed.), *Urban Riots: Violence and Social Change* (New York: Vintage, 1969).

Harold Cruse, *Rebellion or Revolution?* (New York: William Morrow, 1968).

———, *The Crisis of the Negro Intellectual: From Its Origins to the Present* (New York: William Morrow, 1967).

Angela Y. Davis (ed.), *If They Come in the Morning* (New York: New American Library, 1971).

———, *With My Mind on Freedom: An Autobiography* (New York: Bantam, 1975).

Carl N. Degler, *Affluence and Anxiety, 1945–Present* (Glenview, Illinois: Scott, Foresman, 1968).

Vine DeLoria, *Custer Died for Your Sins: An Indian Manifesto* (New York: Macmillan, 1969).

———, *We Talk, You Listen, New Tribes, New Turf* (New York: Macmillan, 1970).

Roberta Yancy Dent (ed.), *Paul Robeson: Tributes and Selected Writings* (New York: Paul Robeson Archives, 1977).

Isaac Deutscher, *Stalin: A Political Biography* (New York: Oxford University Press, 1949).

———, *The Prophet Outcast: Trotsky: 1929–1940* (New York: Vintage, 1963).

John P. Diggins, *The American Left in the Twentieth Century* (New York: Harcourt, Brace, Jovanovich, 1973).

Leonard Dinnerstein and David M. Reimers, *Ethnic Americans: A History of Immigration and Assimilation* (New York: New York University Press, 1977).

G. William Domhoff, *Who Rules America?* (Englewood Cliffs, New Jersey: Prentice-Hall, 1967).

W. E. B. DuBois, *Black Reconstruction in America, 1860–1880* (New York: Atheneum, 1971).

——, *Color and Democracy: Colonies and Peace* (New York: Harcourt, Brace and Company, 1945).

——, *The Autobiography of W. E. B. DuBois: A Soliloquy on Viewing My Life from the Last Decade of Its First Century* (New York: International Publishers, 1968).

——, *The Education of Black People: Ten Critiques, 1906–1960* (New York: Monthly Review Press, 1973).

——, *The World and Africa* (New York: International Publishers, 1946).

Chester E. Eisinger (ed.), *The 1940s: Profile of a Nation in Crisis* (Garden City, New York: Anchor, 1969).

Archie Epps (ed.), *The Speeches of Malcolm X at Harvard* (New York: William Morrow, 1968).

Les Evans and Allen Myers, *Watergate and the Myth of American Democracy* (New York: Pathfinder Press, 1974).

James Farmer, *Freedom—When?* (New York: Random House, 1966).

William Faulkner, Benjamin E. Mays and Cecil Sims, *The Segregation Decisions* (Atlanta: Southern Regional Council, 1956).

Stanley Feldstein and Lawrence Castello (eds.), *The Ordeal of Assimilation: A Documentary History of the White Working Class* (Garden City, New York: Anchor Books, 1974).

Philip S. Foner, *Organized Labor and the Black Worker, 1619–1973* (New York: International Publishers, 1976).

—— (ed.), *The Black Panthers Speak* (Philadelphia: J. B. Lippincott, 1970).

James Forman, *The Making of Black Revolutionaries* (New York: Macmillan, 1972).

Marshall Frady, *Wallace* (New York: New American Library, 1976).

John Hope Franklin, *From Slavery to Freedom: A History of Negro Americans* (New York: Vintage Books, 1969).

Richard Freeman, *Black Elite: The New Market for Highly Qualified Black Americans* (New York: McGraw-Hill, 1977).

Herbert Garfinkel, *When Negroes March* (New York: Atheneum, 1969).

Richard A. Garcia (ed.), *The Chicanos in America, 1540–1974* (Dobbs Ferry, New York: Oceana Press, 1977).

Addison Gayle, Jr., *The Black Situation* (New York: Delta, 1970).

Irene L. Gendzier, *Frantz Fanon: A Critical Study* (New York: Pantheon, 1973).

Eugene D. Genovese, *In Red and Black: Marxian Explorations in Southern and Afro-American History* (New York: Vintage, 1971).

Dan Georgakas and Marvin Surkin, *Detroit: I Do Mind Dying, A Study in Urban Revolution* (New York: St. Martin's Press, 1975).

James Geschwender, *Class, Race and Worker Insurgency: The League of Revolutionary Black Workers* (New York: Cambridge University Press, 1977).

Nikki Giovanni, *Black Feeling, Black Talk, Black Judgement* (New York: William Morrow, 1970).

Douglas G. Glasgow, *The Black Underclass: Poverty, Unemployment and the Entrapment of Ghetto Youth* (New York: Vintage, 1981).

Nathan Glazer, *Beyond the Melting Pot* (Cambridge: MIT Press, 1963).

Peter L. Goldman, *The Death and Life of Malcolm X* (New York: Harper and Row, 1973).

Robert J. Goldstein, *Political Repression in Modern America, 1870 to the Present* (New York: Two Continents Publishing Group, 1978).

Charles Goodell, *Political Prisoners in America* (New York: Random House, 1973).

Lawrence Goodwyn, *The Populist Moment: A Short History of the Agrarian Revolt in America* (New York and London: Oxford University Press, 1978).

Leo Grebler, Joan W. Moore and Ralph C. Guzman, *The Mexican-American People: The Nation's Second Largest Minority* (New York: Free Press, 1971).

Bertram Gross, *Friendly Fascism: The New Face of Power in America* (New York: M. Evans, 1980).

Jesse Parkhurst Guzman (ed.), *Negro Year Book: A Review of Events, Affecting Negro Life, 1941–1946* (Tuskegee Institute, Alabama: Tuskegee Institute, Department of Records and Research, 1947).

Morton H. Halperin, Jerry J. Berman, Robert L. Borosage and Christine M. Marwich, *The Lawless State: The Crimes of the U.S. Intelligence Agencies* (New York: Penguin, 1976).

Richard Handyside (ed.), *Revolution in Guinea: Selected Texts by Amilcar Cabral* (New York: Monthly Review Press, 1969).

Vincent Harding, *The Other American Revolution* (Los Angeles: Center for Afro-American Studies, 1980).

Celia S. Heller, *Mexican-American Youth: Forgotten Youth at the Cross-Roads* (New York: Random House, 1966).

Lillian Hellman, *Scoundrel Time* (Boston: Little, Brown, 1976).

Florette Henri, *Black Migration: Movement North, 1900–1920* (Garden City, New York: Anchor Books, 1976).

John Hillson, *The Battle of Boston: Busing and the Struggle for School Desegregation* (New York: Pathfinder Press, 1970).

Lennox S. Hinds, *Illusions of Justice: Human Rights Violations in the United States* (Iowa City, Iowa: School of Social Work, University of Iowa, 1978).

Bell Hooks, *Ain't I A Woman: Black Women and Feminism* (Boston: South End Press, 1981).

Edwin P. Hoyt, *Paul Robeson: The American Othello* (Cleveland: World, 1967).

Paul Jacobs and Saul Landau. (eds.), *The New Radicals: A Report with Documents* (New York Vintage, 1966).

Sylvia M. Jacobs (ed.), *Black Americans and the Missionary Movement in Africa* (Westport, Connecticut: Greenwood Press, 1982).

Julius Jacobson (ed.), *The Negro and the American Labor Movement* (Garden City, New York: Anchor, 1968).

James Weldon Johnson, *Negro Americans, What Now?* (New York: Viking Press, 1962).

Marcus E. Jones, *Black Migration in the United States with Emphasis on Selected Central Cities* (Saratoga, California: Century Twenty One Publishing, 1980).

V. O. Key, Jr., *Southern Politics in State and Nation* (New York: Vintage, 1949).

Martin Luther King, Jr., *Strength to Love* (New York: Pocket Books, 1964).

———, *The Trumpet of Conscience* (New York: Harper and Row, 1967).

———, *Where Do We Go From Here: Chaos or Community* (New York: Harper and Row, 1967).

———, *Why We Can't Wait* (New York: Harper and Row, 1964).

Harry H. L. Kitano, *Japanese Americans* (Englewood Cliffs, New Jersey: Prentice-Hall, 1969).

Frank Kofsky, *Black Nationalism and the Revolution in Music* (New York: Pathfinder Press, 1970).

Judith Kramer, *The American Minority Community* (New York: Crowell, 1970).

Mark Lane and Dick Gregory, *Code Name Zorro: The Murder of Martin Luther King, Jr.* (New York: Prentice-Hall, 1977).

Steven F. Lawson, *Black Ballots: Voting Rights in the South, 1944–1969* (New York: Columbia University Press, 1976).

Robert Lefcourt (ed.), *Law Against the People* (New York: Vintage, 1971).

Murray B. Levin, *Political Hysteria in America: The Democratic Capacity for Repression* (New York: Basic Books, 1971).

David Lewis, *King: A Critical Biography* (Baltimore: Penguin, 1969).

Claude M. Lightfoot, *Ghetto Rebellion to Black Liberation* (New York: International Publishers, 1968).

C. Eric Lincoln (ed.), *Martin Luther King, Jr.: A Profile* (New York: Hill and Wang, 1970).

———, *My Face is Black* (Boston: Beacon Press, 1964).

———, *The Black Muslims in America* (Boston: Beacon Press, 1961).

Louise E. Lomax, *The Negro Revolt* (New York: Harper, 1963).

———, *To Kill a Black Man* (Los Angeles: Holloway House, 1968).

———, *When The Word is Given* (Cleveland: World Publishing Company, 1963).

Debbie Louis, *And We Are Not Saved: A History of the Movement as People* (Garden City, New York: Anchor, 1970).

John Luckas, *A New History of the Cold War* (Garden City, New York: Anchor Books, 1966).

William Madsden, *The Mexican-Americans of South Texas* (New York: Holt, Rinehart, and Winston, 1964).

S. J. Makielski, Jr., *Beleaguered Minorities: Cultural Politics in America* (San Francisco: W. H. Freeman, 1973).

Malcolm X, *Malcolm X on Afro-American History* (New York: Pathfinder Press, 1970).

———, *The Autobiography of Malcolm X* (New York: Grove Press, 1965).

Eric Mann, *Comrade George: An Investigation into the Life, Political Thought, and Assassination of George Jackson* (New York: Harper and Row, 1972).

Manning Marable, *Blackwater: Historical Studies in Race, Class Consciousness, and Revolution* (Dayton, Ohio: Black Praxis Press, 1981).

———. *From the Grassroots: Social and Political Essays Towards Afro-American Liberation* (Boston: South End Press, 1980).

———, *How Capitalism Underdeveloped Black America: Problems in Race, Political Economy and Society* (Boston: South End Press, 1983).

Gene Marine, *The Black Panthers* (New York: New American Library, 1969).

Stanley Masters, *Black-White Income Differentials* (New York: Academic Press, 1975).

Donald R. McCoy, *Coming of Age: The United States during the 1920s and 1930s* (New York: Penguin, 1973).

August Meier, *Negro Thought in America, 1890–1915: Racial Ideologies in the Age of Booker T. Washington* (Ann Arbor, Michigan: University of Michigan Press, 1963).

August Meier and Elliott Rudwick, CORE: *A Study in the Civil Rights Movement, 1942–1968* (New York: Oxford University Press, 1973).

——, *From Plantation to Ghetto*, Revised Edition (New York: Hill and Wang, 1970).

William Robert Miller, *Martin Luther King, Jr.: His Life, Martyrdom and Meaning for the World* (New York: Avon Books, 1968).

Joan W. Moore, *Mexican-Americans* (Englewood Cliffs, New Jersey: Prentice-Hall, 1970).

Wayne Moquin and Charles van Doren, *Documentary History of the Mexican American* (New York: Praeger, 1972).

Robert Mullen, *Blacks in America's Wars: The Shift in Attitudes from the Revolutionary War to Vietnam* (New York: Pathfinder Press, 1974).

Benjamin Muse, *The American Negro Revolution* (Bloomington, Indiana: University of Indiana Press, 1968).

Michael Myerson, *Nothing Could be Finer* (New York: International Publishers, 1978).

William E. Nelson, Jr., and Philip J. Meranto, *Electing Black Mayors: Political Action in the Black Community* (Columbus, Ohio: Ohio State University Press, 1977).

Herbert Northrup (ed.), *Negro Employment in Basic Industry: A Study of Racial Policy in Six Industries* (Philadelphia: University of Pennsylvania Press, 1970).

Julius Nyerere, *Ujamaa—Essays on Socialism* (New York: Oxford University Press, 1968).

Earl Ofari, *The Myth of Black Capitalism* (New York: Monthly Review Press, 1970).

Elena Padilla, *Up from Puerto Rico* (New York: Columbia University Press, 1958).

Nelson Perry, *The Negro National Colonial Question* (Chicago: Workers Press, 1975).

Frances Fox Piven and Richard Cloward, *Regulating the Poor: The Functions of Public Welfare* (New York: Random House, 1971).

Richard Polenberg, *One Nation Divisible: Class, Race, and Ethnicity in the United States Since 1938* (New York: Penguin Books, 1980).

Michael B. Preston, Lenneal J. Henderson, Jr. and Paul Puryear (eds.), *The New Black Politics: The Search for Political Power* (New York: Longman, 1982).

Dudley Randall (ed.), *The Black Poets* (New York: Bantam, 1972).

Mark Reisler, *By the Sweat of their Brow: Mexican Immigrant Labor in the United States, 1900–1940* (Westport, Connecticut: Greenwood Press, 1976).

Feliciano Rivera, *The Chicanos: A History of Mexican Americans* (New York: Hill and Wang, 1972).

Caroline Ross and Ken Lawrence, *J. Edgar Hoover's Detention Plan: The Politics of Repression in the United States, 1939–1976* (Jackson, Mississippi: Anti-Repression Resource Team, 1978).

John R. Salter, Jr., *Jackson, Mississippi: An American Chronicle of Struggle and Schism* (Hicksville, New York: Exposition-Banner, 1979).

Don A. Schanche, *The Panther Paradox: A Liberal's Dilemma* (New York: D. McKay, 1970).

Bobby Seale, *Seize the Time* (New York: Vintage, 1970).

Mario Seton, *Paul Robeson* (London: Dobson, 1958).

John Shockley, *Chicano Revolt in a Texas Town* (Notre Dame, Indiana: University of Notre Dame Press, 1974).

James W. Silver, *Mississippi: The Closed Society* (New York: Harcourt, Brace and World, 1966).

Thomas Sowell, *Ethnic America: A History* (New York: Basic Books, 1981).

———, *Markets and Minorities* (New York: Basic Books, 1981).

———, *Race and Economics* (New York: Longman, 1975).

Charles Spencer, *Blue Collar: An Internal Examination of the Workplace* (Chicago: Workers Press, 1978).

Stan Steiner, *La Raza: The Mexican-Americans* (New York: Harper and Row, 1970).

———, *The New Indians* (New York: Harper and Row, 1968).

Melvin Steinfeld (ed.), *Our Racist Presidents* (San Ramon, California: Consensus Publishers, 1972).

Gerald D. Suttles, *The Social Order of the Slum* (Chicago: University of Chicago Press, 1968).

W. A. Swanberg, *Norman Thomas: The Last Idealist* (New York: Charles Scribner's Sons, 1976).

Clyde Taylor (ed.), *Vietnam and Black America: An Anthology of Protest and Resistance* (Garden City, New York: Anchor, 1973).

Athan Theoharis, *Spying on America: Political Surveillance from Hoover to the Houston Plan* (Philadelphia: Temple University Press, 1978).

U.S. Commission on Civil Rights, *Racism in America* (Washington, D.C.: U.S. Government Printing Office, 1970).

Thomas Wagstaff (ed.), *Black Power* (Beverly Hills, California: Glencoe Press, 1969).

Hanes Walton, Jr., *Black Politics: A Theoretical and Structural Analysis* (Philadelphia: J. B. Lippincott, 1972).

———, *The Political Philosophy of Martin Luther King, Jr.* (Westport, Connecticut: Greenwood Press, 1971).

Robert Penn Warren, *Who Speaks for the Negro?* (New York: Random House, 1965).

Wilcomb E. Washburn, *The Indian in America* (New York: Harper and Row, 1975).

Chancellor Williams, *The Destruction of Black Civilization* (Dubuque, Iowa: Kendall/Hunt, 1971).

Daniel T. Williams and Carolyn L. Redden, *The Black Muslims in the United States: A Selected Bibliography* (Tuskegee, Alabama: Tuskegee Institute, 1964).

John A. Williams and Charles F. Harris (eds.), *Amistad 2* (New York: Vintage, 1971).

Walter E. Williams, Loren A. Smith and Wendell Wilkie Gunn, *Black America and Organized Labor: A Fair Deal?* (Washington, D.C.: Lincoln Institute for Research and Education, 1980).

William Julius Wilson, *The Declining Significance of Race: Blacks and Changing American Institutions* (Chicago: University of Chicago Press, 1978).

Robert L. Woodson (ed.), *Black Perspectives on Crime and the Criminal Justice System* (Boston: G. K. Hall, 1977).

C. Vann Woodward, *The Strange Career of Jim Crow* (New York: Oxford University Press, Third Revised Edition, 1974).

ARTICLES

Hussein M. Adam, "Frantz Fanon: His 'Understanding,'" *Black World* 21 (December 1971): 4–14.
Muhammad Ahmad (Max Stanford), "We Are All Prisoners of War," *Black Scholar* 4 (October 1972): 3–5.
Abdul Alkalimat (Gerald McWorter), "What Lies Ahead for Black Americans?" *Negro Digest* 19 (November 1969): 21.
Mark Allen, "James E. Carter and the Trilateral Commission: A Southern Strategy," *Black Scholar* 8 (May 1977): 2–7.
Robert L. Allen, "A Reply to Harold Baron," *Socialist Review* 8 (January–February 1978): 120–4.
———, "Black Liberation and the Presidential Race," *Black Scholar* 4 (September 1972): 2–6.
———, "Politics of the Attack on Black Studies," *Black Scholar* 6 (September 1974): 2–7.
———, "Racism and the Black Nation Thesis," *Socialist Revolution* 6 (January–March 1976): 145–50.
Tomás Almaguer, "Chicano Politics in the Present Period," *Socialist Review* 8 (July–October 1978): 137–41.
———, "Historical Notes on Chicano Oppression: The Dialectics of Racial and Class Oppression in North America," *Atzlán* 5 (Spring and Fall 1974): 27–56.
S. E. Anderson, "Black Students: Racial Consciousness and the Class Struggle, 1960–1976," *Black Scholar* 8 (January–Februrary 1977): 35–43.
Ladun Anise, "The Tyranny of a Purist Ideology," *Black World* 24 (May 1975): 18–34.
Anonymous, "Episodes From The Attica Massacre," *Black Scholar* 4 (October 1972): 34–9.
Obi Antarah, "A Blueprint for Black Liberation," *Black World* 22 (October, 1973): 60–6.
Earl Anthony, "Interview: Eldridge Cleaver," *Players* 8 (February 1982): 27–35.
Stanley Aronowitz, "Remaking the American Left, Part One: Currents in American Radicalism," *Socialist Review* 13 (January–February 1983): 9–51.
James Baldwin, "The Dangerous Road Before Martin Luther King," *Harper's Magazine* (February 1961).
Barbara Banks, "Wanted: Killer of Black Men Still At Large in City," *Buffalo Challenger* (2 October 1980).
Dennis Banks, Interview, *Black Scholar* 7 (June 1976): 29–36.
Imamu Amiri Baraka (LeRoi Jones), "Black Nationalism: 1972," *Black Scholar* 4 (September 1972): 23–9.
———, "The National Black Assembly and the Black Liberation Movement," *Black World* 26 (March 1975): 22–7.
———, "Toward the Creation of Political Institutions for all African People," *Black World* 21 (October 1972): 54–78.
Harold Baron, "The Retreat from Black Nationalism: A Response to Robert L. Allen," *Socialist Review* 8 (January–February 1978): 109–19.
Bruce Bartlett, "Assault on Federal Spending," *Society* 19 (July–August 1982): 39–43.
A. H. Beller, "The economics of enforcement of an anti-discrimination law: Title

VII of the Civil Rights Act of 1964," *Journal of Law and Economics* 21 (October 1978): 359–80.

Lerone Bennett, Jr., "SNCC: Rebels With a Cause," *Ebony* 20 (June 1965): 146–53.

Janice Bevien, "Notes on Current Struggles Against Repression," *Black Scholar* 12 (January–February 1981): 82–4.

Ken Bode, "Carter's Chosen Path," *New Republic* 180 (27 January 1979): 12–14.

——, "Glad Old Party," *New Republic* 180 (17 February 1979): 13–15.

Benjamin P. Bowser, "Black People and the Future: A Summary of the Major Trends," *Black Books Bulletin* 4 (Summer 1976): 6–10.

Herb Boyd, "Blacks and the Police State: A Case Study of Detroit," *Black Scholar* 12 (January–February 1981): 58–61.

Anne Braden, "Lessons From a History of Struggle," *Southern Exposure* 8 (Summer 1980): 8–13.

Demetri Brown, "Black Man Found Near Lake Stirs Rumors," *Jackson Advocate* (15–21 October 1981).

Robert Brown, "Black Land Loss: The plight of black ownership," *Southern Exposure* 2 (Fall 1974): 112–21.

Tony Brown, "Is Integration Killing Black Colleges?" *African-American News and World Report* (5 September 1980).

Pat Bryant, "Justice vs. the Movement," *Southern Exposure* 8 (Summer 1980): 31–9.

Herrington J. Bryce, "Are Most Blacks in the Middle Class?" *Black Scholar* 5 (February 1974): 32–6.

Jim Campen, "Economic Crisis and Conservative Economic Policies: U.S. Capitalism in the 1980s," *Radical America* 15 (Spring 1981): 32–54.

Rodney Carlisle, "Black Nationalism: An Integral Tradition," *Black World* 22 (February 1973): 4–10.

Frank Carroll, "OSHA Under the Gun," *Political Affairs* 60 (September 1981): 28–33.

Cesar Chavez, "The California Farm Workers' Struggle," *Black Scholar* 7 (June 1976): 16–19.

Robert Chrisman, "George Jackson," *Black Scholar* 3 (October 1971): 2–4.

Imani Clairborne, "Racial Violence as Reported in the Black Press During the Autumn of 1981," *Racially Motivated Random Violence* 1 (November–December 1981): 1–11.

John Henrik Clarke, "The Rise of Racism in the West," *Black World* 19 (October 1970): 4–10.

Eldridge Cleaver, "On Lumpen Ideology," *Black Scholar* 4 (November–December 1972): 2–10.

Mark Colvin, "The Contradictions of Control: Prisons in Class Society," *Insurgent Sociologist* 10 (Summer–Fall 1981): 33–45.

M. R. Cramer, "Race and Southern white worker's support for unions," *Phylon* 39 (December 1978): 311–21.

Harold Cruse, "Black and White: Outlines of the Next Stage," *Black World* 20 (January 1971): 19–41, 66–71.

——, "The Little Rock National Black Political Convention," *Black World* 23 (October 1974): 10–17, 82–8.

——, "The Methodology of Pan-Africanism," *Black World* 24 (January 1975): 4–20.

Elliott Currie, "The Politics of Jobs: Humphrey–Hawkins and the Dilemmas of Full Employment," *Socialist Review* 7 (March–April 1977): 93–114.

Ronald V. Dellums, interview, "Peace, Justice, and Politics," *Plain Speaking* (16–31 May 1982).

Elaine Douglas, "The Conversion of Eldridge Cleaver," *Encore* 2 (2 February 1976): 9–15.

St. Clair Drake, "The Black Diaspora in Pan-African Perspective," *Black Scholar* 7 (September 1975): 2–13.

W. E. B. DuBois, "A History of the Negro Vote," *Crisis* 40 (June 1933): 128–9.

——, "Bound by the Color Line," *New Masses* 58 (12 February 1946): 8.

——, "Civil Rights Legislation Before and After the 14th Amendment," *Lawyers' Guild Review* 6 (November–December 1946): 640–2.

——, "Negroes and the Crisis of Capitalism in the United States," *Monthly Review* 4 (April 1953): 478–85.

——, "Reconstruction and Its Benefits," *American Historical Review* 15 (July 1910): 781–99.

——, "Reconstruction, Seventy-Five Years After," *Phylon* 4 (1943): 205–12.

——, "The Choice That Confronts America's Negroes," *National Guardian* (13 February 1952).

——, "The Negro in America Today," Five-part Essay, *National Guardian* (16, 23, 30 January; 13 February; 5 March 1956).

——, "The Thirteenth, Fourteenth and Fifteenth Amendments," *Lawyers' Guild Review* 9 (Spring 1949): 92–5.

——, "There Must Come a Vast Social Change in the United States," *National Guardian* (11 July 1951).

Barbara Easton, Michael Kazin and David Plotke, "Desperate Times: The Peoples Temple and the Left," *Socialist Review* 9 (March–April 1979): 63–73.

Frank Elam, "Attacks on Blacks: Death Toll Climbs," *Guardian* (22 October 1980).

Glen Ford, "Reagan and South Africa," *Black Communicator* 1 (Spring 1981): 15–16.

——, "The Need for a Black Women's Movement," *Black Communicator* 1 (Spring 1981): 4–7.

Raymond S. Franklin, "The Political Economy of Black Power," *Social Problems* 16 (Winter 1969): 286–301.

Jeff Frieden, "The Trilateral Commission: Economics and Politics in the 1970s," *Monthly Review* 29 (December 1977): 1–18.

Hoyt Fuller, "Another Fork in the Road," *Black World* 23 (October 1974): 49–50, 97.

Mario T. Garcia, "On Mexican Immigration, the United States and Chicano History," *Journal of Ethnic Studies* 7 (Spring 1979): 80–8.

——, "Racial Dualism in the El Paso Labor Market, 1880–1920," *Atzlán* 6 (Fall 1975): 197–218.

Richard A. Garcia, "The Chicano Movement and the Mexican-American Community, 1972–1978: An Interpretive Essay," *Socialist Review* 8 (July–October 1978): 117–36.

James Garrett, "A Historical Sketch: The Sixth Pan African Congress," *Black World* 26 (March 1975): 4–20.

Joe Gilyard, "White Man Who Shot Two Black Girls Is Awarded $5,000 For His Trouble," *Cleveland Call and Post* (17 October 1981).

Nathan Glazer, "Ethnicity—North, South, West," *Commentary* 73 (May 1982): 73-8.

Lawrence Goodwyn, "Jimmy Carter and 'Populism,'" *Southern Exposure* 5 (Spring 1977): 45-6.

A. James Gregor, "Black Nationalism: A Preliminary Analysis of Negro Radicalism," *Science and Society* 26 (Fall 1963): 415-32.

Bertram M. Gross, "Profits Without Honor: The Secret Success of Jimmy Carter," *Nation* 228 (2 June 1979): 623-4.

Bob Hall, "Jimmy Carter: Master Magician," *Southern Exposure* 5 (Spring 1977): 43-4.

Charles V. Hamilton, "Black Americans and the Modern Political Struggle," *Black World* 19 (May 1970): 5-9, 77-9.

Nathan Hare, "A Critique of Black Leaders," *Black Scholars* 3 (March–April 1972): 2-5.

Richard G. Hatcher, "Black Politics in the 70s," *Black Scholar* 4 (September 1972): 17-22.

L. J. Henderson, "The impact of the Equal Employment Opportunity Act of 1972 on employment opportunities for women and minorities in municipal government," *Policy Studies Journal* 7 (Winter 1978): 234-43.

John Herbers, "Poverty Rate, 7.4% Termed Highest Since '67," *New York Times* (26 July 1982).

Herbert Hill, "Race and Labor: The AFL-CIO and the Black Worker Twenty-Five Years After the Merger," *Journal of Intergroup Relations* 10 (Spring 1982): 5-78.

James J. Horgan, "Voter Literacy Tests: Hail the Passing, Guard the Tomb," *Southern Exposure* 10 (July–August 1982): 62-6.

Mathew Hutchins and Lee Sigelman, "Black Employment in State and Local Governments: A Comparative Analysis," *Social Science Quarterly* 62 (March 1981): 79-87.

Florence B. Irving, "The Future of the Negro Voter in the South," *Journal of Negro Education* 26 (Summer 1957): 390-9.

C. L. R. James, "Kwame Nkrumah: Founder of African Emancipation," *Black World* 21 (July 1972): 4-10.

Jacquelyne Johnson Jackson, "Death Rates of Aged Blacks and Whites, United States, 1964-1978," *Black Scholar* 13 (January–February 1982): 36-48.

John Judis and Alan Wolfe, "American Politics at the Crossroads: The Collapse of Cold-War Liberalism," *Socialist Review* (March–April 1977): 9-37.

Maulana Ron Karenga, "Black Art: A Rhythmic Reality of Revolution," *Negro Digest* 17 (January 1968): 5-9.

———, "Overturning Ourselves: From Mystification to Meaningful Struggle," *Black Scholar* 4 (October 1972): 6-14.

Kaidi Kasirika and Maharibi Muntu, "Prison or Slavery," *Black Scholar* 3 (October 1971): 6-12.

Muhammad Isaiah Kenyatta, "The Impact of Racism on the Family as a Support System," *Catalyst* 2 (1980): 37-44.

Martin Kilson, "Black Power: Anatomy of a Paradox," *Harvard Journal of Negro Affairs* 2 (1968): 30-4.

Martin Luther King, Jr. "Behind the Selma March," *Saturday Review* 16 (3 March 1965): 16-17.

———, "Fumbling on the New Frontier," *Nation* 194 (3 March 1962): 190-3.

———, "Let Justice Roll Down," *The Nation* 206 (15 March 1965): 269-74.

268 SELECT BIBLIOGRAPHY

————, "Next Stop: The North," *Saturday Review* 16 (13 November 1965): 33–5.
B. Sung Lee, "A differential index of black/white income inequality, 1965–74," *Review of Black Political Economy* 9 (Fall 1978): 90–4.
Edward A. Leonard, "Ninety-Four Years of Non-Violence," *New South* 20 (April 1965): 4–7.
Kirk Loggins and Susan Thomas, "The Menace Returns," *Southern Exposure* 8 (Summer 1980): 2–6.
Chokwe Lumumba, "Short History of the U.S. War on the R.N.A.," *Black Scholar* 12 (January–February 1981): 72–81.
Clifford M. Lytle, "The History of the Civil Rights Bill of 1964," *Journal of History* 51 (October 1966): 275–96.
Haki Madhubuti (Don L. Lee), "Enemy: From the White Left, White Right, and In-Between," *Black World* 23 (October 1974): 36–47.
————, "The Death Walk Against Afrika," *Black World* 22 (October 1973): 28–36.
————, "The Latest Purge: The Attack on Black Nationalism and Pan-Afrikanism by the New Left, the sons and daughters of the Old Left," *Black Scholar* 6 (September 1974): 43–56.
Malcolm X (Malcolm Little) and James Farmer, "Separation or Integration: A Debate," *Dialogue Magazine* 2 (May 1962): 14–18.
Manning Marable, "Black Conservatives and Accommodation: Of Thomas Sowell and Others," *Negro History Bulletin* 45 (April–June 1982): 32–5.
————, "Justice is on Trial in Greensboro," *San Francisco Sun Reporter* (10 September 1981).
————, "Martin Luther King's Ambiguous Legacy," WIN magazine 19 (15 April 1982): 15–19.
————, "Reaganomics," *Umoja Sasa* 3 (Spring 1981): 25, 28.
————, "The Crisis of the Black Working Class: An Economic and Historical Analysis," *Science and Society* 46 (Summer 1982): 130–61.
————, "The Question of Genocide," *Journal of Intergroup Relations* 10 (Autumn 1982): 19–29.
John L. Marshall, "1872 Law Used to Prosecute Police Gadfly: Ex-Black Panther Accused of Trying to Turn Crowd Against Police," *Los Angeles Times* (6 May 1982).
Andrew Marx and Tom Tuthill, "Resisting the Klan: Mississippi Organizes," *Southern Exposure* 8 (Summer 1980): 25–8.
August Meier, "Negro Protest Movements and Organizations," *Journal of Negro Education* 32 (Fall 1963): 437–50.
————, "On the Role of Martin Luther King," *New Politics* 4 (Winter 1965): 52–9.
————, "The Dilemmas of Negro Protest Strategy," *New South* 21 (Spring 1966): 1–18.
————, "The Revolution Against the NAACP," *Journal of Negro Education* 32 (Spring 1963): 146–52.
Martin B. Miller, "Sinking Gradually into the Proletariat: The Emergence of the Penitentiary in the United States," *Crime and Social Justice* no. 14 (Winter 1980): 37–43.
David Moberg, Alexander Cockburn and James Ridgeway, "Cult Politics Comes of Age," *Santa Barbara News and Review* (30 November 1978).
Dhoruba Moore, "Strategies of Repression Against the Black Movement," *Black Scholar* 12 (May–June 1981): 10–16.

D. R. Morgan and M. R. Fitzgerald, "A casual perspective on school segregation among American States: A Research Note," *Social Forces* 58 (1979): 329–35.

Marietta Morrissey, "Ethnic Stratification and the Study of Chicanos," *Journal of Ethnic Studies* 10 (Winter 1983): 71–99.

Askia Muhammad (Rolland Snellings), "Behind the Washington Siege: Civil War in Islamic America," *Nation* 224 (11 June 1977): 721–4.

C. Lynn Munro, "Le Roi Jones: A Man in Transition," CLA Journal 17 (September 1973): 58–78.

Samuel L. Myers and E. Kenneth Phillips, "Housing segregation and black employment: another look at the ghetto dispersal strategy," *American Economic Review* 69 (May 1979): 298–301.

Julius K. Nyerere, "Capitalism or Socialism? The Rational Choice," *Black World* 23 (March 1974): 38–48.

Imari Obadele (Richard Henry), "The Struggle of the Republic of New Africa," *Black Scholar* 5 (June 1974): 32–41.

J. K. Obatala, "How Carter Should Pay His Debt," *Nation* 223 (27 November 1976): 550–2.

John H. O'Connell, Jr., "Black Capitalism," *Review of Black Political Economy* (Fall 1976): 67–84.

Earl Ofari, "Black Labor: Powerful Force For Liberation," *Black World* 22 (October 1973): 43–7.

——, "W. E. B. DuBois and Black Power," *Black World* 19 (August 1970): 26–8.

Alexander Okanlawon, "Africanism—A Synthesis of the African World-View," *Black World* 21 (July 1972): 40–4.

John O'Loughlin, "Black Representation and the Seat-Vote Relationship," *Social Science Quarterly* 60 (June 1979): 72–86.

Roxanne Dunbar Ortiz, "Land and Nationhood: The American Indian Struggle for Self-Determination and Survival," *Socialist Review* 12 (May–August 1982): 105–20.

Alfred E. Osborne, Jr., "A Note on Black Well-Being in the North and West," *Review of Black Political Economy* 7 (Fall 1976): 85–92.

Brenda Payton, "Police Use of Deadly Force in Oakland," *Black Scholar* 12 (January–February 1981): 62–4.

Peoples College, "Imperialism and Black Liberation," *Black Scholar* 6 (September 1974): 38–42.

T. F. Pettigrew, "Racial change and social policy," *Annals of the American Academy of Political and Social Science* 441 (January 1979): 114–31.

Kenneth Porter, "Relations Between Negroes and Indians Within the Present Limits of the United States," *Journal of Negro History* 17 (July 1932): 287–367.

Alejandro Portes, "Illegal Immigration and the International System: Lessons From Recent Legal Mexican Immigrants to the United States," *Social Problems* 26 (April 1979): 425–38.

Popular Economics Research Group, "Barefoot and Pregnant Women and Reaganomics," WIN magazine 18 (15 April 1982): 12–14.

A. Philip Randolph Institute, "An Appeal by Black Americans for United States Support of Israel," *Black World* 19 (October 1970): 42–4.

Jack L. Roach and Janet K. Roach, "Mobilizing the Poor: Road to a Dead End," *Social Problems* 26 (December 1978): 160–71.

Gene Roberts, "The Story of Snick: From 'Freedom Rides' to 'Black Power,'" *New York Times Magazine* (25 September 1966): 27–9.

Paul Robeson, "Voting for Peace," *Masses and Mainstream* (January 1952): 7–14.

E. O'Neill Robinson, "Jury Convicts Utah Murderer of Joggers," *Baltimore Afro-American* (26 September 1981).

Walter Rodney, "Guyana: The making of the labour force," *Race and Class* 22 (Spring 1981): 331–52.

Sheila Rule, "Black Middle Class Slipping, Study by Urban League Says," *New York Times* (4 August 1982).

———, "New York Blacks Focusing on Equal Opportunity," *New York Times* (22 August 1982).

Bayard Rustin, "'Black power' and Coalition Politics," *Commentary* 42 (September 1966): 35–40.

———, "The meaning of the March on Washington," *Liberation* 8 (October 1963): 11–13.

Kalamu Ya Salaam, "In the Face of Oppression: A Case Study of New Orleans," *Black Scholar* 12 (January–February 1981): 65–7.

———, "Tell No Lies, Claim No Easy Victories," *Black World* 23 (October 1974): 18–34.

William Seraile, "The Assassination of Malcolm X: The View from Home and Abroad," *Afro-Americans in New York Life and History* 5 (January 1981): 43–58.

Mohan L. Sharma, "Martin Luther King: Modern America's Greatest Theologian of Social Action," *Journal of Negro History* 53 (July 1968): 257–63.

Baxter Smith, "New Evidence of FBI 'Disruption' Program," *Black Scholar* 6 (July–August 1975): 43–8.

———, "The Resurgence of the KKK," *Black Scholar* 12 (January–February 1981): 25–30.

Damu Smith, "The Upsurge of Police Repression: An Analysis," *Black Scholar* 12 (January–February 1981): 35–57.

Mark Smith, "A Response to Haki Madhubuti," *Black Scholar* 6 (January–February 1975): 45–52.

Frederic Solomon, Walter L. Walker, Garrett J. O'Connor and Jacob R. Fishman, "Civil Rights Activity and Reduction in Crime among Negroes," *Archives of General Psychiatry* 12 (1965): 227–36.

Yusufu Sonebeyatta (Joseph F. Brooks), "Ujamaa For Land and Power," *Black Scholar* 3 (October 1971): 13–20.

Thomas Sowell, "Myths About Minorities," *Commentary* 68 (August 1979): 33–7.

———, "The Uses of Government for Racial Equality," *National Review* 33 (4 September 1981): 1009–16.

Johnny Spain, "The Black Family and the Prisons," *Black Scholar* 4 (October 1972): 18–31.

Robert Staples, "Black Manhood in the 1970s: A Critical Look Back," *Black Scholar* 12 (May–June 1981): 2–9.

Chuck Stone, "Black Political Power in the Carter Era," *Black Scholar* 8 (January–February 1977): 6–15.

Chinta Strausberg, "White Sheriff Denies Rights to Black Religious Group," *Chicago Defender* (22 September 1981).

William Strickland, "The Gary Convention and the Crisis of American Politics," *Black World* 21 (October 1972): 18–26.

————, "Watergate: Its Meaning for Black America," *Black World* 23 (December 1973): 4–14.

D. H. Swinton, "A labor force competition model of racial discrimination in the labor market," *Review of Black Political Economy* 9 (Fall 1978): 5–42.

Leonard Sykes, Jr., "Jim Crow, Lynchings and a Return to Business as Usual," *Black Books Bulletin* 7 (Fall 1981): 18–20.

Abigail M. Thernstrom, "The odd evolution of the Voting Rights Act," *Public Interest* no. 55 (Spring 1979): 49–76.

Jim Thomas, David Stribling, Ra Rabb Chaka, Edmond Clemons, Charlie Secret and Alex Neal, "Prison Conditions and Penal Trends," *Crime and Social Justice* no. 15 (Summer 1981): 49–55.

June Manning Thomas, "Miami: Harbinger of Rebellion?" *Catalyst* 3 (1981): 37–56.

John Trinkl, "Racist acquitted in Jordan Shooting," *Guardian* (1 September 1982).

Kenneth N. Vines, "Courts and Political Change in the South," *Journal of Social Issues* 22 (January 1966): 59–62.

K. Vinodgopal, "Anti-Black attacks rise in Boston," *Guardian* (1 September 1982).

Don Wallace, "The Political Economy of Incarceration Trends in Late U.S. Capitalism: 1971–1977," *Insurgent Sociologist* 10 (Summer–Fall 1981): 59–65.

Ronald Walters, "African-American Nationalism: A Unifying Ideology," *Black World* 22 (October 1973): 9–27, 84.

Hanes Walton, Jr., "The Political Leadership of Martin Luther King, Jr.," *Quarterly Review of Higher Education Among Negroes* 36 (July 1968): 163–71.

Joseph R. Washington, Jr., "Black Nationalism: Potentially Anti-Folk and Anti-Intellectual," *Black World* 22 (July 1973): 32–9.

Richard A. Wasserstrom, "Federalism and Civil Rights," *University of Chicago Law Review* 33 (Winter 1966): 411–13.

J. C. Webb, "Weber, Sears and the Fight for Affirmative Action," *Political Affairs* 58 (June 1979): 13–16.

Bernard L. Weinstein and John Rees, "Reaganomics, Reindustrialization, and Regionalism," *Society* 19 (July–August 1982): 33–8.

Steven R. Weisman, "Reagan Says Blacks Were Hurt by Works of the Great Society," *New York Times* (16 September 1982).

Jitu Weusi, "Jonestown Massacre—An Act of Genocide," *Black Thoughts* 10 (May–June 1979): 1, 30–1.

Roy Wilkins, "Whither 'Black Power'?," *Crisis* (August–September 1966): 354.

Roy Wilkins et al., "Crisis and Commitment," *Crisis* (November 1966): 474–9.

Eddie N. Williams, "Black Impact on the 1976 Elections," *Focus* 4 (November 1976).

Franklin H. Williams, "On Death Cars," *Milwaukee Courier* (12 June 1982).

Robert F. Williams, "1957: The Swimming Pool Showdown," *Southern Exposure* 8 (Summer 1980): 22–4.

————, "USA: The Potential of a Minority Revolution," *The Crusader Monthly Newsletter* 5 (May–June 1964): 1–7.

Ann Withorn, "Retreat From The Social Wage: Human Services in the 1980s," *Radical America* 15 (Spring 1981): 23–31.

M. Frank Wright, "The National Question: A Marxist Critique," *Black Scholar* 5 (February 1974): 43–53.

Nathan Wright, Jr. "Another Look At Leon Sullivan: A Leader Among Us," *Fort Lauderdale Westside Gazette* (2 September 1982).

Richard Wright, "A Blueprint for Negro Writing," *New Challenge* 11 (1937): 53–65.

Robert L. Zangrando, "From Civil Rights to Black Liberation: The Unsettled 1960s," *Current History* 62 (November 1969): 281–6, 299.

Howard Zinn, "Registration in Alabama," *New Republic* 149 (26 October 1963): 11–12.

Sam Zuckerman, "House backs 'soak-the-poor' budget," *Guardian* (23 June 1982).

Index

Pictorial
Encyclopedia
of
JAPANESE
LIFE and EVENTS

Gakken

STAFF

Editorial Consultant
    Nakayama Kaneyoshi
    (Professor of English, Tokoha Gakuen Fuji Junior College)
Translation
    Gaynor Sekimori (Logostiks)
Book Design
    Nakamura Yoichi
Photography
    Yajima Yasuji
Illustrations
    Shiba Yuji

Managing Editor
    Anzai Tatsuo
Publishing Manager (Planning)
    Sato Shunji
Editorial Assistant
    Ohtsuka Takao

Pictorial Encyclopedia of JAPANESE LIFE and EVENTS

Published by GAKKEN CO., LTD.
4-40-5 Kami-ikedai, Ohta-ku, Tokyo 145, Japan

Overseas Distributor : Japan Publications Trading Co., Ltd.
P. O. Box 5030 Tokyo International, Tokyo, Japan

Distributors :
United States : Kodansha America Inc., through Farrar, Straus & Giroux,
19 Union Square West, New York, NY 10003
Canada : Fitzhenry & Whiteside Ltd.,
195 Allstate Parkway, Markham, Ontario L3R 4T8
British Isles and the European Continent : Premier Book Marketing Ltd.,
1 Gower Street, London WC1E 6HA
Australia and New Zealand : Bookwise International,
54 Crittenden Road, South Australia 5023
The Far East and Japan : Japan Publications Trading Co., Ltd.,
1-2-1, Sarugaku-cho, Chiyoda-ku, Tokyo 101

First Edition 1993
First Printing 1993
ISBN : 0-87040-921-2
ISBN : 4-05-151582-6 (in Japan)
Printed in Japan

CREDITS

We are grateful to the following for their cooperation and their permission to reproduce
the photographs :

Asahi Shimbun Publishing Co., Boncolor Photo Agency, Chichibu Shrine Office, Chichibu
Tourist Association, Gifu City Office, Kashima-cho Town Office (Shimane), Kofu Tourist
Association, Kyodo Photo Service, Mitsukoshi Ltd. (Yokohama Branch), Nachikatsuura
Town Office (Wakayama), Shimoda City Office, Takizawa Village Office (Iwate), The
Chamber of Commerce and Industry of Hakata, The Sanwa Bank, Ltd., The Mainichi
Newspapers, The Walt Disney Company, Tokyo Fire Department, Gakken Co., Ltd.
(Photo Department, New Culture Editorial Department, and "Sozai de Ryori" by Life &
Foods Editorial Department)

INTRODUCTION

The world is rapidly becoming a borderless society. What is essential in such an environment is accurate understanding among people of different societies and a good quality of communication based upon such understanding. We are in what is undoubtedly an age of communication, which means that the ability to achieve deeper communication depends on the possession of correct information about others.

This volume has been compiled to meet the express demand of people both in Japan and overseas for accurate information about a Japan very much in need of good communication.

I have been involved as editorial supervisor now on three books published by Gakken : "Pictorial Encyclopedia of Modern Japan," "Pictorial Encyclopedia of Japanese Culture," and "The Beauty of Japan." All three were planned to provide information from a comparative viewpoint between Japanese and western cultures. Each treated the subject from different angles but they shared a depth in terms of the quality of the information they gave. We hope that they have been instrumental in promoting more profound communication through their in-depth picture of Japan and the Japanese, and have enabled readers to understand at a deeper level how the Japanese look at their world, what their feelings are toward nature, and how they think about and lead their lives.

This book, "Pictorial Encyclopedia of Japanese Life and Events", contains the most current information necessary for an understanding of Japan. Overall it is divided into two sections. Part 1 examines those events which are common to Japan as a nation, together with certain traditional observances like festivals which are the proud possessions of particular localities. We have deliberately made plentiful use of photographs, considering them one of the best means of making understanding easier. We have also thought it important to explain why such events and observances occur, so that the reader will be able to understand how the Japanese feel about the underlying elements of their life and how they perceive that which is traditional.

Part 2 focuses on the modern Japanese and their lives. The Japanese, like the rest of the world, are experiencing phenomenal change in their lives and ways of thinking. Here we deal with what is undergoing the greatest change, in particular life style and consciousness about what life means. We have also included a section on words and expressions that the Japanese use most often in their daily lives, to show how the Japanese react to circumstances and to demonstrate how easy it is to make mistakes when a usage is not understood adequately. Thus Part 2 provides extremely useful data for understanding the changing life, customs and attitudes of Japanese people.

We hope that this book will be an effective tool in promoting good communication with the Japanese, based on an understanding of the traditional and the modern in Japanese life and a deeper comprehension of Japanese national characteristics.

C O N T E N T S

JAN

THE FIRST SUNRISE *-Hatsu hinode-*

On the first day of the year, people still tend, after making their first visits to shrines or temples, to climb a nearby hill and pay respects to the sun as it rises, praying for prosperity and a good harvest. The most famous place for observing the first sunrise is Futamigaura in Mie Prefecture, quite near Ise Jingu, one of Japan's oldest shrines. Traditionally an agricultural society, the Japanese set great store on the sun and water, both indispensable for the growth of plants.

The first sunrise of the year at Futamigaura.

JAN

THE NEW YEAR -Shogatsu-

The first and most important event of the year for the Japanese is *Shogatsu*, the New Year, when they welcome the *toshigami*, the deity of the incoming year. Towards the end of December, people begin to prepare for the New Year celebrations by cleaning out their houses, preparing the special New Year's food called *osechiryori*, and placing pine decorations, *kadomatsu*, in front of gates or doorways. On the first day of the New Year, called *Ganjitsu*, family members sit down together with the visiting *toshigami* to a feast of traditional new year dishes, toast the *toshigami* and each other with spiced sake called *toso*, and eat the festive soup, *zoni*. During the day they make their first shrine or temple visit of the year to pray for good luck for the coming year. Most women and girls wear colorful kimono, one of the few occasions during the year that most of them will do so. New Year's cards (*nengajo*) arrive from the first day of the year, bringing news of relatives and friends. Many people decorate their cards with woodblock prints they have made themselves, and these excite admiration. Nowadays, the New Year holidays generally last from December 29 to January 3, and at that time virtually all government offices and businesses are closed. Because

Kagamimochi. Piled cakes of pounded rice, an indispensable decoration at the New Year.

Hatsumode. On January 1, shrines and temples are packed with people making their first visit of the year.

so many people return to their ancestral homes in the countryside at this time, the cities are quiet, with very few cars on the roads.

People greet each other with the words *Akemashite omedeto gozaimasu,* literally, "New Year Congratulations." Children receive *otoshidama,* money placed in colorful envelopes, from parents and relatives. Traditional children's games played at the New Year are kite-flying, top-spinning, *hanetsuki,* a game played with a battledore and shuttlecock, and a card game called *karuta.* Today, though, they are being played by fewer and fewer children.

Though the expression "Shogatsu" originally applied to the whole month of January, it is now the custom to limit it to the first three days of the year.

JAN

KADOMATSU

Kadomatsu, made of pine branches, bamboo and straw, are placed beside the gates or doorways of homes at the New Year. They are considered to act as a guide to the god of the New Year, the protector of household prosperity. The pine symbolizes long life, and the bamboo, strength. The majority of families, though, tend to decorate their front doors with an arrangement of rice straw called *shimekazari*, instead of placing a *kadoma-tsu* at the entrance to the house. The *shimekazari* also demarcates the sacred place prepared for the visit of the god of the New Year.

KAKIZOME

The first formal calligraphy of the New Year is usually done on January 2. In many cases it has become a calligraphy exercise for children. People write auspicious phrases suitable for the New Year, such as *hatsu hinode* (first sunrise) or *kibo no funade* (hopes for a new start). Many people attend events such as *kakizome* meets and *kakizome* exhibitions, where children display *en masse* the calligraphy they have done at home. Of old, the Japanese would spend the first day of the year quietly, before resuming their work or study on the second. *Kakizome* therefore has the broader meaning of commencing studies.

The first calligraphy of the year.

NEW YEAR'S CARDS *-Nengajo-*

Greeting cards are sent at the beginning of the year to friends, teachers, relatives and business acquaintances. Most are delivered on New Year's Day. Virtually all Japanese send New Year's cards, and the cards mailed out each year number in the vicinity of four billion for the whole of Japan. The cards, in the shape of a post-card, are generally decorated with a picture of the animal representing the coming year, according to the Chinese zodiac, and a greeting.

illustrations. The deck for *Hyakunin Isshu* is made up of two hundred cards, one hundred containing *tanka* (poems with a metrical arrangement of 5-7-5, 7-7 syllables) written by one hundred poets between the seventh and thirteenth centuries and the portrait of the poet, and another one hundred containing only the second part (7-7 syllables) of the poem. In both games, the first set of cards is retained by the reader, and the second set is spread out on a flat surface. The reader selects a card from the first pile and reads the phrase or poem and the players must try to locate the corresponding card as quickly as possible. The person who has most cards at the end is the winner. *Hyakunin Isshu* is played not only in the home but also at regional or school contests.

OTOSHIDAMA

At the New Year, children receive from parents and relatives sums of money placed in small envelopes. A ten-year-old child receives an average of between twenty and thirty thousand yen. The element *tama* (*-dama*) means spirit, and refers to the spirit received by the head of the family from the god of the New Year. Now it has come to mean a present given children by their elders.

Hyakunin isshu. Part of a formal game conducted as a ritual at Yasaka Shrine, Kyoto.

KARUTA AND HYAKUNIN ISSHU

Karuta and *Hyakunin Isshu* are card games played at the New Year. Karuta consists of one hundred cards, fifty containing a proverb or something similar, and fifty containing matching

New Year's cards.

Gleeful children with their *otoshidama*.

JAN

NEW YEAR'S FOOD -Osechi ryori-

The festive food made for the New Year celebrations is presented in special boxes called *jubako*, consisting of from two to five layers stacked one on top of the other. *Osechi* refers to the food eaten on important festive occasions. It is served to the whole family in the presence of the god of the New Year. Traditional dishes include *tazukuri*, small dried sardines coated with a glaze of shoyu, mirin, and sugar ; *kobu maki*, vegetables or fish wrapped in small rolls of flat seaweed ; *onishime*, vegetables cooked in shoyu ; *takenoko*, bamboo shoots ; *kuromame*, black beans ; *kazunoko*, herring roe ; *kuri kinton*, chestnuts in a paste made of sweet potatoes ; *renkon*, lotus root ; and *yatsugashira* and *sato imo*, varieties of taro. *Osechi* sets are sold at department stores for those families who do not have the time to cook themselves ; nevertheless, most housewives still spend the last days of the year in a welter of preparation of a large variety of New Year's food.

ZONI

Zoni, New Year's soup.

New Year's food.

Zoni is a soup eaten at the New Year. Its main ingredient is *mochi*, glutinous rice pounded into a variety of shapes ; it may also contain vegetables, fish, meat, and other ingredients. It is the custom in most households to serve *zoni* as the main dish for the first three days of the year. *Zoni* originally referred to the foods that had been offered to the god of the New Year that were then cooked together in a pot and eaten by all the members of the family. Each region and each family has its own variant of the soup.

JAN

DEZOMESHIKI

Dezomeshiki is an event held at the beginning of the year when people associated with the fire-fighting service turn out to give an exhibition of fire-fighting techniques and the traditional art of ladder-climbing. Fire-fighters clad in traditional *happi* coats whose design dates back to the Edo period (17th-19th centuries) perform acrobatic feats on the top of tall bamboo ladders.

Firemen also stage mock fires, and demonstrate the latest of their equipment. New fire engines are on show, as are helicopters and powerful hoses which shoot water high into the sky. In a land where the majority of houses are wooden and fires break out often, fire-fighting is held in great esteem.

Reenactment of an Edo period *dezomeshiki*.

Firemen with hoses.

Spraying water from a ladder truck.

DARUMA FAIRS -Daruma ichi-

Daruma refers to Bodhidharma, the Indian priest who is said to have spent nine years meditating in a Chinese temple

A coming-of-age ceremony.

in his effort to attain enlightenment. *Daruma* dolls are painted red with the features of the priest. They are round, with no arms or legs, and are weighted at the bottom so that they rebound as soon as they are knocked over. Because they return immediately to the upright position, they are popular throughout the country as a talisman ensuring eventual success. *Daruma* fairs are held from the end of the year to March. *Daruma* dolls are great favorites with a wide range of people, particularly shopkeepers. The two largest fairs are held at Takasaki in Gunma Prefecture and at Fuji in Shizuoka Prefecture. The eyes of the *daruma* are left unpainted ; people buy them and paint in one eye to wish for success in an examination or an election, for example, and when the wished-for success has been achieved, they paint in the other.

A Daruma fair.

COMING-OF-AGE DAY

Coming-of-Age Day is a national holiday which falls on January 15. On this day large-scale coming-of-age ceremonies are held in all parts of Japan. Young men and women who have had their twentieth birthdays over the year gather together to hear celebratory messages from the heads of local government ; then one of the young people, speaking on behalf of the others, verbalizes their awareness that they have reached adulthood and pledges their determination to become good members of society. This national holiday was created in 1948, and is described in the National Holidays Act as the day on which young people are made aware of their achievement of adulthood, and congratulated upon it. At the age of twenty, young people receive the right to vote, and to smoke and drink, but they also must bear the responsibilities of adults.

Coming-of-age rituals were carried out from ancient times, in ceremonies called *gempuku* for boys between the ages of thirteen and sixteen, and *mogi* for girls between twelve and sixteen, on which occasion they formally adopted adult styles of hair and clothing.

15

JAN

SUMO

Sumo, traditional Japanese wrestling, has a 1,500 year-old history. It became the Japanese national sport in the late nineteenth century. Two wrestlers, naked except for a *mawashi*, a belt that doubles as a breechclout, climb onto the *dohyo*, a square mound made of packed clay, and grapple with each other, using a variety of techniques such as pushing, throwing, and pulling to beat their opponent either by thrusting him out of the center circle of the *dohyo* or causing him to touch the ground with any part of his body other than the soles of his feet. Official tournaments are held six times a year, each fifteen days in length. The first tournament of the year, called *hatsubasho*, takes place at the Kokugikan in Ryogoku, Tokyo. Sumo is not simply a sport ; traditionally it was a ritual to forecast the nature of the year's harvest and to call upon the *kami* to descend. For this reason, wrestlers have always worn their long hair tied in the old *chonmage* topknot style, upheld traditional rituals and supported the rule that forbids women to mount the *dohyo*. At the same time, there has been increasing internationalization of Sumo in recent years, with wrestlers from Hawaii, Taiwan and other countries attracting considerable interest. The Grand Sumo Exhibition Tournament held in London in 1991 was a resounding success.

Inside the Kokugikan.

Throwing salt into the ring before the bout.

Akebono, a Hawaiian-born wrestler whose real name is Chad Rowan, became the first non-Japanese *yokozuna*, the highest rank in tradition-bound Sumo, in Jan 1993.

Sumo wrestlers in action.

FEB

BEAN-SCATTERING CEREMONY -Setsubun-

Setsubun refers to the eve of *Risshun* (the first day of spring according to the lunar calendar ; around February 4th according to the solar calendar). In the past, *Risshun* marked the beginning of the new year, and was generally thought of as New Year's Day. It was thus important that evil be exorcised before the new year began. Such unseen evil forces were called *oni* ("demons"). On the evening of *Setsubun*, people fling roasted beans at the invisible demons lurking in the dark outside, at the same time chanting *oni wa soto* (Demons, out!). After dispersing the demons, they scatter beans inside the house to attract fortune within, this time chanting *fuku wa uchi* (Good luck, in!). This ceremony is still carried out in a large number of homes. It is also the custom for large shrines and temples to conduct their own bean-scattering ceremonies. The rite is thought to have its origins in a Chinese exorcism ceremony called *tsuina* (Ch : *zhuinuo* or *chui-no*), used to drive away pestilence and ill fortune, that was brought to Japan by the official emissaries who conducted trade and diplomatic missions between the two countries in the years 630 to 894.

NATIONAL FOUNDATION DAY

In the nineteenth century the Meiji government decided to specify a day on which to celebrate the founding of the nation, basing its calculations upon the accession of the mythological first emperor of Japan, Jimmu, said to have been January 1, 660 B.C. Adjusted to the modern calendar, the day, called *Kigensetsu*, fell

Symposia are held on National Foundation Day to reflect on events of the past.

on February 11. Despite the fact that Jimmu has no historical basis, his accession was commemorated in order to stress, both domestically and abroad, the legitimacy of a national government centered on the emperor. *Kigensetsu*, being closely associated with prewar nationalism and militarism, was abolished in 1948 as being unsuited to the aspirations of the new Constitution, with its advocacy of the

Throwing beans at a shrine.

Throwing beans in the home. The deity of good fortune, on the right, pelts the demon on the left with beans, and chases him.

principles of freedom and democracy. A later movement which sought to restore the national day brought upon itself accusations from historians and others of attempting to restore emperor-centered nationalism. Nevertheless, in 1967 the government decided to reinstitute the national day as "Kenkoku Kinenbi" (literally, "commemoration of the founding of the nation"). Even now, groups for and against the holiday hold meetings on that day every year to discuss the meaning of National Foundation Day and the problems that it engenders.

ST. VALENTINE'S DAY

The celebration of St. Valentine's Day on February 14 has only a short history in Japan. On that day, women make presents of chocolate to men as an expression of their warm feelings. As the day approaches, cake shops and the sweets sections of department stores are packed with women buying chocolate in the shape of hearts or popular cartoon characters. It has in fact become the custom for women to give chocolates to superiors and co-workers out of duty (and so there has evolved the expression *giri-choco*, "duty chocolates") rather than as a token of real feeling. March 14 is gradually taking root as "White Day," when men who have received Valentine Day chocolate must reciprocate the gift with candy or marshmallows.

Young girls throng chocolate shops several days before St. Valentine's Day.

FEB

A palace made of packed snow.

SAPPORO SNOW FESTIVAL

The Sapporo Snow Festival in Hokkaido has been held every year since 1950 over four days culminating on the first Sunday of February. It is the largest event held in Hokkaido, and attracts visitors from all over Japan and abroad. Various groups and organizations construct snow figures and ice sculptures, such as scale models of famous buildings from around the world. Visitors are amazed that such grandeur and detail can be achieved using snow as a medium. Traditionally, Japan had very few winter festivals, but in recent years people have begun to look on winter as a time when life can be enjoyed, rather than merely endured. The festival has taken on an international flavor as more and more people from overseas are participating in the event.

Night view of the Snow Festival.

FEB

EXAMINATION HELL

More than ninety percent of students move on from junior high school to senior high school, and entry to all senior high schools, as well as universities, public and private alike, is by examination. They are the reason that even elementary school students are attending cram school every day after regular school. The preparations they make are not unlike the training a sportsman or woman does for the Olympics. In today's Japan, job requirements are virtually unrelated to a person's actual ability, or to his father's profession, position or wealth. People dream therefore of gaining a good job and rising to a high position through having graduated from a good school, however poor their parents might be. In addition, the Japanese have traditionally been a people who like reading and writing and who value their culture, and so they tend to think highly of the merits of education. As a result, students compete to continue their education and, since most aspire to university, the continuation rate is high and the competition is enormous, giving rise to the expression, "examination hell." Living in a society which places so much emphasis on the scholastic record, people tend to look on entrance into a high ranking university, such as the pinnacle, Tokyo University, as a passport to a rosy future. Thus the university dominates work and marriage as well. A student who fails the university entrance examination may become a *ronin* ("masterless samurai") for one or two years, attending cram school and waiting for his next chance. In Japan it is difficult to enter university, but relatively easy to

The university entrance examination.

graduate from it. Some even call it a four-year vacation. Because entering a good university is regarded as being so important, cram schools are a flourishing business, to the extent that there are even some which are so large that they use satellite broadcasting to transmit televised lectures by famous teachers to branch schools.

NEEDLE MEMORIAL SERVICE -*Hari kuyo-*

On February 8 or December 8, or in some places on both days, there is a widespread custom that women do not do any sewing. They stick their old or broken needles into *tofu* (bean curd) or *konnyaku* (devil's tongue jelly), praying for improvement in their skill at sewing, before pre-

A successful student being tossed by his friends.

A shrine scene on the first Day of the Horse.

senting them to shrines or allowing them to float away in a river. The connection between needles and shrines, particularly those in the Awashima Shrine lineage, is related to the deity of the main Awashima Shrine in Wakayama, a female deity called *Harisainyo*. The custom of dedicating needles took root during the nineteenth century among those learning traditional Japanese sewing. The Japanese believe that spirits dwell even within such things as dolls, wooden clogs, and needles, and since ancient times they have held memorial services to them in appreciation of the function they perform. The needle memorial service is one such.

Women dedicating their needles.

HATSUUMA

The first "day of the horse" falls around the beginning of February and is celebrated at Inari shrines around the country. Of the roughly 80,000 Shinto shrines in Japan, some 40 per cent are Inari shrines. Inari is a deity worshiped as a guardian of agriculture, fishing, and commerce. The deity's messenger is believed to be a fox. The custom of instituting the first "horse day" of February as the festival of Inari originates in the tradition that the deity of the Fushimi Inari Shrine in Kyoto was enshrined at Inariyama on that day in the year 711. *Hatsuuma* was originally a rite held in farming villages to pray for a good harvest of rice. The festival at the Fushimi Inari Shrine is one of the largest and most solemn, and it attracts crowds of worshipers. It is associated in people's minds with the ending of the rigors of winter and the coming of spring.

23

DOLL FESTIVAL -Hinamatsuri-

Hinamatsuri is held on March 3. On that day, households with daughters set up a tiered platform covered with red felt and display on it dolls representing the emperor, empress, court ladies and attendants dressed in the flamboyant robes of the Heian court. This they do to pray for the health and sound growth of their daughters. In ancient times people would exorcise themselves by transferring their impurities to paper images, called *hitogata*, rubbing them against the body and then throwing them into a river. During the Heian period (794-1191), it became the custom to decorate these "dolls," and in the Edo period (1603-1867) dolls were dressed to new heights of magnificence.

The Doll Festival, originally an urban celebration, became commercialized during and after the Meiji period (1868-1912) and spread throughout the country. Food, such as *kusamochi*, a rice-cake made with *yomogi* (mugwort), and *hishimochi* (a diamond shaped rice-cake), is arranged before the tiered platform, together with *shirozake*, a drink made from rice malt and sake. Because the festival coincides with the blooming of the peach blossom, branches of peach blossom are also placed on the platform, and an alternative name for the Doll festival is *Momo no Sekku* (Peach Festival). The dolls are left on display for about one week.

Hina dolls displayed on a tiered platform. ▶

The custom of throwing *hitogata* into a river survives in Tottori Prefecture.

OMIZUTORI

Omizutori (lit. "drawing of water") is the name of the central rite of a series of ceremonies called *shunie*, held in the Nigatsudo Hall of Todaiji in Nara between March 1 and 14 to pray for national peace and the happiness of the people. It is a fire festival which takes place on the evening of March 12. Young priests set alight large torches (*taimatsu*) and wave them from the high platform surrounding the Nigatsudo, so that sparks fall over the heads of the crowd below. These sparks are said to have the power to drive away all that is inauspicious. Around 2 a.m. on the thirteenth, priests emerge from where they have been conducting austerities and draw water from a nearby well, which they place in five jars in the sanctuary as an offering to the Buddha. The water is also given to worshipers, and it is believed to drive away disease.

Large torches being brandished during the *Omizutori* rite.

MAR

HIGAN

Buddhism refers to the present life as "this shore" and to the life of enlightenment as the "other shore" (Jap. *higan*). *Higan* is a seven-day long time of memorial services for the dead, centering on two periods, the vernal equinox (around March 21) and the autumnal equinox (around September 21). The Japanese have long had the custom of revering at those times their ancestors whom they believe to be in the "other world" of the west where the sun sinks. People visit their family graves, clean them, place flowers, incense and food on them, and reverence the dead. A kind of rice dumpling called *ohagi*, flavored with sweet bean paste or soybean flour, is also placed before the graves. A proverb, "Heat and cold end at Higan" associates the equinox with the change of the seasons, and people believe that after that time, summer heat or winter cold will fade away.

Ohagi, rice dumplings eaten during Higan.

Bowing before the family Buddhist altar.

Visiting the family grave.

GRADUATION CEREMONIES

In March, elementary and junior and senior high schools, as well as universities, hold their graduation ceremonies. During the ceremonies, school principals and university presidents offer their congratulations and encouragement to graduating students, and the students, in a mood both joyful and emotional, sing their school song, *Hotaru no hikari* (By the Firefly's Light), a song praising diligence set to the melody of "Auld Lang Syne," and *Aogeba totoshi*, which tells of a student's gratitude to his teachers. A student representing the year below the graduating class reads a farewell speech written in the form of a long scroll, which records the memories and gratitude of the lower classes toward the seniors. A representative from the graduates then makes a reply. They then receive their graduation certificates and a commemorative album. After the graduation ceremony, students attend parties called *shaonkai* to which they invite their teachers. At this time the newspapers feature articles such as what the president of Tokyo University spoke about in his graduation ceremony address, how a small elementary school deep in the mountains was graduating only one student, and concerning the graduation of a seventy-year-old woman from university. For example, the words of a former president of Tokyo University encouraging his students to be "lean Socrates rather than fat pigs" drew much comment from the media, who also like to feature pictures of graduating female students wearing the traditional *hakama* (split skirt) of seventy or eighty years ago.

A graduating student receiving her graduation certificate from the principal.

Graduating students being farewelled by their teachers and lower graders.

Women dressed in hakama after their university graduation ceremony.

29

SCHOOL ENTRANCE CEREMONIES

In Japan six-year-olds begin school at the beginning of April. Because many countries throughout the world have a school year beginning in September, some people in Japan are of the opinion that Japan should do likewise. However there is considerable opposition to the idea of changing the beginning of the school year from April, at the height of the cherry-blossom season, to September, when the heat of summer can be still quite oppressive. Mothers dressed in their best clothes escort their children, wearing new clothes slightly too big for them, large name tags pinned to their chest, and bright smiles full of anticipation. At that time parents buy their children satchels, stationery and study-desks, and friends and relatives give them gifts to celebrate their starting school. It is a very happy time for the new students.

New first graders with their mothers on their way to their entrance ceremony.

A teacher and new first graders shaking hands.

New employees listening to the company president.

COMPANY ENTRANCE CEREMONIES

April marks not only the start of the new school year, but the beginning of the year for public offices and companies as well. Therefore companies hold their entrance ceremonies at this time also. The new employees listen to words of encouragement from company presidents and directors, and one of their number makes a vow on behalf of his fellows to serve the company with their best efforts. Because lifetime employment is still the norm in Japan, most students want to work for large corporations, in the spirit of the proverb "Take shelter under a large tree." The goal of young Japanese who have undergone the honing of the examination hell is to find a good job. People do not think that a person who does not change jobs lacks ability, as is the case in the United States. Only a few will leave the large corporation into which they were recruited for another position. After four unfettered years at university, the young people go through the company training programs and metamorphose into worker bees. However, the ratio of young people who value their own interests, privacy and home life over promotion within their companies is increasing year by year, and there is a tendency for company loyalty to be weaker and the number of people changing jobs to rise.

PROFESSIONAL BASEBALL

Baseball is one of Japan's most popular sports.

Professional baseball is organized into two leagues, the Central and the Pacific, made up of six teams each. The teams are owned by such organizations as newspaper companies, railway companies and supermarket chains. The twelve teams each play 130 games between early April, when the so-called "pennant race" begins, and October. The regular season is followed in October by the Japan Series between the two league champions.

Other popular sports are soccer and Sumo.

Many professional baseball players are American.

APR

CHERRY VIEWING

Places famous for their cherry blossom are to be found all over Japan. Large numbers of people enjoy holding flower-viewing parties under the blossoming cherry trees. The custom began at court during the Heian period, and became a widespread and popular event in the Edo period. Families and friends from the neighborhood or the company find a spot under a suitable tree and spread out straw mats or vinyl sheets on the ground to sit on. They bring food, sake and *karaoke* sets and have a noisy time drinking and singing and dancing. Modern people appreciate the cherry blossom for its beauty, but the nobility of old saw in its brief period of glory a metaphor for the transiency of life, while the samurai regarded the fall of the blossom while still unwithered to represent their values of bravery and purity. It seems to be typical of Japan that the weather reports carried on television and in newspapers at this time always show the "cherry blossom front" as it moves from south to north, pinpointing the places where the flowers are blossoming at that moment.

People enjoying *karaoke* beneath the cherry trees.

Cherry blossoms at Sumida Park, Tokyo.

FLOWER FESTIVAL -Hanamatsuri-

Many Buddhist temples celebrate the birth of the Buddha on April 8. A small statue of the Buddha is placed within a small flower-decorated shrine called a *hanamido* and worshipers pour sweet tea (*amacha*) made of hydrangea seeds three times over the Buddha's head, using a bamboo water-scoop. Most temples offer visitors and children cups of *amacha* to drink. There are also parades of children wearing festival clothes. The Buddha, the founder of Buddhism, was born in the 5th century B.C. At the age of twenty-nine he abandoned his wife and child in order to seek the way to bring people deliverance from their suffering. After his enlightenment he spent his whole life spreading his teachings far and wide.

Children pouring sweet tea over a statue of the Buddha.

33

APR

FESTIVAL OF LORD SHINGEN -Shingenko matsuri-

The Festival of Lord Shingen is held in honor of Takeda Shingen (1521-1573), a famous general of the Sengoku period (1467-1568), at Kofu in Yamanashi Prefecture. It centers on the anniversary of Shingen's death, April 12, and a 1,300 strong procession depicting Shingen's cavalry and a parade including folk songs and dancing are held on the Saturdays and Sundays preceding and following that day. Takeda Shingen commanded what was reputed to have been the strongest cavalry unit of his time and he is known for his heroism and his skill as a military leader. He belonged to the generation before the famous generals Oda Nobunaga and Tokugawa Ieyasu, and it was not until after Shingen's death through illness that they began to occupy center-stage in the country's affairs. The Japanese regard Takeda Shingen as the ideal figure of a military commander.

The samurai parade wends its way through the streets.

MAY

GOLDEN WEEK

The holiday-studded period between the end of April and the early part of May is called Golden Week. The national holidays are Greenery Day (April 29), Constitution Memorial Day (May 3) and Children's Day (May 5). Though not a national holiday as such, May 4 has also been made a holiday, called a "rest day." Large corporations in many cases have a ten day holiday at this time, incorporating Saturdays, Sundays, and paid vacation time. With the New Year's holiday (end of December-beginning of January) and the Obon holiday (the middle of August), it is one of the major holiday periods in Japan. At this time people from all around the nation throng popular resorts, families with children flock to amusement parks and zoos, and Narita Airport is packed with tourists traveling to overseas destinations such as Hawaii. Japanese fathers spend their "rest day" tiring themselves out on family outings.

Children flock to the zoo on holidays.

Traffic jams many kilometers long hold up traffic exiting cities during Golden Week.

MAY DAY

May Day, the international day of worker solidarity, has been celebrated in Japan since 1920. It was suppressed in 1938 in an environment of growing militarism, but reinstituted in 1946 after the Second World War. In the past it has been associated with pointed political demands and some violence at times, but today it has become a festival for workers and their families.

Greenery Day

April 29 has been a national holiday since the ascension of Emperor Showa (1901-1989). After his death, though the national holiday for the Emperor's Birthday changed to December 23, the day remained a holiday, promulgated in 1990 as "Greenery Day." It recalls the previous emperor, a botanist as well as a marine biologist, and provides a focus for heightening people's awareness of the importance of plant life.

Cheerful-faced young workers participating in May Day activities. ▶

◀ The world's first Disneyland outside the United States is always filled with visitors on holidays.
©The Walt Disney Company

37

MAY

CHILDREN'S DAY

In earlier times, May 5 was celebrated as Boys' Day, just as March 3 was celebrated as Girls' Day. Today though the day is a festival for both boys and girls, called Children's Day, and it is counted as a national holiday. As Children's Day approaches, carp streamers (*koinobori*) made of paper or cloth can be seen trailing bravely in the sky in every part of Japan.

The carp is believed to have a strong life-force, and so is regarded as symbolizing worldly success. This idea comes from the Chinese fable that tells how only the carp, of all the fish who had swum up together in a vast school from the lower reaches of the great river, could negotiate the rapids and waterfalls and become in the end a dragon. Parents therefore set up carp streamers in the hope that their child will grow up to be strong and successful like the carp. Those families with sons also display large warrior dolls decked out in helmet and armor, so that their sons might also grow up sturdy and brave. Other customs on this day are hanging irises from the eaves in order to ward away evil influences and eating *chimaki* (rice cakes wrapped in bamboo leaves) and *kashiwa mochi* (rice cakes filled with sweet bean paste and wrapped in oak leaves).

Carp streamers fluttering against the blue sky. ▶

Many families display warrior dolls in the hope that their sons will grow up healthy and strong.

Mother's Day

On Mother's Day, held on the second Sunday in May, children give their mothers red carnations, or place white carnations on their *Butsudan* (small Buddhist altars) if deceased. In the language of flowers, a white carnation signifies a mother's love. The celebration of Mother's Day began in the United States in 1907. It has taken root as a Japanese event, being completely in accord with Japanese sentiment.

Red and white carnations.

MAY

HAKATA DONTAKU

The Hakata Dontaku is a festival of singing and dancing by the townspeople of Fukuoka on May 4 and 5. The name "Dontaku" derives from the German Zontag (Sunday). Before this name became popular in the late nineteenth century, the festival was called *Matsubayashi*. It was originally a ritual celebrating spring, when the merchants of Hakata paraded with the Seven Deities of Good Fortune to offer New Year greetings to their lord. The *matsubayashi*, now designated an intangible cultural property, is a procession of adults and children dressed in traditional costume leading floats of the Seven Deities of Good Luck accompanied by musicians playing flutes, drums, and *shamisen*. The highlight of the procession is when various groups of people in all kinds of traditional or fancy-dress costume join in, singing to the accompaniment of the *shamisen* and the clack of wooden ladles.

The Hakata Dontaku Festival.

Parade, Yokohama Port Festival. ▶

YOKOHAMA PORT FESTIVAL

The Yokohama Port festival, lasting from May 3 to July 20, is Yokohama's largest festival. It celebrates the opening of Yokohama as a port on June 2, 1859 following the signing of the Harris Treaty in 1858, the first commercial treaty between Japan and the United States. One of the main attractions is a parade on May 3, which stretches two kilometers and features more than two thousand people, Japanese and foreign, dressed in the costume of the mid-nineteenth century or wearing the national clothing of many different countries. This parade used to take place on June 2, the anniversary of the opening of the port, but was put forward to the National Holiday because the rainy season generally starts in early June. Bazaars and other events take place during the festival period. It closes on July 20 with a large fireworks display.

Yokohama port is also known for the beauty of the Bay Bridge, which is illuminated at night and is a mecca for dating couples. Yokohama and Kobe are Japan's largest trading ports.

The Shimoda Black Ships Festival.

BLACK SHIPS FESTIVAL

The Black Ships Festival is a tourist attraction held every year between May 16 and 18 at Shimoda in Shizuoka Prefecture and commemorates the arrival in 1853 of the squadron of ships of the United States navy under Commander Matthew Perry. It began in 1934 to celebrate eighty years of Japanese-American friendship. During the festival American naval ships visit Shimoda, and a ceremony is held in Shiroyama Park, attended by the American and other ambassadors. There is a parade of American marines and other events of an international flavor. When the former president of the United States, Jimmy Carter, was visiting Japan in 1979, he visited Shimoda because of its associations with Commander Perry.

MAY

AOI MATSURI

The Aoi Matsuri, celebrated by the two Kamo Shrines, is one of the three great Kyoto festivals. It unfolds like a scroll depicting the manners and customs of the Heian period. The highlight of the festival is the procession which departs from the Kyoto Imperial Palace at ten o'clock on May 15. The participants, numbering over one hundred and all dressed in ancient costume, take the part of imperial envoys, law enforcement officials, members of the old Bureau of Imperial Storehouses, women court attendants, and the High Priestess of the Kamo Shrine wearing the ornate twelve-layered kimono. "Aoi" refers to the hollyhock (*Asarum caulescens*), the leaves of which decorate the headgear of the participants and the ox-drawn carriages in the procession, for it is believed the hollyhock has the power to avert lightning and earthquakes. The festival originated about fourteen hundred years ago, when, it was said, the emperor, troubled by the continuing wind and rains that prevented the crops from maturing, sent envoys to the Kamo Shrine. Because the wind and rain then stopped, it became the custom to send imperial envoys to the shrine every year.

Parade, Aoi Festival.

MAY

SANJA MATSURI

The Sanja Matsuri is the festival of the Asakusa Shrine, and is one of the three great festivals of Tokyo. It lasts for three days centering on a Sunday in the middle of May. During the Edo period it was a spring festival held in March. Young men and women wearing happi coats and a band of cloth around their heads carry three great portable shrines (*mikoshi*) and around one hundred smaller ones from six o'clock in the morning to evening, dividing themselves into three groups to transverse the forty-four districts of shrine parishioners. The most spectacular event takes place on the Sunday, within the shrine precincts. The Sanja festival is a good place to experience the spirit of the "Edokko," as the native inhabitants of Tokyo (known as Edo till 1868) are called.

Kaminarimon, entrance to the Asakusa Shrine.

Carrying a portable shrine around the neighborhood. ▶

JUN

THE RAINY SEASON

The rainy season lasts for about forty days, starting some twenty days before the summer solstice, and lasting some twenty days after it. The Japanese call it *baiu* ("plum rain"), because it occurs at the time the plum ripens. The rainfall during the rainy season accounts for one fifth to one quarter of the yearly total, and though such heavy and constant rain often results in flooding or landslides, it provides Japan with an indispensable resource. Rice growing, and Japanese agriculture as a whole, depend on the rainy season. The dampness allows mold to thrive ; and mold has an important role in Japanese food, being responsible for the production of fermented products such as *shoyu* (soy sauce), *sake* and *natto* (fermented soybeans).

The rainy season.

RICE PLANTING

Rice is the most important of all Japan's crops. "Rice planting" refers to the transplanting of seedlings from the nursery beds to the paddy fields. It is a scene of pastoral delight to see long lines of farmers busy planting the rice shoots during the rainy season in June. As rice is the principal food of the Japanese, rice planting is an extremely important task in the minds of the Japanese, and therefore they precede it with rituals to welcome the spirit of the rice plant, which is the god of the rice field. In addition, a great many festivals have incorporated the idea of rice planting. Today, though, rice planting is increasingly being done by machine.

Ancient rice-planting methods are preserved as shrine rituals.

Mechanization marks rice-planting today.

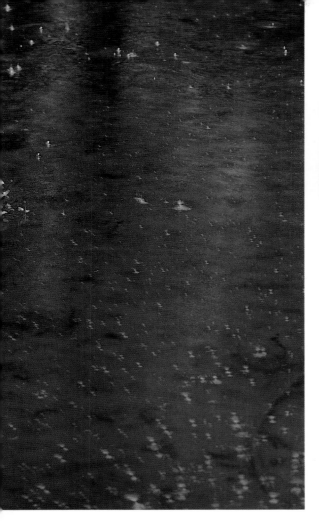

Teruteru Bozu, a charm to bring good weather, made out of white cloth and thread.

A uniform typical of the kind worn until May.

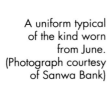

A uniform typical of the kind worn from June. (Photograph courtesy of Sanwa Bank)

CHANGING UNIFORMS *-Koromogae-*

A uniform is worn widely in Japan by the police, nurses, students, and female employees in many businesses. On June 1, it changes from long to short sleeves, and in many cases to a light color suitable for summer. On October 1, the reverse occurs, and people resume wearing the long-sleeved version. The custom of formally changing clothes according to the season (*koromogae*) dates back to ancient aristocratic society. It apparently derives from the Japanese preference to act in groups combined with a sensitivity toward the changing seasons.

JUN

CHAGUCHAGU UMAKKO

The Chaguchagu Umakko is a horse festival held on June 15 in the vicinity of Morioka in Iwate Prefecture. It originated in an event intended to give fatigued horses a rest from their work in the fields. Each family decks out its horse with fine ribbons and ornaments. The horses are mounted by boys wearing short coats and girls wearing colorful kimono, and led by a red bridle to the Sozen Shrine, where all pray for safety and health to the tutelary god of horses enshrined there. After this they walk in procession fifteen kilometers to the Hachiman Shrine in Morioka. The expression "*chagu chagu*" is said to be the sound made by the horses' bells.

A folk-craft item in the form of a *Chaguchagu Umakko*.

Parade of decorated horses.

48

JUL

THE OPENING OF MT. FUJI

Mt. Fuji, symbol of Japan and the country's highest mountain, rises to a height of 3,776 meters. A volcano, it has been dormant since its last eruption in 1707. Of imposing presence and with a beauty that changes with time and season, it has long been the subject for the pens of poets as well as an object of a religious cult which regarded it as sacred. In the past it was forbidden for people to enter freely sacred mountains ; for a limited period only could worshipers climb and venerate them. This short time was called *yamabiraki*, literally "opening of the mountain," and today the expression refers to the beginning of the climbing season, in terms of recreation rather than religion. The "opening" of Mt. Fuji occurs on July 1.

Children, with Mt. Fuji in the background. Mt. Fuji is Japan's most beautiful and loved mountain. It is also the country's most sacred peak. ▶

Local women perform a dance in honor of the deity of the mountain.

Yamabushi, mountain ascetics, wearing *tengu* masks, cut the cord to mark the opening of Mt. Fuji.

The climbing season on Mt. Fuji officially begins, a portable shrine leading the way.

JUL

MIDSUMMER GREETINGS

People send postcards containing summer greetings to friends, teachers, superiors and colleagues, though not to the extent new year cards are exchanged. At the beginning of summer postcards for the purpose go on sale, bearing designs reminiscent of coolness, such as morning glories or wind bells. Though the custom of making summer greetings is somewhat formal, it allows people to confirm and renew acquaintance easily, in the form of short notes asking after those they have not seen for some time and giving news of their own doings.

Summer greeting cards.

Summer gift section in a department store (Mitsukoshi, Yokohama).

SUMMER AND WINTER GIFTS -Ochugen and Oseibo-

Twice a year, in summer and winter, the Japanese send gifts to those to whom they feel some obligation, such as parents, acquaintances, teachers, and superiors and colleagues at work. They do this as an expression of their thanks for favors and apology for any neglect. The summer gift is called *ochugen*, and is made between July 1-15, and the winter gift is *oseibo*, made between December 10-25. In olden times people would call upon each other bearing noodles as a gift, but today it is more usual to eschew the personal visits and to have gifts such as noodles, edible seaweed, salad oil, drinks, socks or shopping vouchers delivered directly by a department store.

Food typical of summer

People prefer food that is cool and refreshing during the summer heat.

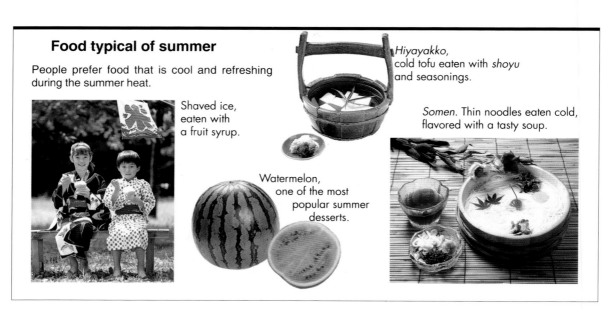

Shaved ice, eaten with a fruit syrup.

Hiyayakko, cold tofu eaten with *shoyu* and seasonings.

Somen. Thin noodles eaten cold, flavored with a tasty soup.

Watermelon, one of the most popular summer desserts.

The Ground Cherry Market, popular with people taking advantage of the cool of the evening.

GROUND CHERRY MARKET -Hozuki ichi-

It is believed that a visit to the Asakusa Kannon temple in Tokyo on July 10 has the same merit as 46,000 visits at other times. This day therefore sees vast crowds of people at the temple. The *hozuki* (ground cherry) market is held on July 9-10, at which time small stalls set up around the temple precincts sell the ground cherry plant. The plant is a perennial of the eggplant family, and stands about 60 to 80 centimeters in height.

After white, five-petalled flowers have bloomed, the calyx expands to become the pod of the fruit and turns a vivid orange when mature. The fruit is used as decoration, and as a noise-making toy made by emptying the pod of its seeds and then pressing it between the tongue and the roof of the mouth. It was traditionally a toy for girls. The *hozuki* can also be drunk as a tea for medicinal purposes, and is said to be good as a laxative; in olden times it was thought to be the best of all such medicines.

JUL

NACHI FIRE FESTIVAL

The Nachi Fire festival occurs on July 14 as part of the festival of Kumano Nachi Taisha (shrine) in Wakayama Prefecture. Twelve huge torches made of bamboo and grasses are shouldered by twelve white-robed priests, who proceed along the main path to the shrine through the forest. At the same time twelve *ogi mikoshi* (literally, "portable shrines with fans"), long and slender in shape (one meter by ten meters), with their framework wrapped with red damask and topped with thirty-two folding fans, descend the pathway. There is a great spectacle when the two groups meet. The spectators watch breathlessly, caught in the heat of the wildly weaving torches. The deity of the Nachi Shrine is the waterfall itself, and the fire festival is a ritual in which the twelve *ogi mikoshi*, symbolizing the shape of the Nachi Fall and serving as the temporary dwelling place of the deity, are purified by the huge torches. There are many shrines in Japan whose gods are natural phenomena, like mountains or waterfalls.

The Nachi waterfall.

The collision between the torches and the portable shrines at The Nachi Fire Festival.

The parade of magnificent floats is famous world-wide.

GION FESTIVAL

The Gion Festival of Kyoto's Yasaka Shrine must be counted as one of Japan's greatest, in terms of scale, splendor, and tradition. It is long, lasting from July 1 to 29, but the most dazzling spectacle occurs on the seventeenth, when huge wheeled floats are pulled through the city. It has its origins in a ritual first performed in 869 to counter an epidemic that was killing large numbers of people. The wheeled floats are of two kinds, *hoko*, topped with a spear-like pole, which number seven, and *yama*, smaller with life-size figures of famous people in legend and history, of which there are twenty-two. The spear-like *naginatahoko* lead the parade, and the boat-shaped *funahoko* bring up the rear. Some years the *hoko* and *yama* are fewer in number than the above figures. The *hoko* and *yama* are believed to summon epidemics to themselves and subdue them. From the *hoko*, leaf-wrapped rice cakes called *chimaki*, thought to dispel disease, are distributed, and amid the haunting tones of the music called *gionbayashi*, sightseers wander around intoxicated by the atmosphere, forgetting the summer's heat.

Yasaka Shrine, Kyoto.
The Gion Festival is the festival of the Yasaka Shrine, but the parade of wheeled floats does not pass in front of the shrine.

JUL

SUMMER HOLIDAYS

With the exception of some of the colder areas of the country, Japanese school children have a summer holiday of 42 days, lasting from July 21 to August 31. Salaried workers, on the other hand, have only between three and ten days, but though Japan is still criticized abroad for allowing its citizens to work too hard, the time available for summer holidays is increasing slowly but surely. During the school holidays, beaches and pools are crowded with holidaying families. Crowds at Tokyo Disneyland can reach forty thousand a day at this time. Once the rush of people leaving to spend holidays abroad has started, more than thirty thousand people, including children, leave Narita each day for destinations such as Hawaii, the American mainland, and Australia. Amid all the enjoyment, the children are afflicted with mountains of homework.

A crowded beach.

EATING EEL -Doyo ushi no hi-

The last week of July and the first week of August are traditionally the hottest part of summer. It is customary for people to eat charcoal broiled eel (*kabayaki*) on the "earth-ox" (*doyo ushi*) day, according to the ancient sexagenary cycle, which falls during this time. Eel has long been considered nourishing and capable of restoring vitality, and so it is widely eaten at the height of summer to prevent any diminution of bodily strength due to the heat.

An eighth century poem mentions that eel was eaten on this day, and the custom became widespread among the common people during the Edo period. According

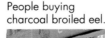

Unadon, rice topped with broiled eel.

People buying charcoal broiled eel.

to the eastern calendar, *doyo* days represent most vigorously the spirit of the season ; they occur each season, but today people are aware only of the summer one.

Catching goldfish.

CATCHING GOLDFISH

Goldfish catching is a favorite attraction at summer events like shrine festivals. Sellers of goldfish set up their stalls, in the form of a small pool full of fish. People are given a ladle whose scoop is made of paper; the skill is to catch as many fish as possible before the paper gets too wet and tears. Usually there is time to catch only one or two. The fish caught are placed with water in small plastic bags to be taken home. A person who catches no fish at all is always given one.

People pulling the cart carrying the drum.

Children taking a break from carrying a small portable shrine.

SUMMER FESTIVALS

Unlike spring and autumn festivals, summer festivals developed in the urban centers. Whereas the former are largely connected with agriculture, centering on prayers for a good crop or thanks for a bountiful harvest, the latter originated to exorcise the evil spirits believed to be responsible for epidemics or floods. During the summer festival, children pull carts on which is placed a large drum, and shoulder small portable shrines through the streets of the neighborhood. The grounds of the shrine are filled with stalls selling candy floss, drinks, masks, yo-yos, and goldfish, and by evening they are packed with families dressed in colorful summer kimonos. In many instances, fireworks displays and Bon dances are held in conjunction with summer festivals.

FIREWORKS DISPLAYS

All Japanese people retain fond memories of summer evenings spent in the garden letting off fire crackers bought at the local store. Large scale fireworks displays are held on riverbanks as a summer attraction throughout Japan. The most famous of these is that held at Ryogoku, on the Sumida river in Tokyo, where every year twenty thousand fireworks light up the night sky to delight crowds which number around 900,000 people. Competitions are also held to test the art of the craftsmen who make the fireworks, and the displays produced are like a great pageant, as beautiful as a field of flowers in full bloom. The Sumida fireworks display is said to have originated in a memorial service to all those who lost their lives on the riverbank when fleeing from the great fires that periodically swept through Edo. People today have forgotten that side of the display and enjoy the fireworks for their own sake as they sit on the riverbank in the cool of the evening and find respite from

Letting off fire crackers at home.

the summer heat. The first Sumida fireworks display held around 1733 had only about twenty rounds of fireworks, but as the years passed the event became more and more elaborate as new techniques were added.

The Sumida River fireworks display.

Extracting the fish from the cormorant's throat.

Cormorant fishing.

CORMORANT FISHING

Cormorant fishing begins on the Nagara river in Gifu Prefecture on May 11, and runs until October 15. A master fisherman, wearing the traditional cap of lacquered fabric called *eboshi* and the *koshimino*, a straw raincoat covering the waist and hips, manipulates up to twelve cormorants. The birds, collared to prevent them from swallowing their catch, take mainly *ayu* (sweetfish), carp, and crucian carp. When the bird surfaces with a fish in its throat, the fisherman hauls it in by rope. During the Heian period, cormorants were used to catch *ayu* for presentation, and were under the protection of the court and great lords. Cormorant fishing used to be done all over Japan, but today the Nagara river event is the most famous. It is a prosperous tourist resource, but it is threatened by the lack of people to carry on the tradition.

NEBUTA

The Nebuta festival, held in Aomori city between August 3-7, is a contest among large floats containing paper images (*nebuta*) of famous figures from Kabuki or of animals. These elaborately designed images are lit by lanterns from within and especially in motion are incomparably beautiful. Dozens of floats, both children's and adults', are drawn through the streets, presenting a fantastic spectacle to those watching. The festival originated in rites to expel ill fortune and to welcome the season of Bon, when the spirits of the ancestors are consoled.

The Nebuta Festival, Aomori. After the festival the paper images are thrown into the sea.

The Kanto Festival, Akita. Forty-eight lanterns are suspended from bamboo poles up to ten meters in length. The total weight can reach 40 kilograms.

KANTO FESTIVAL

The Kanto festival is a lantern festival dating from the early seventeenth century which is celebrated in Akita for three days from August 5 to pray for a bountiful harvest. The "*kanto*" are twelve-meter high bamboo poles hung with 24-48 lanterns suspended on both sides of nine vertical poles. Young men compete among themselves to display the best technique of balancing the *kanto*, which weigh up to fifty kilograms, on some part of their bodies. Under the starry sky the hundred or so "radiant ears of rice," as the *kanto* are called, weave through the streets, an undulating sea of light, accompanied by drums and shouts.

TANABATA

The Tanabata festival derives from an old Chinese legend about the Weaver Star (Vega) and the Cowherd Star (Altair), lovers who are separated on opposite banks of the River of Heaven (the Milky Way) and who can meet only once a year, on July 7. Since in Japan Tanabata fell just before the Bon festival, it was originally a time when markers were erected to call the spirits of the ancestors forth, but today it is better known in terms of the ancient Chinese story. Children and young people place in the garden or somewhere outside the house branches of bamboo decorated with long strips of paper on which they write their hopes concerning health, success, or love. The custom grew out of the tradition that those who write poems or proverbs with a brush and dedicate them to the stars will gain proficiency at calligraphy. The name "*Tanabata*" comes from a native Japanese goddess called *Tanabatatsume*, who excelled at weaving.

Colorful Tanabata festivals are held in shopping districts all around the country. Some areas celebrate Tanabata on August 7, the most famous of these being the city of Sendai in Miyagi Prefecture. Every year between August 6-8 brightly colored decorations fill the streets of Sendai, and more than three thousand bamboo poles are suspended on both sides of the roads. It is a major tourist attraction which draws over three million visitors.

The Tanabata festival, Sendai.
Decorations fill shopping arcades.

AUG

BON

The Bon festival is a Buddhist observance held between July 13-16 (a month later in some areas). It is believed that during this time the spirits of the dead return to their families ; it is therefore a time when people make special offerings at their Buddhist family altars and visit their family graves. The spirits are guided to their homes by a welcoming fire (*mukaebi*), lit on the evening of July 13, and are farewelled on July 16 with the sending-off fire (*okuribi*). On the last day of Bon, lighted lanterns are set afloat in rivers and the sea to guide the spirits safely back to the other world. This is called *toronagashi*. Bon dances (*Bon odori*) are performed in every part of the country to console the ancestral spirits. In recent years they have shed their religious coloring and become a summer leisure event. During this period in August, there is an enormous exodus of city people returning to their family homes in the country, as they combine summer holidays with visiting the ancestral graves.

Bon dance.

DAIMONJI BONFIRE -Daimonji okuribi-

The Daimonji Bonfire is held in Kyoto on August 16. It features a fire which is burned in the shape of an enormous Chinese character signifying "great," on the side of a hill called Nyoigatake. The fire can be seen all over Kyoto. Four other hills also burn fires in other shapes on the same evening. The fires are lit at the end of the Bon season to farewell the ancestral spirits as they return to the other world. Families which preserve traditional customs will also light farewell bonfires at their gates, miniature versions of the large-scale Daimonji Okuribi.

The Daimonji Bonfire, Kyoto.

The Emperor and the Empress honoring the war-dead.

KOSHIEN BASEBALL

On August 8 the All-Japan High School Baseball Championship Tournament, sponsored by Asahi Shimbun Publishing Co. and the Japan High School Baseball Federation, gets under way at the Koshien Stadium near Osaka. Forty-nine teams representing every prefecture take part; they are selected after playoffs between the more than 4,000 participating schools. The event began in 1915, with seventy-three schools participating. The tournament lasts fourteen days, and is followed avidly by people all over the country rooting for their local team of shaven-headed young players. Spectators, composed of students from the schools, fielding teams, follow each point with joy or despondency, depending on which team scores, and if defeat comes,

THE ANNIVERSARY OF THE END OF WORLD WAR II

On August 15, 1945, Japan surrendered unconditionally to the United States, the United Kingdom, and other allied nations, bringing the Second World War to a close. The end of the war is commemorated, together with the memorial days marking the atomic bombings of Hiroshima (August 6) and Nagasaki (August 9), as a pledge by the Japanese people never to wage war again. On August 15 the government holds a memorial service for the war dead in the presence of the emperor. The service is attended by around eight thousand people, including relatives of the dead, the prime minister, and foreign representatives. The pledge for peace is renewed, and one minute's silence is held from midday. The Japanese people at first thought of themselves as victims of the war, but have begun more recently to speak about the importance of acknowledging they caused great damage to neighboring countries during the war's course.

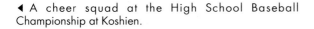

◀ A cheer squad at the High School Baseball Championship at Koshien.

AUG

AWA DANCE -Awa odori-

The Awa Odori is held at Tokushima over four days between August 12-15. Originally a form of Bon dance performed to console the spirits of the ancestors, the festival is thought to have originated in the dancing that accompanied the revelry permitted by Hachisuka Iemasa(1558-1639), the lord of Awa (Tokushima), to celebrate the completion of his castle. For four days the townspeople dance unrestrainedly through the streets to the accompaniment of boisterous music. During the Edo period, the lords of Awa feared that the dance might spur riots which would bring the wrath of the shogunate upon them, and banned it several times. The Awa Odori is also known as the "Fool's Dance," from its song : "You're a fool if you dance, and a fool if you watch, so since you're a fool anyway, you might as well dance!"

The Awa Dance (both photographs).

SEP

DISASTER PREVENTION DAY

September 1, Disaster Prevention Day, commemorates the Tokyo Earthquake of September 1, 1923 and is intended to make people aware of precautions they should take in regard to potential earthquakes and other disasters. On this day fire departments conduct evacuation and fire-extinguishing drills with local residents. There were about 100,000 lives lost in the Tokyo Earthquake, mostly due to fire. An earthquake of the same scale is predicted for Tokyo again some time in the future, but in a country as small as Japan there are few places to escape to.

Drill to train people to put out fires in their earliest stage.

Safety drill by means of a simulated earthquake.

Respect for the Aged Day

September 15 has been a national holiday known as Respect for the Aged Day since 1966. It is defined as the celebration of long life, the day when all can show their love and respect for old people, remembering that it was they who for many years sustained society. The average life expectancy in Japan is around eighty years, and centenarians number a few thousand. This makes Japan one of the world's longest-lived societies. On this day people pray for the health and long life of the old, and express thanks for their efforts. Various functions for the entertainment of the elderly in all parts of Japan mark the occasion. A large number of local governments present old people with money or gifts on this day.

Old people playing gate-ball.

A typhoon.

TYPHOONS

The gale-force winds and rain that come into being in equatorial regions and then bear down on countries on the East Asian seaboard, including Japan, are called "typhoons." They affect Japan particularly between the beginning of September and the beginning of October ; on an average five or six hit Japan directly every year. The largest ever recorded, the Muroto typhoon, came ashore at Cape Muroto in Shikoku on September 21, 1934, with winds at their greatest intensity reaching 61 meters per second. The death toll was 2,700. The Ise Bay typhoon which hit on September 26, 1959, also caused enormous damage. In the United States hurricanes are given people's names, but in Japan typhoons are numbered in the order they arise. It is not at all unusual for the numbering to exceed twenty. Typhoons cause anxiety to farmers for the potential damage they can do to rice, apple, and other crops, but in another sense they are a blessing for the bounty of rainwater they

Typhoon damage at the Itsukushima Shrine, a National Treasure, in 1991.

bring. In recent years there have been many instances of flash flooding and large-scale damage caused by typhoons even though no warning had been issued. This suggests an environmental problem arising out of indiscriminate land-use.

SEP

MOUNTED ARCHERY -*Yabusame*-

The festival of the Tsurugaoka Hachiman Shrine in Kamakura is held between September 14-16. The traditional mounted archery contest called *yabusame* occurs on the last day. This style of archery has existed since the twelfth century. Three archers mounted on galloping horses and dressed in the garb of warriors of that time shoot arrows at three targets 260 meters apart. The event recalls the training in military arts undertaken by the samurai of old.

Yabusame. A rider looses an arrow at the target.

CHRYSANTHEMUM DOLLS

In China, the ninth day of the ninth lunar month was celebrated as the Chrysanthemum Festival, and it was marked by the custom of drinking chrysanthemum wine, made by a special distillation method. The day was made an official event of the Japanese court at the beginning of the ninth century. The chrysanthemum, long a symbol of nobility, comprises the Imperial crest. It is thought that to drink dew that has collected on its petals is efficacious for gaining long life. During the Edo period, people began making "chrysanthemum dolls," figures with the features of popular actors wearing clothes made of chrysanthemums. Today, the Chrysanthemum Doll display at the Ryogoku Kokugikan is an annual autumn event. Department stores and amusement parks also display chrysanthemum dolls representing a particular theme, such as characters from that year's popular historical drama on NHK (Japan's national broadcasting system).

Chrysanthemum dolls representing famous historical figures.

MOON VIEWING -Tsukimi-

On the night of the full moon falling around September 25 (the 15th of the 8th month in the lunar calendar), people erect a small altar on the outside corridor of the house or in the garden so that it faces the direction of the rising moon, place a vase of *susuki* (eulalia) upon it, and make offerings of rice dumplings (*dango*), sweet potatoes, chestnuts, and sometimes sacred sake (*omiki*). The susuki are said to represent ears of rice. Whereas in Japan moon viewing is a rite to pray for a good harvest, in China, from where the custom derived, it had more literary associations. The moon is a favorite topic for *haiku* poetry. There is an old tradition that the markings on the surface of the moon depict two rabbits pounding rice, but since the Apollo landing, the image that the Japanese have about the moon has changed considerably.

Moon viewing.

73

OCT

THE RED FEATHER APPEAL

The Red Feather Appeal, manned by over 2 million volunteers from all parts of the country, is held between October 1 and December 31. During that time Boy and Girl Scouts, students and housewives stand outside stations and on street corners from early morning, calling out "*Onegaishimasu*" (Please give us your help), and businessmen wear red feathers in their lapels. The donations are used, for example, to assist welfare efforts for old people, children, and the handicapped. The media delight in featuring stories and pictures of famous figures, such as the Minister of Health, actresses, and sumo wrestlers adding their voices to the appeal.

HEALTH-SPORTS DAY

Autumn is considered a season conducive to activity, as such expressions as "the season of sports" and "the season for reading books" imply. October 10 is a national holiday called Health-Sports Day. It was promulgated in 1966 to encourage the enjoyment of sport and the cultivation of a healthy mind and body and the day was chosen to commemorate the opening

High school girls calling for donations during the Red Feather Appeal.

ceremony of the Tokyo Olympics of 1964. On that day people can have physical examinations, and participate in tug-o'-war competitions, walking marathons and sports meetings held by communities, schools, and companies. The autumn meet of the annual National Sports Festival (Kokutai) is held at the beginning of October, and competitors from all prefectures vie for the Emperor's and the Empress's Cups. The National Sports Festival consists of three seasonal meets, in winter, summer, and autumn.

The opening ceremony of the Tokyo Olympiad, 1964.

An elementary school sports day.

Hiking during the autumn foliage season.

VIEWING AUTUMN FOLIAGE -Momijigari-

Momijigari is the traditional pastime of enjoying the changing colors of the leaves when the hills are covered with the tints of autumn. Autumn is long in Japan, and because there are many trees, like the maple, whose leaves turn yellow or red at that season, Japan is considered to have some of the most beautiful autumn foliage in the world. Large numbers of families use their free time to go on outings to mountains during this season, and they eat their boxed lunches while enjoying the view.

Like cherry viewing in spring, the custom of viewing autumn foliage grew up among the court nobility during the Heian period. The nobles played music and composed poetry as they delighted in the beautiful colors of the autumn leaves. Unlike the rowdiness that accompanies cherry viewing, viewing autumn foliage is a quiet pastime, allowing thoughtful people to reflect upon change in the natural world.

OCT

NAGASAKI KUNCHI

The Nagasaki Kunchi is a festival held between October 7-9 in the districts centering on the city's Suwa shrines. Tradition says that it was started by the magistrate of Nagasaki with the support of the shogunate as a means of turning the townspeople away from Christianity, which was considered harmful to the feudal system. The Dragon Dance, designated an intangible cultural property, is performed by ten young men wearing Chinese dress and supporting a ten-meter-long dragon on poles, to the accompaniment of the loud music of an assortment of Chinese instruments, including drums, gongs, and trumpets. They are led in a weaving dance by a juggler. Since Nagasaki was the only port in Japan opened to foreign ships during the period of isolation between the 17th and 19th centuries and therefore acted as Japan's door to the rest of the world, its festivals contain many foreign elements not to be seen in other regions. The word "*Kunchi*" stands for the ninth of the ninth month (*kugatsu kokonoka*) ; the festival appears to have been originally associated with the chrysanthemum festival.

The Dragon Dance.

OCT

FESTIVAL OF THE AGES -Jidai matsuri-

The Jidai Matsuri is one of the three great festivals of Kyoto. The festival of the Heian Shrine, it is held on October 22. It is a relatively new event, dating from 1895 when the shrine was built to commemorate the 1,100th anniversary of the city. Twenty-seven years previously the capital had been shifted from Kyoto to Tokyo, and the festival was devised to return some of its traditional vigor to the old city. A procession of people dressed in costumes representing each period between the Heian period and the Meiji Restoration of 1868 leaves the old Imperial Palace grounds, and circles the city before reaching the Heian Shrine. The costumes of the various historical periods are valuable as material to study the history of Japanese manners and customs.

Army drum and fife band at the time of the Meiji Restoration (19th century).

Warriors of the Civil War period (16th century).

Women in the dress of the Edo period (18th-19th centuries).

Women in the costume of the Heian period (10th-11th centuries).

NOV

CULTURE DAY

Culture Day, November 3, is a national holiday. It was promulgated in 1948 to promote culture and the love of peace and freedom, and is the occasion for arts festivals and cultural awards. Before the war the day commemorated Emperor Meiji's birthday. Decorations for cultural achievements were inaugurated in 1937 ; they are awarded to those who have made contributions to culture in the sciences and the arts. On this day some four thousand people receive decorations for their services to the nation or the public. The decorations, including those for cultural merit, are ranked in 28 grades.

Decoration for cultural achievement.

Recipients of awards for cultural achievement after receiving their decoration from the Emperor.

A university campus festival.

SCHOOL FESTIVALS

Between the end of October and the end of November, universities and high schools hold festivals. The school festival is one of the biggest events of the year for students, and it is important for its role in strengthening feelings of solidarity. The campus is dotted with small student-run booths selling food such as hamburgers and fried noodles, and visitors from other universities, high school students, and graduates crowd the scene. During the festival the various student clubs with cultural interests give exhibitions or performances—choir, band, drama, tea ceremony, flower arrangement, and so on—while other clubs give displays of Japanese archery or dancing, for instance. In recent years many universities have been attracting large numbers of visitors by screening famous films or by inviting popular singers or well-known cultural figures and holding concerts and lectures.

An exhibition of paper silhouettes made by junior high school students.

Labor Thanksgiving Day

November 23 is a national holiday called Labor Thanksgiving Day. It was instituted in 1948 to honor labor, celebrate production and make people aware of the gratitude they owe one another. From ancient times the solemn rite of Niinamesai was performed on this day. The emperor celebrates the rice harvest by dedicating the new rice to the deities and then eating that rice in communion with them. This association gives the present Labor Thanksgiving Day the coloring of an agricultural festival, and even today shrines all over the country celebrate Niinamesai on this day.

NOV

SHICHIGOSAN

Shichigosan is observed on November 15 ; on that day boys and girls are taken to shrines to give thanks for their healthy growth so far and to pray for their future good fortune. The name of the festival derives from the children's ages and the stages in their growth. Odd numbers are considered auspicious in Japan. The custom of *Shichigosan* became popular during the Edo period, particularly in Edo (the present Tokyo), but as it spread to other areas, local rituals stressed certain of the years. Though there are variations according to locality, in general three- and five-year-old boys and three- and seven-year-old girls are taken, dressed in their best clothes, by their parents to the shrine of their local deity (*ujigami*). Stalls in the grounds of the shrines sell souvenirs such as good-luck talismans and pink and white *chitose-ame* ("thousand-year candy") in colorful bags.

The ritual to welcome the deities.

The Hakone Daimyo Parade.
Foot soldiers carrying luggage.

HAKONE DAIMYO PARADE

The Hakone Daimyo Parade, held on November 3, recreates the formal procession of an Edo period daimyo (feudal lord) crossing the Hakone mountains. Around 250 people, wearing clothes of the period, proceed slowly up the old stone-paved road that still exists near the town. Men dressed as *ashigaru* (foot soldiers) give displays of wielding lances, and other traditional military skills. During the Edo period the daimyo were required by the shogunate to travel to Edo every other year from their domains; the Hakone Daimyo Parade recalls the scale of their journey.

Festival of the Gods being Present
-Kamiari matsuri-

The Grand Shrine of Izumo in the town of Taisha, Shimane Prefecture, is dedicated to Okuninushi no Mikoto, regarded as the deity of marriage. The shrine is built according to the old-

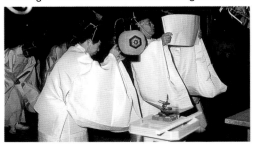

The ritual to welcome the deities.

est style of shrine architecture in the country. Large numbers of unmarried men and women come to the shrine praying to find a marriage partner. Those who are happily married also visit the shrine to give thanks for their fortune and pray that their love may continue. As a result Izumo Shrine is always crowded with newlyweds. The period October 11-17 (according to the lunar calendar, now November) has long been believed to be the time when the gods from every part of Japan gather at Izumo Shrine, and a number of solemn rituals are performed for them. This is the meaning of "*Kamiari*," the gods being gathered together at Izumo. For this reason, the lunar tenth month in other parts of Japan was called *Kannazuki*, the month without gods.

NOV

ROOSTER FAIRS -Tori no ichi-

The Tori no Ichi is held on the days of the rooster (*tori*) in November (which occur twice or three times during the month depending on the year) in the various shrines around the country dedicated to Otori Myojin, the god of good luck. During the festival, booths selling *kumade* (rakes) are set up in the street leading to the shrine, and vendors attract visitors by their lively banter as they extol the virtues of the colorful *kumade*, considered to bring about business prosperity by "raking in" good fortune. The deity of the Otori shrines was worshiped in the past by warriors as the guardian of success in battle. He eventually became the god of good luck, venerated in particular by people in the hotel and restaurant business.

Crowds at the Rooster Fair. ▶

A decorated rake displayed in the home.

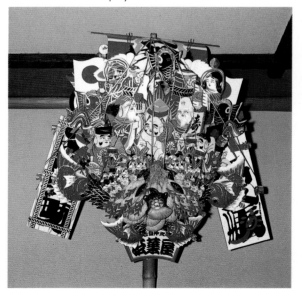

DEC

CHICHIBU NIGHT FESTIVAL

The 300-year-old festival of the Chichibu Shrine, in the city of Chichibu, Saitama Prefecture, takes place on December 3-4. During the day Kabuki performances are given on the festival floats; at night the floats are hung with lanterns and make a beautiful sight. The festival reaches its climax on the night of the third. Six floats rumble out of the shrine to the accompaniment of small drums, flutes, and gongs, parade some two kilometers through the streets, and at the end rush at speed up a steep slope with a 30 degree gradient. The men strain with the effort of it all. If they relax their attention even for an instant, the 7.5-ton float will slip and fall. The drums and flutes combine to make even louder music, as if to encourage the men. When the floats, their weight making the ground reverberate, reach the top, those watching all applaud, and brilliant fireworks explode to light up the night sky. Like numerous other festivals in Japan, this was originally a rite to pray for a bountiful rice harvest.

Kabuki performances by local people during the day.

The Chichibu Night Festival. Despite the cold, people turn out in large numbers.

THE EMPEROR'S BIRTHDAY

The present Emperor (Akihito) was born on December 23, 1933. Since 1990 this day has been a national holiday, the Emperor's Birthday. During the morning the Emperor receives the congratulations of members of the imperial family, the Prime Minister, the speakers of the Houses of Representatives and Councillors, and the Chief Justice of the Supreme Court, in a ceremony known as "*Shukuga no Gi.*" This is followed by the "*Enkai no Gi,*" a banquet to which one hundred representatives of various fields are invited. In the afternoon there is held a celebratory tea party attended by the ambassadors of over one hundred countries, with their wives. During the time when militarism was dominant in the reign of the present Emperor's father, Emperor Showa, the emperor was revered as a divinity (*arahitogami,* "living god") and many countries regarded him as the supreme commander in a war of aggression. In 1946 Emperor Showa renounced his divinity, and under the postwar constitution became "the symbol of the state and the unity of the people." The present emperor fell in love with his wife, the commoner daughter of the chairman of a flour milling company, on the tennis court. They have three children, two boys and a girl. The Emperor is respected by the Japanese as being in touch with the people, seeking a more open life for the imperial family and not subscribing necessarily to the established traditions of the imperial household, as instanced, for example, in the way his children have been brought up. Japanese legend says

The Emperor receiving the congratulations of the people.

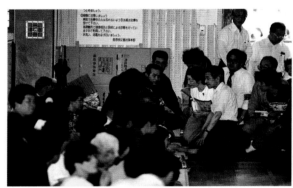

The Emperor and the Empress giving encouragement to victims of a volcanic eruption.

The Emperor's enthronement ceremony, November, 1990.

that the first emperor, Jimmu, ascended the throne in 660 B.C.; the present emperor is 125th in direct line from him.

The Imperial family.

Crown Prince Naruhito and Masako Owada, a Harvard-educated diplomat, announcing their engagement at a press conference in January 1993.

Emperor Showa, who died in 1989.

DEC

CHRISTMAS

The majority of Japanese are not Christian, and Christmas has entered their lives not as a religious feast but as an exotic festival. Shopping districts hold Christmas bargain sales, and the sound of "Jingle Bells" can be heard everywhere. Children eagerly await their "presents from Santa Claus" which are placed beside them as they sleep. Homes with young children decorate Christmas trees and eat Christmas cake and other festive food. Some young people hold Christmas parties for friends, acquaintances, and associates, and in recent years it has become increasingly popular among young couples to spend Christmas Eve partying luxuriously at a hotel, or something similar, a tendency deplored by thinking people.

YEAR-END PARTIES -Bonenkai-

Between the middle of December and the end of the month two important events occur. The first is a massive cleaning effort in homes and businesses in preparation for the new year. The second is the year-end party, a noisy affair where everyone eats, drinks and sings and forgets about all the trials and tribulations of the past year. At this time many businessmen are occupied every night attending year-end parties held by companies, neighborhood associations, and friends. Year-end parties are deemed important by Japanese society because they serve to strengthen the bonds between people, confirm the sense of company solidarity, and act as a measure of the vitality of the organization.

A Christmas tree decorates the streets.

Salaried workers at a year-end party.

A family seated around the *kotatsu*.

KOTATSU

It is impossible to think of winter in Japan without the *kotatsu*, a form of heater attached to the wooden frame of a Japanese table, over which is draped a quilted cover and topped by the table surface. Family members sit around it, their feet snug under the table and the quilt tucked up around them, to eat their meals, drink tea, watch television, or play cards. Sitting around the *kotatsu*, watching television and eating *mikan* (tangerines) is the favorite depiction of everyday life during winter.

RICE-POUNDING -*Mochitsuki*-

At the New Year people eat *mochi*, cakes of glutinous rice, instead of ordinary rice. It is believed that the deity of the incoming year (*toshigami*) resides within the *mochi*, and to eat it assures a healthy and prosperous year. The mochi can be eaten in *ozoni*, the festive soup, or grilled and eaten with *shoyu* and *nori*, dried seaweed. In the past most households possessed a mortar and pestle, and so *mochi*

A family pounds rice.

was pounded at home. Today though it tends to be sold in vacuum packs at supermarkets, and it is increasingly rare to see traditional rice-pounding.

Women enjoying *karaoke*.

Karaoke

No Japanese party is complete without *karaoke*. The expression means literally "empty orchestra," and refers to a prerecorded tape of the accompaniment to a song for people to sing to. It rapidly became popular during the 1970s, and the sight of people holding a microphone absorbed in their song became a common sight in bars and restaurants as well as in the home. Today, film backing is provided by laser disc, and the words of the songs are shown on a television screen. *Karaoke* has now become popular in many countries overseas. In Japan *karaoke* contributes to some extent to the ever-present problem of sound pollution.

DEC

BATTLEDORE MARKET -Hagoita ichi-

Hanetsuki is a game like badminton played by girls during the New Year holiday season. It has a history of at least five hundred years. The making of lavishly decorated battledores dates from the end of the 17th century, when designs made of silk collage based on the faces of kabuki actors were particularly popular. Today *hanetsuki* has completely disappeared from the urban landscape, but the craft of making elaborate battledores to be used as ornaments remains alive.

Battledores are decorated with the faces of beautiful women or of popular Kabuki actors.

Crowds throng the Battledore Market. ▶

DEC

NAMAHAGE

Namahage is a custom observed on New Year's Eve in Oga, Akita Prefecture. Two or three young men, called *namahage*, wearing straw capes and fierce demon masks, carrying heavy cleavers and wooden pails, and uttering fierce shouts, visit each house in the village to warn children not to be lazy. Very young children cry in fright. The head of each family gives the *namahage* sake and rice-cakes.

Namahage go from house to house.

These demons are in fact the distant ancestors visiting to give notice of the coming of the new season, and their menacing aspect derives from the hope that children can be dissuaded from laziness and encouraged to try their best.

OMISOKA

The year closes for government offices and large companies on December 28. This day is spent in cleaning up the office, rather than on the regular round of work. At home, the family spends the next three days in a rush of cleaning, shopping, and cooking, preparing for the New Year. Everything is finished by the night of the 31st, when most people watch the annual Red and White contest between male and female singers and entertainers on television and eat *toshikoshi soba* ("year-crossing noodles") in the hope that good fortune and life may be extended like the long and thin noodles. At midnight Buddhist temples in every district ring their bells 108 times (*joya no kane*) to expel the 108 defilements and greet the new year. Radio and television broadcast live the peals rung at famous temples around the country. The custom of *joya no kane* entered Japan during the Edo period and is based upon a Buddhist ritual that was performed in China. Many people set off to make their first shrine and temple visits of the year with the sound of the *joya no kane* ringing in their ears.

95

JAPANESE WEDDINGS

The decorated envelope in which is placed money for the bride and groom.

Marriage

Marriages are basically of two types, that between two people who have married for love, and that where the couple has been introduced through the offices of a go-between (*nakodo*). In the past the majority of marriages were arranged (*miai*), but today "love-marriages" make up 70% of the total. All the same, businesses specializing in computerized matchmaking are fairly popular. In some country villages, men have been unable to find marriage partners locally because most of the women have left to go to work in the cities, and have brought brides from other Asian countries, such as the Philippines and Korea. The average age at which people first marry is steadily rising ; at the moment it is 28 for men and 26 for women, the second highest in the world after Sweden. One result of this trend has been a decline in the birthrate. Most newlyweds favor such places as the west coast of the United States, Hawaii, Europe or Australia for their honeymoon.

The reception.

Wedding Gifts

People invited to a wedding reception make gifts of money to the newlywed couple. The money is placed inside specially decorated envelopes and handed to guests who have been designated to be in charge of greeting those invited and who man a table set at the entrance to the reception room. At this time guests sign their names, using the traditional brush, in a special book for recording their names. It is a widespread custom in Japan to give gifts of money as an expression of one's good wishes and concern.

A Japanese style wedding ceremony.

Wedding Ceremonies

Most wedding ceremonies are conducted according to Shinto rites, immediately before the wedding reception. The Shinto priest purifies the participants, the groom reads the wedding contract, and the bride and groom ritually exchange sacred *sake* poured into cups by a shrine attendant (*miko*) and place wedding rings on each other's fingers. Though Christian ceremonies have become increasingly popular in recent years, Shinto rites are still overwhelmingly followed.

JAPANESE FUNERALS

The altar.

The hearse takes the deceased to the crematorium.

Funerals

When a person dies, a candle is lit at his or her head, a vase of flowers and offerings of food and water placed on a small table, and close relatives and friends come to pay their last respects, burning incense and bowing toward the deceased. In the evening a Buddhist priest comes to recite sutras and give the person a posthumous Buddhist name (*kaimyo*).

The scene outside the place where a funeral is being held.

The body is generally placed in the coffin the following day, and it has become the custom recently to fill the remaining space with different kinds of flowers. That evening the wake is held ; neighbors and acquaintances visit with gifts of money (*koden*), and offer incense at the altar which has been set up, and on which a photo of the deceased occupies the center space. The funeral service takes place the next day, at home, in a temple, or at a funeral hall. During the service, a Buddhist priest chants sutras, a funeral address is read, and incense is offered by all participants. Following it, close relatives accompany the coffin to the crematorium.

The ashes (actually pieces of bones) are placed in a jar (*kotsutsubo*), and are interred after a specific period, either 35 or 49 days. Memorial services are held on the first, third, seventh, and seventeenth years after the death; at that time relatives make offerings to the deceased and afterwards eat together. Most people make either the 33rd or the 50th memorial service the last. After that the deceased is considered to have become a deity (*kami*), the protector of his or her descendants.

Koden

People attending wakes (*tsuya*) and funeral services take with them money (*koden*, literally "incense money") placed in a special white envelope tied with knotted black and white strings. The money is used to contribute toward funeral expenses.

An envelope for *koden*.

THE LIFE OF A SALARIED WORKER

A day in the life of a salaried worker

The day of the salaried worker (*sarariman* in Japanese) begins early. Most companies start work between eight and nine o'clock, but because an hour's commute is not unusual, most people leave the house before seven. Many company employees gulp down a hasty breakfast of noodles or suchlike at the station. The train journey is valuable time for it enables commuters to glance through the newspaper, getting an idea of the main stories and picking out useful information. What with the multiple changes of transport that are perhaps necessary and the tremendous crowds of the rush hour, many people arrive at their office exhausted. Even when work is finished it is not unusual for workers not to return home until around midnight. Some go off

Rush hour.

to drink with colleagues and friends, and others go and entertain company guests. Taking out company guests for golf on Sundays is also part of the work round.

Characteristics of life within the company

1. **Management and the ordinary worker** There is no great gap between management and the ordinary worker. Offices, car parks, cafeterias, toilets and uniforms are all the same, because of the value placed on mutual understanding and a harmonious workplace.

2. **Business cards** Businessmen always exchange cards when they first meet. These cards contain, besides the person's name, his company, his section, and his position.

3. **The company as family** The company is not merely a place where a person works and receives money for his labor. It is supported by a sense of family among those who work in it; management and labor cooperate for the sake of the company's wellbeing, and if the company prospers, so do its employees. Because of the system of lifetime employment, employees are not readily laid off when business is bad. Employees maintain the same loyalty to the company whether times are good or bad, and work hard for its prosperity. The company also promotes friendly relations through staff sports meetings, company outings, and in-company cultural festivals.

4. **Salary and bonuses** Salary is paid monthly. The amount basically depends on the length of time the employee has been working with the company, though there are differences according to position and type of work, and there is also payment according to ability. Most firms pay bonuses twice a year, in June and December. Salary and bonuses are paid in most cases by bank transfer. One of the

reasons for the husband's loss of authority in the home is attributed to the disappearance of the old custom of the man receiving his wages in cash and taking them home to hand over to his wife.

5. **Overtime** Though companies specify the number of paid holidays to which an employee is entitled, employees rarely take the whole of that entitlement. Because the Japanese have been accused of working too hard, large firms in particular are acting to implement a working year of 1,800 hours and are reducing the hours worked. There are a number of reasons why employees rarely take all the paid holidays they are entitled to and why the amount of overtime worked is so great.

(a) The atmosphere within the company is not conducive to taking paid holidays.

(b) Workers want the overtime allowance.

(c) Workers do not wish to leave the office before their superiors.

(d) Workers want to attract the attention of their superiors by their zeal for work.

(e) Work is enjoyable.

(f) Due to the poor housing conditions that most live in, workers do not have any place to relax alone when they get home.

Reasons why the Japanese work hard

From ancient times a social consciousness which regards labor as an ethical value has permeated the Japanese people as a whole. It has been supported by Buddhist and Confucian teachings concerning the fullness of a life in which labor has been undertaken sincerely and painstakingly, and by the experience of an agricultural people that life cannot be sustained without hard work. Another factor is the abolition of the strict social class system of the Edo period with the coming of the social revolution of the Meiji Restoration (1868). As a result, status and

Salaried workers taking a walk during the lunch break.

class lost their importance, and people felt that anyone could advance to a high place in society if only he worked hard. Today, not only salaried workers but people at all levels of the social spectrum share the trait of seeking to advance by working or studying to the best of their ability.

Members who happen to belong to the same group, defined in terms of workplace, will pull together when faced with a difficult problem or an urgent task and put aside their private concerns. This sense of being destined as it were to being a member of the particular community of the company is partly responsible for the development of the "company man" and the excess of overtime worked. All the same growing numbers of people are beginning to demand that they be able to enjoy a more leisured life, one dictated by their own ideas and interests rather than those of an outside agency. Seeking psychological satisfaction, young people are increasingly choosing jobs for reasons other than the salary, such as vacation time, the firm's image, and the nature of the working environment.

MODERN WOMEN

Working women

Every year more and more Japanese women are appearing in the work force. Some reasons for this trend include :(i) the popularization of ideas of male and female equality in Japan, as in other advanced societies,(ii) the increased social consciousness of women as they go further and further in their education,(iii) the decrease in the number of children a woman has to care for, and(iv) the need for women to work in order to alleviate the labor shortage caused by Japan's modernization and economic development.

The life of a female office clerk

Women are making remarkable inroads into society, and among university graduates, even more women than men are seeking employment. All the same, some 70 percent of these women are working as office assistants, the ubiquitous OL ("office lady"), who pours tea and does odd jobs such as making copies. There is a great deal of dissatisfaction, since office assistants are seldom given responsible posts. Women with an eye on specialized work are increasing, and there is a heightening tendency for them to prefer a self-fulfilling job over the joys of marriage. As a result, women are marrying much later.

Marriage and work

A large number of women wish to continue to work after they marry. The birth rate is declining, and now the average is 1.5 children per family. Reasons for the decline include poor housing conditions,

A housewife working part-time.

A young working woman.

the high cost of education, and the lack of facilities for working mothers. The child-care leave law passed in 1991 allows both men and women to take up to one year off to look after a newborn child. The government gives child allowances and is actively encouraging women to have more children, but many difficulties remain for women trying to juggle home and work, for child care facilities and the work environment are far from ideal.

For many women with older children, going out to work is not just a means of supplementing the household budget but an opportunity to seek mental independence and a goal in life outside the home. The power of modern women is being recognized, to the extent there are some who would call this the age of Woman.

THE LIFE OF A MOTHER

A mother hands her daughter her packed lunch.

The busy round of a mother

It is impossible to comment on the life of mothers in a wholesale manner. Those mothers who hold down a job outside the home are incredibly busy. In families where both husband and wife go out to work, the husband's understanding and cooperation regarding child care and household chores are essential. The life of women whose children are under school age, in particular, is a constant battle from morning to night. Mothers prepare meals, make packed lunches, clean the house, do the washing, keep household accounts, and go shopping, as well as raise children, help with homework and practice, attend PTA meetings at school, go to children's activities, maintain good relations with the neighbors, and act as officers in the local neighborhood associations. In fact the entire responsibility for daily life falls on the mother's shoulders. It is expected that the wife manages the family's budget. She gets up early in the morning to make breakfast for her husband and children, and packs their lunches thinking of their nutrition. She is also ready to serve meals whenever they are needed, for her children studying after school at special classes, or for her husband when he comes home late from work.

Enjoying spare time

Young wives who do not work are free during the day when their husbands and children are out of the house. Their most popular pastimes are visiting friends, playing tennis, or doing aerobics. Many of the housewives who hold the purse-strings of the family keep steadily-growing "secret savings" (*hesokuri*). Salaried workers have their earnings transferred into their bank accounts, and the husband receives an allowance from the wife. In middle age she gives psychological support to her adolescent children as they begin to make decisions about their future, and she is responsible for bringing up the children and for their discipline. Yet once the children are past infancy, many women begin taking classes in something or go out to work. Women who have lived through the hardships of the immediate postwar era are, like their husbands who have supported Japan's rapid development, patient and hard-working. Women go to culture centers, where they improve their knowledge or cultivate a hobby, and at times take trips or visit hot springs. Those with such time on their hands are usually the newly-married or women whose children have finished their education.

Mothers attending an aerobics class.

THE LIFE OF CHILDREN

High school students.

Elementary school students

Children attending public elementary schools usually live within walking distance of the school. Four 45-minute classes are held in the morning, and, depending on age, either one or two periods in the afternoon. Children clean their classrooms and the school premises after classes. Older children attend clubs when school is over. After school, many children go to coaching classes, play sports (like swimming, tennis or soccer), or take piano, violin, ballet or *soroban* (abacus) lessons. In the cities, children who will be sitting for the entrance examinations to elite private junior high schools may attend special coaching classes every day. A lot of children wear glasses, their eyesight weakened by too much study.

Elementary school children wearing headbands printed with the words "examination success" taking a trial examination.

Senior high school students

Senior high schools are of two types, the general and the vocational, of which there are the full-day type and the part-time type. Students must pass examinations to enter. Most schools require that a uniform be worn, and school life is governed by many regulations. Hair must be worn in a certain style, and skirts of a certain length. So minute are the regulations that there is a growing demand for the more severe ones to be revised. Most schools forbid students to take part-time jobs, requiring them to devote themselves to their studies rather than making money. After school there are club activities. These clubs give special displays at the annual school sports day or culture festival. Sports and cultural activities, such as baseball, judo, volleyball, swimming, choral work and English debate, are encouraged at a national level by Japan-wide competitions.

Students studying for entrance exams

Student life varies considerably depending on the direction the student takes. Those who are aiming at university must pass the barrier of the entrance examinations. A well-known expression has it that students who sleep for four hours a night or less will pass their exams, but those who sleep for five or more will fail. Studying for university entrance examinations is almost synonymous with little sleep and midnight snacks of hot noodles and rice balls.

CHILDREN'S GAMES

Children play traditional games as well as those that have developed more recently.

Traditional games : playing house, playing shops, *origami*, *karuta* (traditional card games), juggling beanbags (girls), *kendama* (cup and ball game), cat's cradle, cards, swings, slides, sand pits, marbles, skipping (singly and in groups), hide and seek, ball games, *Darumasan ga koronda* (like "What's the time, Mr. Wolf") and dodge ball.

Games that have become popular in recent years : video games, game centers, skateboards, soccer, baseball, collecting cards and stickers, etc.

Fewer children are playing games they have devised themselves outdoors. Reasons for this include fewer hours for play, because children are attending coaching schools and after-school classes, the superfluity of material things in their possession, the fewer children in families, and the lack of open areas to play. Children prefer to stay indoors, playing video games, reading comics, and watching television, or to spend their recreation time at game centers. The inclination of children to play passively, indoors and alone, with items that have been ready-made, is increasing.

Playing on a swing.

Skipping.

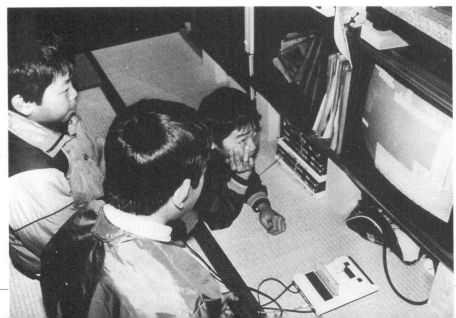
Absorbed in a video game.

THE LIFE OF A JAPANESE PERSON

Birth Most women give birth in a maternity hospital. The child's name is generally chosen by the parents, though in some cases they will ask relatives or a shrine priest to select it.

Omiyamairi *Omiyamairi* is the first formal visit a child pays to the shrine of the local tutelary deity. It usually takes place on the 100th day after birth. Rites are performed to enable the parents to give thanks for the safe delivery of the baby and to pray for his or her continuing wellbeing.

Kindergarten Most children enter neighborhood kindergartens at either three or four.

Shichigosan The Seven-Five-Three festival celebrates the healthy growth of children and takes place at shrines. Parents pray for the continuing wellbeing of their offspring. Though there is some local variation in the custom, in general girls of three and seven years old, and boys of three and five are taken, dressed in their best clothes, by their parents to the shrine to pray.

School education After two or three years at kindergarten, children enter elementary school. Compulsory education consists of six years at elementary school and three at junior high school. Most children continue on to senior high school. Therefore most receive sixteen years of education, and nineteen if we count kindergarten.

Ronin *Ronin* (literally, "masterless warrior") are students who have failed their university entrance examinations and are spending one or two years studying at coaching schools in order to retake them.

Coming-of-age Day Ceremonies to welcome new adults are held all over the country on January 15. Those who have turned twenty over the past year are formally congratulated. It is a time also when the new adults can think about their freedom, their duties and their responsibilities. At the age of twenty, people can legally vote, drink and smoke, but they have also at that time to shoulder the obligations of adults.

The first job High school graduates take their first job at eighteen, and university graduates at twenty-two or three.

Marriage Women are now marrying in their late twenties. Some are preferring to follow a career rather than marry, and since there are fewer marriageable women than men anyway, men are facing difficulties in finding marriage partners.

The housing problem Newlyweds cannot buy a house, because the prices are so high, and it is virtually impossible to aspire to a home in the metropolitan areas of large cities. It is not unusual to find that people live more than two hours commute from their place of work. In recent years there has been a rapid increase in the numbers of long-distance commuters traveling to work by the high speed Shinkansen.

Job transfers Job transfers are part of the life of a salaried worker. Many people are transferred overseas.

Temporary transfers without family Unlike in western countries, it is almost impossible for families to accompany the husband when he is transferred. The biggest factors in this are the problems of education and housing. It is difficult for students to transfer freely from one senior high school to another, and so fathers with children approaching the university entrance examinations are forced to live alone when they are transferred. There are even cases where the husband takes up an overseas posting without his family. Lucky is the father who can spend the weekends with his family. Such cases will continue as long as business keeps expanding.

Child rearing Because the husband is absorbed in his work, the burden of child rearing falls on the wife. The husband has lost his place in the family, and his links with his children have become unavoidably weakened.

Retirement In Japan, 60 is the average age of retirement. According to statistics, many of those approaching 60 would like to work until around 70.

Divorce Divorce is becoming an increasing possibility as the husband approaches retirement, and is around the home more. When her children become independent, the wife is questioning the meaning of her life, and realizes that there is very little that binds her and her husband together. As women become financially autonomous, the divorce rate will rise.

Living on a pension Those who have contributed to a pension fund for more than 25 years receive an annuity after they turn 65. All the same, it is extremely difficult financially to spend one's old age supported by this annuity alone.

Kanreki, kiju, beiju Just as the growth of children is celebrated by a number of festivals, old age is congratulated at certain set times—at 60 (*kanreki*, marking the completion of a sexagenary cycle, and the beginning of a new one), at 77 (*kiju*, celebration of long life), and 88 (*beiju*, celebration of long life). People can become members of old people's clubs once they have turned 70, and take part in

service activities in the community and in sports such as gateball, a Japanese version of croquet.

The Life of a Japanese Person

Omiyamairi: On the 100th day after birth, parents pray that their baby will grow up healthy.

Kindergarten: Kindergartens, to train infants in social and academic skills, take children from the age of three or four.

Shichigosan: Girls of three and seven Boys of three and five

School education: Elementary school starts at the age of six (six years) Junior high school starts at the age of twelve (three years) Senior high school starts at the age of fifteen (three years) Technical college starts at the age of fifteen (five years) University starts at the age of eighteen (generally four years)

Coming-of-Age Day: On January 15, the official adulthood of twenty-year-olds is celebrated. The young people are reminded of their duties and responsibilities as adults.

The first job: Young people may start work at fifteen, after they have completed their nine years of compulsory education at elementary and junior high school. Most people begin work between the ages of eighteen and twenty-two.

Marriage: The average age for the first marriage is 25.9 years for women and 28.4 years for men (1991). Men face problems finding marriage partners because the number of unmarried males exceeds that of unmarried females.

Retirement: Seventy per cent of Japanese companies require their employees to retire at sixty. With the average life expectancy of men at 76 years and that of women at 82 years, the life after retirement is very long.

Kanreki, etc.
Kanreki: the 60th birthday
Kiju: the 77th birthday
Beiju: the 88th birthday

JAPANESE INNS AND HOT SPRINGS

The Japanese inn (ryokan)

The *ryokan* provides overnight accommodation for travelers. In contrast to the western-style hotel, it offers Japanese-style facilities. The rooms are covered with *tatami* (straw matting), and *yukatas* (cotton kimonos) are provided for guests to wear on the premises. Instead of beds, mattresses are rolled out at night on the *tatami* to sleep on. The employees of the *ryokan* wear traditional Japanese clothing, and the meals, which are prepared in the Japanese way, are brought individually to each room. It is the

Family style room service at an inn.

Traditional Japanese dishes served at the inn.

employees who provide the characteristic family-style room service associated with the *ryokan*, and are responsible for greeting and farewelling guests, bringing meals and laying out the bedding.

Hotels have been built in great numbers from the time of the Tokyo Olympics in 1964, and now most *ryokan* near stations have been converted into business hotels. At tourist centers, *ryokan* are turning more to a western type of accommodation, permitting guests to wear shoes indoors, and providing western style rooms with beds and bathrooms. At the same time though there is a trend back to the traditional, and the atmosphere of the Japanese inn surrounded by a Japanese-style garden has an important place in modern urbanizing society.

Unlike city inns, which cater for small functions or to guests staying there on business, inns in hot spring resorts possess large bathrooms, and spacious halls where groups of visitors can eat and drink together. Tourist inns can be found in places of scenic beauty and spots with historical connections.

Hot springs

In Japan, natural springs with a temperature over 25 degrees centigrade are called *onsen*, "hot springs." In European countries designated hot springs are 20 degrees and more, and in the United States, 21.1 degrees (70 degrees F). Perhaps because of its volcanic activity, Japan has more than 2,000 hot spring areas. The popularity of hot springs is in no small way related to the Japanese love for bathing, and tourist resorts have developed around hot springs, sometimes, as in the case of Atami and Beppu, growing into large cities. More than a billion people stay at hot springs annually.

Entrance to an inn.

The lobby of an inn.

An inn garden.

Young and old, men and women alike, delight in visiting hot springs to bathe in the communal baths and enjoy regional cooking at the inns there. Reports about hot springs are featured on television and in women's and travel magazines the year around. Hot springs are also considered to have medicinal value and many people use them for convalescence and rehabilitation, as well as for their effectiveness for stomach complaints, skin diseases, and nervous and gynecological problems.

Outdoor hot springs

Many of Japan's hot springs are to be found outdoors. People bathe naked in these outdoor pools, called *rotenburo*, surrounded by the beauties of nature, often drinking *sake* as they do so. Far from the hustle and bustle of the cities, people find relaxation communicating with others directly and naturally. There are many unique kinds of *rotenburo*, such as those constructed in the sea and in rivers, or those in the basin of a waterfall.

Public baths

Public baths, places where people bathe after paying a fee, grew in popularity between the 14th and 16th centuries. By the latter part of the eighteenth century, they had spread throughout the country, providing an important place for social intercourse among the common people. In modern times the public bath has been an indispensable part of city life, and large numbers existed. Since around 1965 though, most homes have been built with their own bath, resulting in the rapid decline of bath-house customers. As a result many public baths have closed down due to economic difficulty.

People take their own soap and towel to the public bath, which is divided into male and female halves with separate entrances. They pay their money to the proprietor, who sits at a raised desk between the two entrances. After taking off their clothes in the dressing room, they enter the bath proper. Many baths feature large murals of Mt. Fuji. Even today when most homes have their own bath, old people prefer to go to the public bath because it gives them the chance to chat with their friends. The water in the bath is very hot, and many non-Japanese find it too hot to enter.

An outdoor hot spring.

JAPANESE PEOPLE AND THEIR CULTURE

Characteristics of the Japanese people

Racial uniformity : The Japanese, though not a single race in the strictest sense of the word (the Ainu for instance have lived in Japan from ancient times), are, compared with a multiracial society like the United States, racially very uniform, despite a population of 130 million occupying a country smaller than the state of California.

Group consciousness : Because historically the government has regulated life down to the smallest detail, the Japanese tend to think in terms of the group, the society or the nation, rather than the individual. They avoid confrontations with others, and prefer to do whatever others are doing. The harmony of the group is prized, and so those with a strong individuality are regarded as heretical and are ejected from the group. Such thinking is well illustrated by the proverb "A protruding nail should be pounded down."

Group activities : The Japanese like taking part in group activities, such as outings, school trips, sports meetings, radio callisthenics, and organized overseas travel. They feel comfortable within the group ; a current joke has one Japanese saying to another "If everyone crossed the street at the red light, I wouldn't be afraid to cross either!" The ability to act in groups is definitely advantageous when the interests of a company, for example, are to be furthered, since members are able to negate their own individuality for the broader interests of the group.

Uniforms : Most public high school students, and the majority of children from kindergarten age attending private schools, wear uniforms. The acceptance of uniforms is aided by the strength of group consciousness, a tradition which prizes a standardized esthetic, and sheer economic practicality. Many companies even provide uniforms for their employees, and, reflecting the way all ranks work together in the same physical space, there is no difference between the uniforms worn by management and by ordinary workers.

Education : The Japanese are extremely enthusiastic about education. Ninety-nine percent of the school-age population attends school, and 30% of students go on to university. Until the end of the Second World War, all children studied from the same, authorized textbooks. Even today, children use textbooks selected from

Company employees taking part in radio calisthenics. Exercising together with no one out of rhythm, these people seem an apt symbol of Japanese group consciousness with its respect for group activities and discipline.

among a number approved by the Ministry of Education, and, another measure of the preference for uniformity, educators make efforts to ensure that education is kept at a particular level.

The discipline of the group : Elementary school students are divided according to grade, based on age, and relations between older and younger students, and even the language used, are very distinct. The junior-senior relationships fostered in school are in general maintained in society in terms of the seniority rule within companies.

Exclusivity : Because of the way the Japanese form groups at all levels, it can be very hard for outsiders to penetrate the groups. Today though, with more Japanese working abroad and foreigners flowing into Japan than at any other time during Japan's history, there has inevitably been a revolution in ideas among ordinary people as a result of this rapid internationalization. A mark of this growing international consciousness is the greater willingness of people to contribute to overseas charities and to take part in volunteer activities.

Foreign and Japanese students. As links with foreign countries strengthen, the sense of exclusivity of the Japanese is slowly weakening.

The multilayered Japanese culture

Japanese culture is multilayered, marked by the coexistence and merging of completely different influences.

Dress : People normally wear western dress, but on ceremonial occasions Japanese dress is worn as well as western clothing. Those occupations which regard themselves as being especially Japanese, such as restaurants serving Japanese style food, traditional inns, and Sumo, maintain strict adherence to Japanese styles of dress.

Food : People enjoy food and cooking from all over the world. In the home, Chinese and western dishes are every bit as common as Japanese. Restaurants specializing in a particular style of cooking such as Chinese or French are popular, as are fast food outlets selling hamburgers and pizzas.

The home : Western and Japanese elements are mixed in domestic architecture, and most homes blend eastern and western. Kitchens and children's rooms, and the living room in the newer type of home, tend to be western in design. Bathrooms are basically Japanese, but combine western ideas in so far as showers are added. Western style lavatories are now predominant, but they are never to be found in the bathroom, as in America. Even in western style homes, shoes are taken off in the entry hall. At school, also, students generally remove their shoes at the entrance, place them in special racks, and change into indoor shoes. However, it is not usual to remove shoes at universities, companies, and other public institutions.

Elementary school children changing their footwear. It is the custom in the majority of Japanese elementary schools for children to change into indoor shoes at the school's entrance.

UNDERSTANDING JAPANESE PSYCHOLOGY THROUGH LANGUAGE

Dochira made

A common exchange, which does not seem to mean much in logical terms, that is often heard in the street is :

"*Dochira made?*"

(Where are you going?)

"*Chotto soko made*" (Just a little way.)

Of course the answer might just as well be "To the dentist's," or something, and it would be a signal for the beginning of a conversation. In most cases the phrases above are exchanged simply as a greeting and there is no sense of inquisitiveness about the other's behavior. The reaction of non-Japanese to answer such a question with "It's none of your business" is understandable, but incipient anger can easily be avoided with a little knowledge of the cultural background.

Ganbaru

Ganbaru means to carry through one's task, putting up with difficulties and striving to overcome all hardships. The Japanese love the word, and use it all the time. The virtue of *ganbaru* has long been encouraged in Japan, where it is taught as a valuable human attitude. People playing in sports and competitions are urged on before the game with *Ganbatte!*, an idea quite different from the "Good luck" of the English-speaking world. The first word of greeting that new employees utter when taking up their new post is *Ganbarimasu!*, and *Ganbatte!* is what friends call out to newlyweds departing on their honeymoon. When we consider these usages we can only wonder in what sense people are being urged to strive to overcome hardships!

Osewa ni narimasu

When a wife meets her husband's superiors or colleagues, she will always say *Shujin ga osewa ni narimasu*, literally, "Thank you for the help you have given my husband." Similarly, when a parent meets her children's teachers or their friends' parents, he or she will say *Uchi no musuko (musume) ga osewa ni narimasu* (Thank you for the help you have given my son [daughter]) Again, a person in a business situation will answer the phone with *Osewa ni narimasu* (Thank you for your assistance.) In most cases there is little connection between the phrase and any help that may have been received ; all the same it is widely used as a conversational lubricant. A common answer would be *Kochira koso* (literally, "Thank *you* for *your* help"). Unless a person is being really perverse, you will not hear anyone say *Watashi wa nani mo sewa shite inai* (I've done nothing to help you).

Sumimasen

(1) Meaning "I'm sorry." Etymologically, the meaning is closer to "however much I apologize, I cannot offer enough excuses." The Japanese use *sumimasen* all the time. If they do not apologize for even trifling mistakes but rather try to justify themselves, they tend to be judged intractable, arrogant, stubborn, childish, and lacking in character. Just as westerners

protect their position by asserting themselves, the Japanese seem to protect themselves unconsciously by apologizing. With the growth in self-assertion in recent years, there is more of a western-style resistance to apologizing, but it remains true that the social climate prefers a *sumimasen* for a trifling mistake. Indeed, so much is *sumimasen* used in daily affairs, that visitors to Japan have commented what a strange way the Japanese have of greeting each other! Yet the usage remains confined to public life in interactions with strangers, and is much less frequently used within the family, where true feelings are expressed without reserve.

(2) Meaning "thank you." Though *sumimasen* is used as an expression of gratitude, there is a strong apologetic nuance, in the sense of "Thank you. I'm sorry to trouble you." For example, when someone gives up their seat on the train, they are thanked with *sumimasen* rather than the more straightforward *arigato gozaimasu*, and *sumimasen* is commonly heard in any situation where someone has received something. It has a nuance that is a compound of gratitude, apology and shame, and the very moderation of the expression suits Japanese feelings.

Domo

Domo is perhaps the most convenient word in Japanese. Originally it was used as an intensifier in expressions of thanks or apology, like *domo arigato* (thank you very much) and *domo sumimasen* (I'm very sorry), but now it is used by itself to express those emotions. The word can also be doubled, as in *domo domo*, and substituted for *konnichiwa*(hello), *sayonara* (goodbye), *ojama shimashita* (sorry to have disturbed you), and *osewa ni narimashita* (thank you for your help). Friends meeting by chance in the street will also exchange

the word :
  "*Domo.*"
  "*Domo.*"

Nani mo arimasen ga

When a person serves food to guests he or she will say *nani mo arimasen ga....* (It's nothing, but....). It seems a rather strange expression to use when there is a feast spread upon the table, but we should interpret it as meaning "There is nothing here that I have confidence in saying is especially delicious, but...." Japanese contains many such expressions of modesty ; for example, when giving a present, a person will say *Tsumaranai mono desu ga* (lit. "It's nothing much, but...."), or when serving tea, *Socha desu ga* (lit. "It's poor quality tea, but....").

Yoroshiku onegaishimasu

This all-purpose phrase is widely used when asking something of someone, and it is difficult to find an English expression that covers its different nuances. It is used when asking others for help, or when seeking their indulgence, and it also contains a strong measure of respect for the person addressed. Politicians find it a convenient, if euphemistic, phrase to use when soliciting votes or donations. *Yoroshiku onegaishimasu* can be used in the following situations :

(1) When meeting a person for the first time, in the hope that the future relationship will be successful : -

Hajimemashite. Yoroshiku onegaishimasu.

(2) When asking that something be done, in the hope that it will eventuate : -

"The material has to be ready by April 3. *Yoroshiku onegaishimasu.*"

(3) As a parting phrase after a business transaction : -

Dewa, yoroshiku onegaishimasu.

Boku

There are dozens of words in Japanese that express "I." The most commonly used are *watakushi*, *boku*, and *ore*. Women tend to use *watashi* or *watakushi*, while men will use any of the three. Unlike the neutral English "I" though, each of the Japanese words has a particular nuance, and sometimes it is difficult to choose which to use.

(1) *boku* Used widely by males of all ages, from young children to adults. It has a serious, straightforward nuance.

(2) *ore* Used by males, particularly teenagers and adults, when talking with friends. It has a slightly rough impact, and should not be used when speaking to superiors or seniors. It is not unusual to hear mothers advising sons to say *boku* rather than *ore*.

(3) *watashi* Used by females of all ages, from young children to adults. *Watakushi* is a polite word. Men will also use *watashi* or *watakushi* in formal situations or when speaking with clients at the office, without any sense of femininity.

NATIONAL HOLIDAYS IN JAPAN

New Year's Day	January 1
Coming-of-Age Day (Adults' Day)	January 15
National Foundation Day	February 11
Vernal Equinox Day	March 20
Greenery Day	April 29
Constitution Memorial Day	May 3
Children's Day	May 5
Respect for the Aged Day	September 15
Autumnal Equinox Day	September 23
Health-Sports Day	October 10
Culture Day	November 3
Labor Thanksgiving Day	November 23
Emperor's Birthday	December 23